Shojo Beat

Natsume's BOOK of FRIENDS

STORY and ART by
Yuki Midorikawa

VOLUME 26

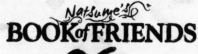

Natsume's BOOK of FRIENDS

VOLUME 26 CONTENTS

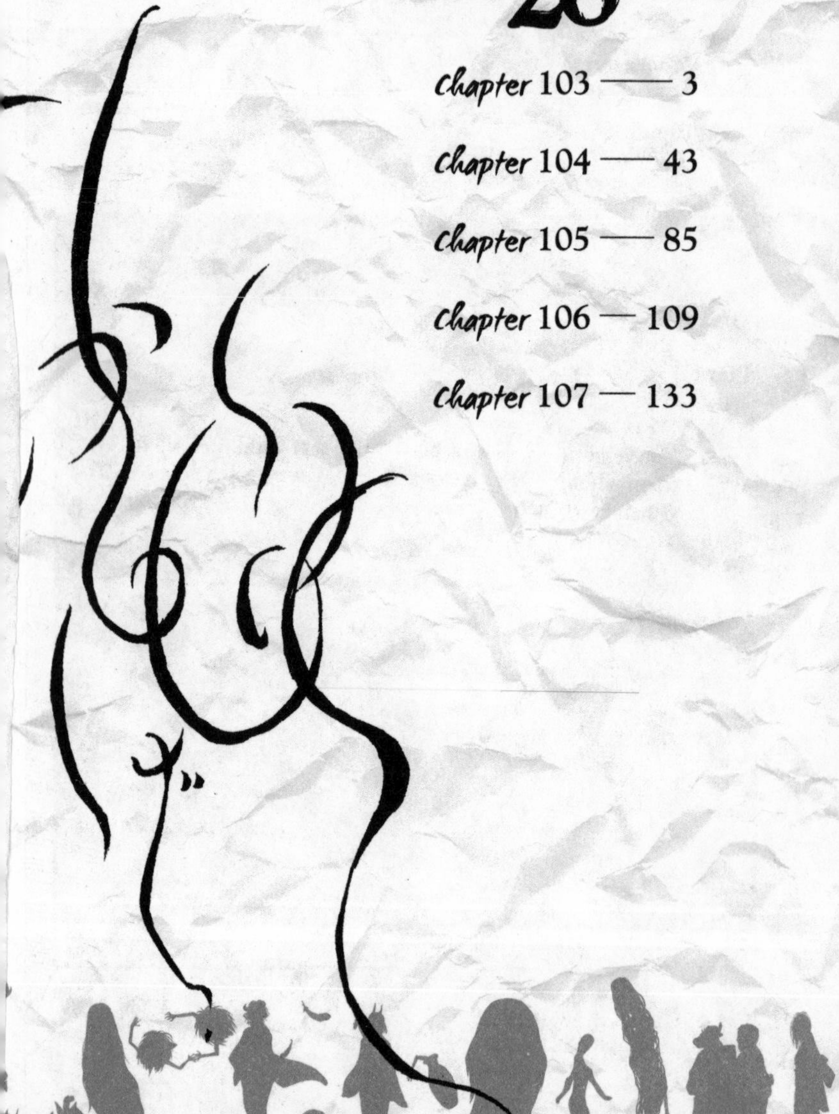

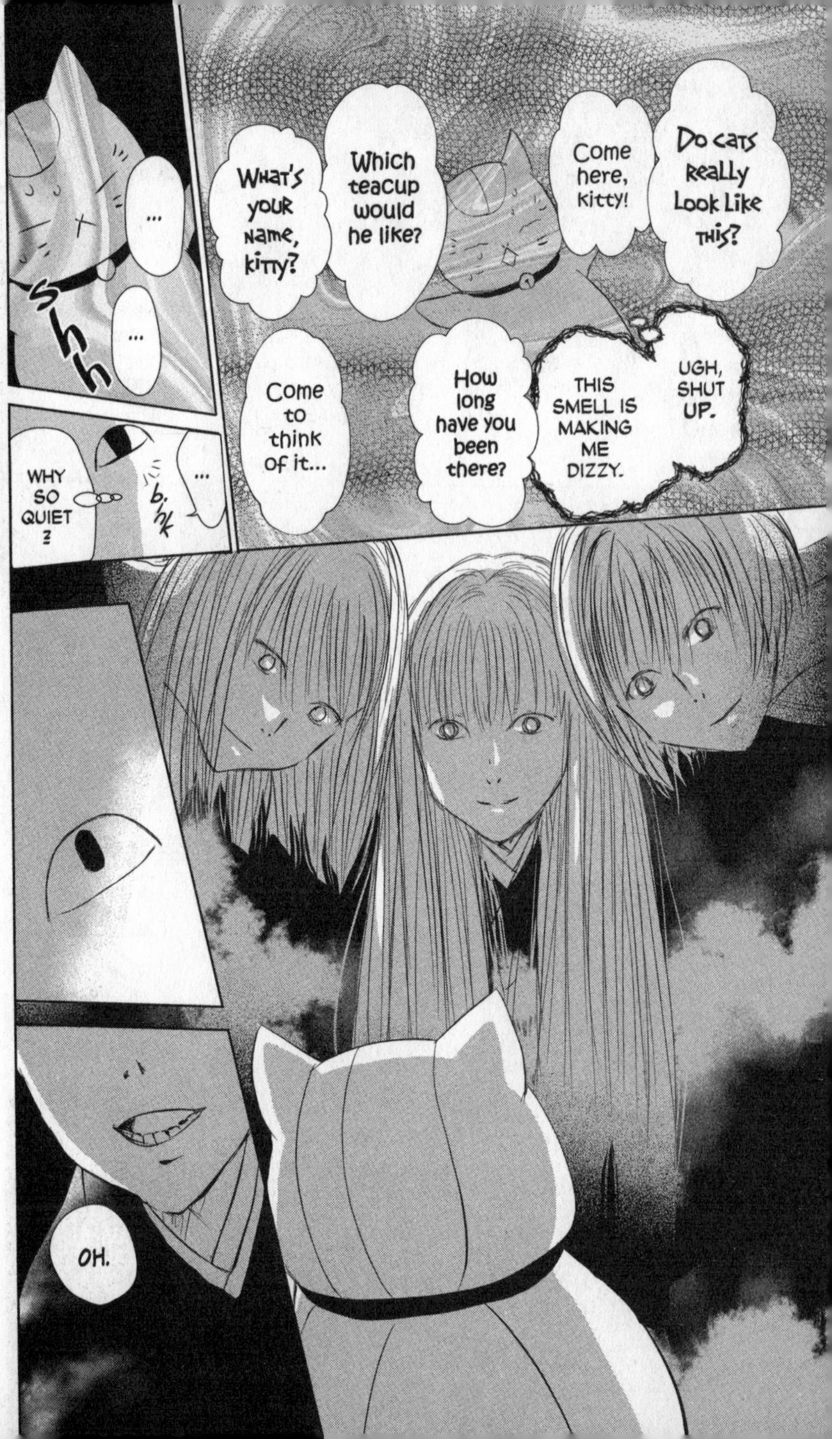
Do cats really Look Like this?
Come here, kitty!
Which teacup would he like?
What's your name, kitty?
UGH, SHUT UP.
THIS SMELL IS MAKING ME DIZZY.
How long have you been there?
Come to think of it...
...
shh
...
...
blink
WHY SO QUIET?
OH.

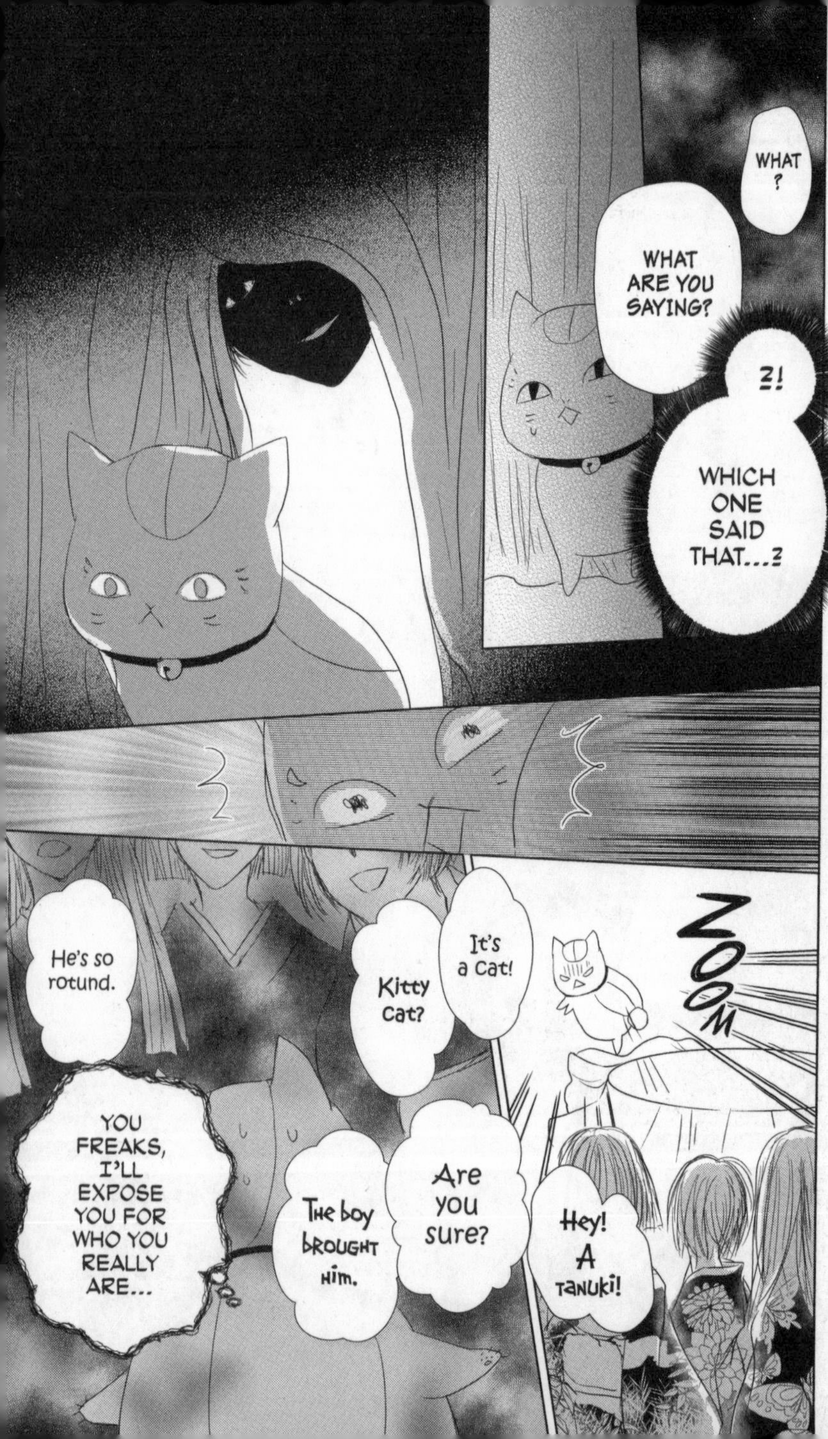
WHAT ?
WHAT ARE YOU SAYING?
?!
WHICH ONE SAID THAT...?
ZOOM
It's a cat!
Kitty cat?
He's so rotund.
Hey! A tanuki!
Are you sure?
The boy brought him.
YOU FREAKS, I'LL EXPOSE YOU FOR WHO YOU REALLY ARE...

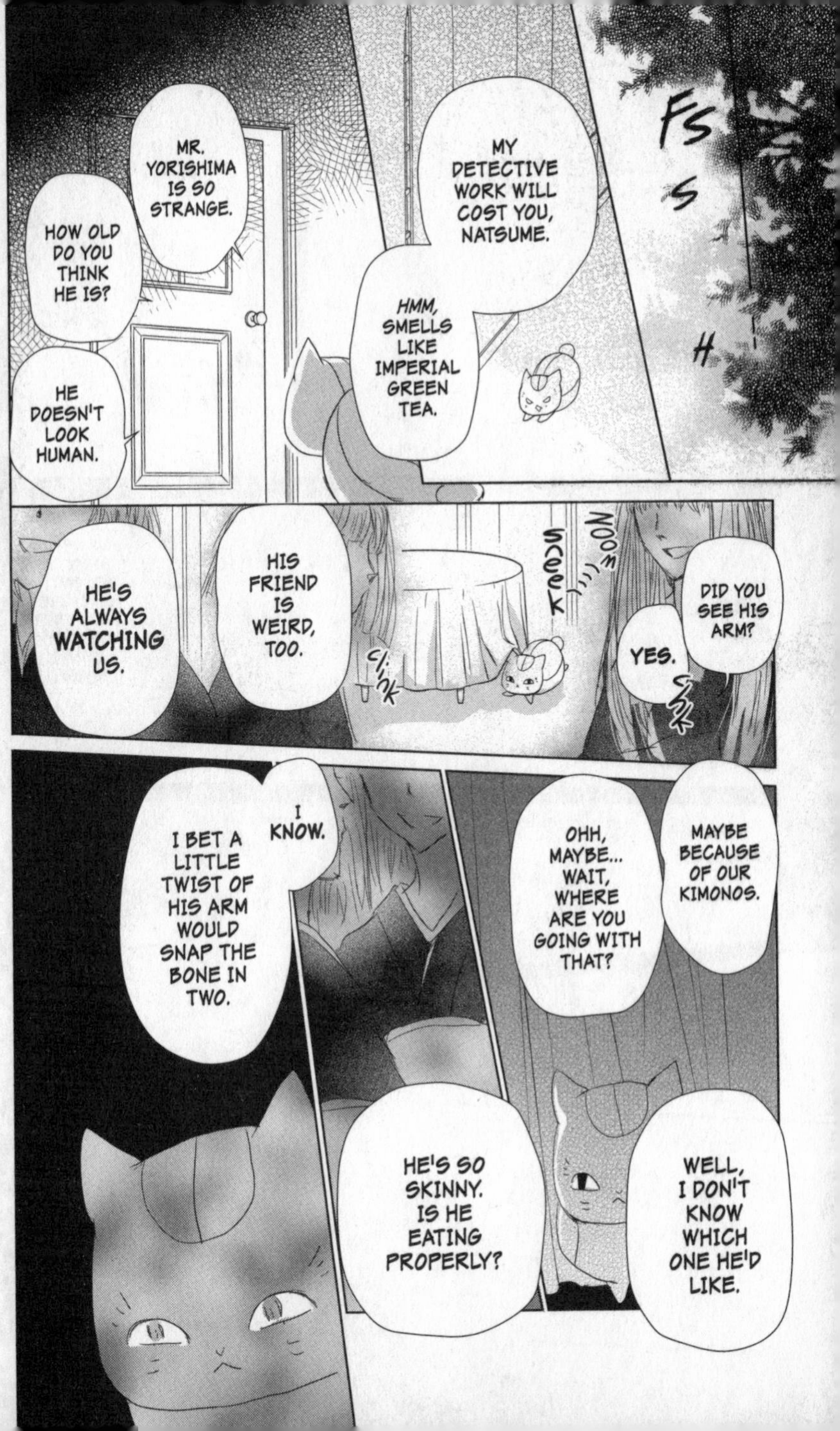
FSSSH
MY DETECTIVE WORK WILL COST YOU, NATSUME.
HMM, SMELLS LIKE IMPERIAL GREEN TEA.
MR. YORISHIMA IS SO STRANGE.
HOW OLD DO YOU THINK HE IS?
HE DOESN'T LOOK HUMAN.
DID YOU SEE HIS ARM?
YES.
CLINK
CLINK
HIS FRIEND IS WEIRD, TOO.
HE'S ALWAYS WATCHING US.
MAYBE BECAUSE OF OUR KIMONOS.
OHH, MAYBE... WAIT, WHERE ARE YOU GOING WITH THAT?
WELL, I DON'T KNOW WHICH ONE HE'D LIKE.
HE'S SO SKINNY. IS HE EATING PROPERLY?
I KNOW.
I BET A LITTLE TWIST OF HIS ARM WOULD SNAP THE BONE IN TWO.

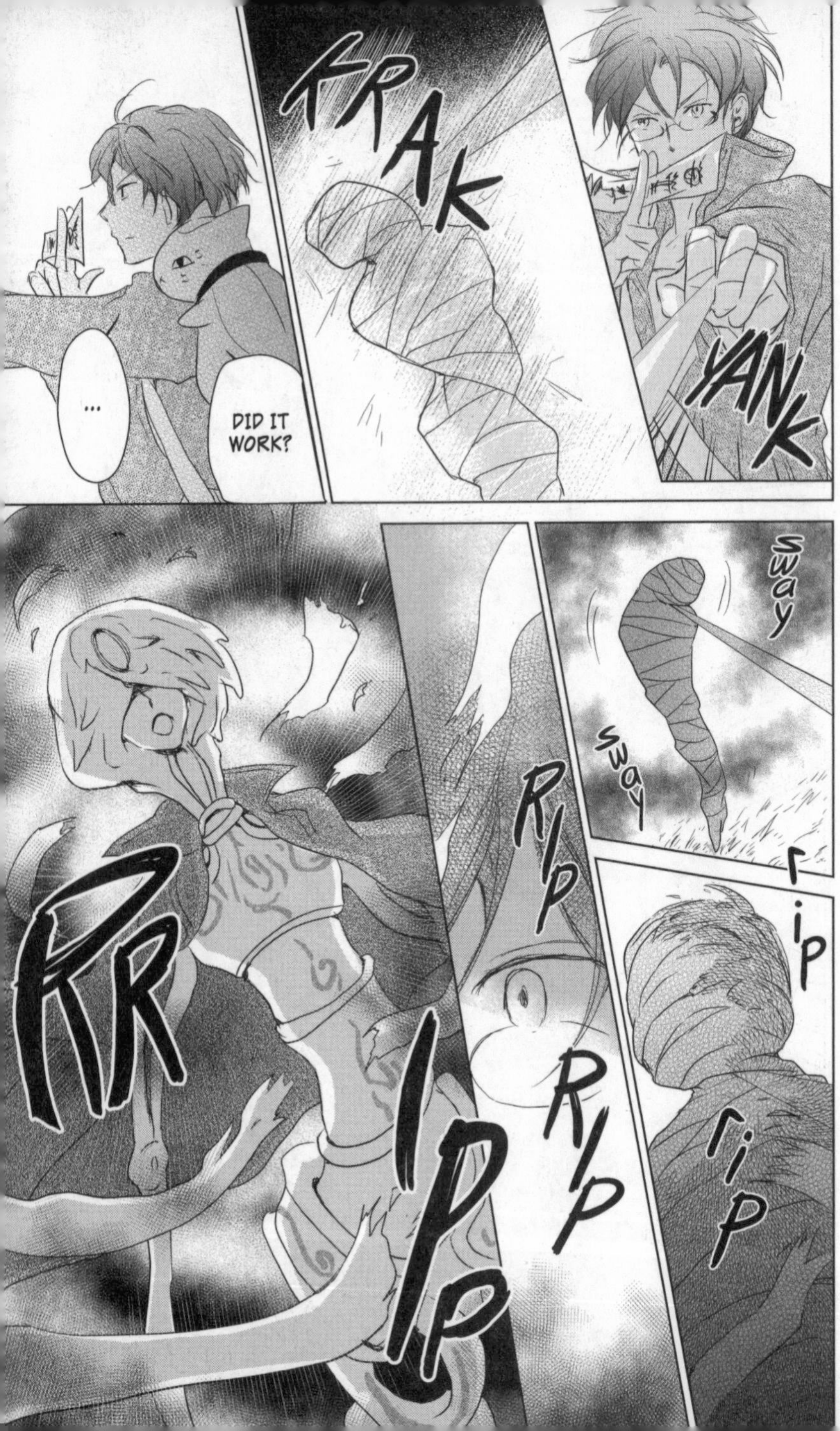
YANK
KRAK
DID IT WORK?
...
sway
sway
rip
rip
RIP
RIP
RRIPP

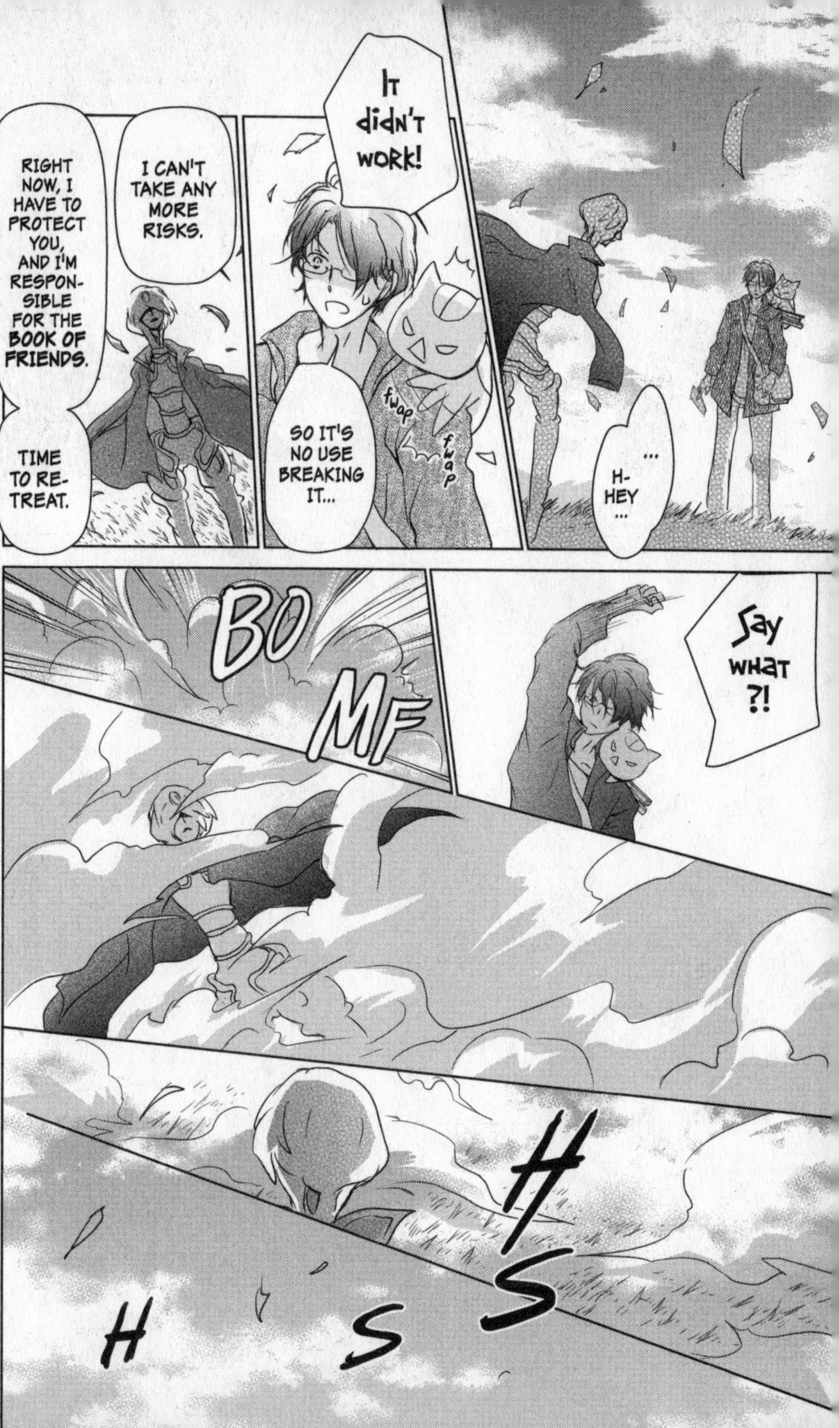
... H-HEY ...
It didn't work!
fwap
fwap
SO IT'S NO USE BREAKING IT...
I CAN'T TAKE ANY MORE RISKS.
RIGHT NOW, I HAVE TO PROTECT YOU, AND I'M RESPONSIBLE FOR THE BOOK OF FRIENDS.
TIME TO RETREAT.
Say what?!
BOMF
H S
H S

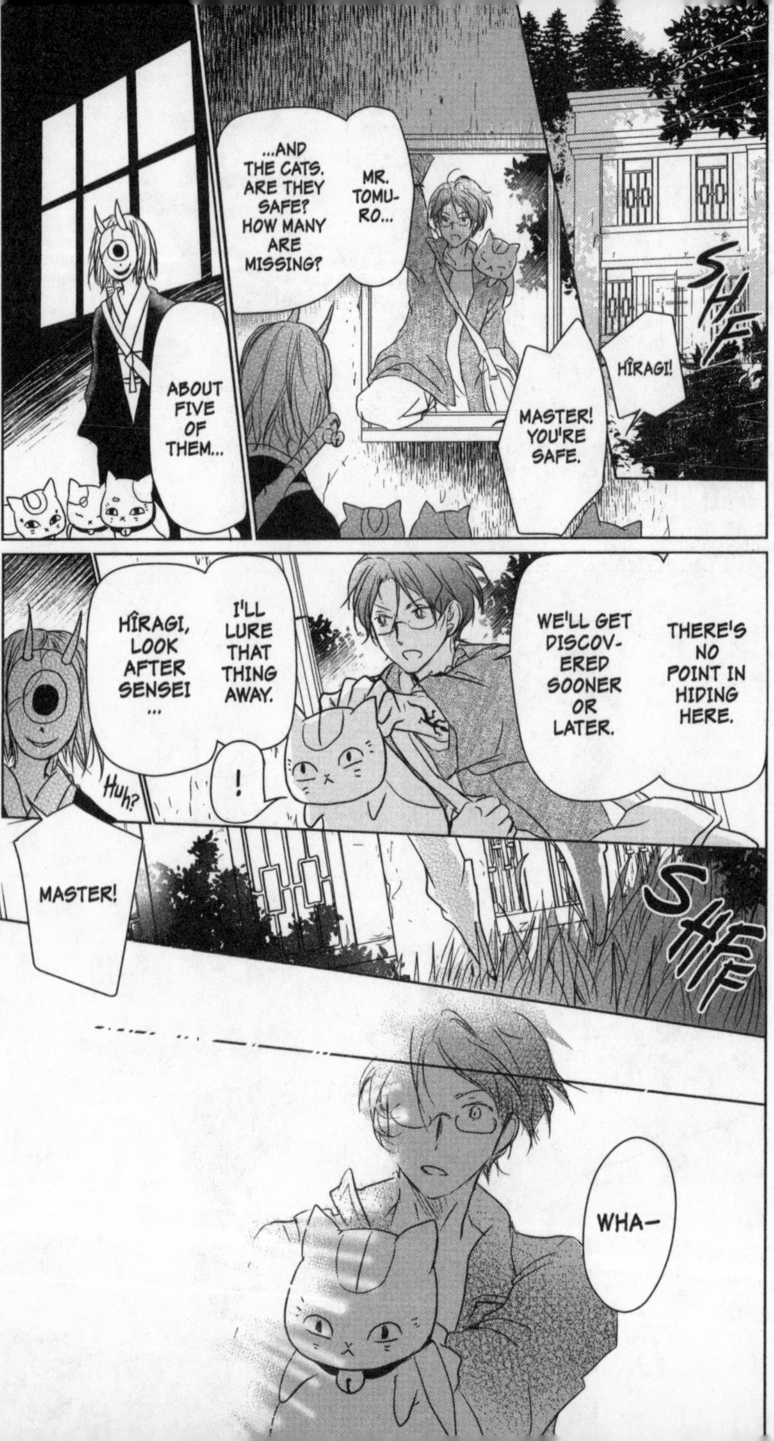
SHF
HÎRAGI!
MASTER! YOU'RE SAFE.
MR. TOMU-RO...
...AND THE CATS. ARE THEY SAFE? HOW MANY ARE MISSING?
ABOUT FIVE OF THEM...
THERE'S NO POINT IN HIDING HERE.
WE'LL GET DISCOV-ERED SOONER OR LATER.
I'LL LURE THAT THING AWAY.
HÎRAGI, LOOK AFTER SENSEI...
!
Huh?
SHF
MASTER!
WHA—

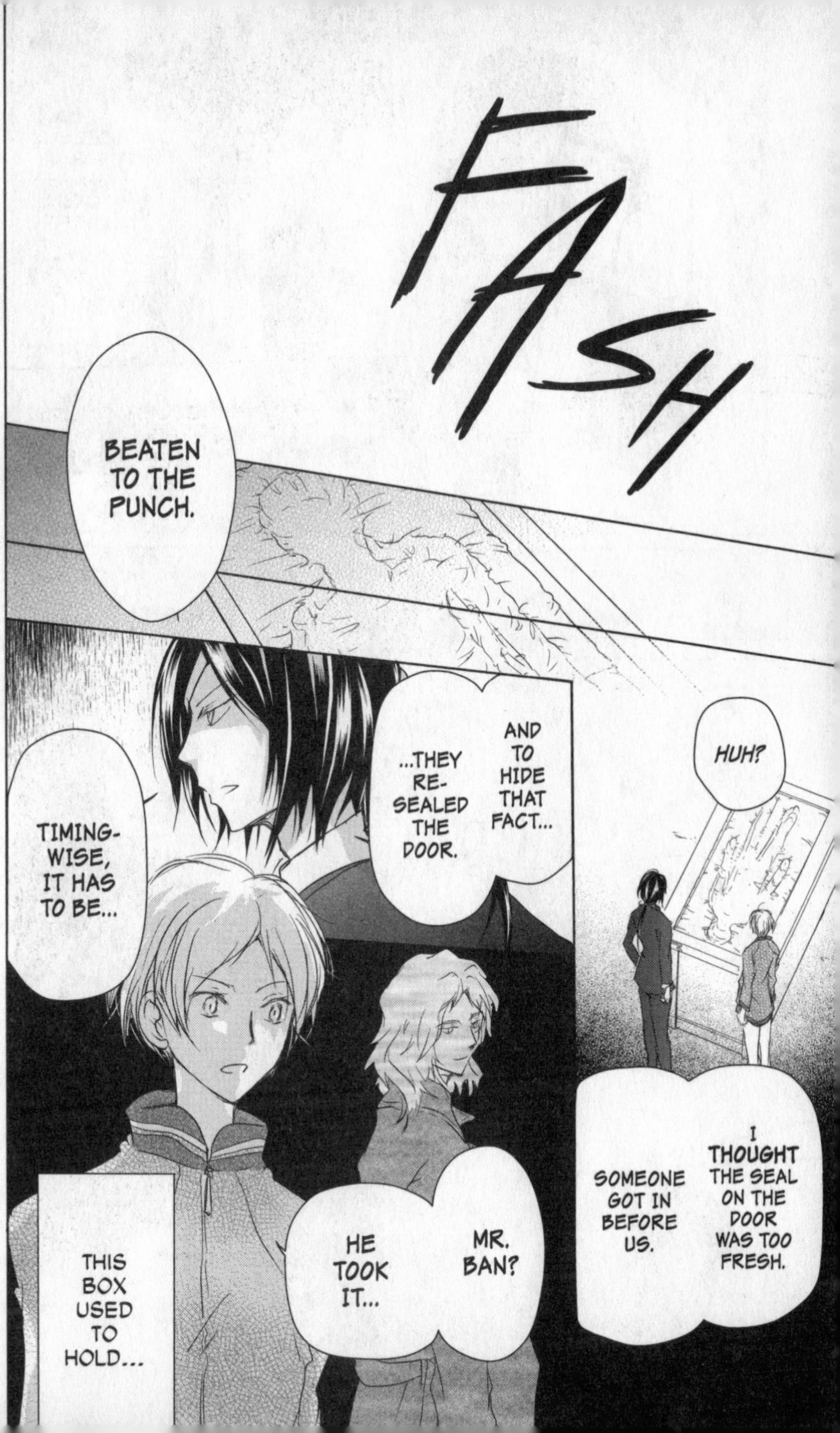
FASH
BEATEN TO THE PUNCH.
HUH?
I THOUGHT THE SEAL ON THE DOOR WAS TOO FRESH.
SOMEONE GOT IN BEFORE US.
AND TO HIDE THAT FACT...
...THEY RE-SEALED THE DOOR.
TIMING-WISE, IT HAS TO BE...
MR. BAN?
HE TOOK IT...
THIS BOX USED TO HOLD...

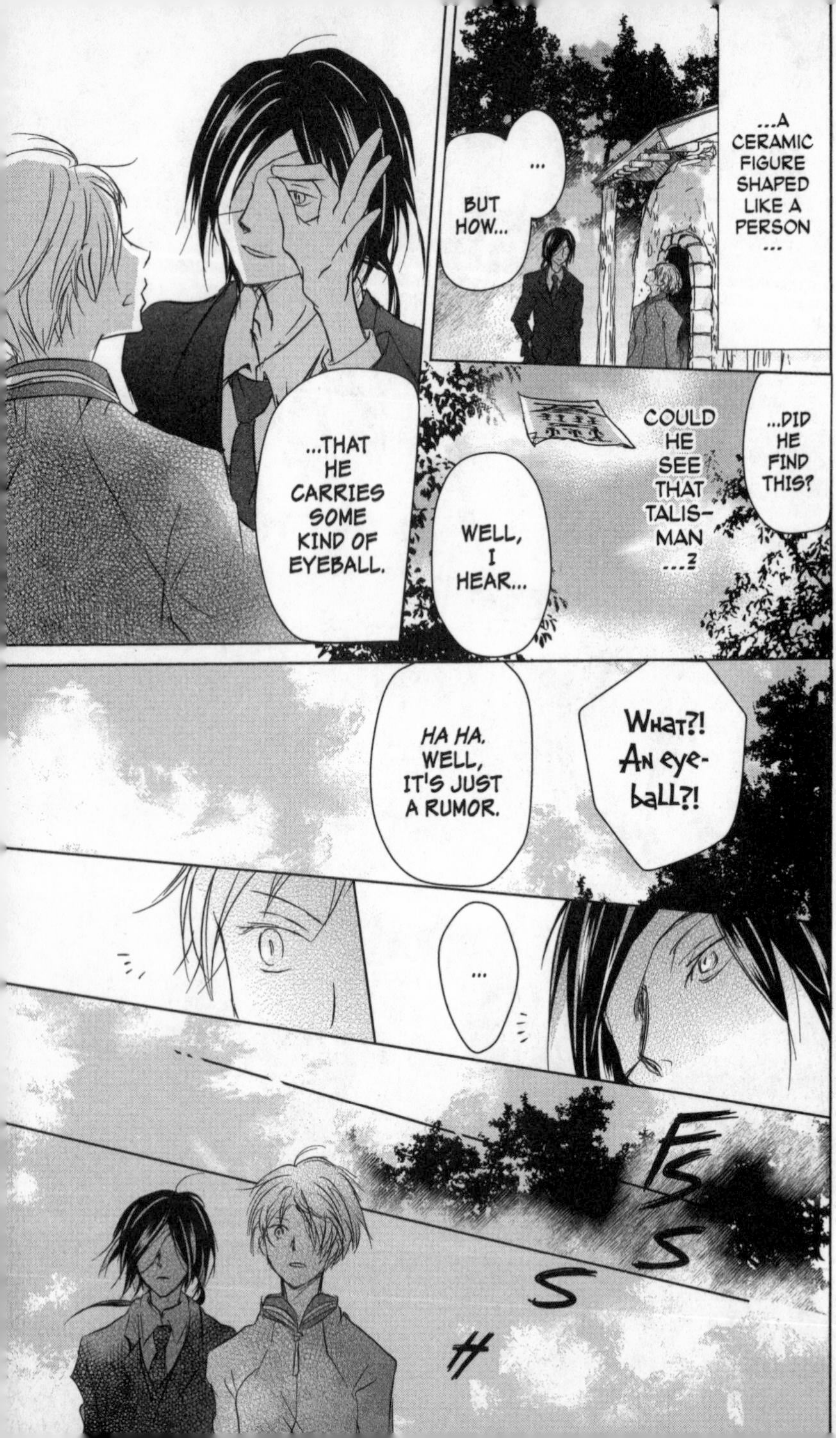
...A CERAMIC FIGURE SHAPED LIKE A PERSON...
...
BUT HOW...
...DID HE FIND THIS?
COULD HE SEE THAT TALIS-MAN...?
WELL, I HEAR...
...THAT HE CARRIES SOME KIND OF EYEBALL.
WHAT?! AN EYE-BALL?!
HA HA. WELL, IT'S JUST A RUMOR.
...
FSSSH

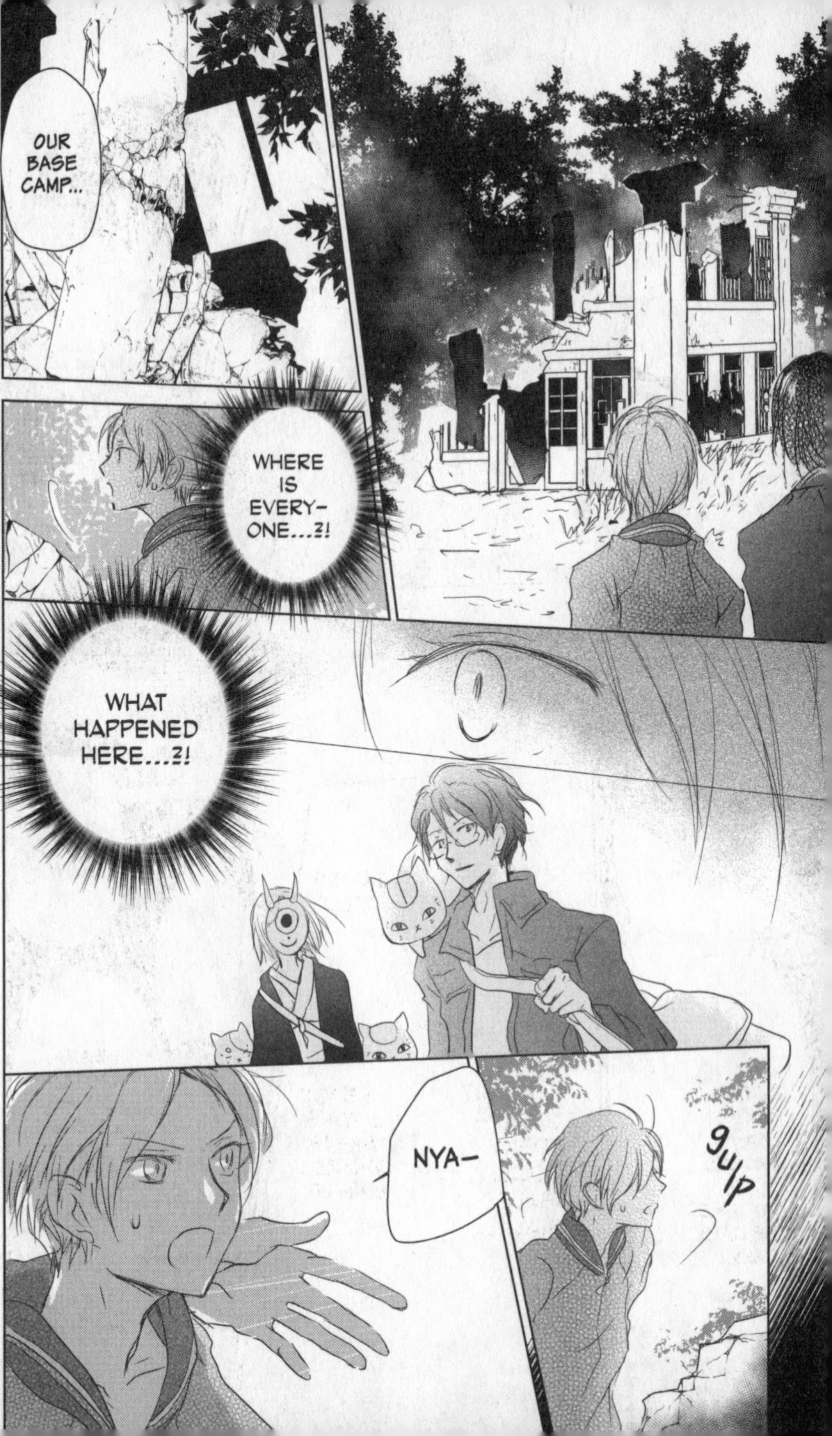
OUR BASE CAMP...
WHERE IS EVERYONE...?!
WHAT HAPPENED HERE...?!
NYA-
gulp

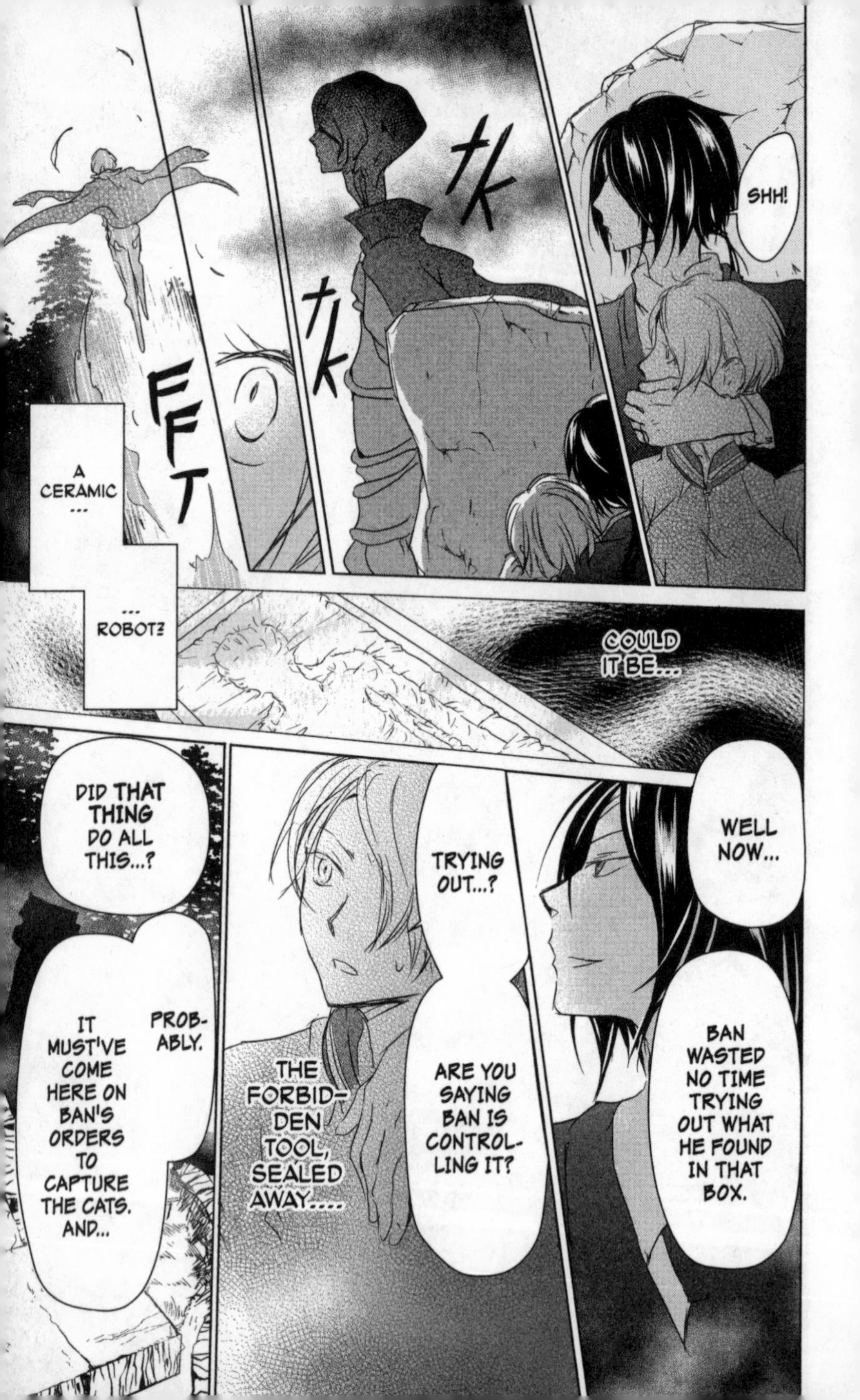
SHH!
tk
tk
FFT
A CERAMIC...
...ROBOT?
COULD IT BE...
WELL NOW...
BAN WASTED NO TIME TRYING OUT WHAT HE FOUND IN THAT BOX.
TRYING OUT...?
ARE YOU SAYING BAN IS CONTROLLING IT?
THE FORBIDDEN TOOL, SEALED AWAY....
DID THAT THING DO ALL THIS...?
PROBABLY.
IT MUST'VE COME HERE ON BAN'S ORDERS TO CAPTURE THE CATS. AND...

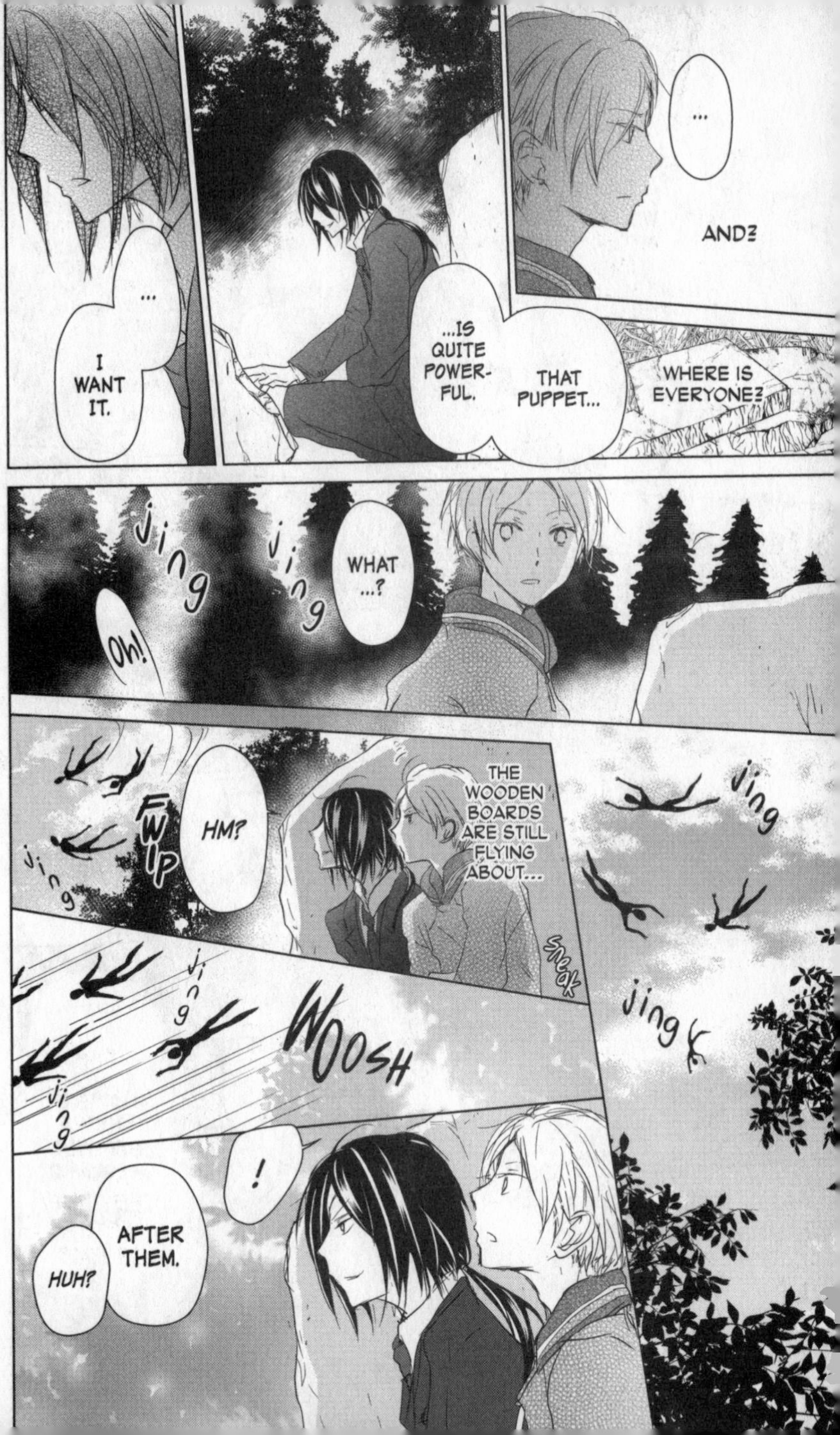
...
AND?
WHERE IS EVERYONE?
THAT PUPPET...
...IS QUITE POWERFUL.
...
I WANT IT.
WHAT ...?
jing
jing
Oh!
jing
THE WOODEN BOARDS ARE STILL FLYING ABOUT...
HM?
FWIP
jing
sneak
jing
jing
WOOSH
jing
!
AFTER THEM.
HUH?

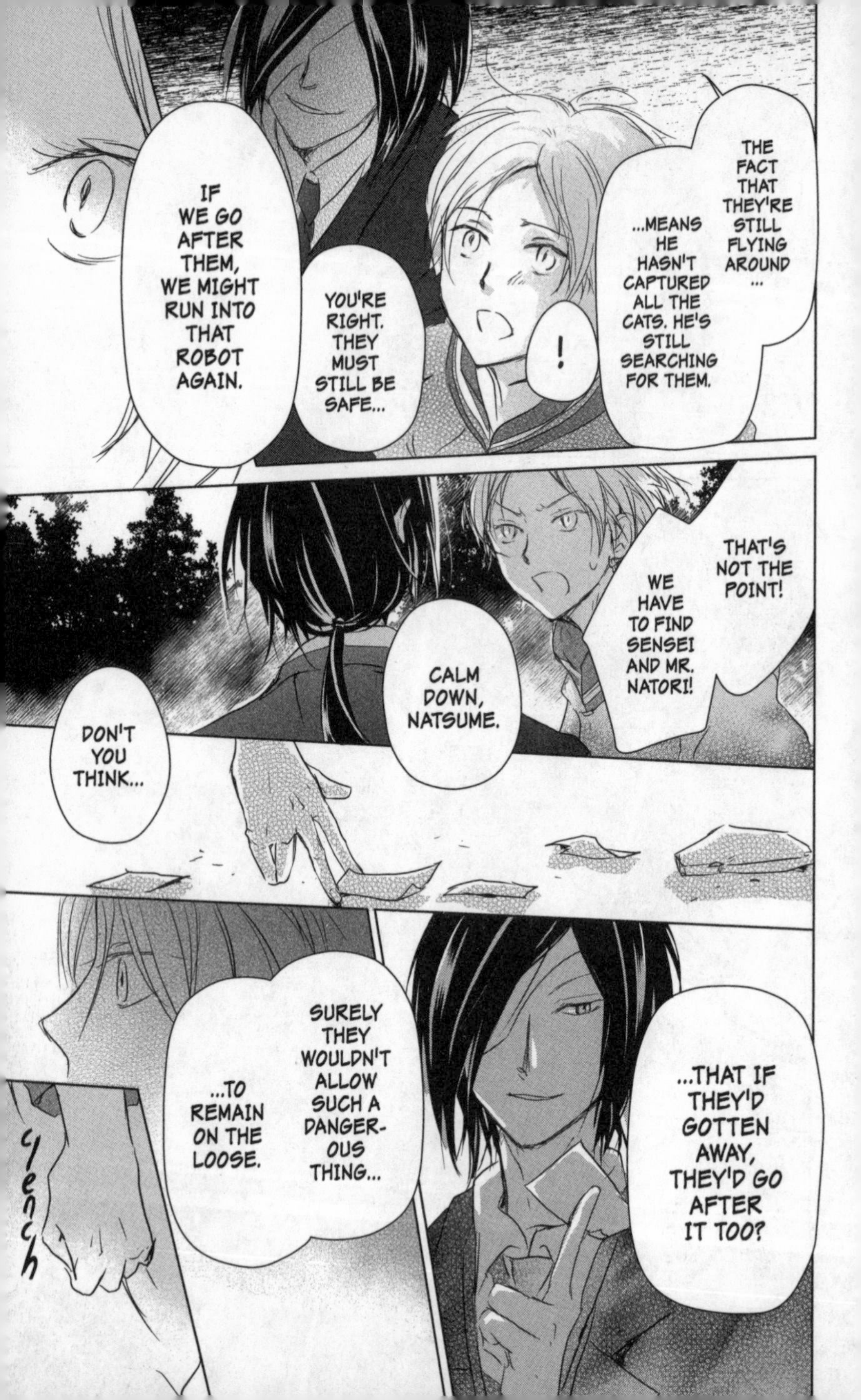
THE FACT THAT THEY'RE STILL FLYING AROUND...
...MEANS HE HASN'T CAPTURED ALL THE CATS. HE'S STILL SEARCHING FOR THEM.
!
YOU'RE RIGHT. THEY MUST STILL BE SAFE...
IF WE GO AFTER THEM, WE MIGHT RUN INTO THAT ROBOT AGAIN.
THAT'S NOT THE POINT!
WE HAVE TO FIND SENSEI AND MR. NATORI!
CALM DOWN, NATSUME.
DON'T YOU THINK...
...THAT IF THEY'D GOTTEN AWAY, THEY'D GO AFTER IT TOO?
SURELY THEY WOULDN'T ALLOW SUCH A DANGER-OUS THING...
...TO REMAIN ON THE LOOSE.
clench

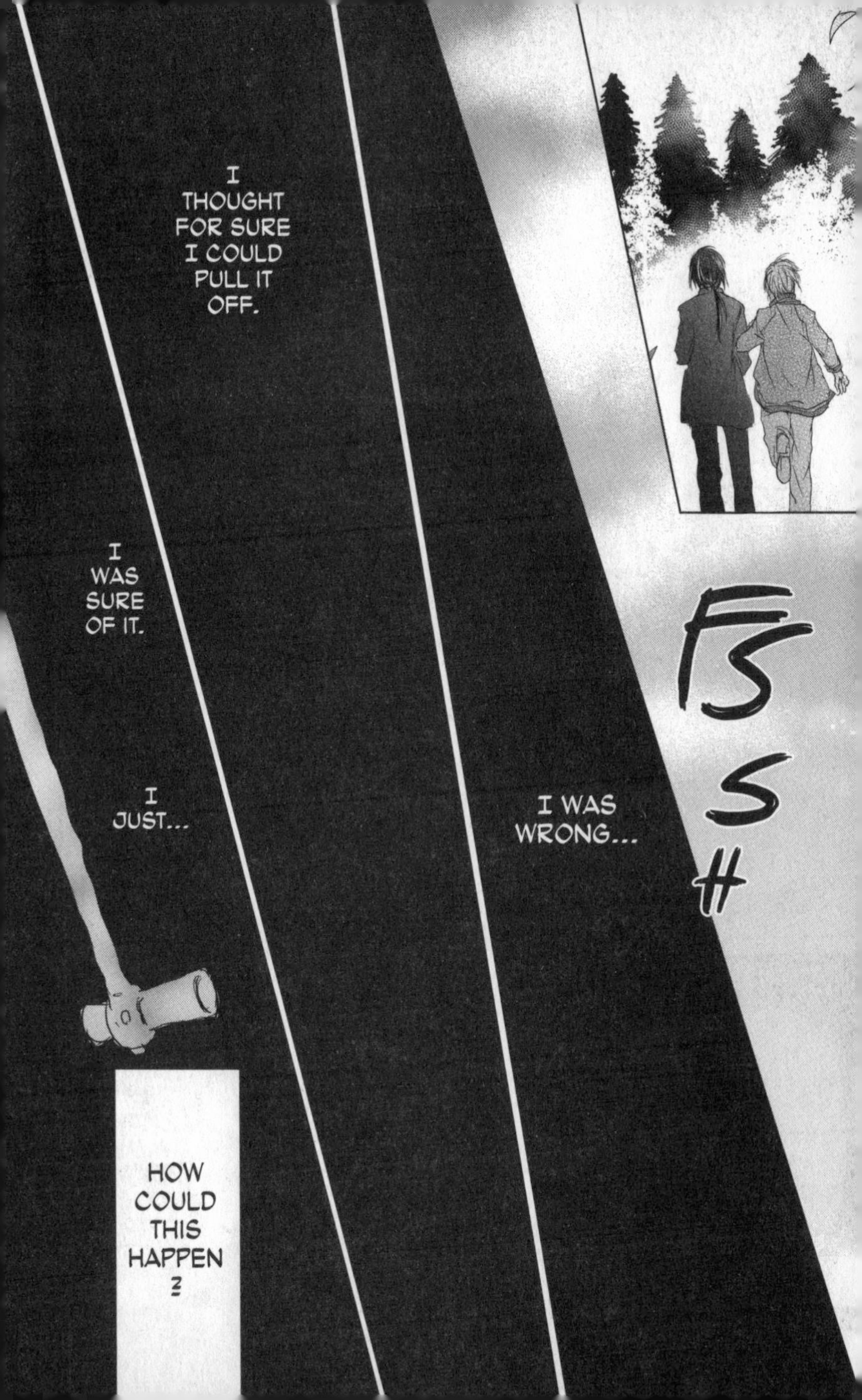
FSSH
I WAS WRONG...
I THOUGHT FOR SURE I COULD PULL IT OFF.
I WAS SURE OF IT.
I JUST...
HOW COULD THIS HAPPEN?

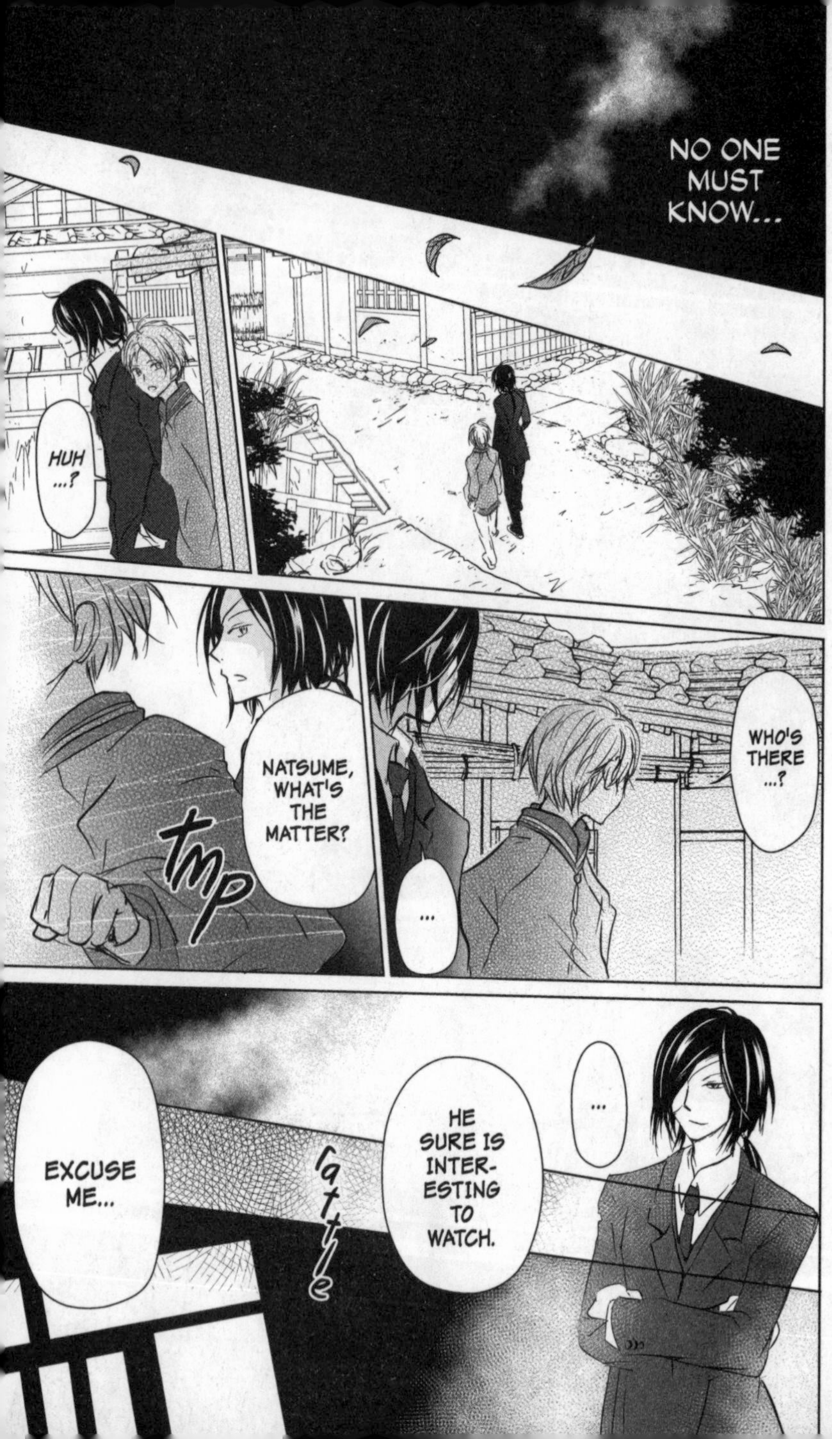
NO ONE MUST KNOW...
HUH ...?
WHO'S THERE ...?
...
NATSUME, WHAT'S THE MATTER?
tmp
...
HE SURE IS INTER-ESTING TO WATCH.
rattle
EXCUSE ME...

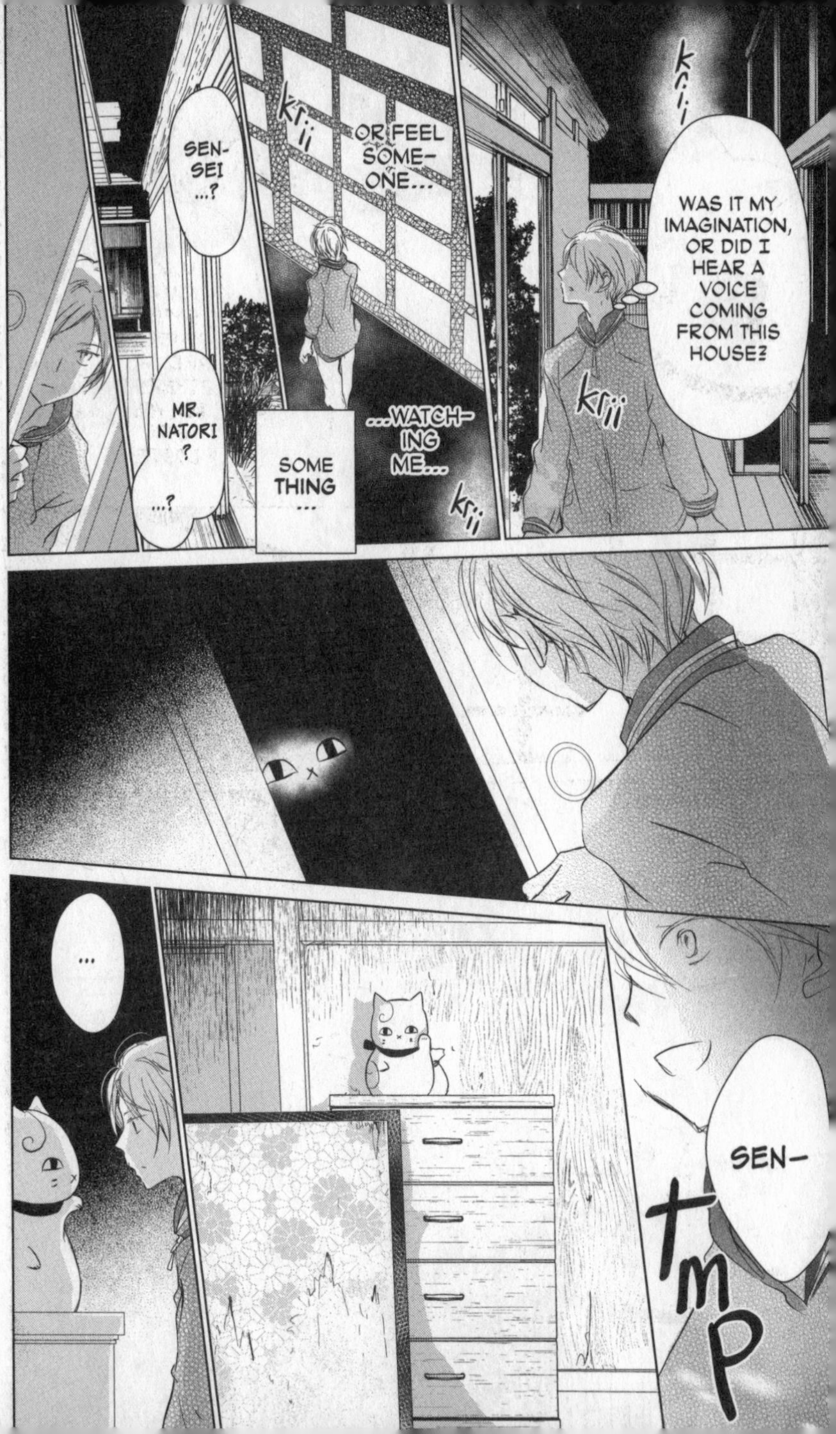
krii
WAS IT MY IMAGINATION, OR DID I HEAR A VOICE COMING FROM THIS HOUSE?
krii
krii
OR FEEL SOME-ONE...
...WATCH-ING ME...
SOME THING ...
krii
SEN-SEI ...?
MR. NATORI ?
...?
SEN-
tmp
...

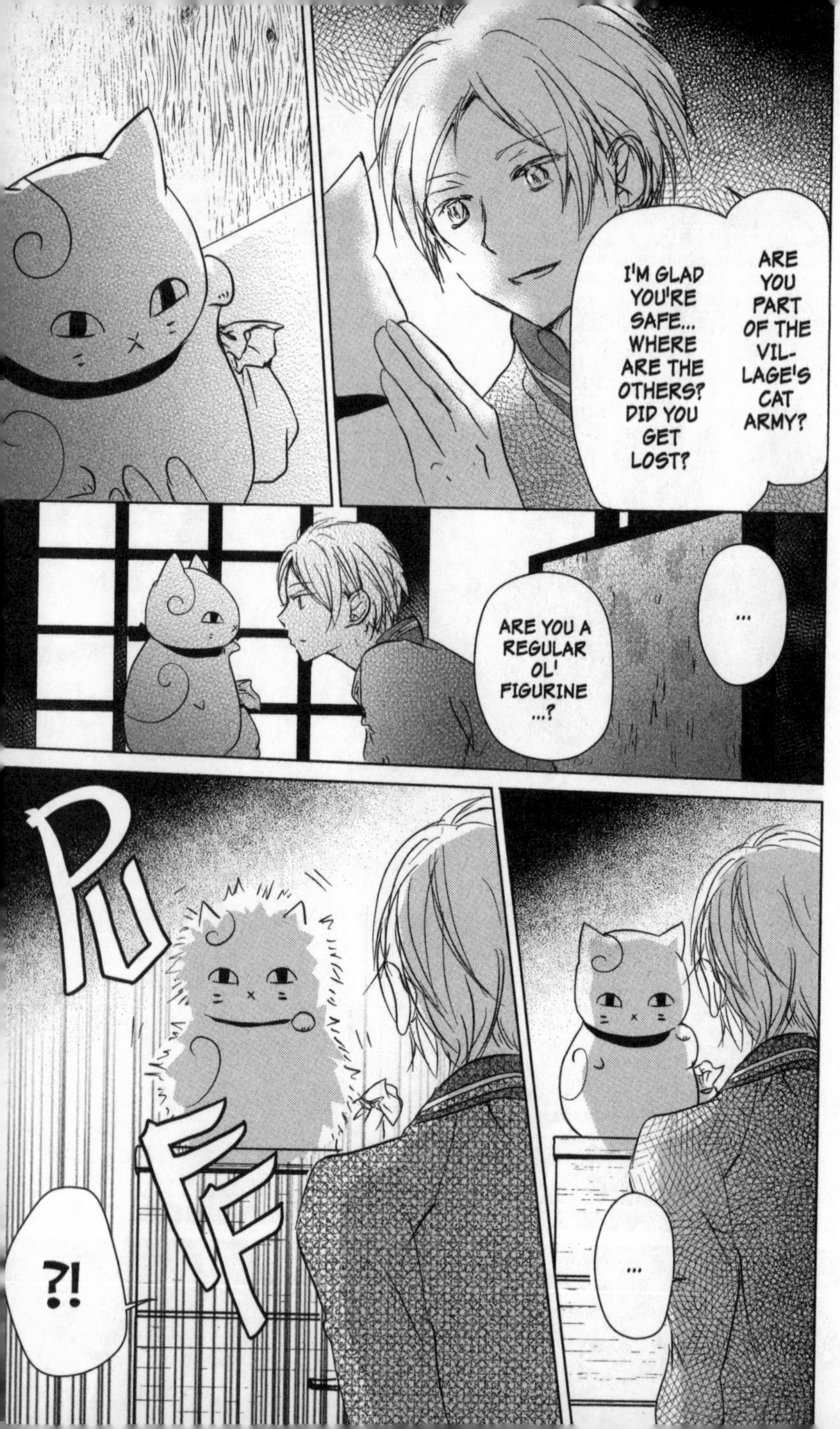
I'M GLAD YOU'RE SAFE... WHERE ARE THE OTHERS? DID YOU GET LOST? ARE YOU PART OF THE VIL-LAGE'S CAT ARMY?
...
ARE YOU A REGULAR OL' FIGURINE ...?
...
PUFF
?!

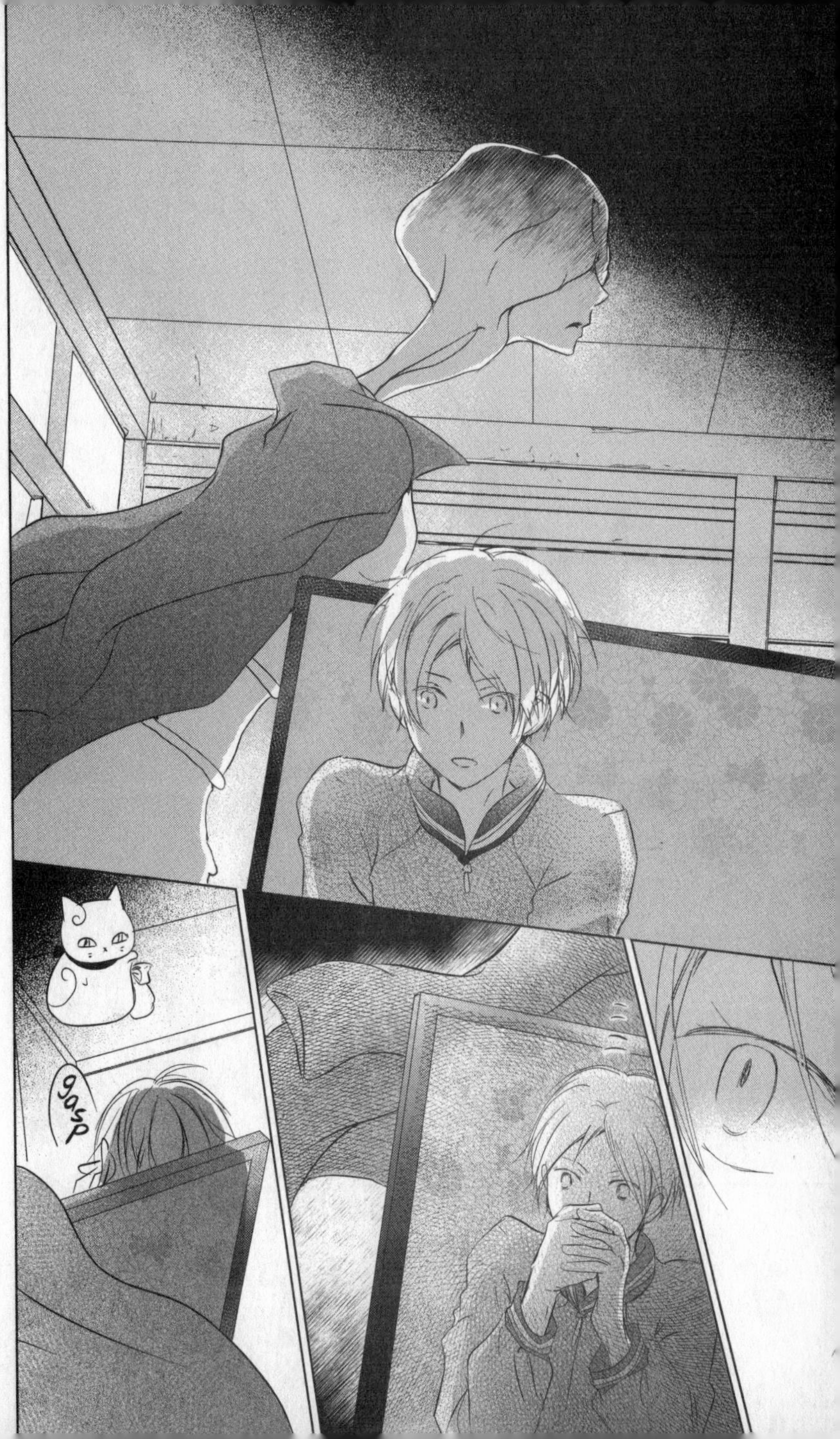
gasp

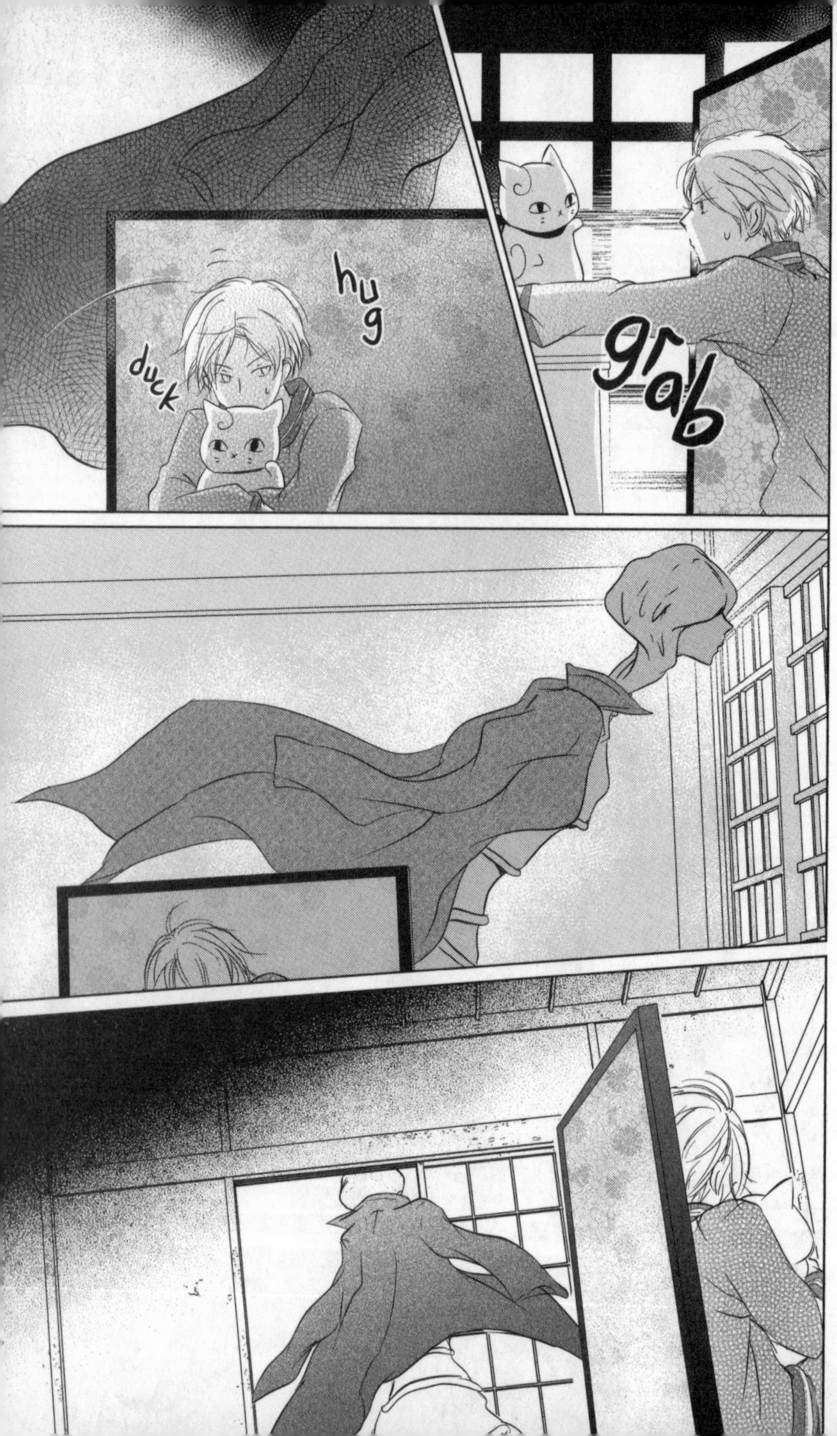
grab
hug
duck

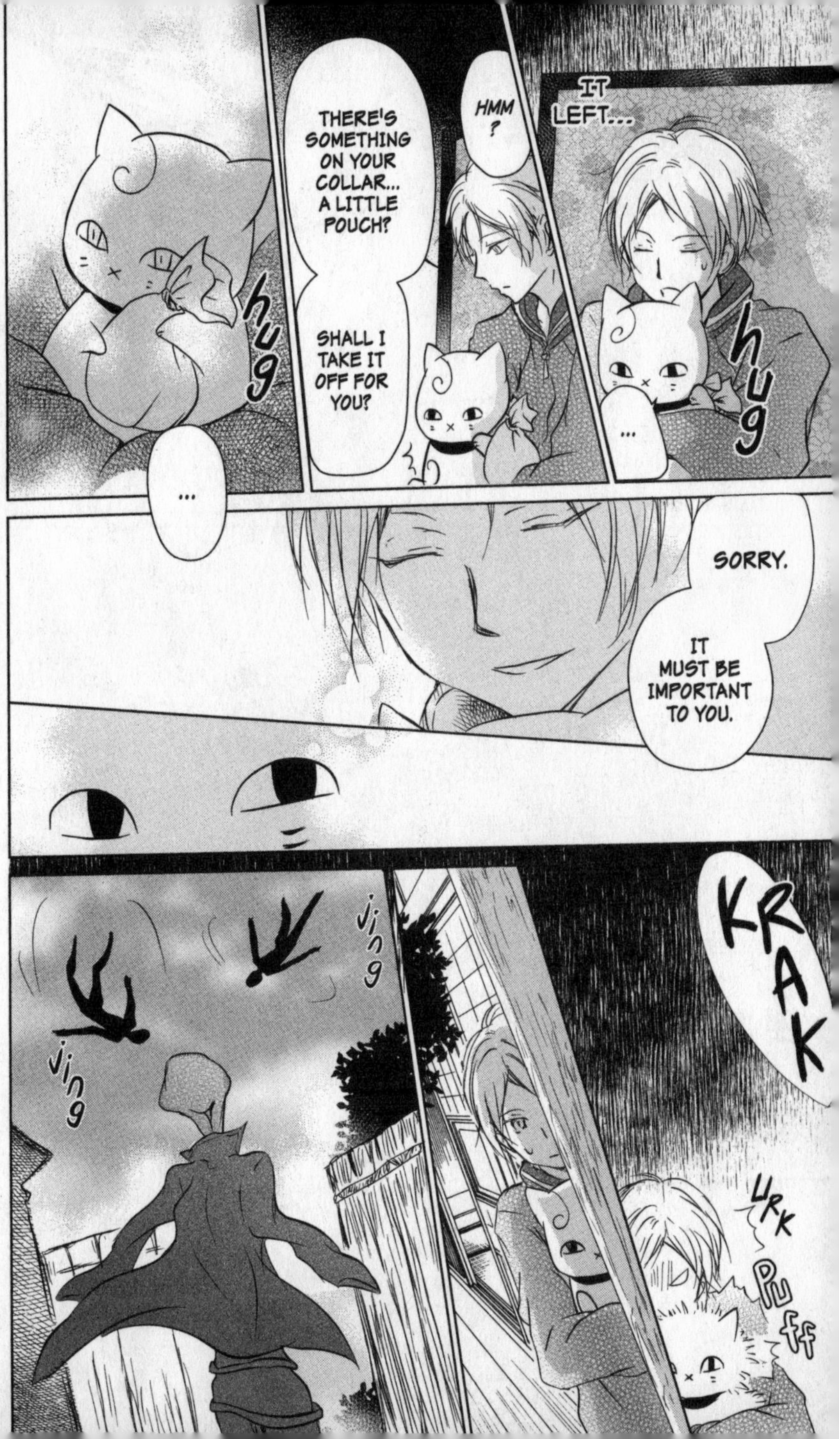
I-IT LEFT...
hug
...
HMM?
THERE'S SOMETHING ON YOUR COLLAR... A LITTLE POUCH?
SHALL I TAKE IT OFF FOR YOU?
hug
...
SORRY.
IT MUST BE IMPORTANT TO YOU.
KRAK
URK
Puff
jing
jing

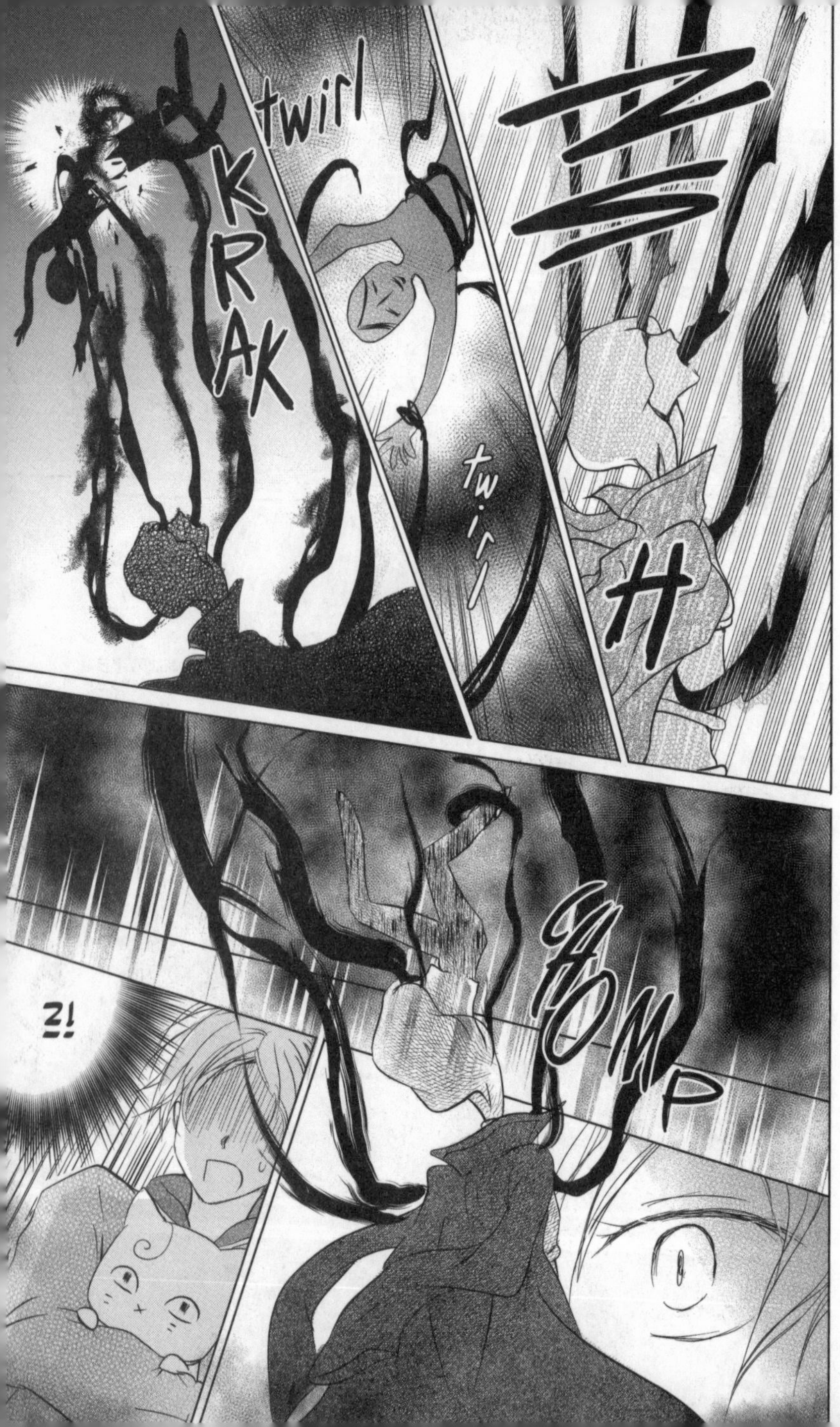
ZSH
twirl
twirl
KRAK
CHOMP
Z!

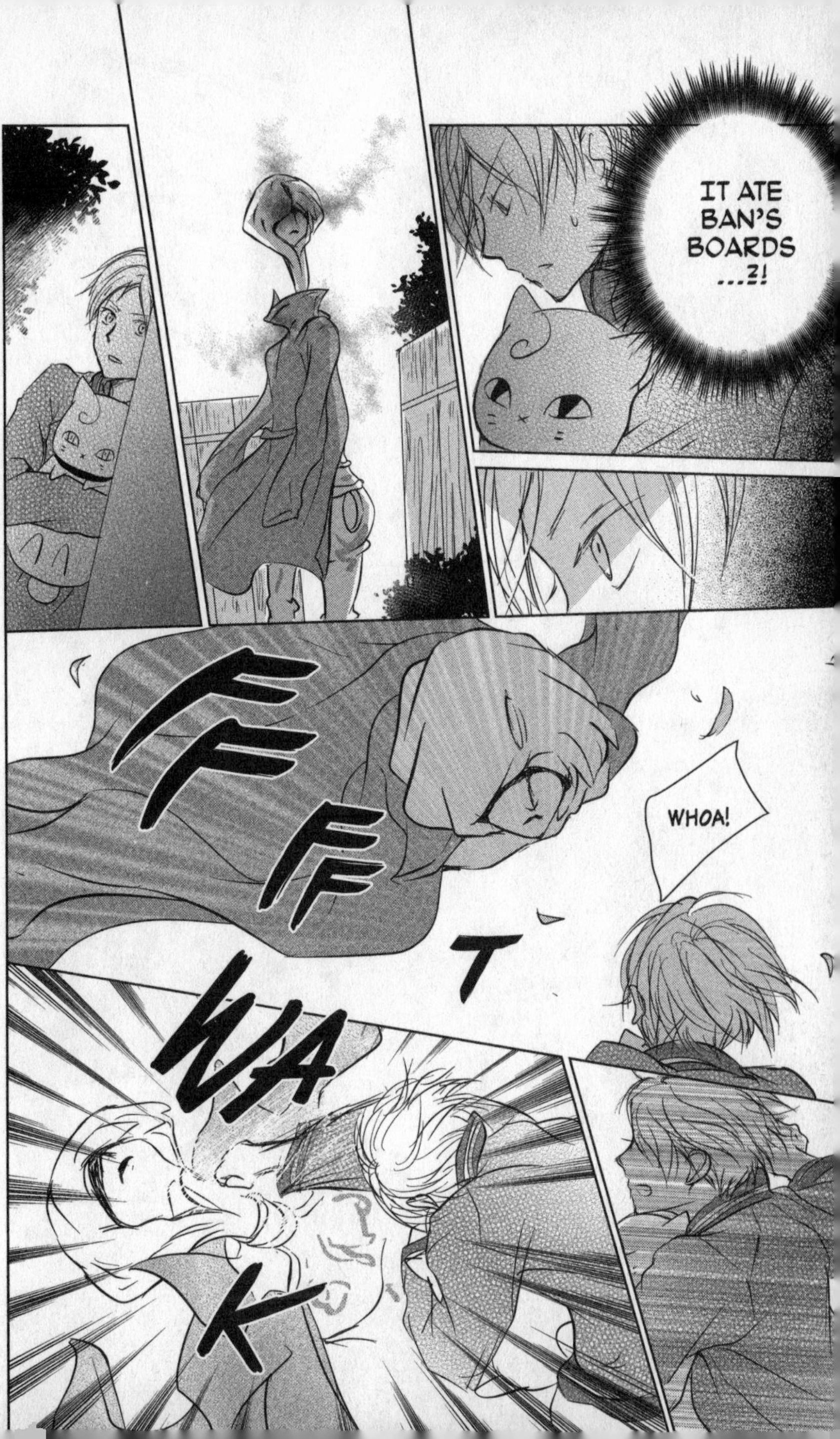
IT ATE BAN'S BOARDS ...?!
WHOA!
FFFWAT
FFF
WA
T
K

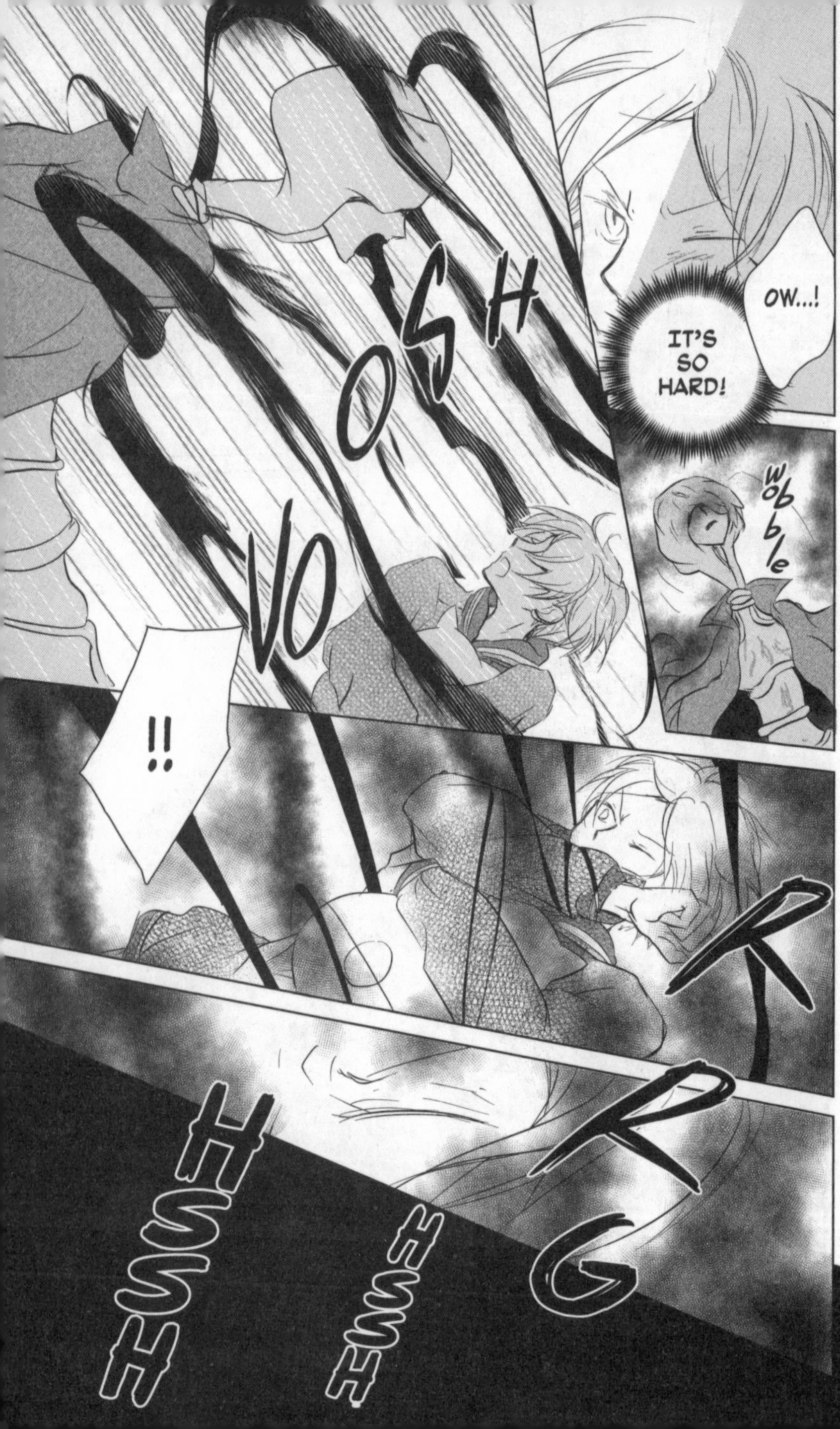
OW...!
IT'S SO HARD!
wobble
VOOSH
!!
RRG
HISSH
HISSH

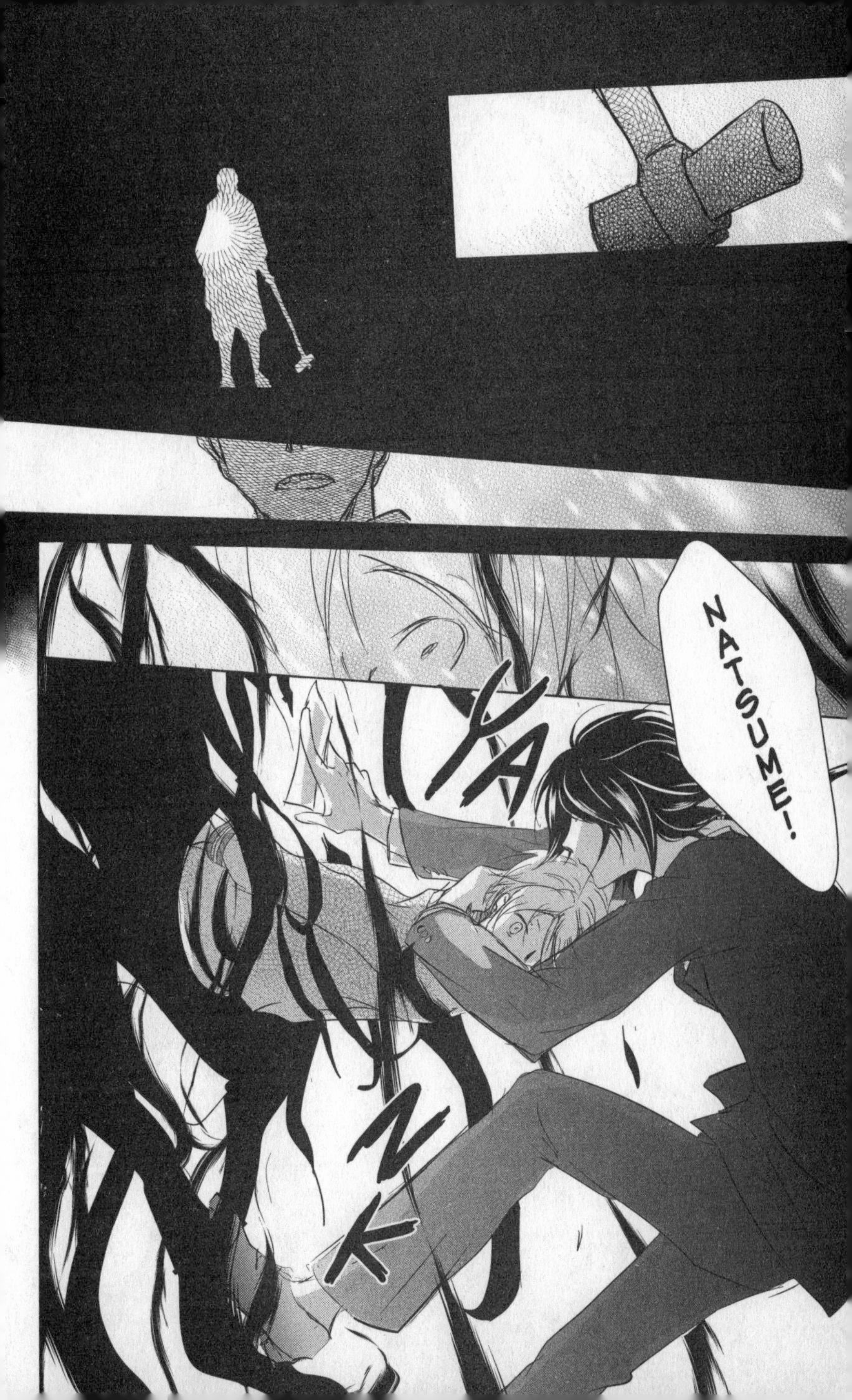
NATSUME!
YANK

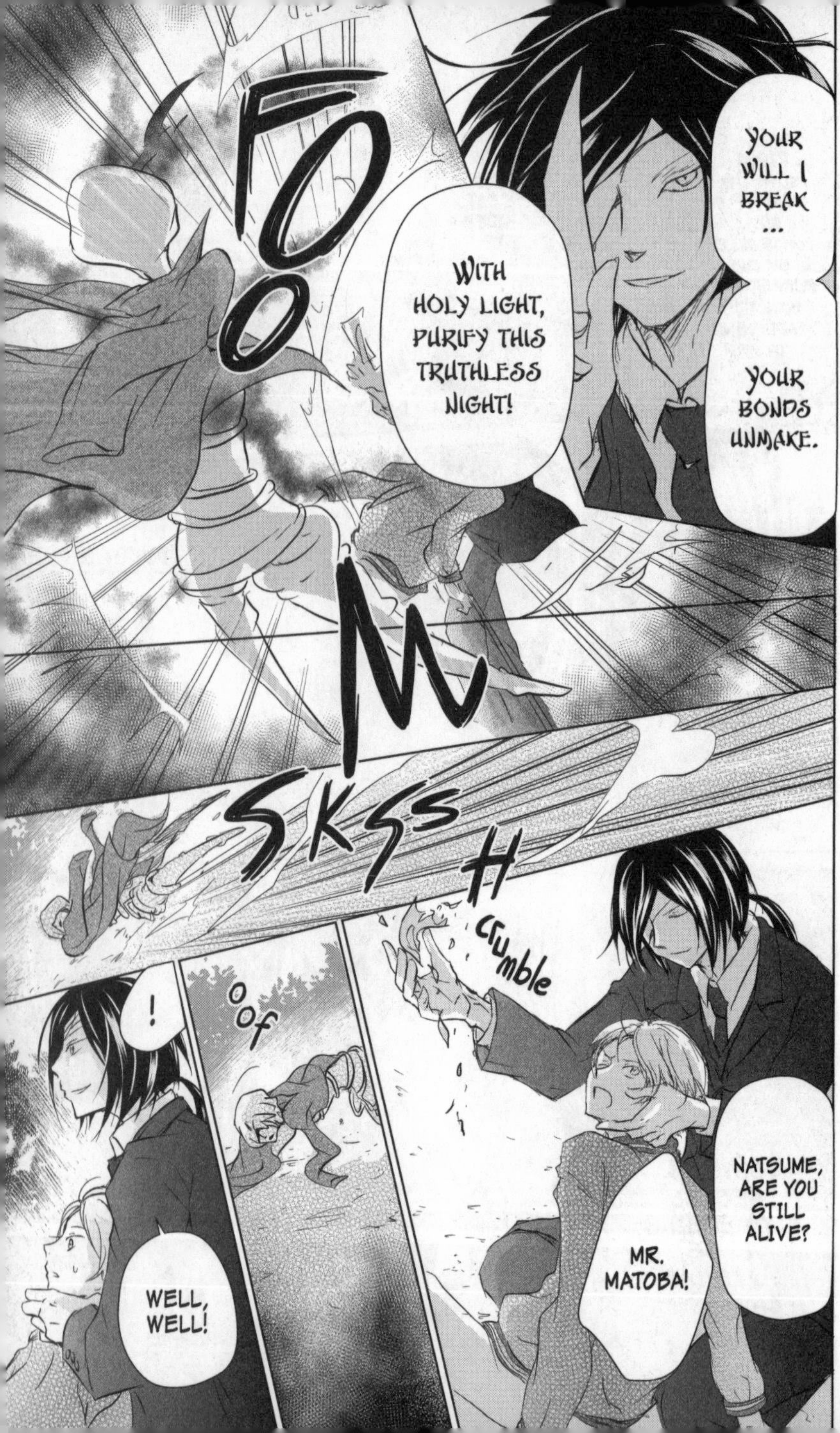
YOUR WILL I BREAK ...
YOUR BONDS UNMAKE.
WITH HOLY LIGHT, PURIFY THIS TRUTHLESS NIGHT!
FOOOM
SKSSH
crumble
NATSUME, ARE YOU STILL ALIVE?
MR. MATOBA!
oof
!
WELL, WELL!

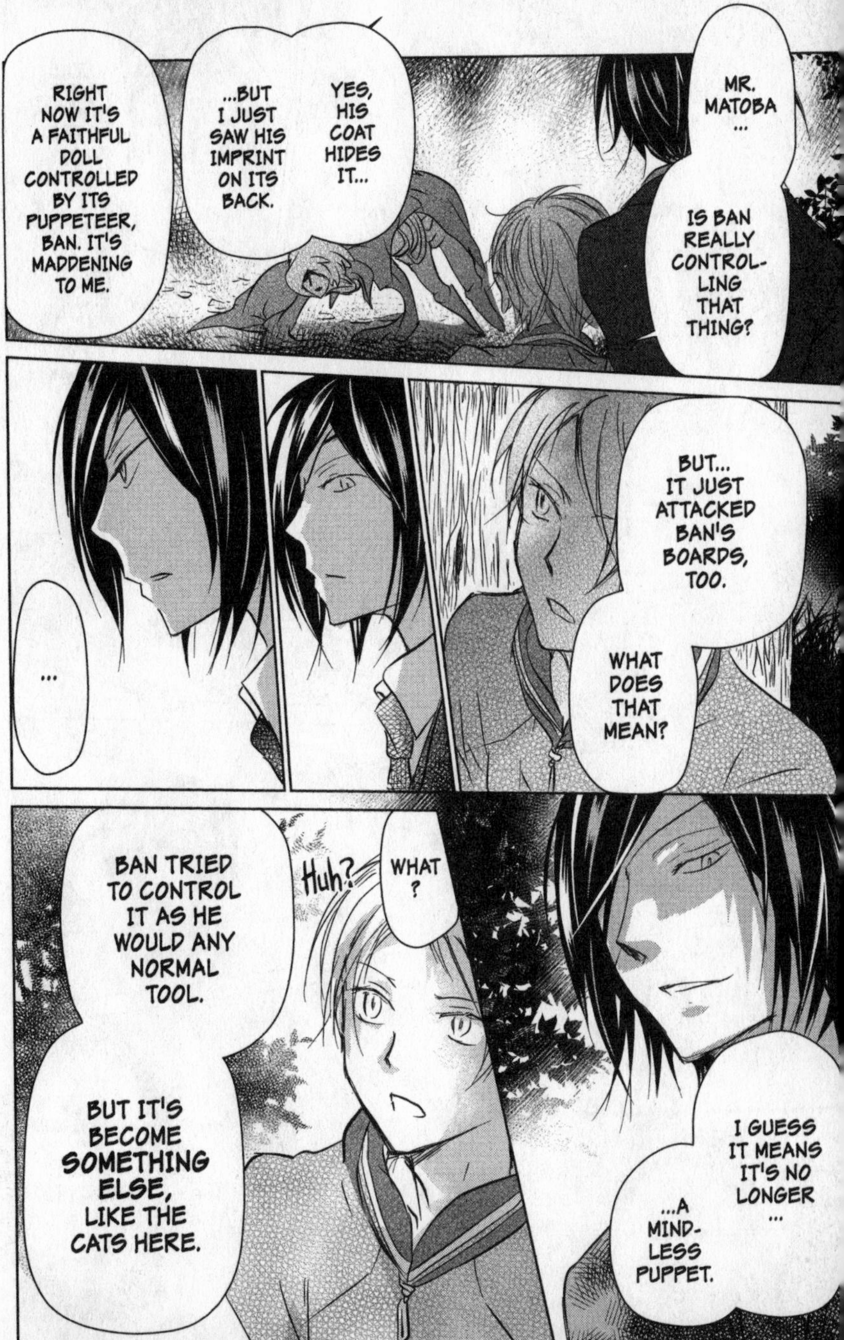
MR. MATOBA ...
IS BAN REALLY CONTROL-LING THAT THING?
YES, HIS COAT HIDES IT...
...BUT I JUST SAW HIS IMPRINT ON ITS BACK.
RIGHT NOW IT'S A FAITHFUL DOLL CONTROLLED BY ITS PUPPETEER, BAN. IT'S MADDENING TO ME.
BUT... IT JUST ATTACKED BAN'S BOARDS, TOO.
WHAT DOES THAT MEAN?
...
I GUESS IT MEANS IT'S NO LONGER ...
...A MIND-LESS PUPPET.
WHAT ?
Huh?
BAN TRIED TO CONTROL IT AS HE WOULD ANY NORMAL TOOL.
BUT IT'S BECOME SOMETHING ELSE, LIKE THE CATS HERE.

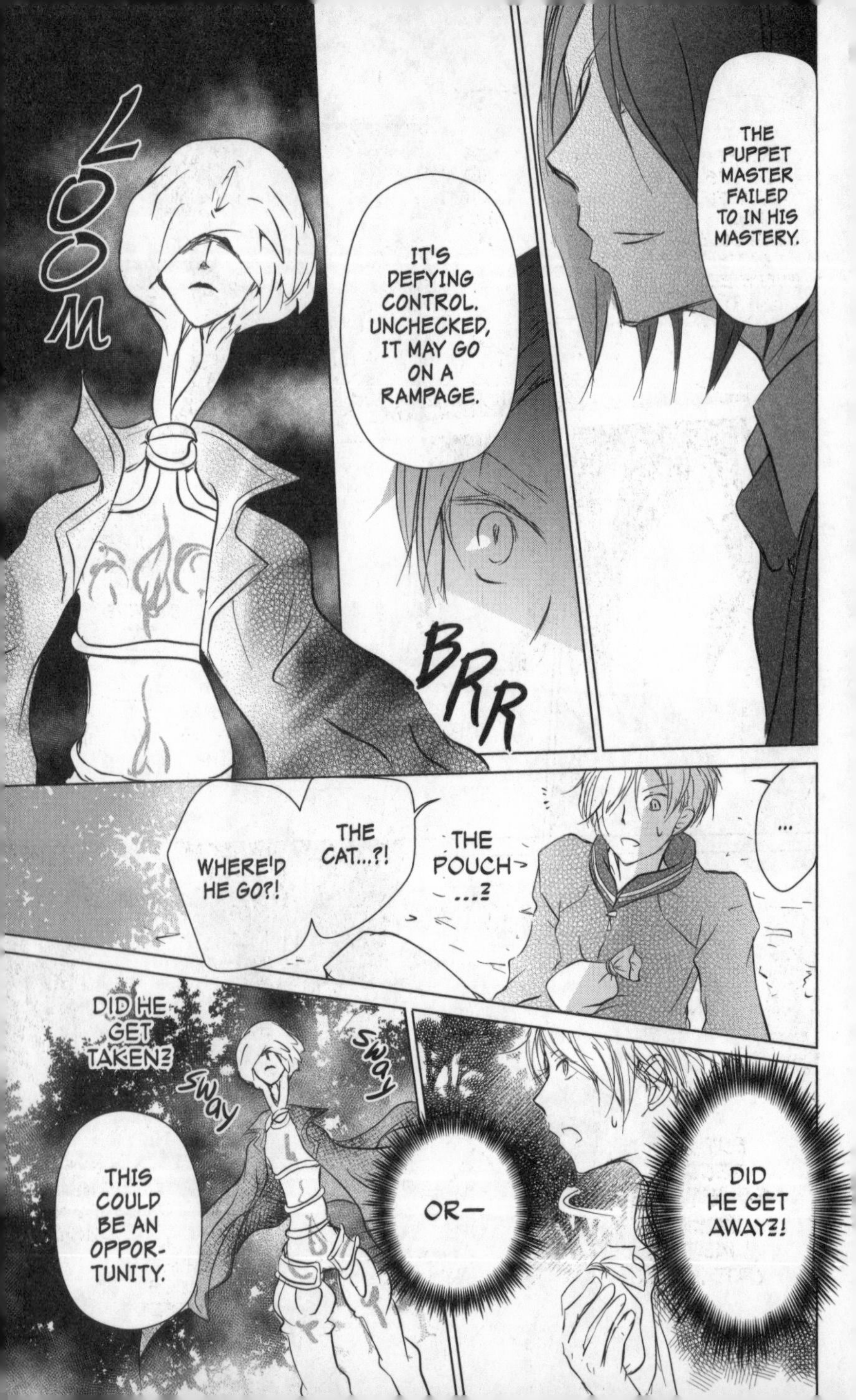
THE PUPPET MASTER FAILED TO IN HIS MASTERY.
IT'S DEFYING CONTROL. UNCHECKED, IT MAY GO ON A RAMPAGE.
BRRR
LOOM
...
THE POUCH ...?
THE CAT...?!
WHERE'D HE GO?!
DID HE GET AWAY?!
OR—
DID HE GET TAKEN?
SWAY
SWAY
THIS COULD BE AN OPPOR-TUNITY.

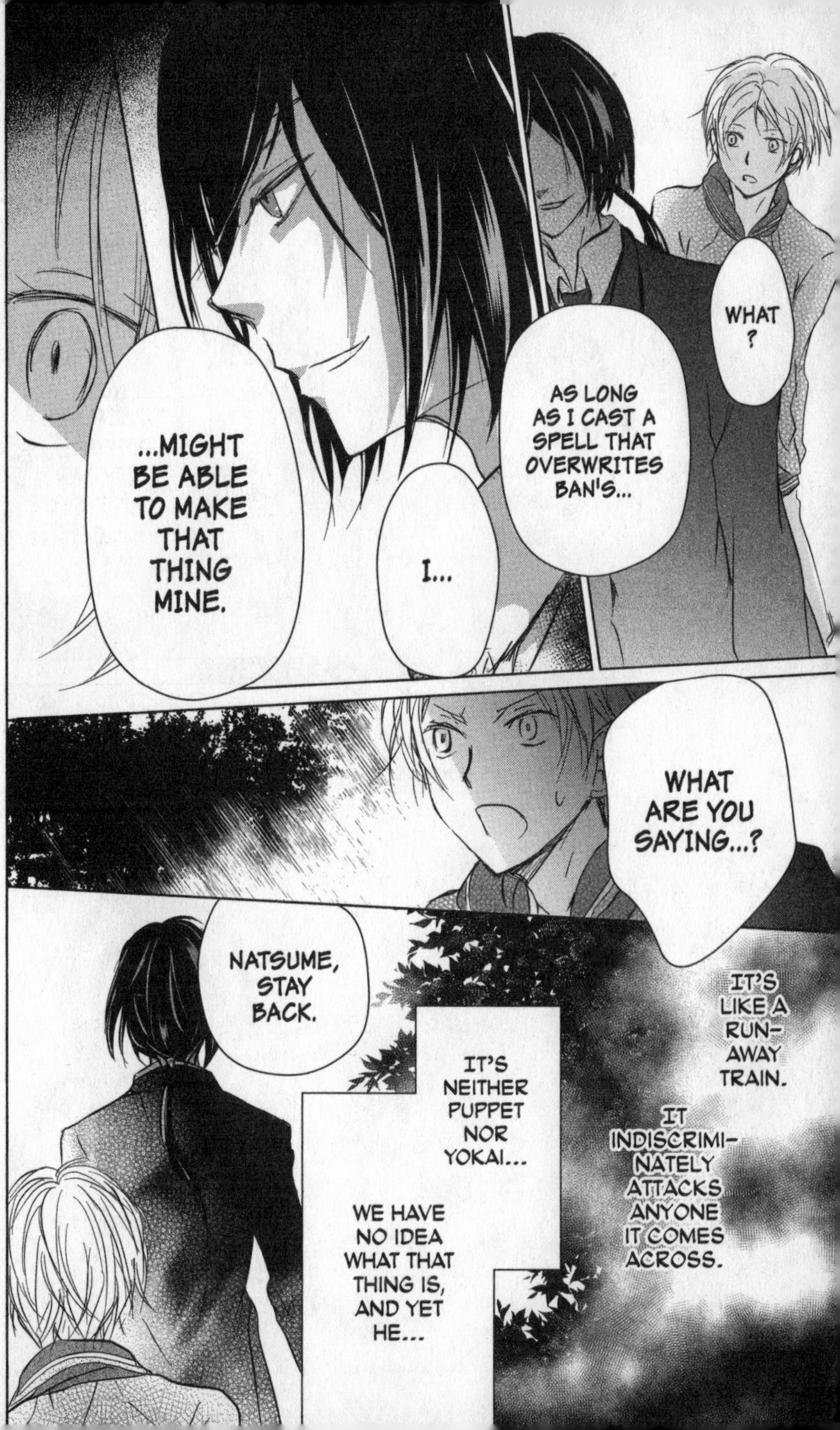
WHAT?
AS LONG AS I CAST A SPELL THAT OVERWRITES BAN'S...
I...
...MIGHT BE ABLE TO MAKE THAT THING MINE.
WHAT ARE YOU SAYING...?
IT'S LIKE A RUN-AWAY TRAIN.
IT INDISCRIMI-NATELY ATTACKS ANYONE IT COMES ACROSS.
NATSUME, STAY BACK.
IT'S NEITHER PUPPET NOR YOKAI...
WE HAVE NO IDEA WHAT THAT THING IS, AND YET HE...

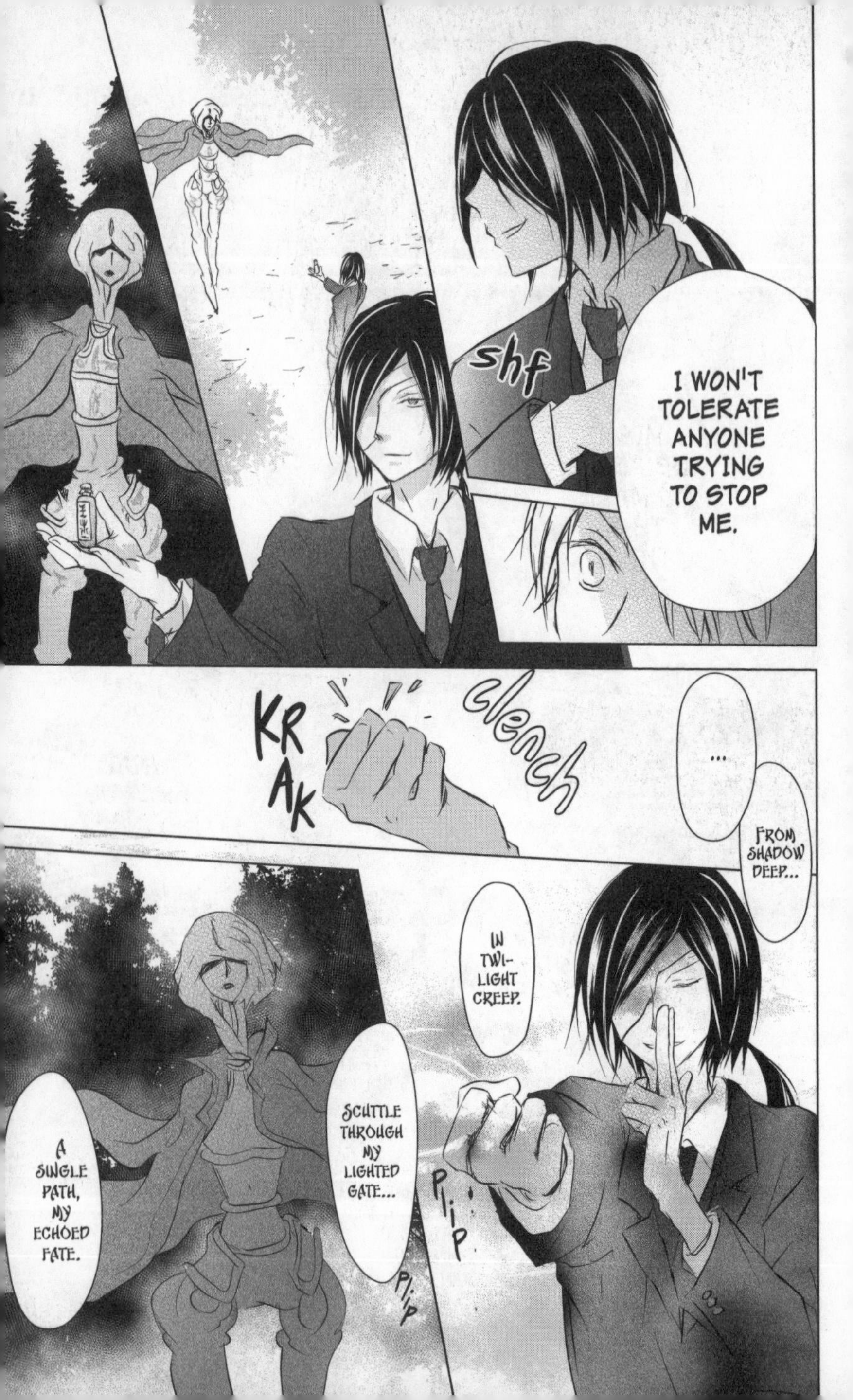
shf
I WON'T TOLERATE ANYONE TRYING TO STOP ME.
...
clench
KRAK
FROM SHADOW DEEP...
IN TWI-LIGHT CREEP.
SCUTTLE THROUGH MY LIGHTED GATE...
A SINGLE PATH, MY ECHOED FATE.
Plip
Plip

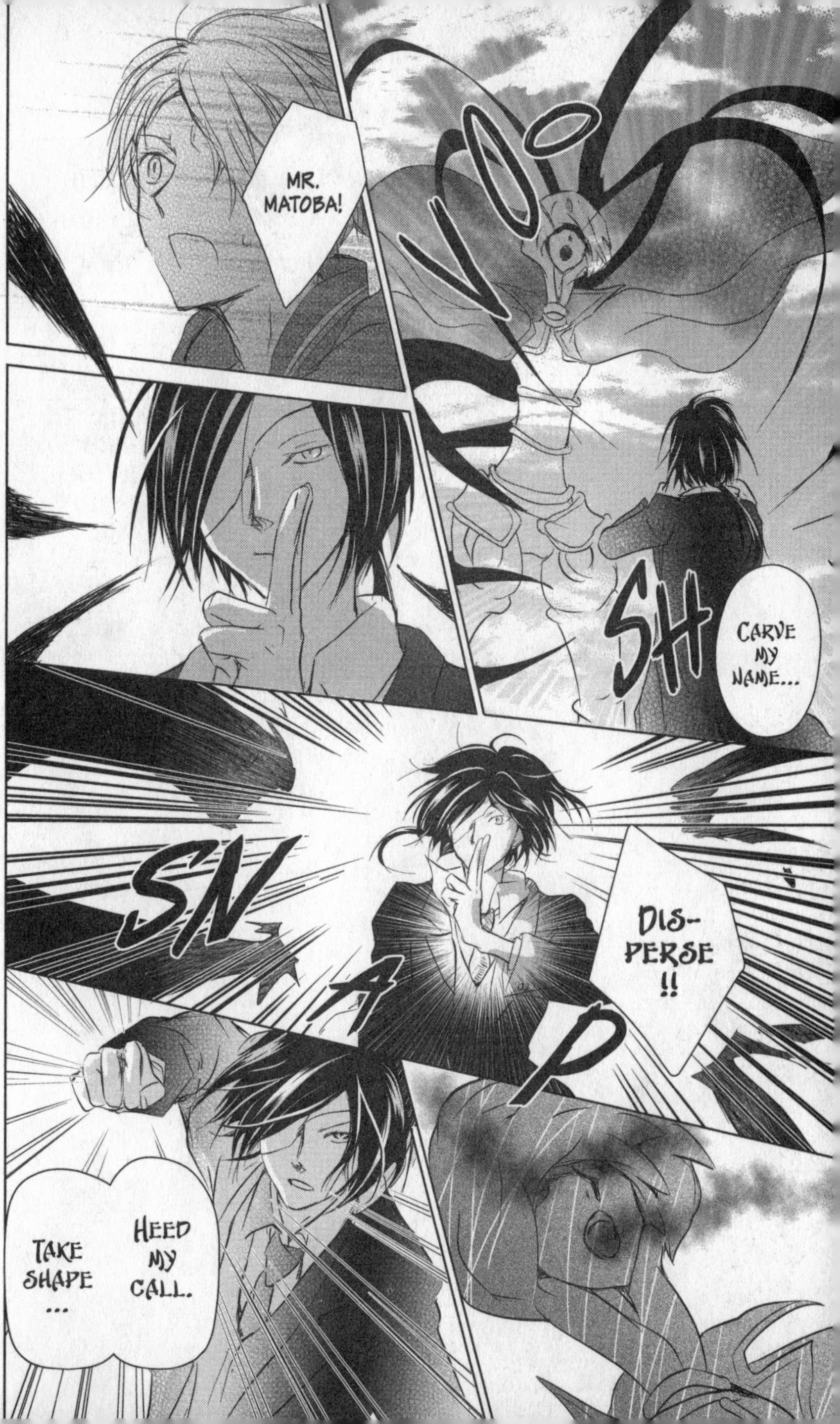
VOOO
MR. MATOBA!
SH
CARVE MY NAME...
DIS-PERSE!!
SNAP
HEED MY CALL.
TAKE SHAPE...

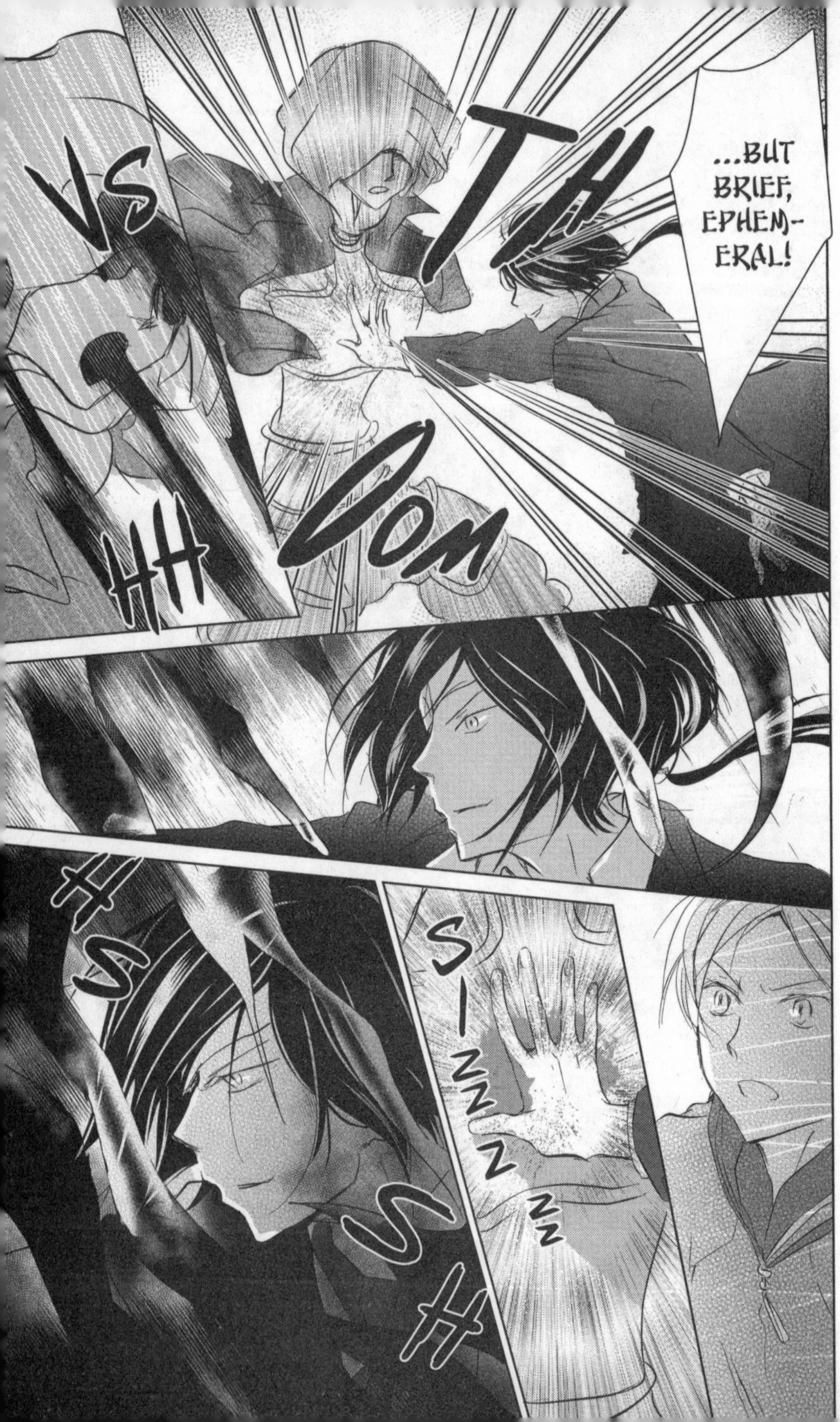
...BUT BRIEF, EPHEMERAL!
THOOM
VSHH
SIZZZZZZZ

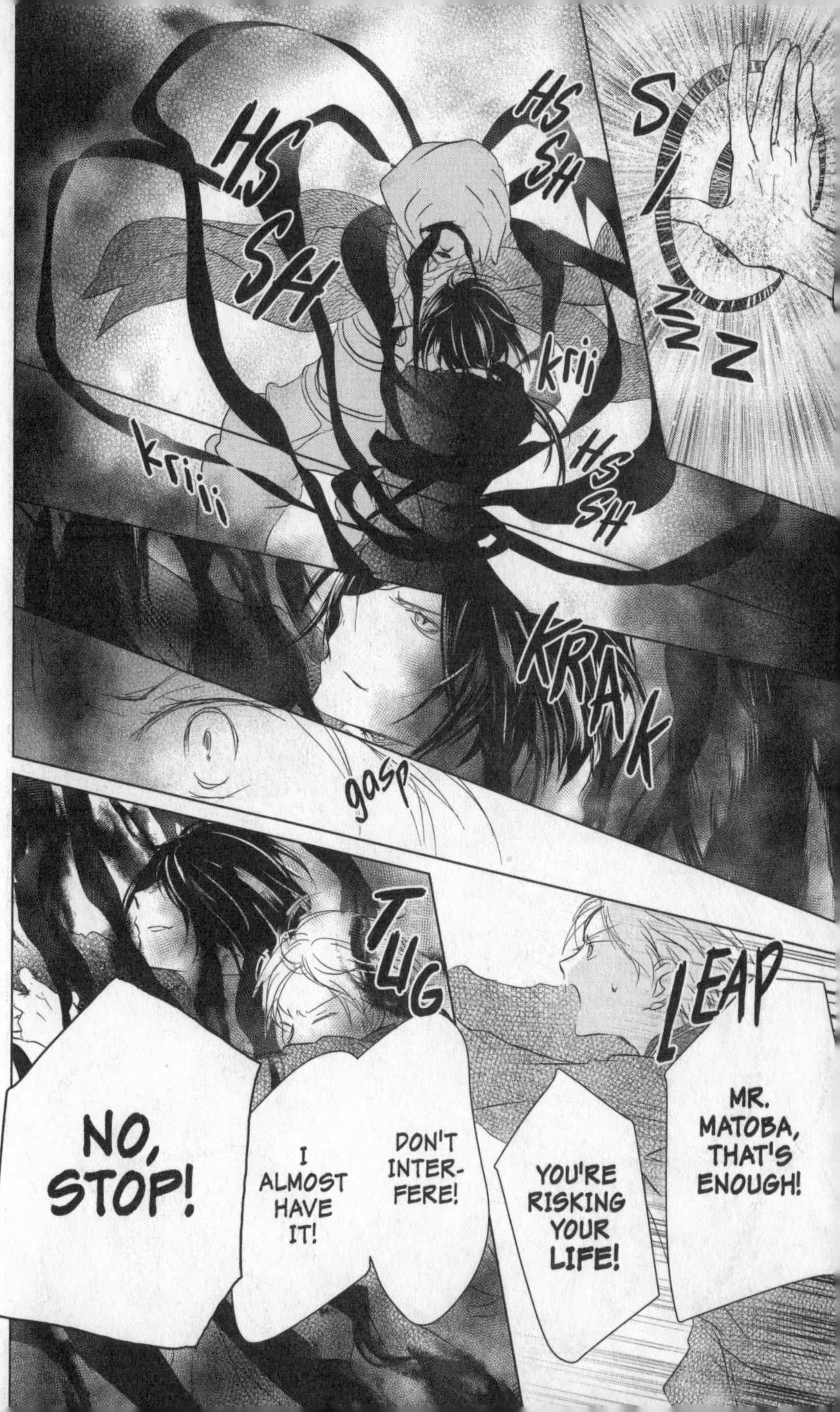
SIZZZZ
HS SH
HS SH
kriii
kriii
HS SH
KRAK
gasp
LEAP
MR. MATOBA, THAT'S ENOUGH!
YOU'RE RISKING YOUR LIFE!
TUG
DON'T INTER-FERE!
I ALMOST HAVE IT!
NO, STOP!

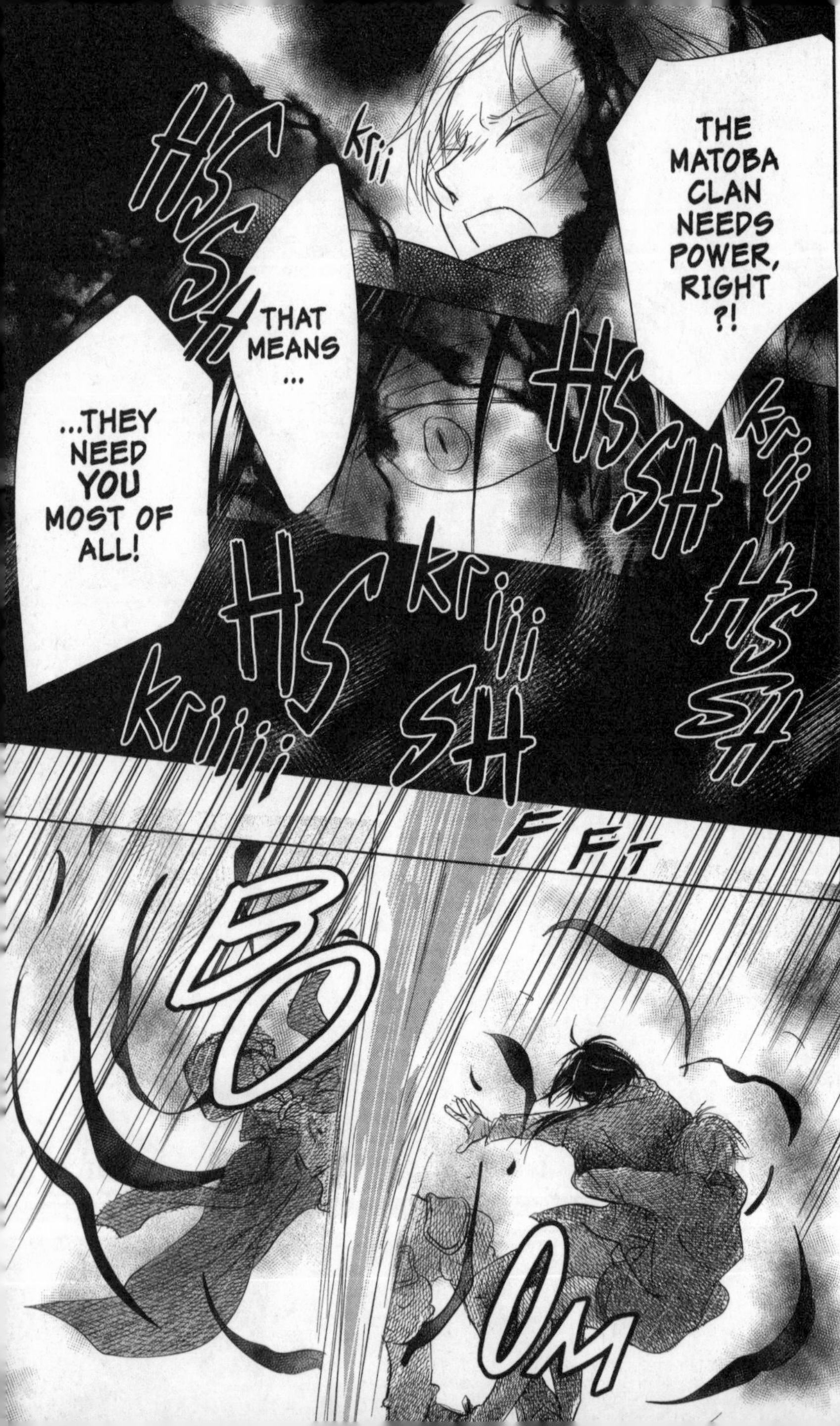
THE MATOBA CLAN NEEDS POWER, RIGHT?!
kriii
HSSH
THAT MEANS...
...THEY NEED YOU MOST OF ALL!
HSSH
kriiii
HSSH
HSSH
kriiii
HSSH
kriiiii
FFFT
BOOM

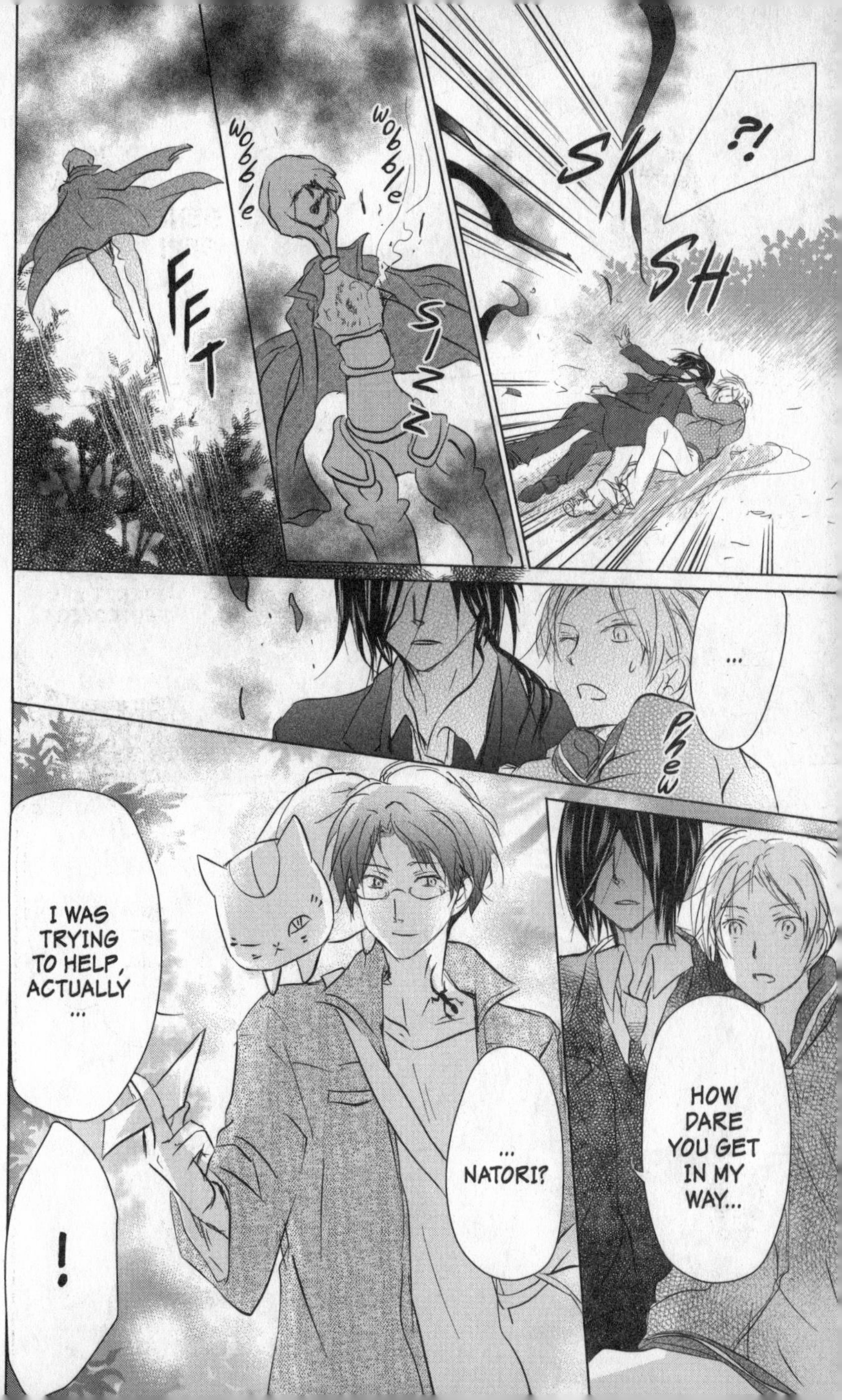
?!
SKSH
wobble
wobble
SIZZ
FFT
...
Phew
HOW DARE YOU GET IN MY WAY...
... NATORI?
I WAS TRYING TO HELP, ACTUALLY ...
!

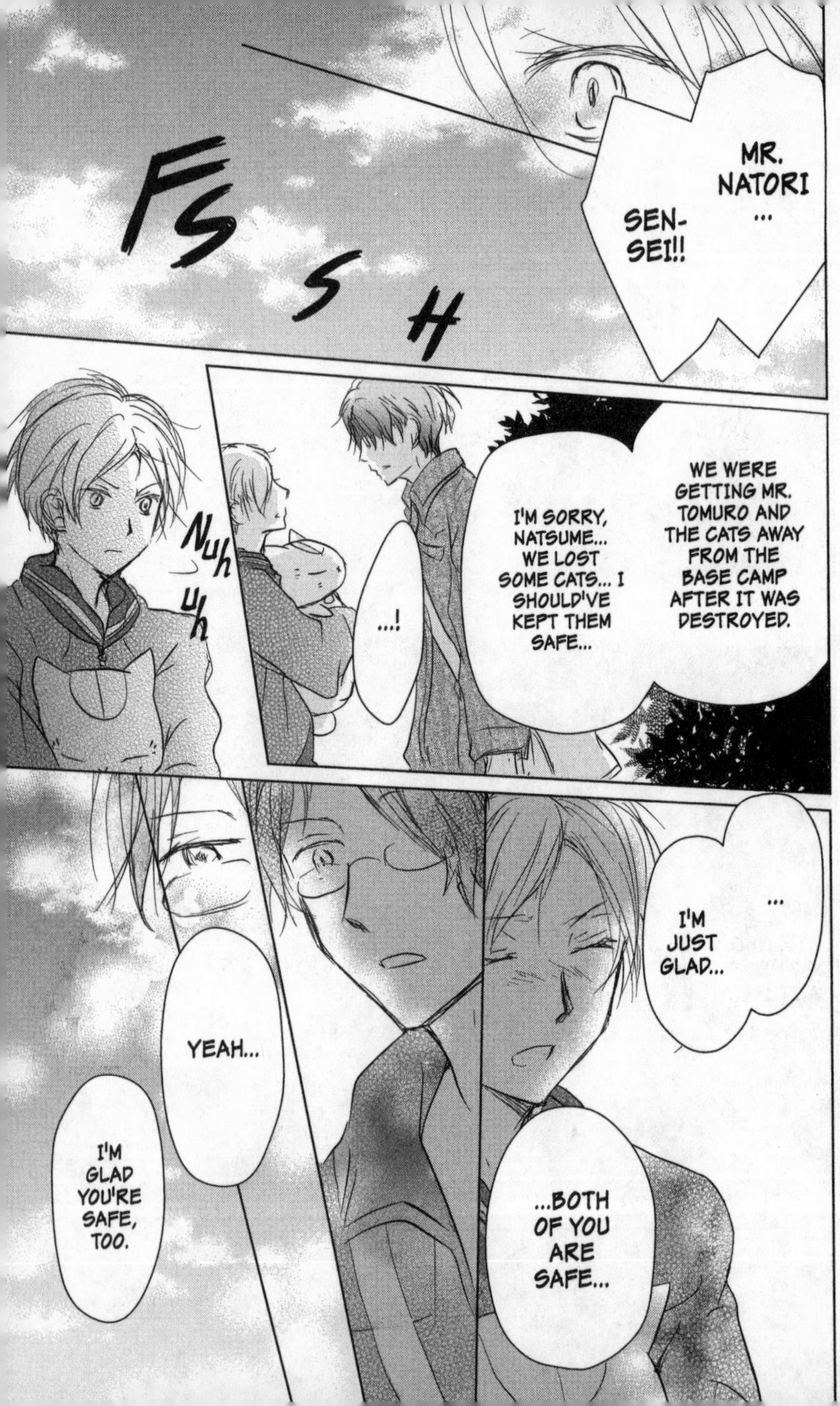
FSSH
MR. NATORI ...
SEN-SEI!!
WE WERE GETTING MR. TOMURO AND THE CATS AWAY FROM THE BASE CAMP AFTER IT WAS DESTROYED.
I'M SORRY, NATSUME... WE LOST SOME CATS... I SHOULD'VE KEPT THEM SAFE...
...!
Nuh uh uh
... I'M JUST GLAD...
...BOTH OF YOU ARE SAFE...
YEAH...
I'M GLAD YOU'RE SAFE, TOO.

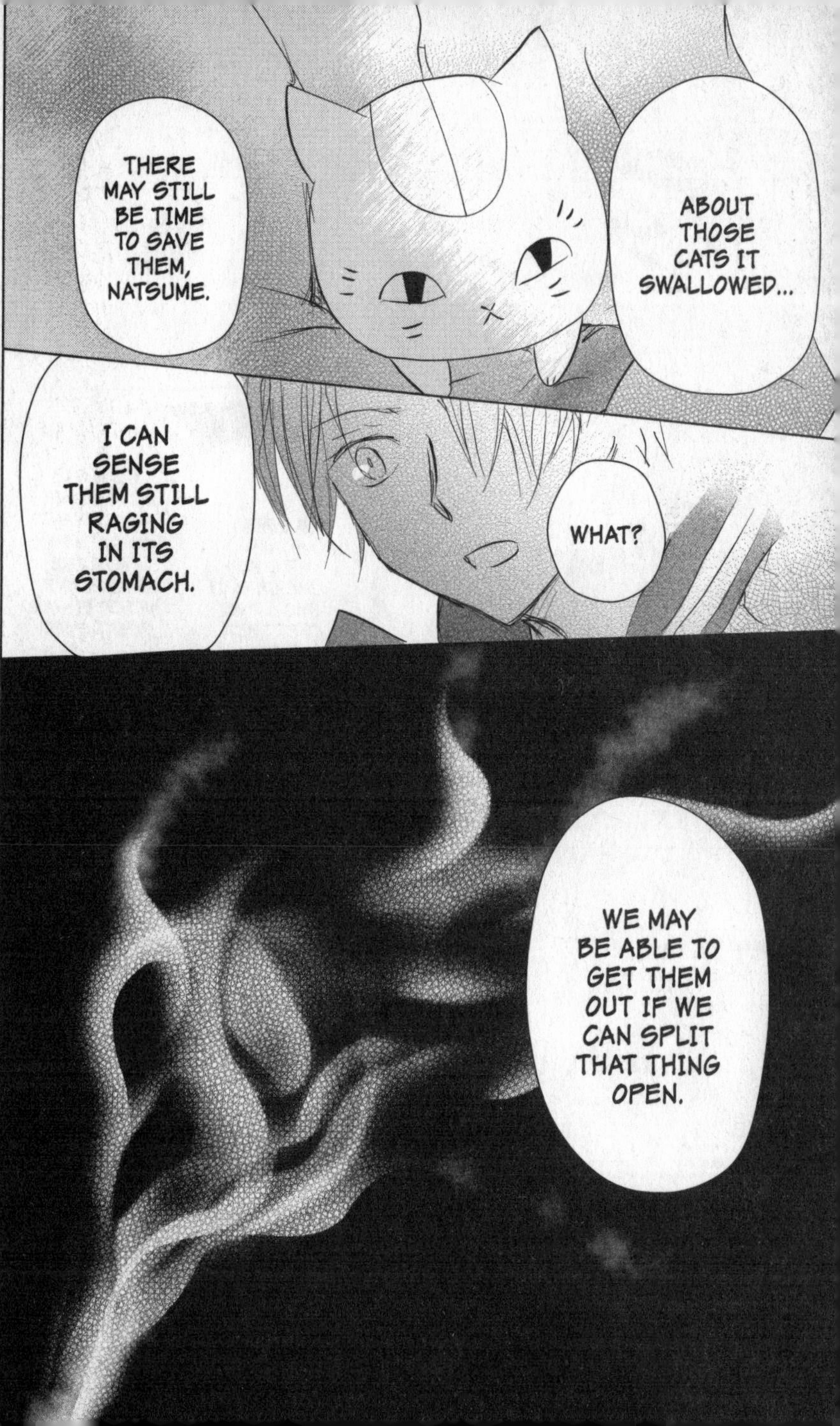
ABOUT THOSE CATS IT SWALLOWED...
THERE MAY STILL BE TIME TO SAVE THEM, NATSUME.
WHAT?
I CAN SENSE THEM STILL RAGING IN ITS STOMACH.
WE MAY BE ABLE TO GET THEM OUT IF WE CAN SPLIT THAT THING OPEN.

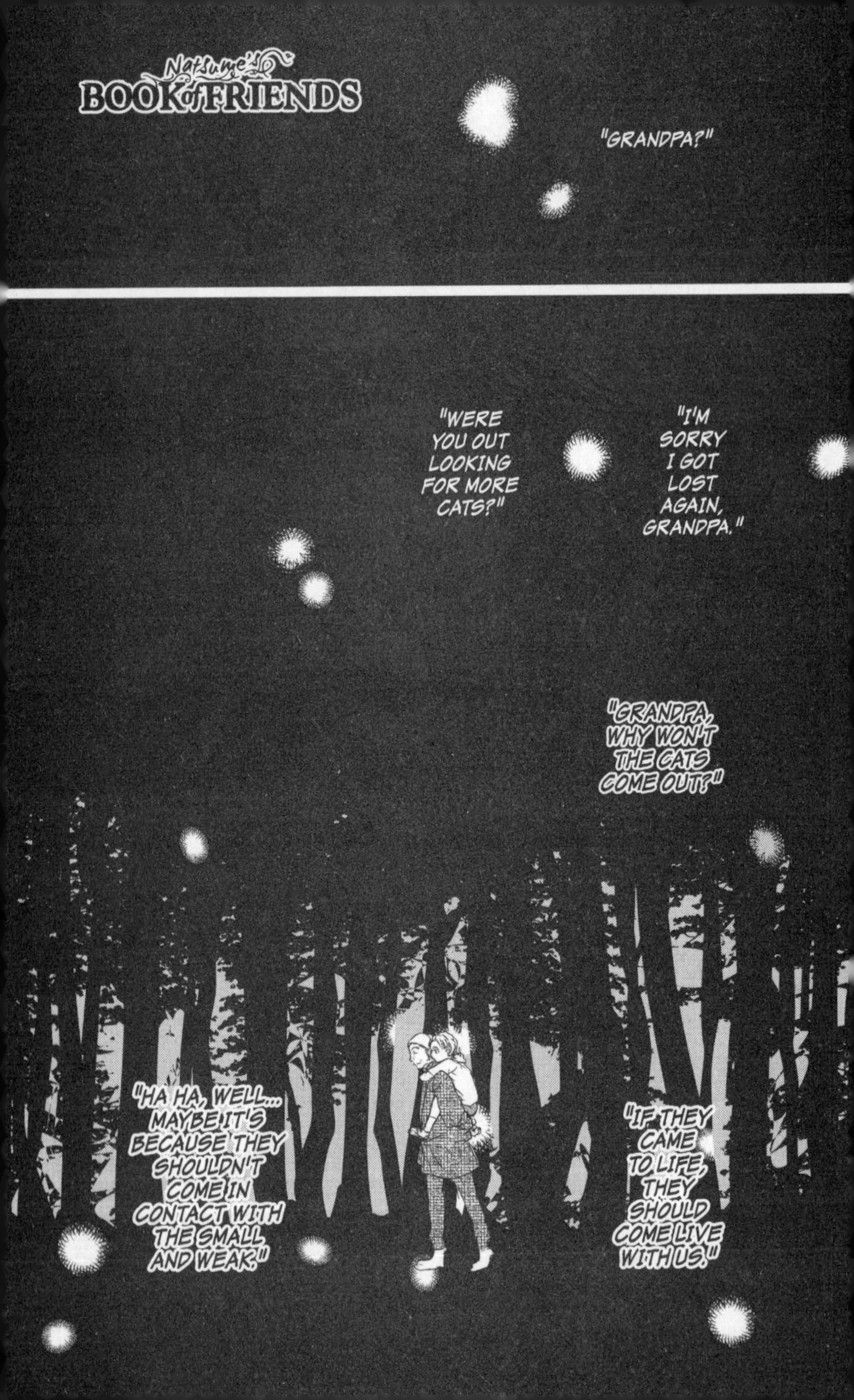
"GRANDPA?"
"I'M SORRY I GOT LOST AGAIN, GRANDPA."
"WERE YOU OUT LOOKING FOR MORE CATS?"
"GRANDPA, WHY WON'T THE CATS COME OUT?"
"IF THEY CAME TO LIFE, THEY SHOULD COME LIVE WITH US."
"HA HA, WELL... MAYBE IT'S BECAUSE THEY SHOULDN'T COME IN CONTACT WITH THE SMALL AND WEAK."

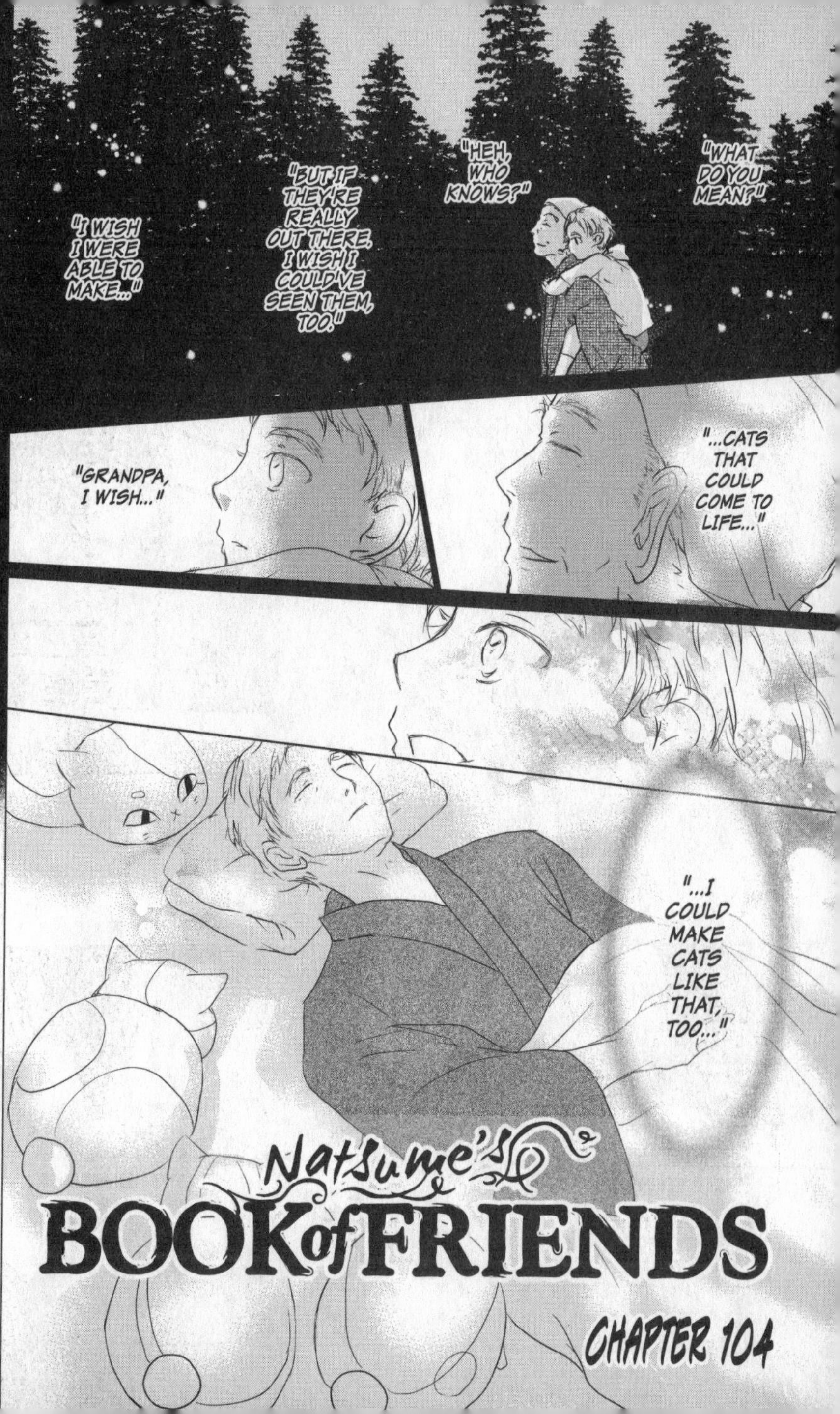
"WHAT DO YOU MEAN?"
"HEH, WHO KNOWS?"
"BUT IF THEY'RE REALLY OUT THERE, I WISH I COULD'VE SEEN THEM, TOO."
"I WISH I WERE ABLE TO MAKE..."
"...CATS THAT COULD COME TO LIFE..."
"GRANDPA, I WISH..."
"...I COULD MAKE CATS LIKE THAT, TOO..."
Natsume's
BOOK of FRIENDS
CHAPTER 104

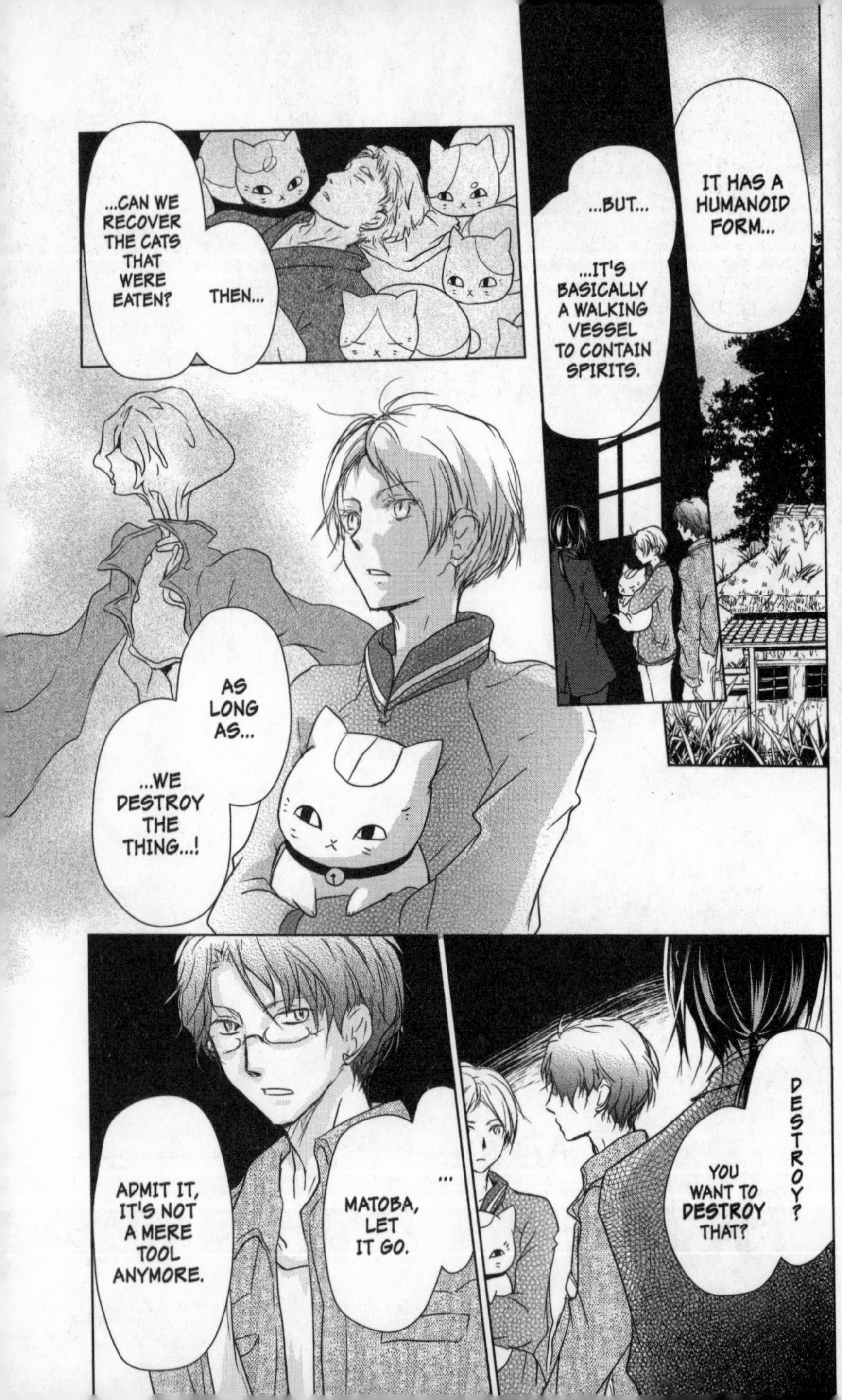
IT HAS A HUMANOID FORM...
...BUT...
...IT'S BASICALLY A WALKING VESSEL TO CONTAIN SPIRITS.
THEN...
...CAN WE RECOVER THE CATS THAT WERE EATEN?
AS LONG AS...
...WE DESTROY THE THING...!
DESTROY?
YOU WANT TO DESTROY THAT?
...
MATOBA, LET IT GO.
ADMIT IT, IT'S NOT A MERE TOOL ANYMORE.

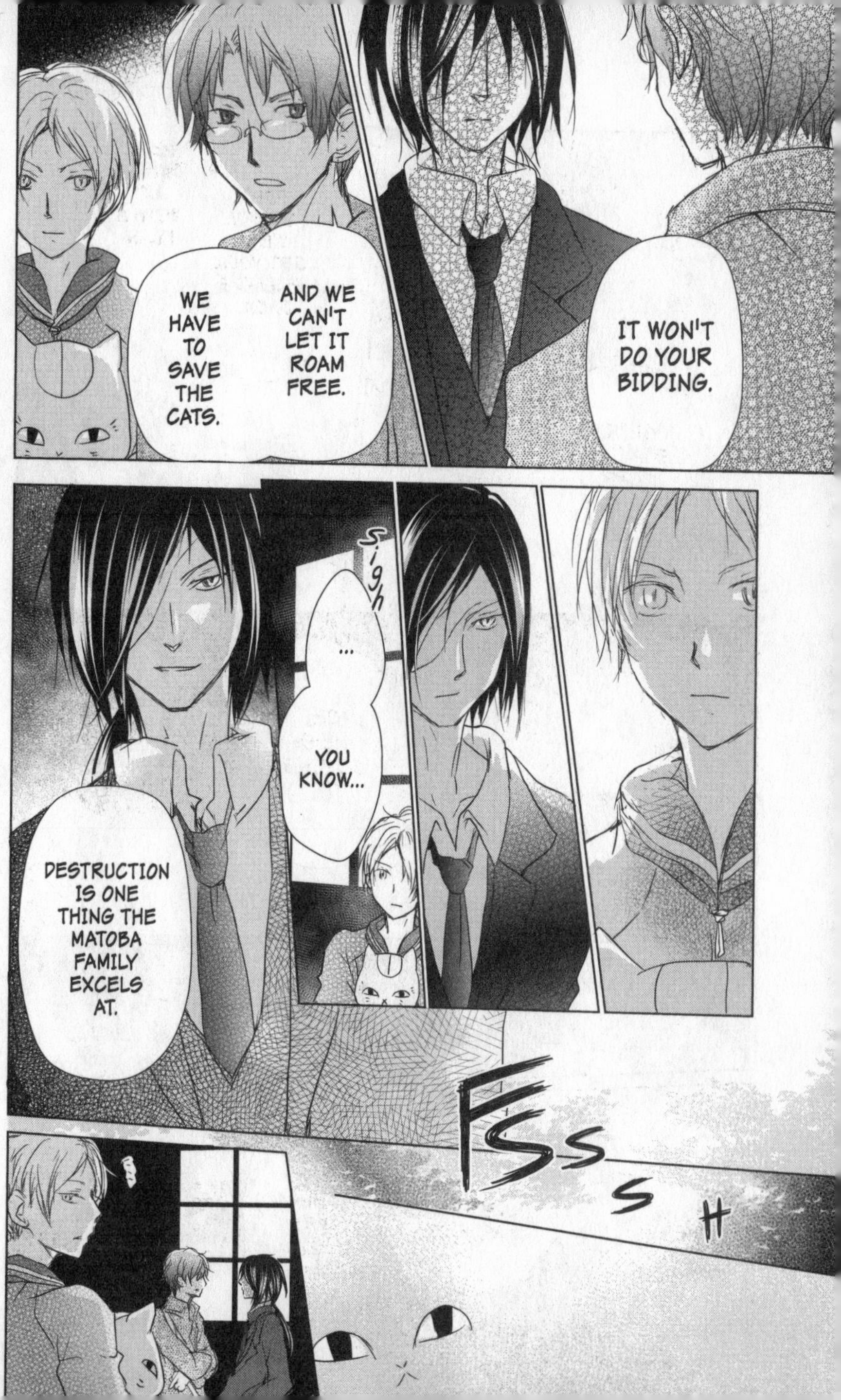
IT WON'T DO YOUR BIDDING.
WE HAVE TO SAVE THE CATS.
AND WE CAN'T LET IT ROAM FREE.
sigh
...
YOU KNOW...
DESTRUCTION IS ONE THING THE MATOBA FAMILY EXCELS AT.
FSSSSH

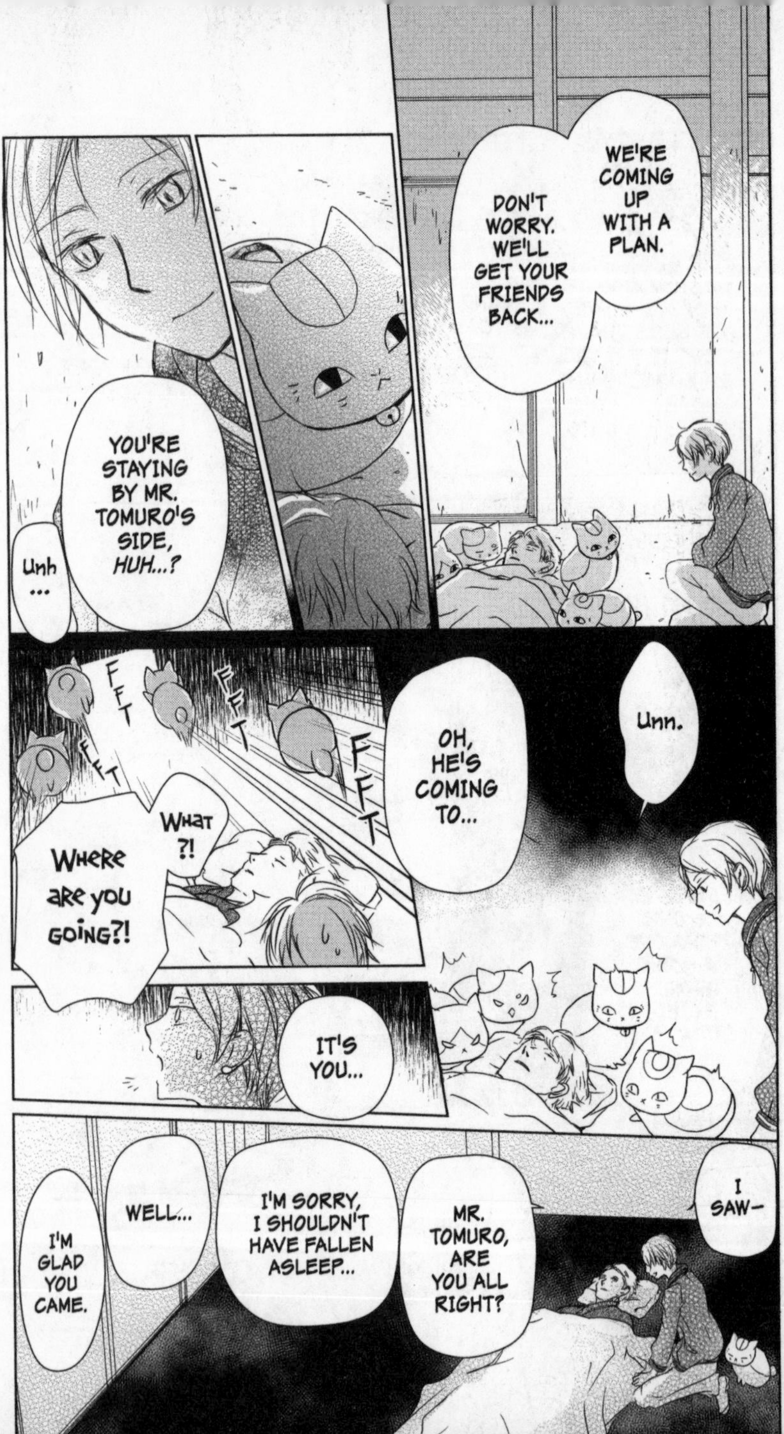
WE'RE COMING UP WITH A PLAN.
DON'T WORRY. WE'LL GET YOUR FRIENDS BACK...
YOU'RE STAYING BY MR. TOMURO'S SIDE, HUH...?
Unh...
Unn.
OH, HE'S COMING TO...
FFT
FFT
FFT
FFT
What?!
Where are you going?!
IT'S YOU...
I SAW—
MR. TOMURO, ARE YOU ALL RIGHT?
I'M SORRY, I SHOULDN'T HAVE FALLEN ASLEEP...
WELL...
I'M GLAD YOU CAME.

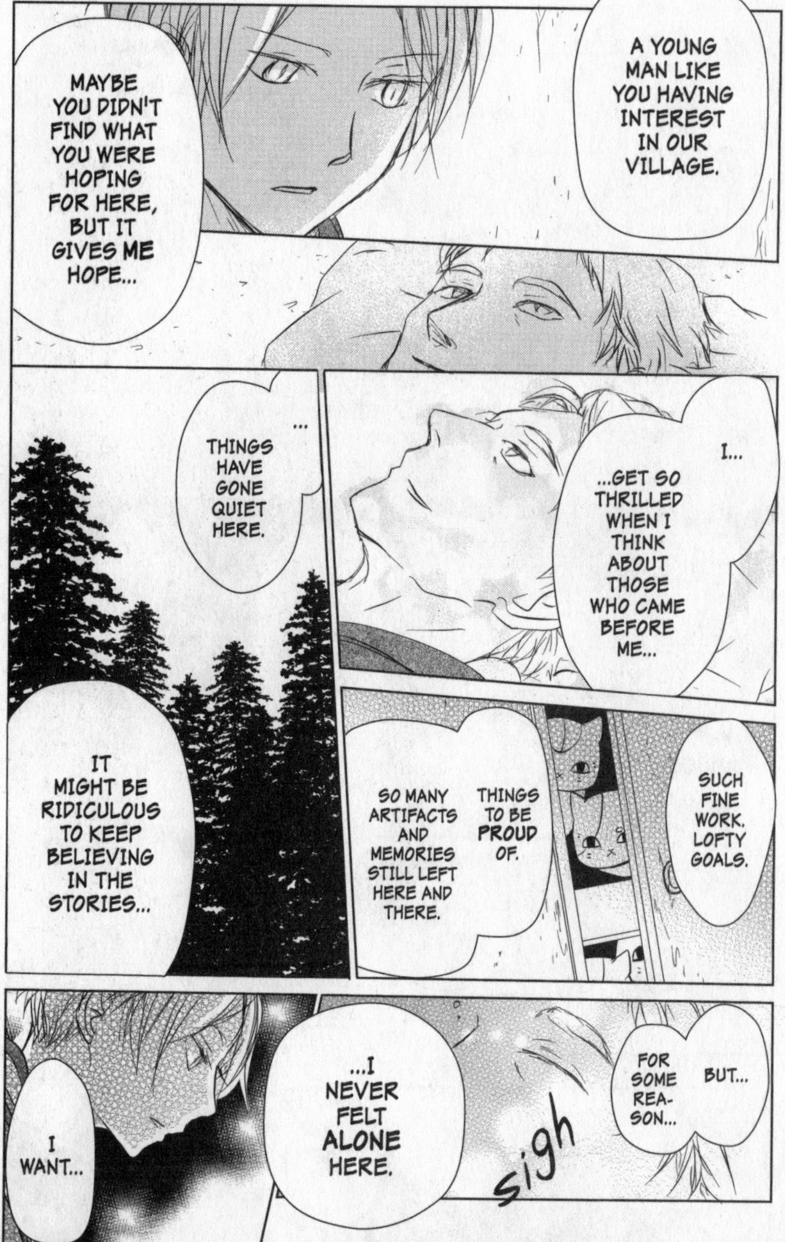
A YOUNG MAN LIKE YOU HAVING INTEREST IN OUR VILLAGE.
MAYBE YOU DIDN'T FIND WHAT YOU WERE HOPING FOR HERE, BUT IT GIVES ME HOPE...
I...
...GET SO THRILLED WHEN I THINK ABOUT THOSE WHO CAME BEFORE ME...
SUCH FINE WORK. LOFTY GOALS.
THINGS TO BE PROUD OF.
SO MANY ARTIFACTS AND MEMORIES STILL LEFT HERE AND THERE.
...
THINGS HAVE GONE QUIET HERE.
IT MIGHT BE RIDICULOUS TO KEEP BELIEVING IN THE STORIES...
BUT...
FOR SOME REA-SON...
sigh
...I NEVER FELT ALONE HERE.
I WANT...

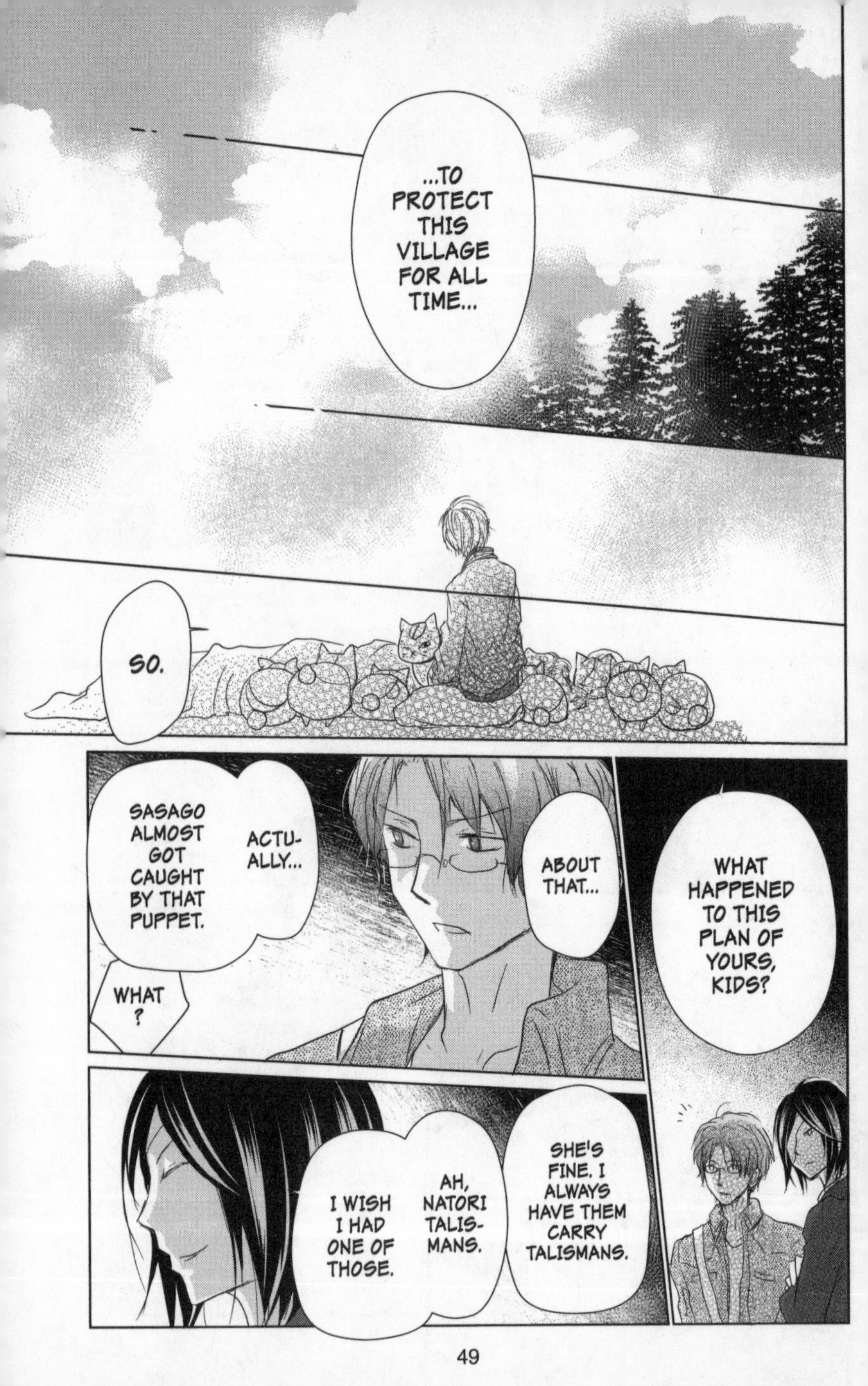
...TO PROTECT THIS VILLAGE FOR ALL TIME...
SO.
WHAT HAPPENED TO THIS PLAN OF YOURS, KIDS?
ABOUT THAT...
ACTUALLY...
SASAGO ALMOST GOT CAUGHT BY THAT PUPPET.
WHAT?
SHE'S FINE. I ALWAYS HAVE THEM CARRY TALISMANS.
AH, NATORI TALISMANS.
I WISH I HAD ONE OF THOSE.

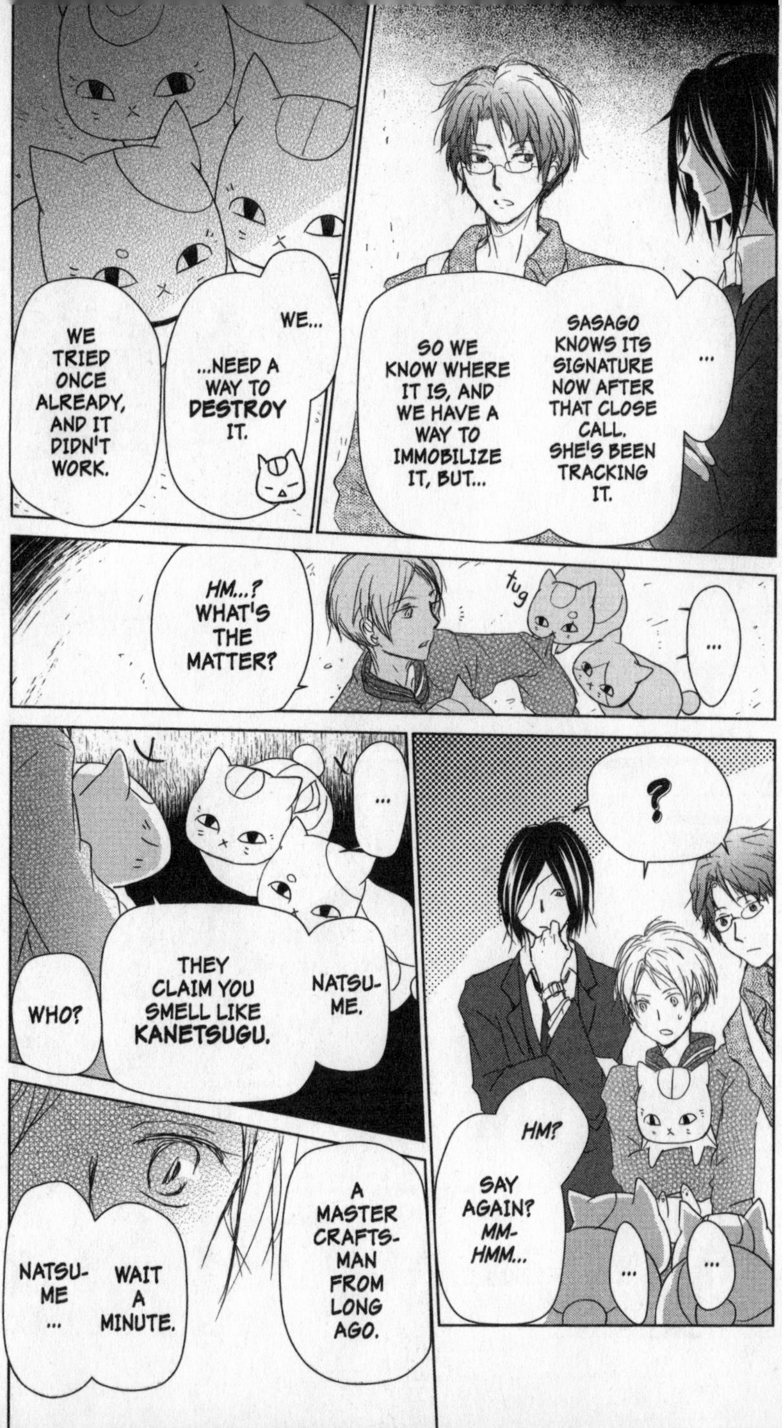
...
SASAGO KNOWS ITS SIGNATURE NOW AFTER THAT CLOSE CALL. SHE'S BEEN TRACKING IT.
SO WE KNOW WHERE IT IS, AND WE HAVE A WAY TO IMMOBILIZE IT, BUT...
WE...
...NEED A WAY TO DESTROY IT.
WE TRIED ONCE ALREADY, AND IT DIDN'T WORK.
...
tug
HM...? WHAT'S THE MATTER?
?
HM?
SAY AGAIN? MM-HMM...
...
...
...
NATSU-ME.
THEY CLAIM YOU SMELL LIKE KANETSUGU.
WHO?
A MASTER CRAFTS-MAN FROM LONG AGO.
WAIT A MINUTE.
NATSU-ME ...

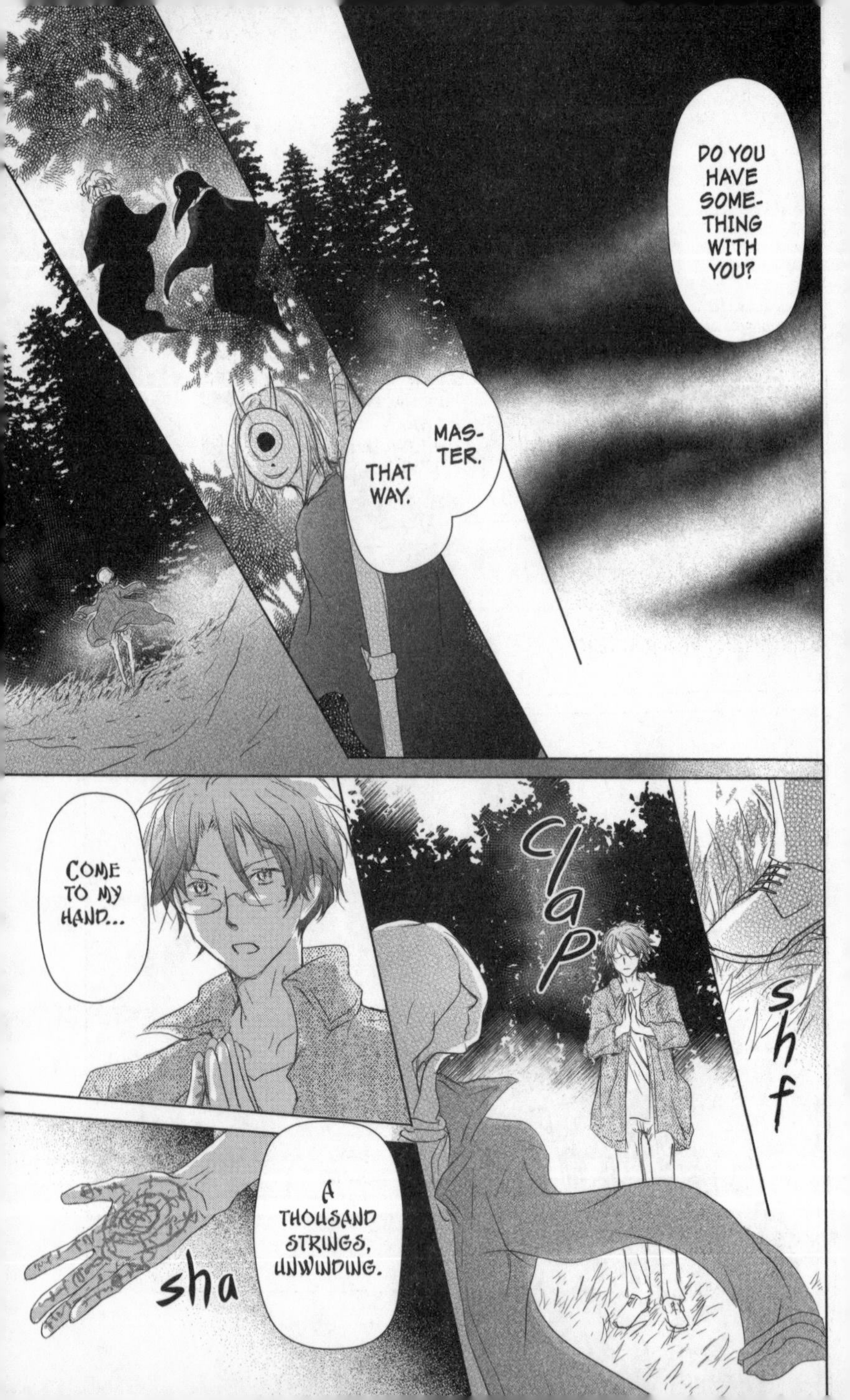
DO YOU HAVE SOME-THING WITH YOU?
MAS-TER. THAT WAY.
shf
clap
COME TO MY HAND...
A THOUSAND STRINGS, UNWINDING.
sha

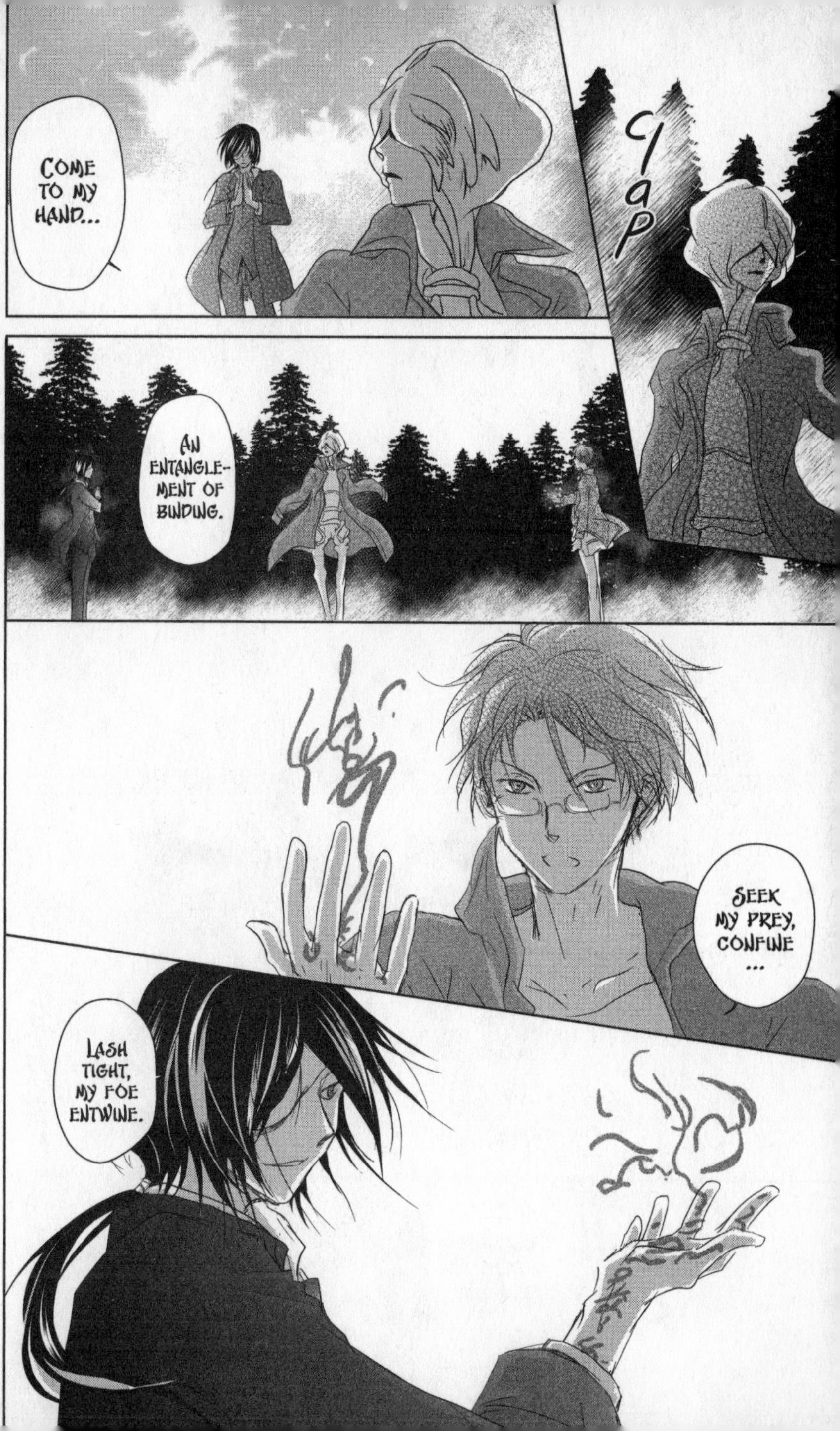
Clap
Come to my hand...
An entangle-ment of binding.
Seek my prey, confine ...
Lash tight, my foe entwine.

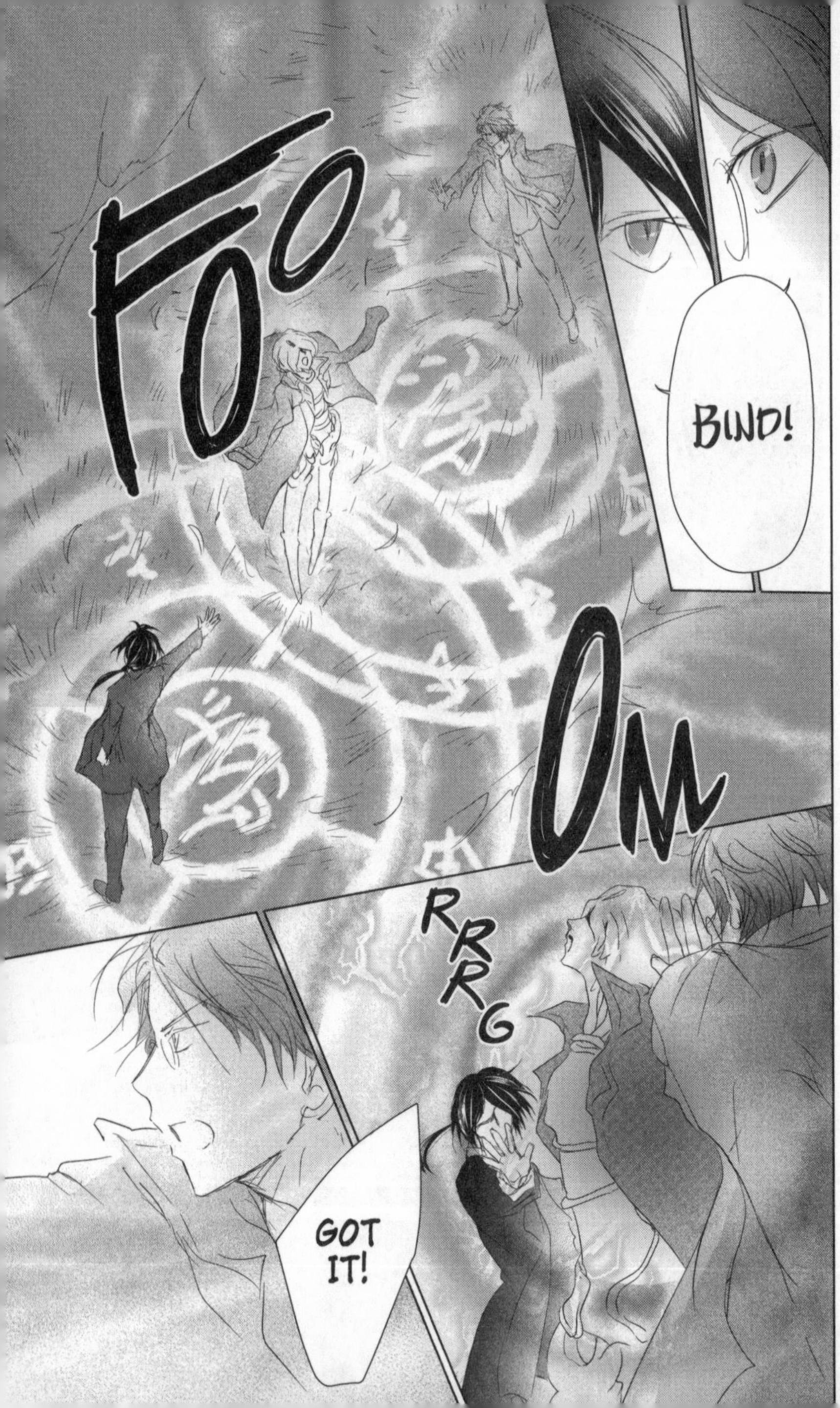
BIND!
FOOOOM
RRRG
GOT IT!

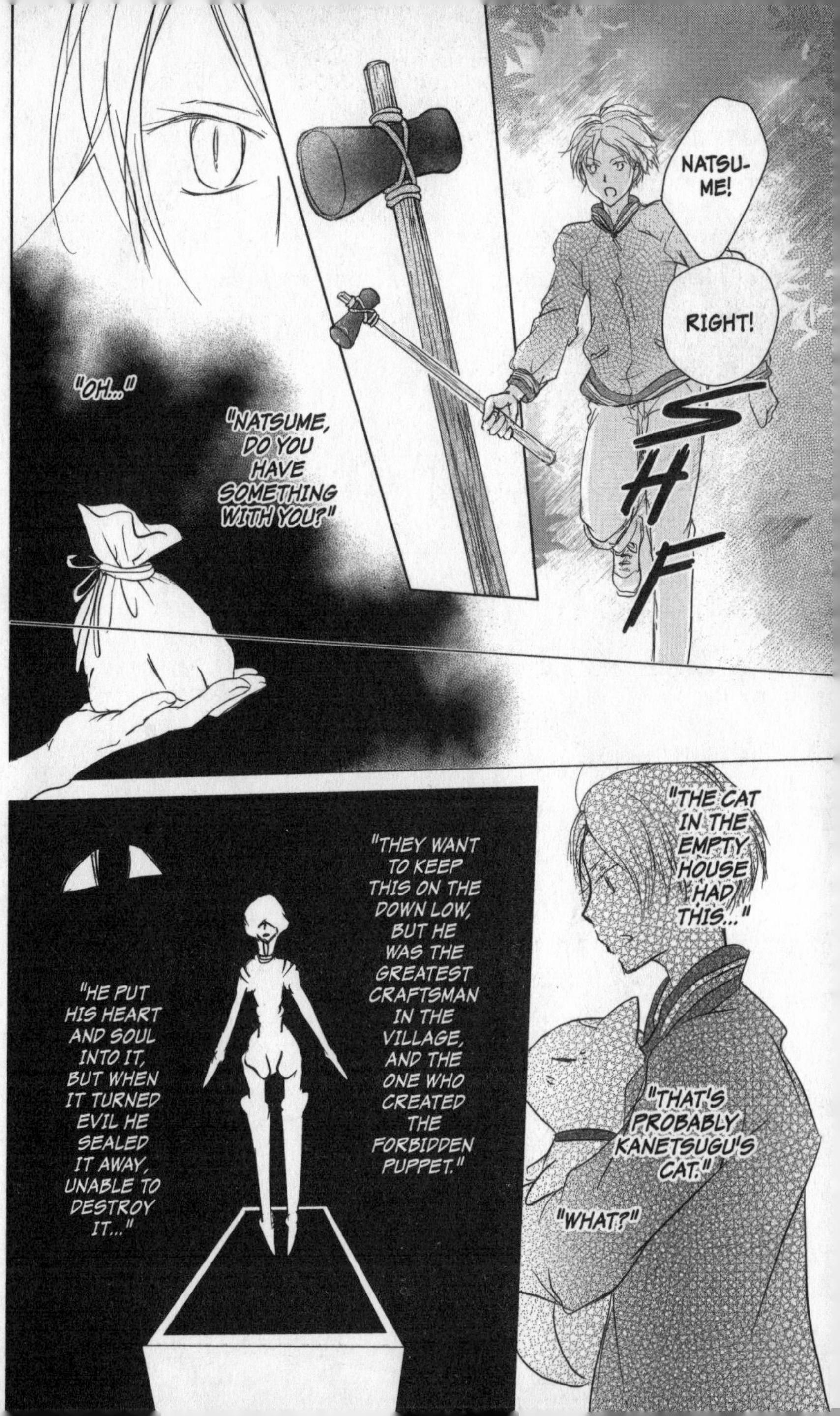
NATSU-ME!
RIGHT!
SHF
"OH..."
"NATSUME, DO YOU HAVE SOMETHING WITH YOU?"
"THE CAT IN THE EMPTY HOUSE HAD THIS..."
"THAT'S PROBABLY KANETSUGU'S CAT."
"WHAT?"
"THEY WANT TO KEEP THIS ON THE DOWN LOW, BUT HE WAS THE GREATEST CRAFTSMAN IN THE VILLAGE, AND THE ONE WHO CREATED THE FORBIDDEN PUPPET."
"HE PUT HIS HEART AND SOUL INTO IT, BUT WHEN IT TURNED EVIL HE SEALED IT AWAY, UNABLE TO DESTROY IT..."

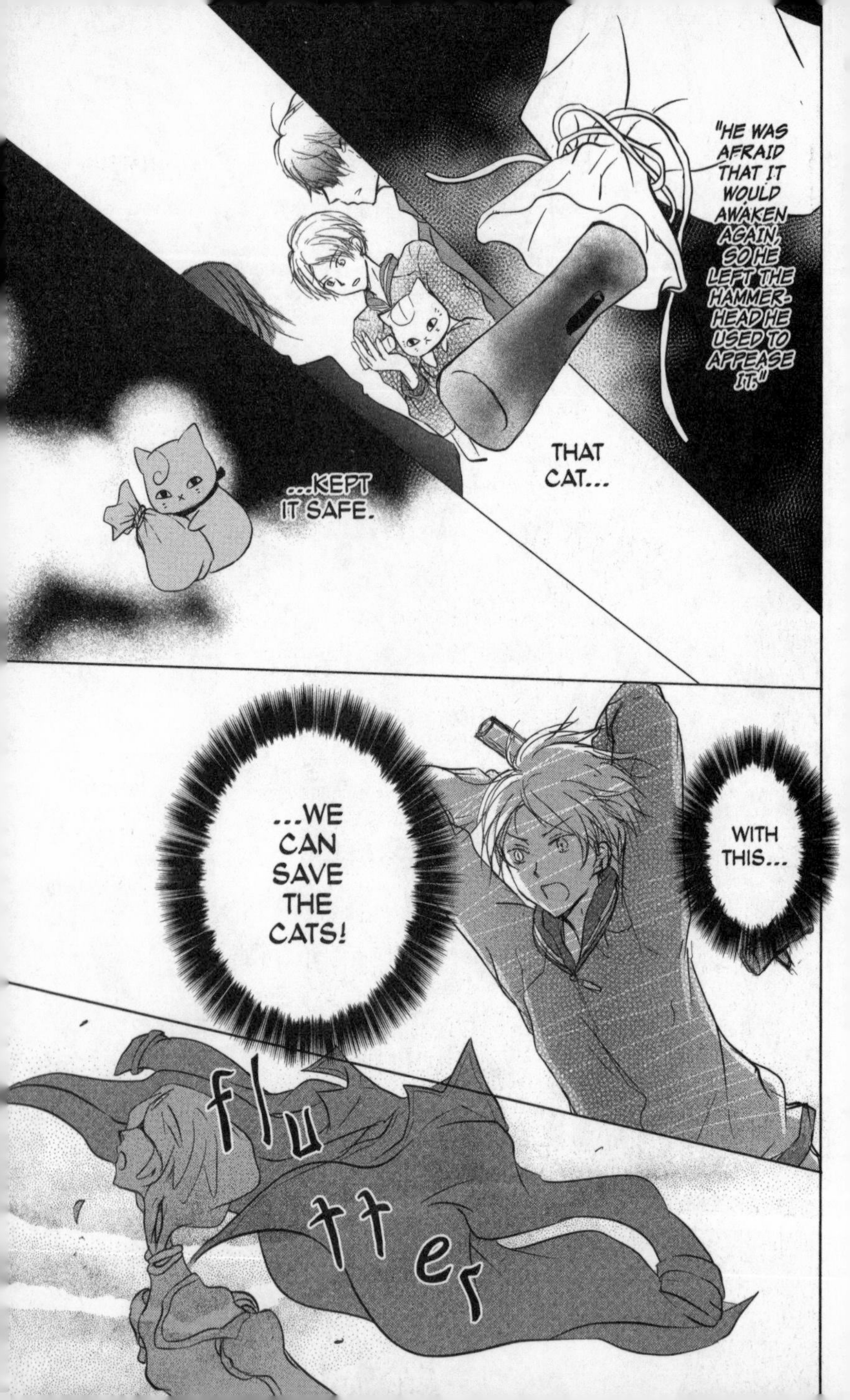
"HE WAS AFRAID THAT IT WOULD AWAKEN AGAIN, SO HE LEFT THE HAMMER-HEAD HE USED TO APPEASE IT."
THAT CAT...
...KEPT IT SAFE.
WITH THIS...
...WE CAN SAVE THE CATS!
flutter

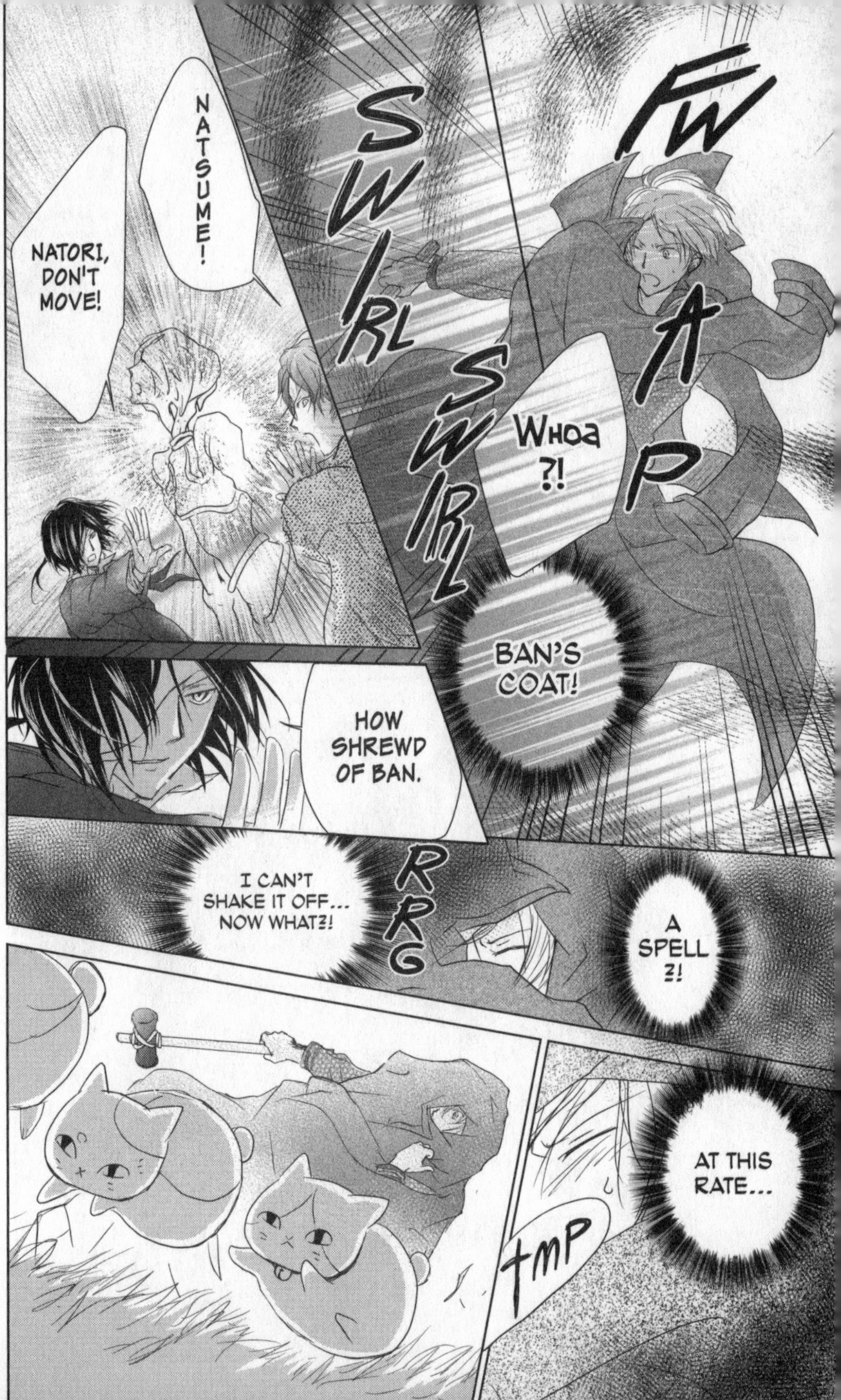
FWAP
WHOA?!
SWIRL
SWIRL
NATSUME!
NATORI, DON'T MOVE!
BAN'S COAT!
HOW SHREWD OF BAN.
A SPELL?!
RRG
I CAN'T SHAKE IT OFF... NOW WHAT?!
AT THIS RATE...
tmp

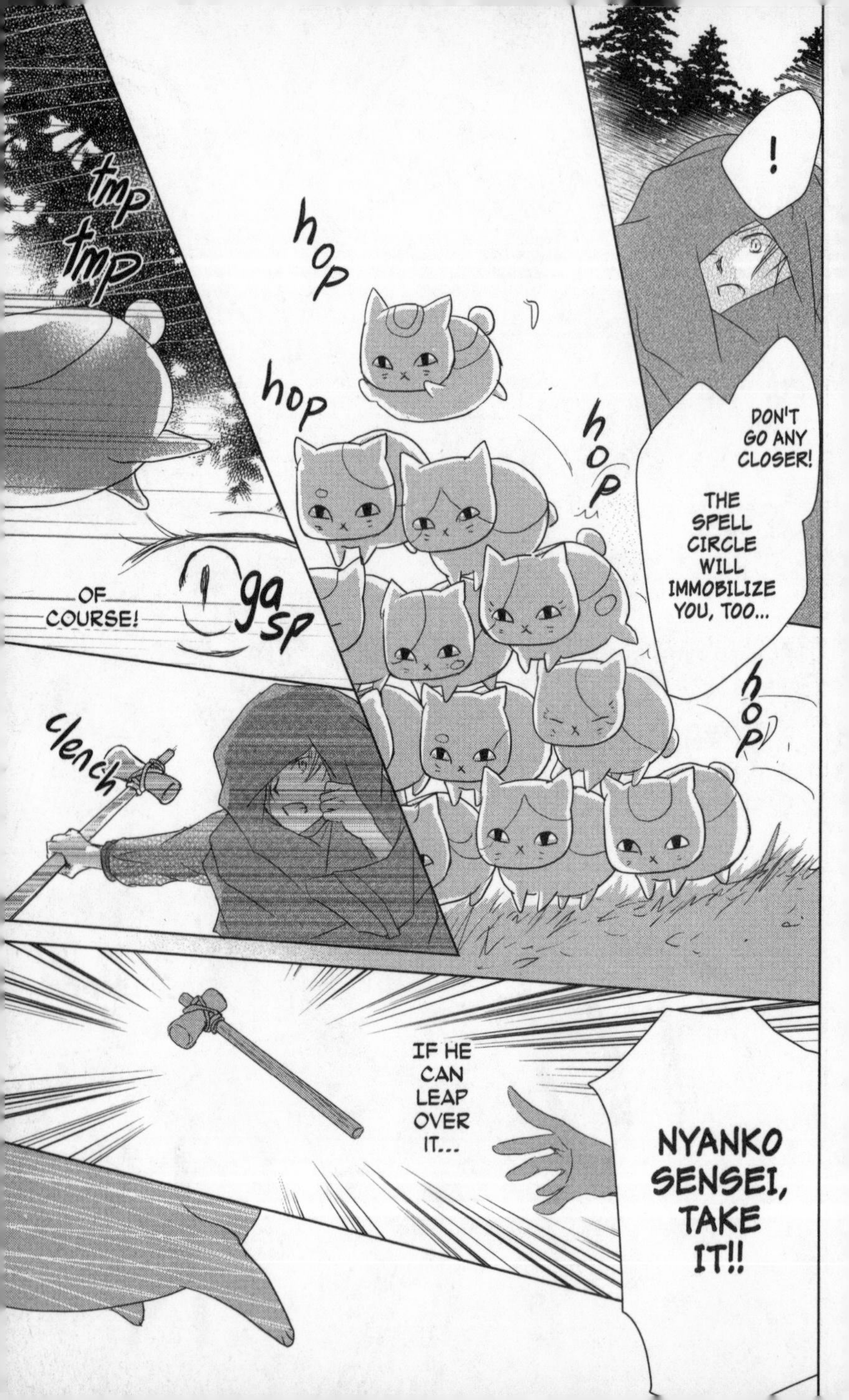
!
DON'T GO ANY CLOSER!
THE SPELL CIRCLE WILL IMMOBILIZE YOU, TOO...
hop
hop
hop
hop
tmp tmp
gasp
OF COURSE!
clench
NYANKO SENSEI, TAKE IT!!
IF HE CAN LEAP OVER IT...

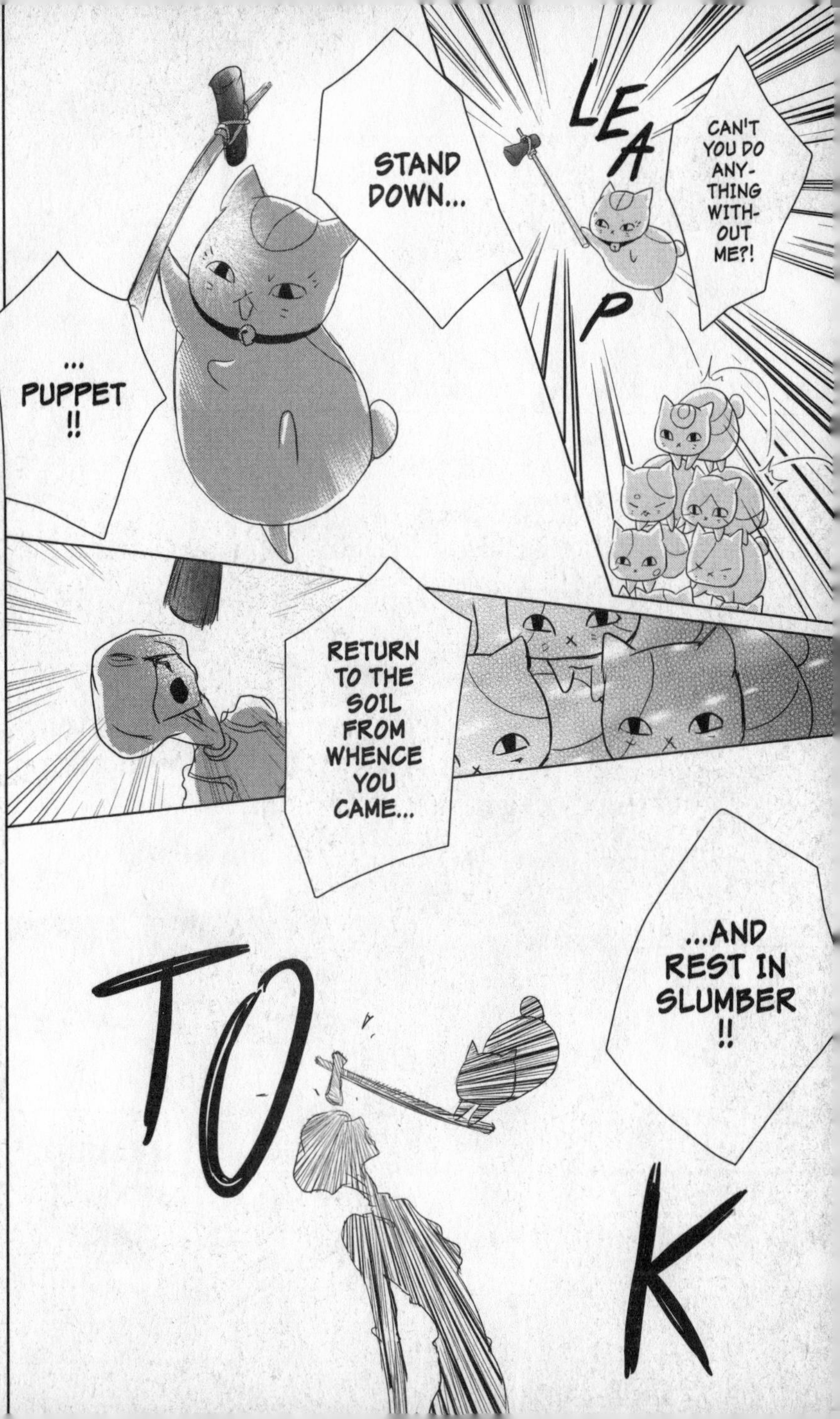
LEAP
CAN'T YOU DO ANY-THING WITH-OUT ME?!
STAND DOWN...
...PUPPET!!
RETURN TO THE SOIL FROM WHENCE YOU CAME...
...AND REST IN SLUMBER!!
TOK

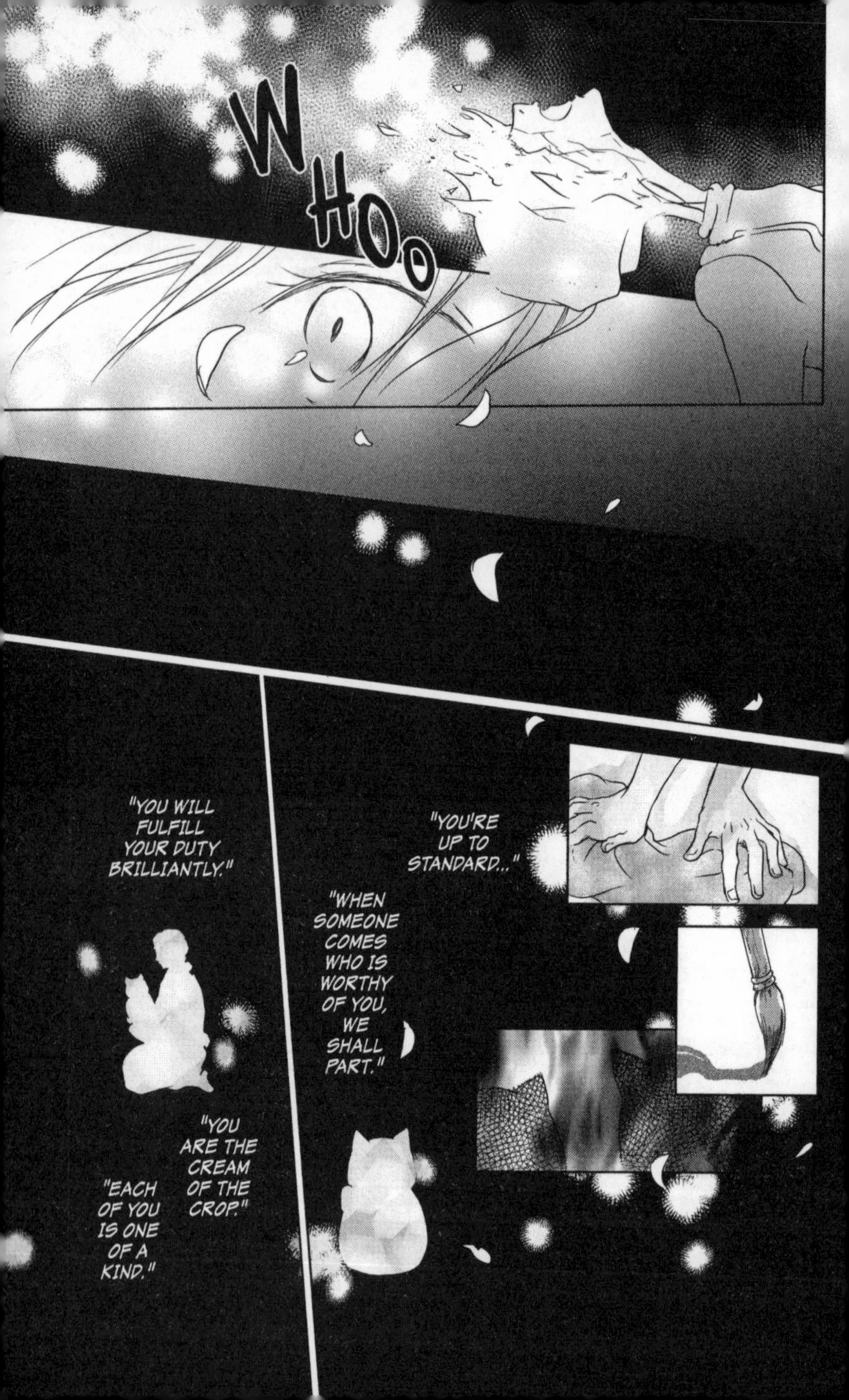
WHOOO
"YOU'RE UP TO STANDARD..."
"WHEN SOMEONE COMES WHO IS WORTHY OF YOU, WE SHALL PART."
"YOU WILL FULFILL YOUR DUTY BRILLIANTLY."
"YOU ARE THE CREAM OF THE CROP."
"EACH OF YOU IS ONE OF A KIND."

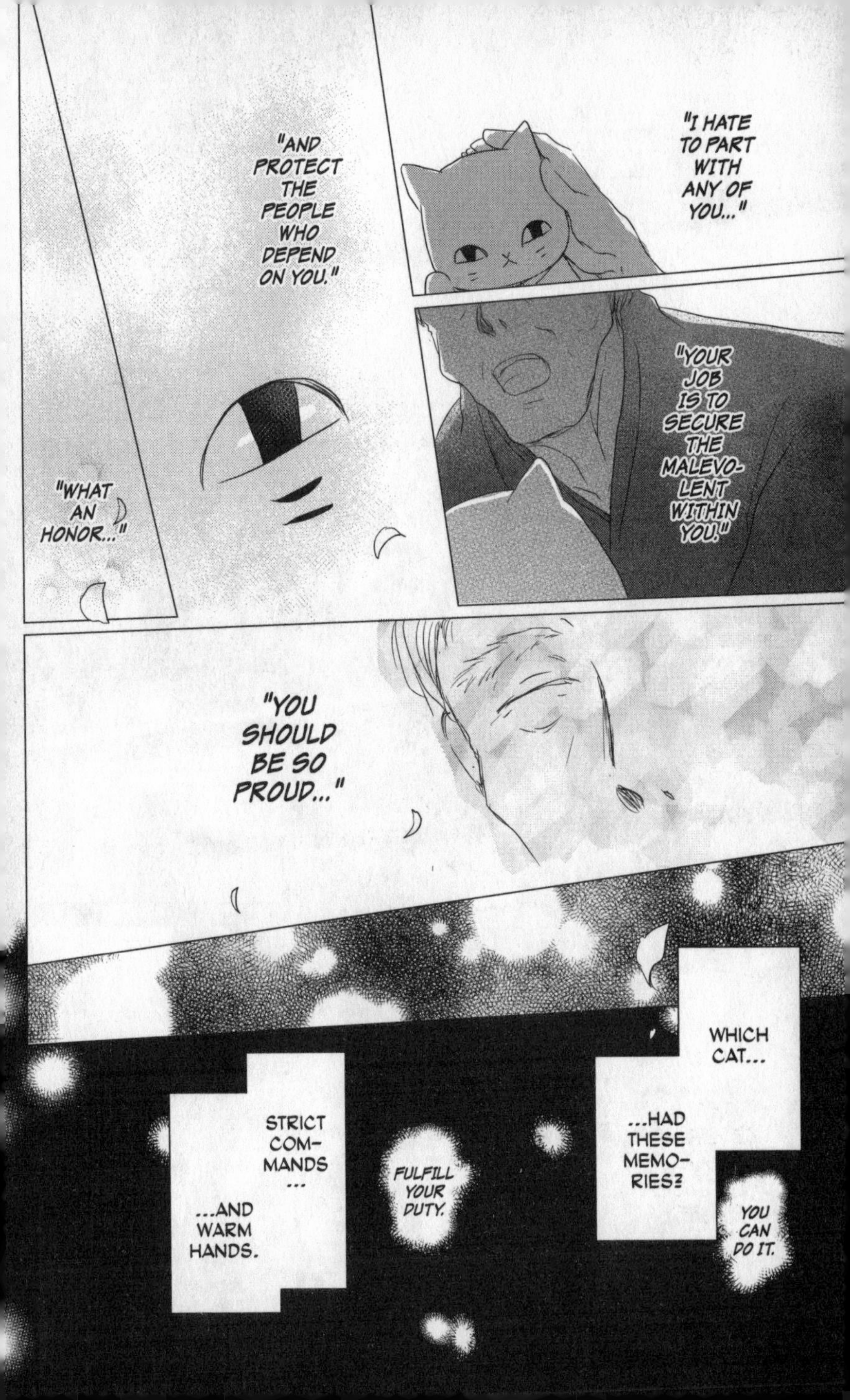
"I HATE TO PART WITH ANY OF YOU..."
"YOUR JOB IS TO SECURE THE MALEVOLENT WITHIN YOU."
"AND PROTECT THE PEOPLE WHO DEPEND ON YOU."
"WHAT AN HONOR..."
"YOU SHOULD BE SO PROUD..."
WHICH CAT...
...HAD THESE MEMORIES?
YOU CAN DO IT.
FULFILL YOUR DUTY.
STRICT COMMANDS...
...AND WARM HANDS.

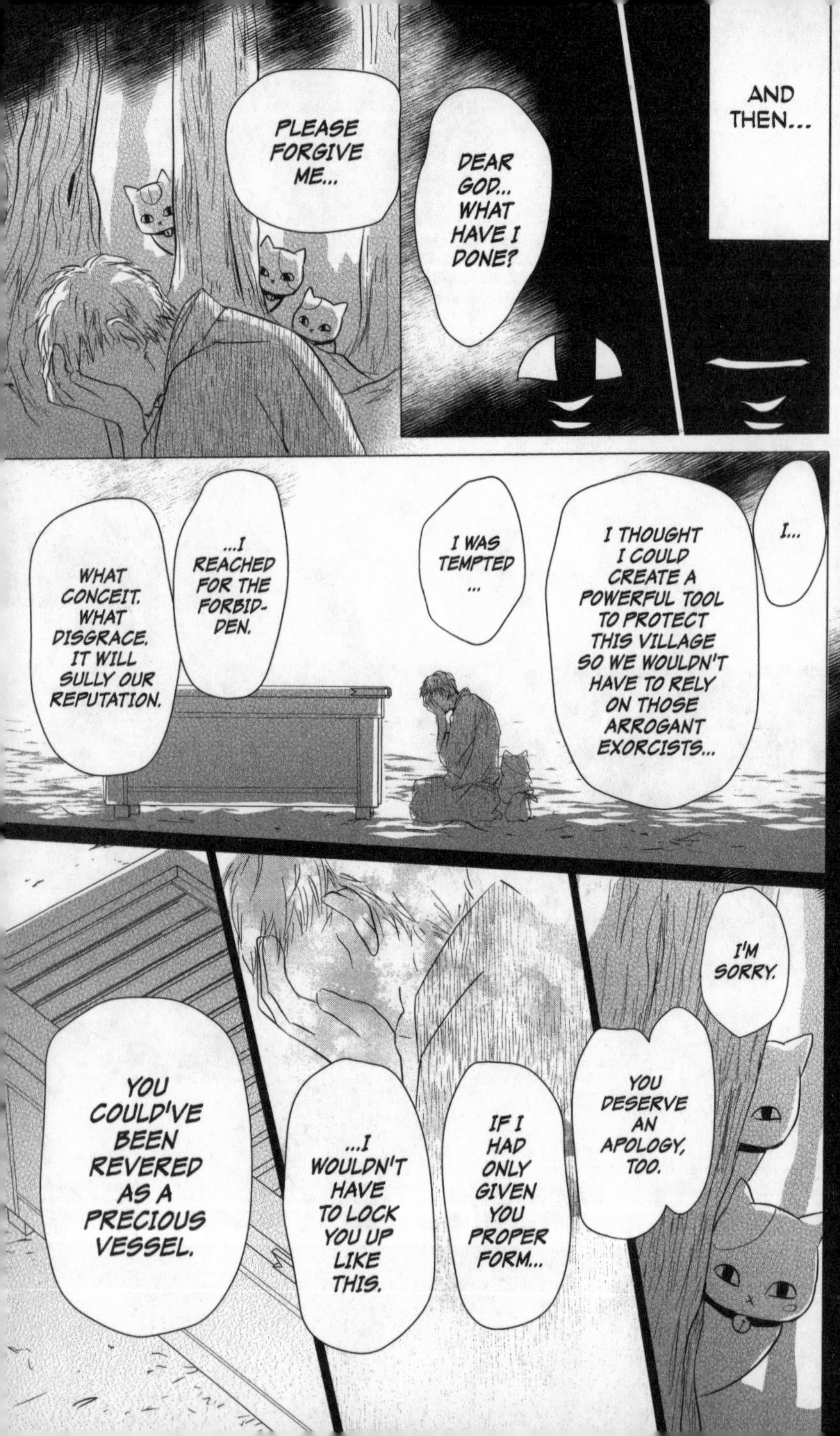
AND THEN...
DEAR GOD... WHAT HAVE I DONE?
PLEASE FORGIVE ME...
I...
I THOUGHT I COULD CREATE A POWERFUL TOOL TO PROTECT THIS VILLAGE SO WE WOULDN'T HAVE TO RELY ON THOSE ARROGANT EXORCISTS...
I WAS TEMPTED ...
...I REACHED FOR THE FORBID-DEN.
WHAT CONCEIT. WHAT DISGRACE. IT WILL SULLY OUR REPUTATION.
I'M SORRY.
YOU DESERVE AN APOLOGY, TOO.
IF I HAD ONLY GIVEN YOU PROPER FORM...
...I WOULDN'T HAVE TO LOCK YOU UP LIKE THIS.
YOU COULD'VE BEEN REVERED AS A PRECIOUS VESSEL.

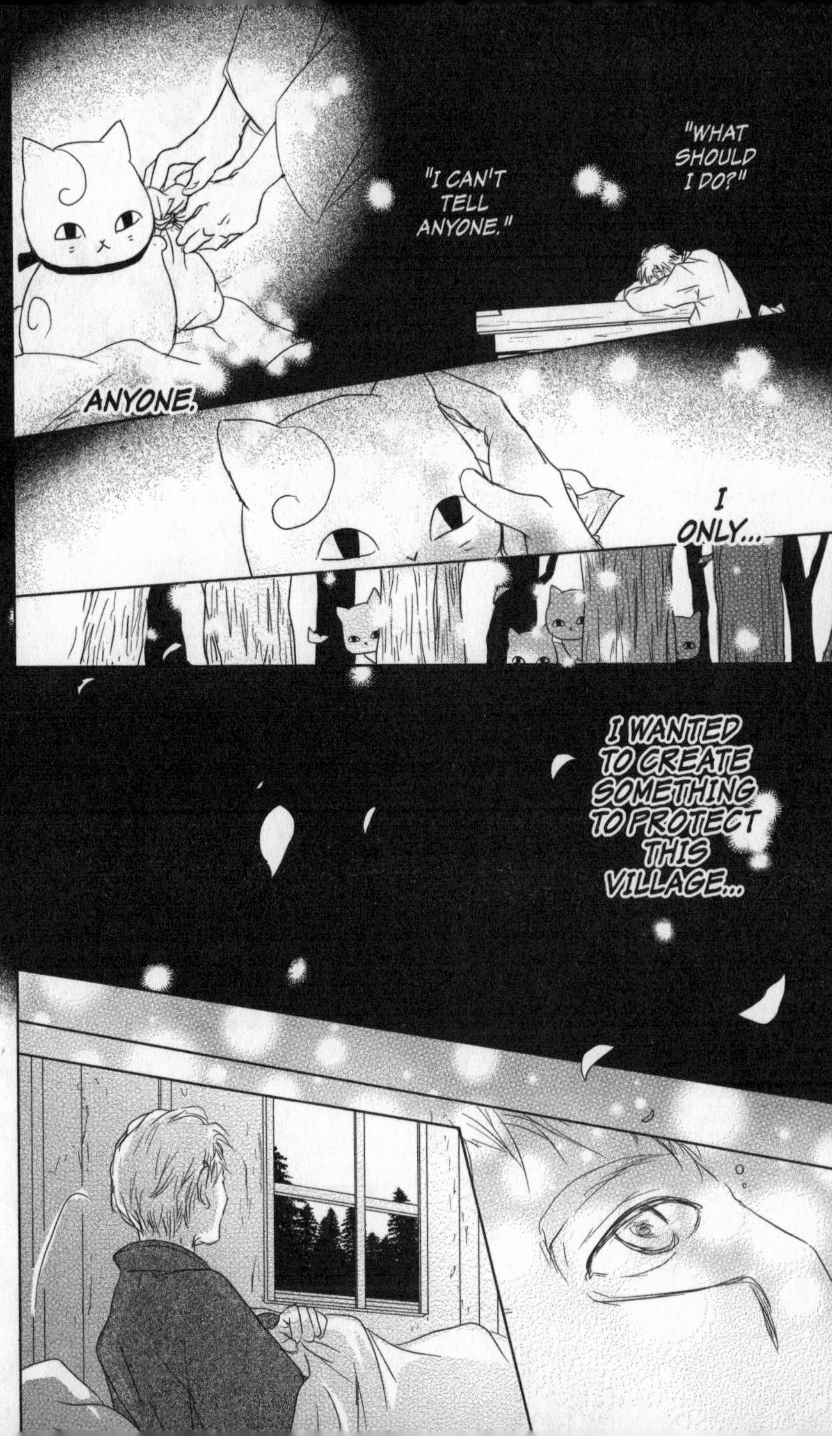
"WHAT SHOULD I DO?"
"I CAN'T TELL ANYONE."
ANYONE.
I ONLY...
I WANTED TO CREATE SOMETHING TO PROTECT THIS VILLAGE...

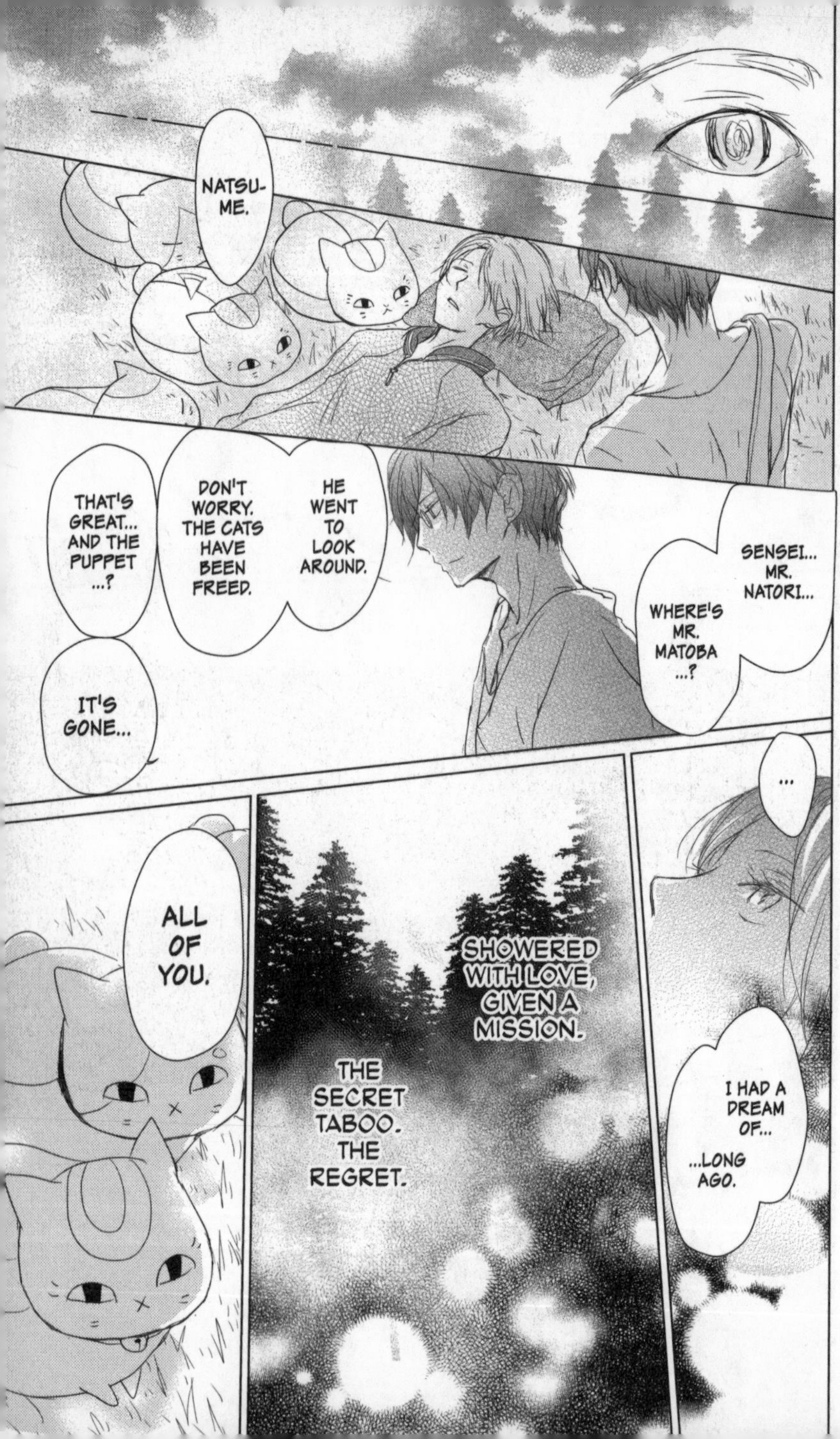
NATSU-ME.
SENSEI... MR. NATORI...
WHERE'S MR. MATOBA ...?
HE WENT TO LOOK AROUND.
DON'T WORRY. THE CATS HAVE BEEN FREED.
THAT'S GREAT... AND THE PUPPET ...?
IT'S GONE...
...
I HAD A DREAM OF...
...LONG AGO.
SHOWERED WITH LOVE, GIVEN A MISSION.
THE SECRET TABOO. THE REGRET.
ALL OF YOU.

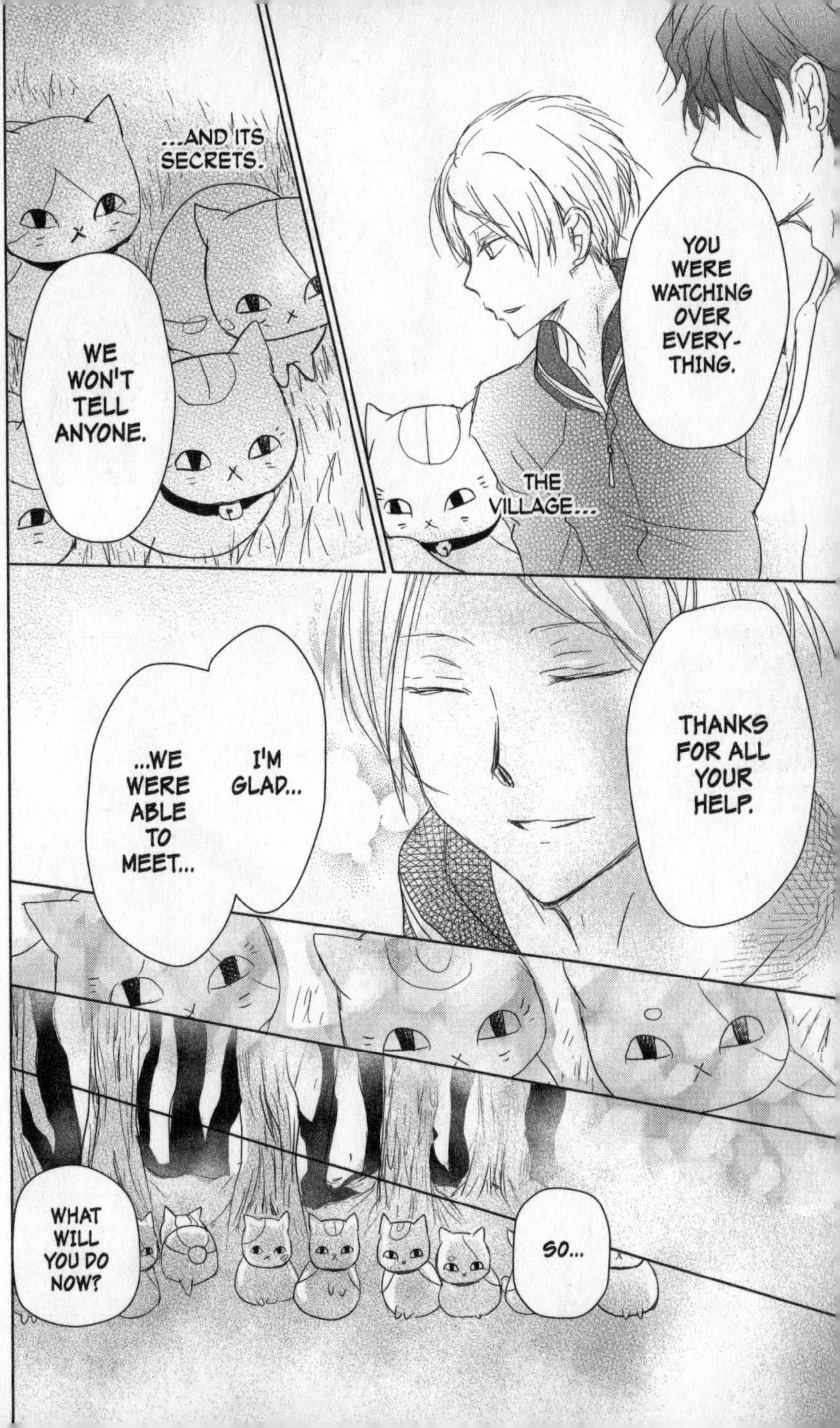
YOU WERE WATCHING OVER EVERY-THING.
THE VILLAGE...
...AND ITS SECRETS.
WE WON'T TELL ANYONE.
THANKS FOR ALL YOUR HELP.
I'M GLAD...
...WE WERE ABLE TO MEET...
SO...
WHAT WILL YOU DO NOW?

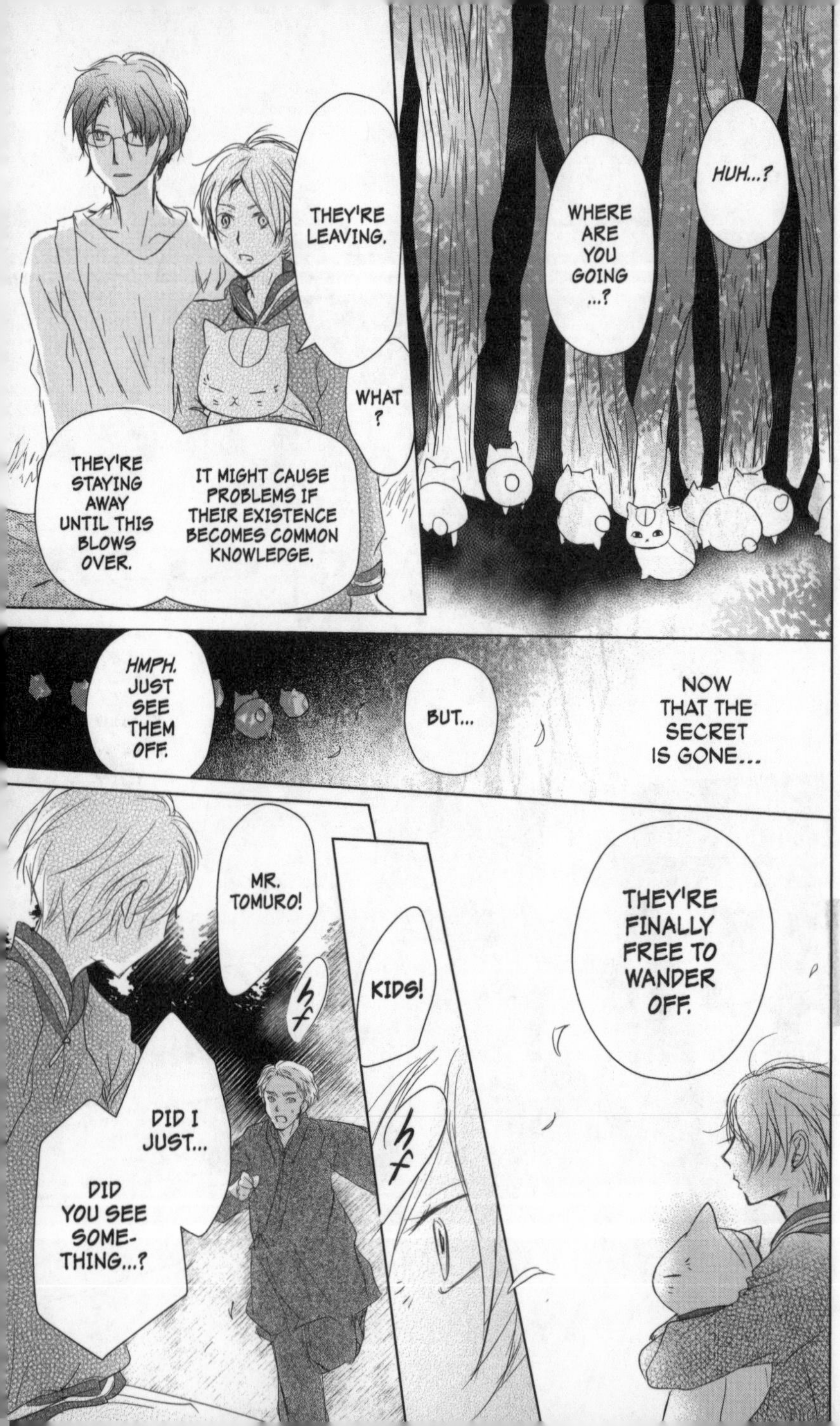
HUH...?
WHERE ARE YOU GOING ...?
THEY'RE LEAVING.
WHAT ?
IT MIGHT CAUSE PROBLEMS IF THEIR EXISTENCE BECOMES COMMON KNOWLEDGE.
THEY'RE STAYING AWAY UNTIL THIS BLOWS OVER.
NOW THAT THE SECRET IS GONE...
BUT...
HMPH. JUST SEE THEM OFF.
THEY'RE FINALLY FREE TO WANDER OFF.
KIDS!
MR. TOMURO!
DID I JUST...
DID YOU SEE SOME-THING...?

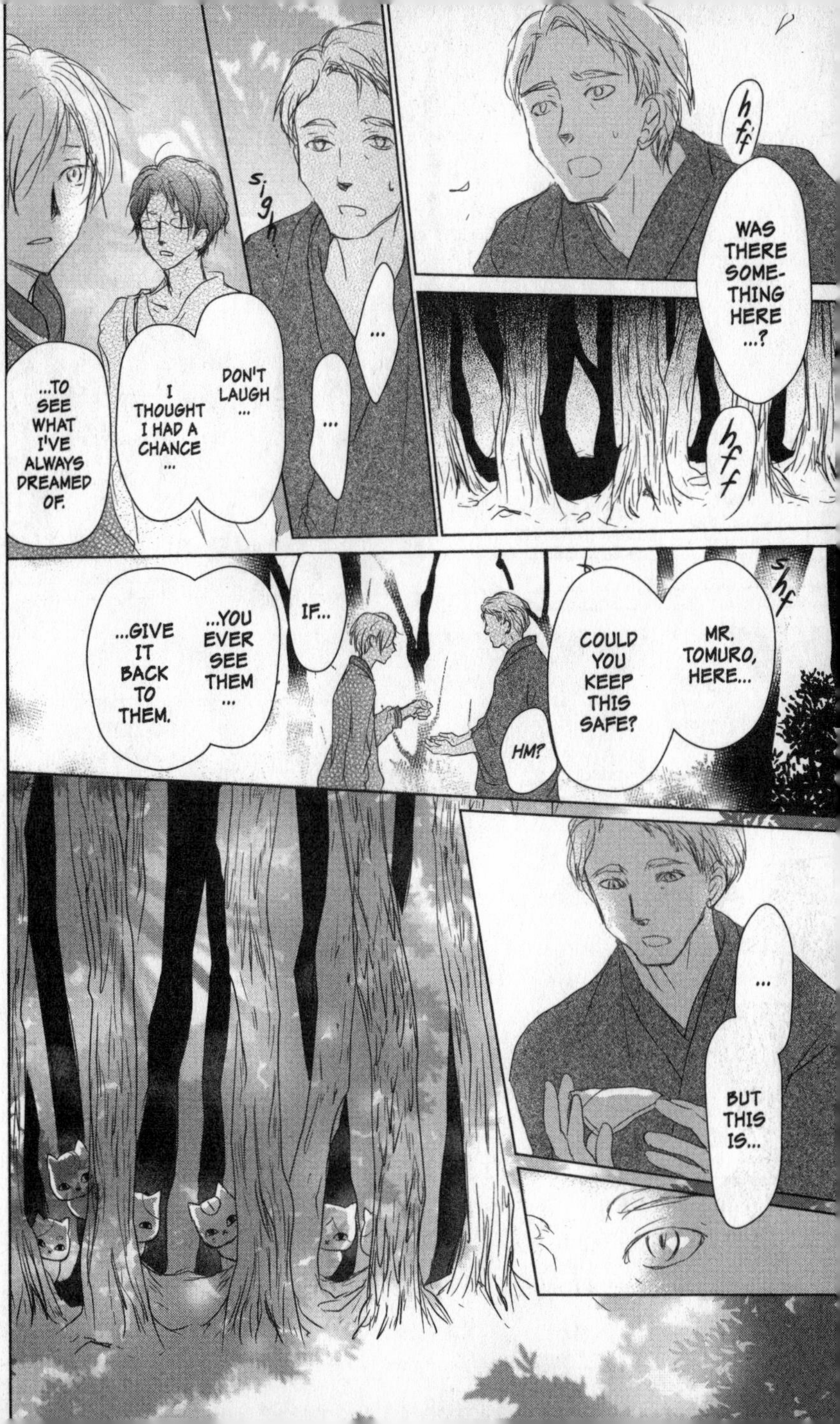
hff
WAS THERE SOMETHING-THING HERE ...?
hff
sigh...
...
...
DON'T LAUGH ...
I THOUGHT I HAD A CHANCE ...
...TO SEE WHAT I'VE ALWAYS DREAMED OF.
shf
MR. TOMURO, HERE...
COULD YOU KEEP THIS SAFE?
HM?
IF...
...YOU EVER SEE THEM ...
...GIVE IT BACK TO THEM.
...
BUT THIS IS...

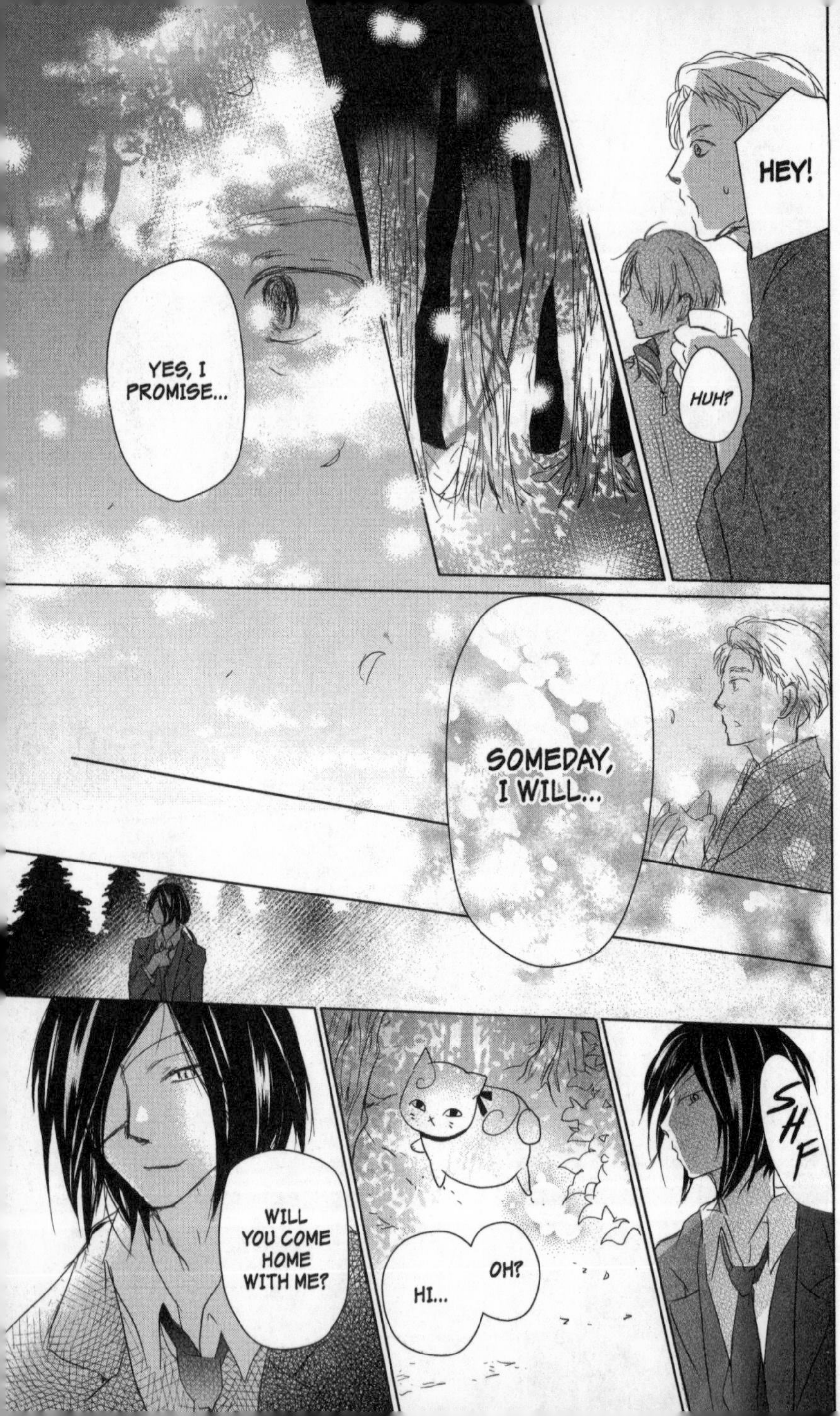
HEY!
HUH?
YES, I PROMISE...
SOMEDAY, I WILL...
SHF
OH?
HI...
WILL YOU COME HOME WITH ME?

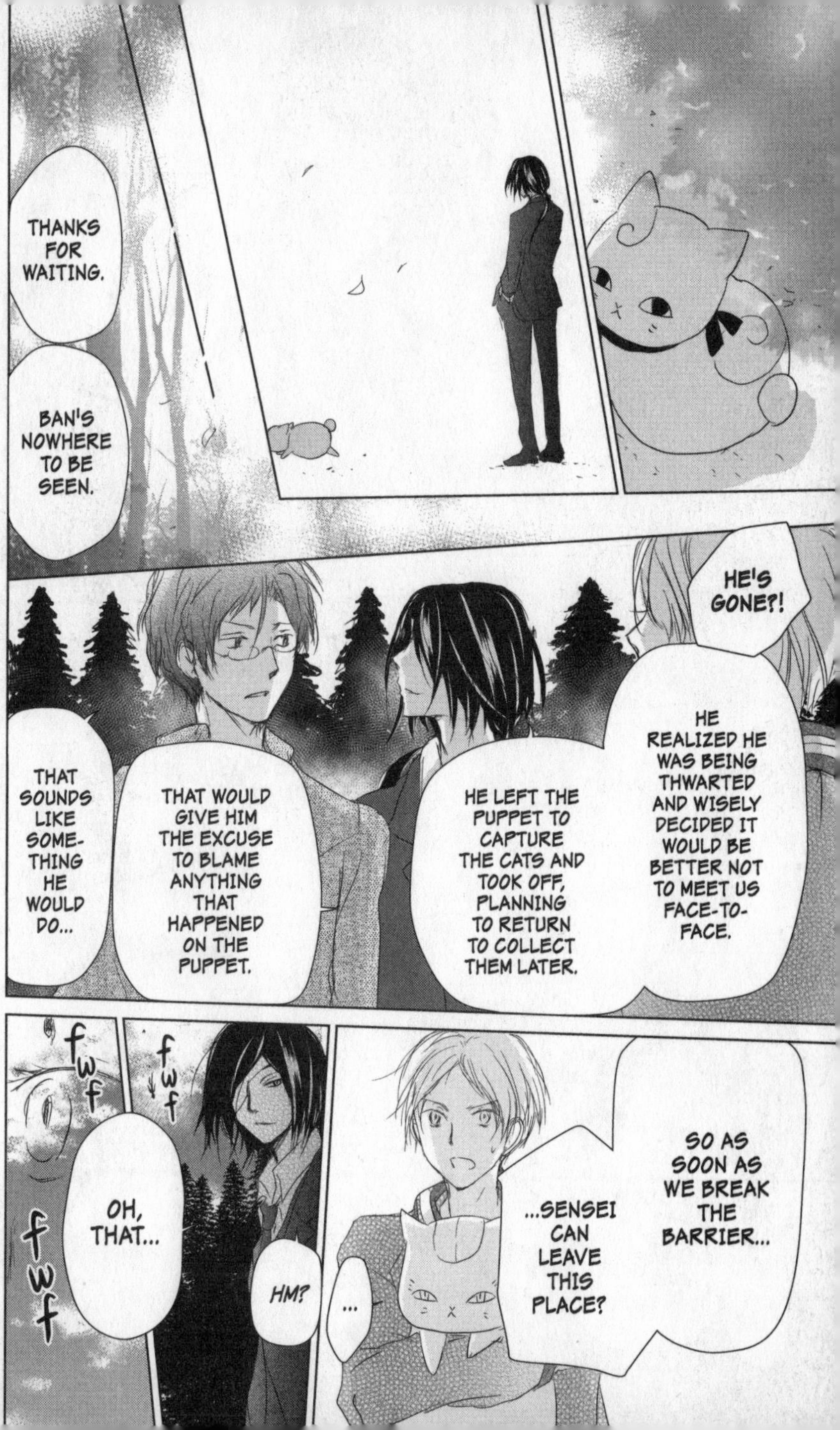
THANKS FOR WAITING.
BAN'S NOWHERE TO BE SEEN.
HE'S GONE?!
HE REALIZED HE WAS BEING THWARTED AND WISELY DECIDED IT WOULD BE BETTER NOT TO MEET US FACE-TO-FACE.
HE LEFT THE PUPPET TO CAPTURE THE CATS AND TOOK OFF, PLANNING TO RETURN TO COLLECT THEM LATER.
THAT WOULD GIVE HIM THE EXCUSE TO BLAME ANYTHING THAT HAPPENED ON THE PUPPET.
THAT SOUNDS LIKE SOME-THING HE WOULD DO...
SO AS SOON AS WE BREAK THE BARRIER...
...SENSEI CAN LEAVE THIS PLACE?
...
HM?
fwf
OH, THAT...
fwf
fwf

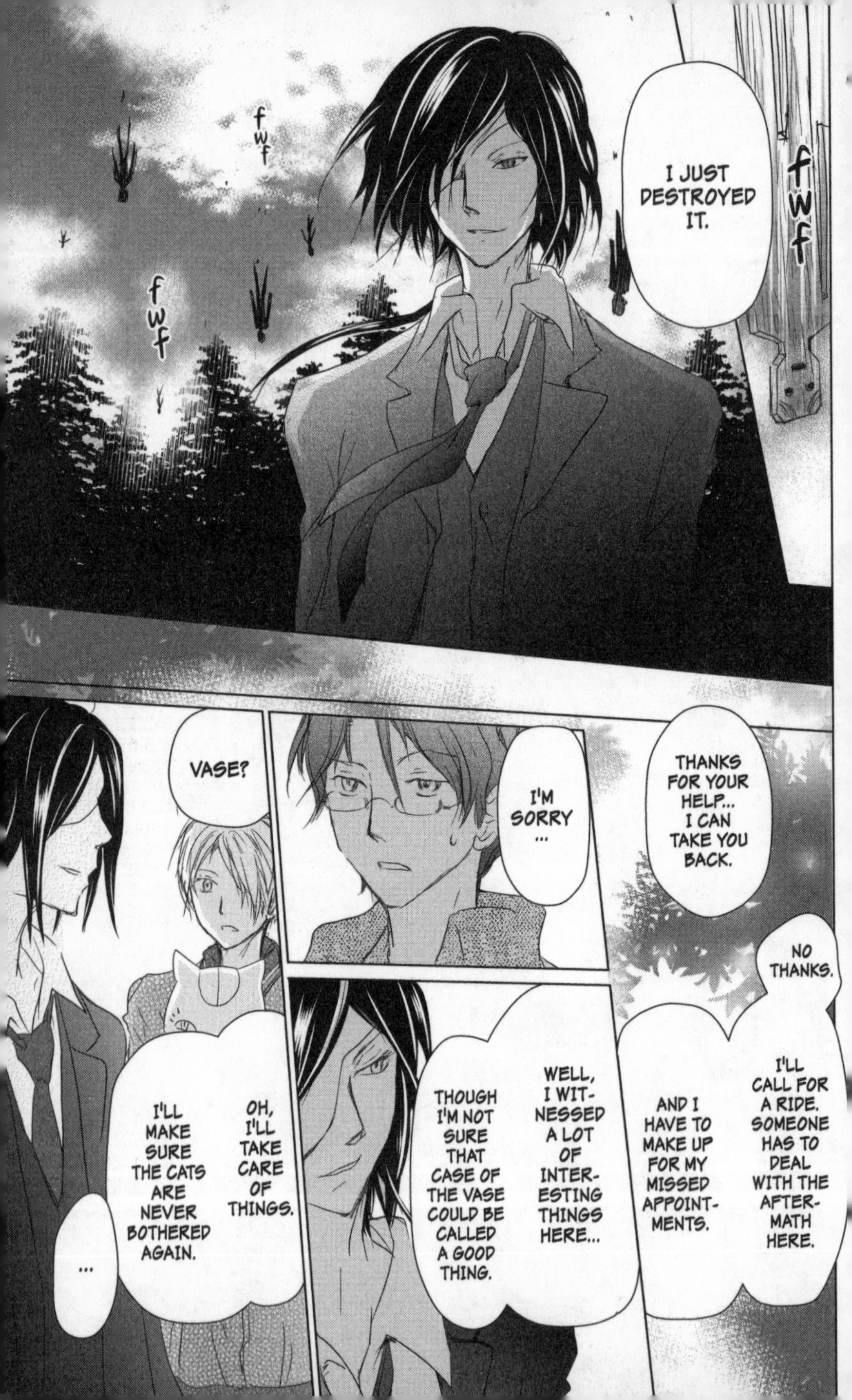
fwf
I JUST DESTROYED IT.
fwf
fwf
THANKS FOR YOUR HELP... I CAN TAKE YOU BACK.
I'M SORRY ...
NO THANKS.
I'LL CALL FOR A RIDE. SOMEONE HAS TO DEAL WITH THE AFTERMATH HERE.
AND I HAVE TO MAKE UP FOR MY MISSED APPOINTMENTS.
WELL, I WITNESSED A LOT OF INTERESTING THINGS HERE...
THOUGH I'M NOT SURE THAT CASE OF THE VASE COULD BE CALLED A GOOD THING.
VASE?
OH, I'LL TAKE CARE OF THINGS.
I'LL MAKE SURE THE CATS ARE NEVER BOTHERED AGAIN.
...

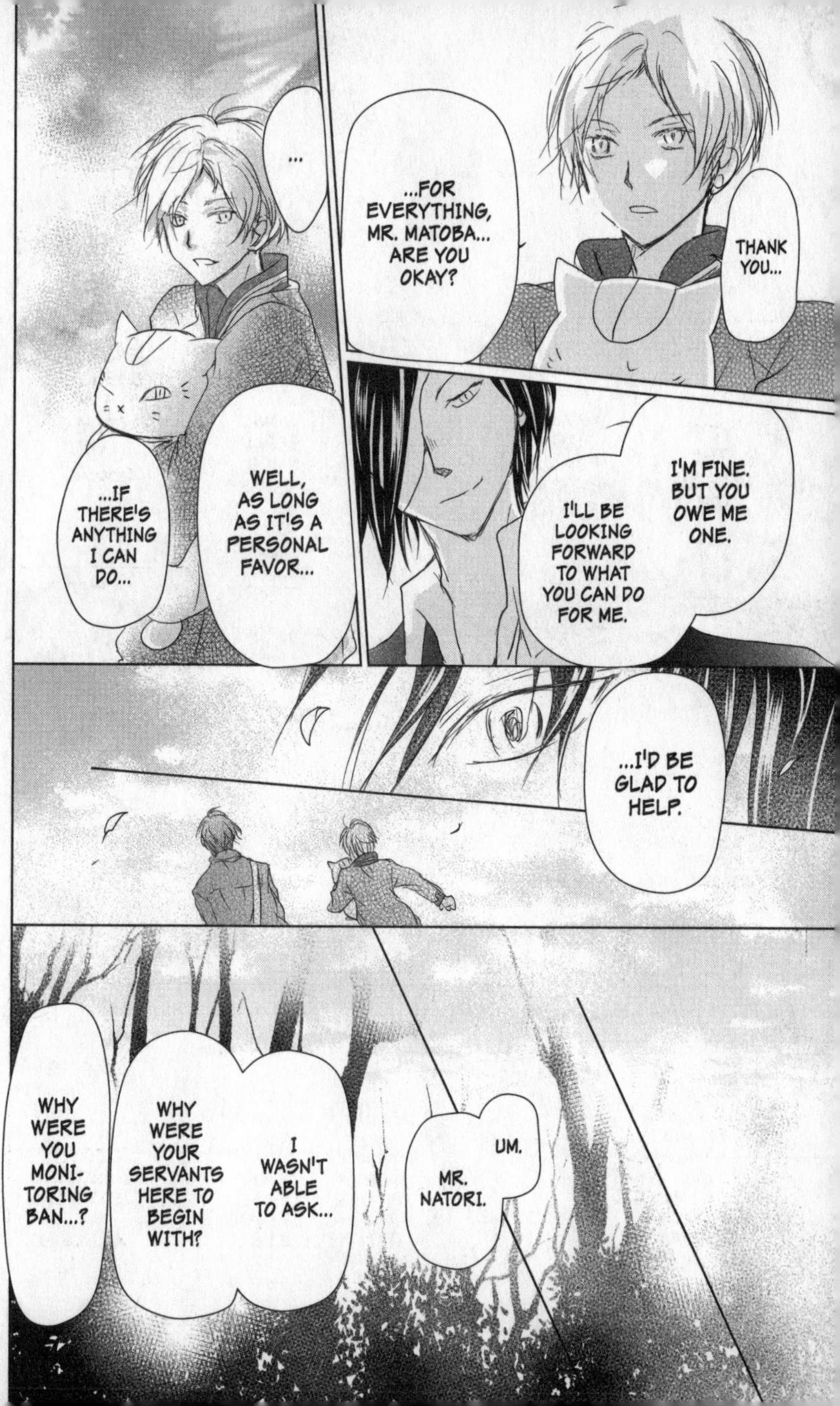
THANK YOU...
...FOR EVERYTHING, MR. MATOBA... ARE YOU OKAY?
I'M FINE. BUT YOU OWE ME ONE.
I'LL BE LOOKING FORWARD TO WHAT YOU CAN DO FOR ME.
...
WELL, AS LONG AS IT'S A PERSONAL FAVOR...
...IF THERE'S ANYTHING I CAN DO...
...I'D BE GLAD TO HELP.
UM.
MR. NATORI.
I WASN'T ABLE TO ASK...
WHY WERE YOUR SERVANTS HERE TO BEGIN WITH?
WHY WERE YOU MONITORING BAN...?

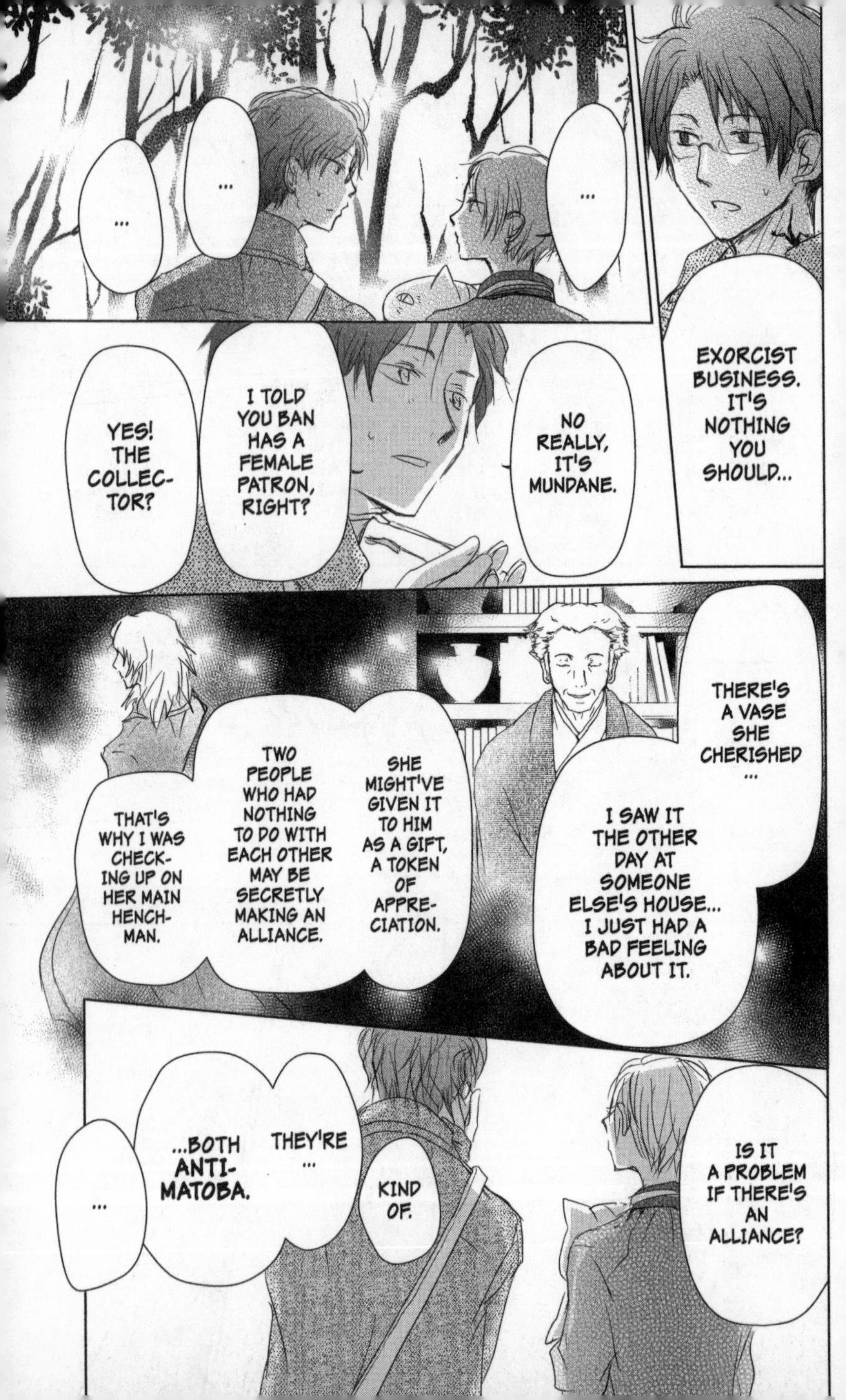
EXORCIST BUSINESS. IT'S NOTHING YOU SHOULD...
...
...
...
NO REALLY, IT'S MUNDANE.
I TOLD YOU BAN HAS A FEMALE PATRON, RIGHT?
YES! THE COLLECTOR?
THERE'S A VASE SHE CHERISHED...
I SAW IT THE OTHER DAY AT SOMEONE ELSE'S HOUSE... I JUST HAD A BAD FEELING ABOUT IT.
SHE MIGHT'VE GIVEN IT TO HIM AS A GIFT, A TOKEN OF APPRE-CIATION.
TWO PEOPLE WHO HAD NOTHING TO DO WITH EACH OTHER MAY BE SECRETLY MAKING AN ALLIANCE.
THAT'S WHY I WAS CHECK-ING UP ON HER MAIN HENCH-MAN.
IS IT A PROBLEM IF THERE'S AN ALLIANCE?
KIND OF.
THEY'RE...
...BOTH ANTI-MATOBA.
...

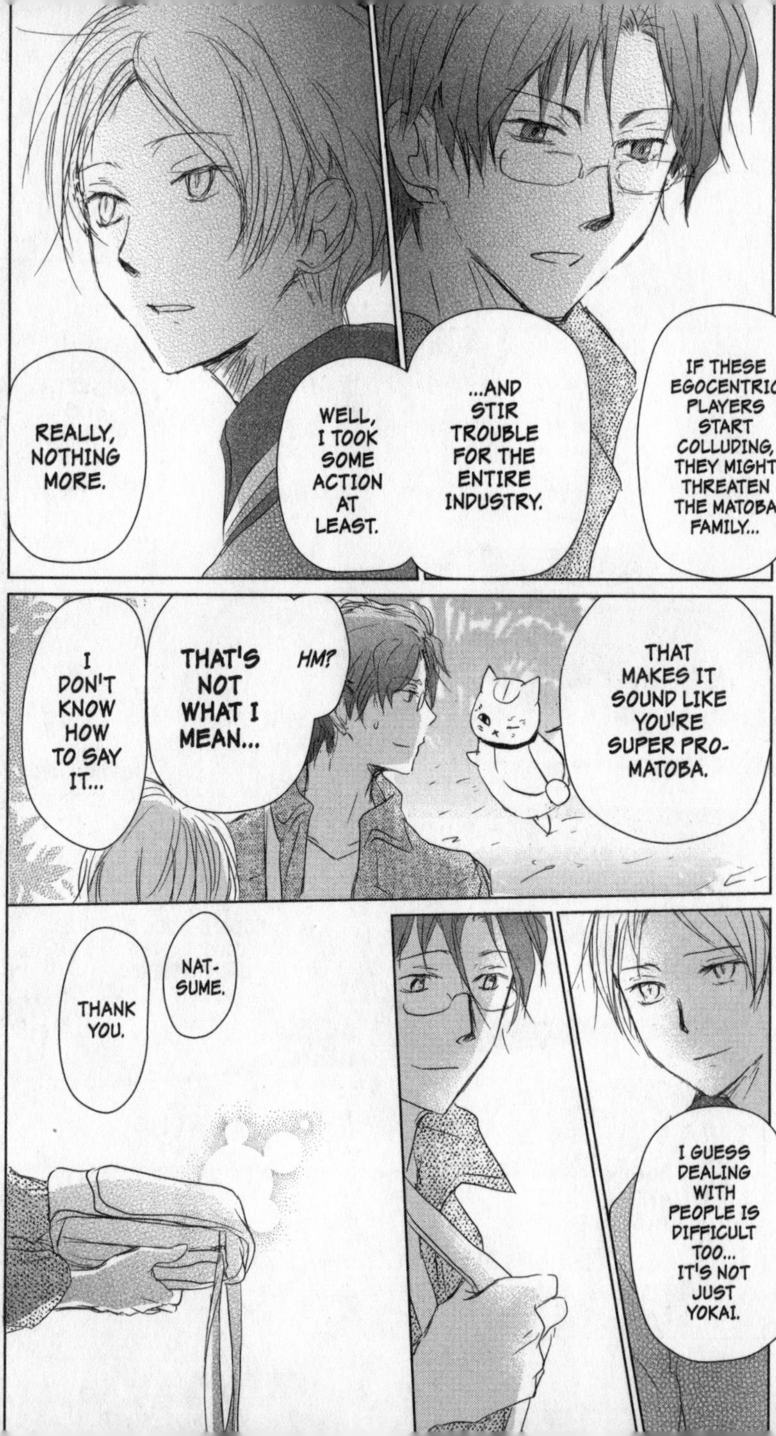
IF THESE EGOCENTRIC PLAYERS START COLLUDING, THEY MIGHT THREATEN THE MATOBA FAMILY...
...AND STIR TROUBLE FOR THE ENTIRE INDUSTRY.
WELL, I TOOK SOME ACTION AT LEAST.
REALLY, NOTHING MORE.
THAT MAKES IT SOUND LIKE YOU'RE SUPER PRO-MATOBA.
HM?
THAT'S NOT WHAT I MEAN...
I DON'T KNOW HOW TO SAY IT...
I GUESS DEALING WITH PEOPLE IS DIFFICULT TOO... IT'S NOT JUST YOKAI.
NAT-SUME.
THANK YOU.

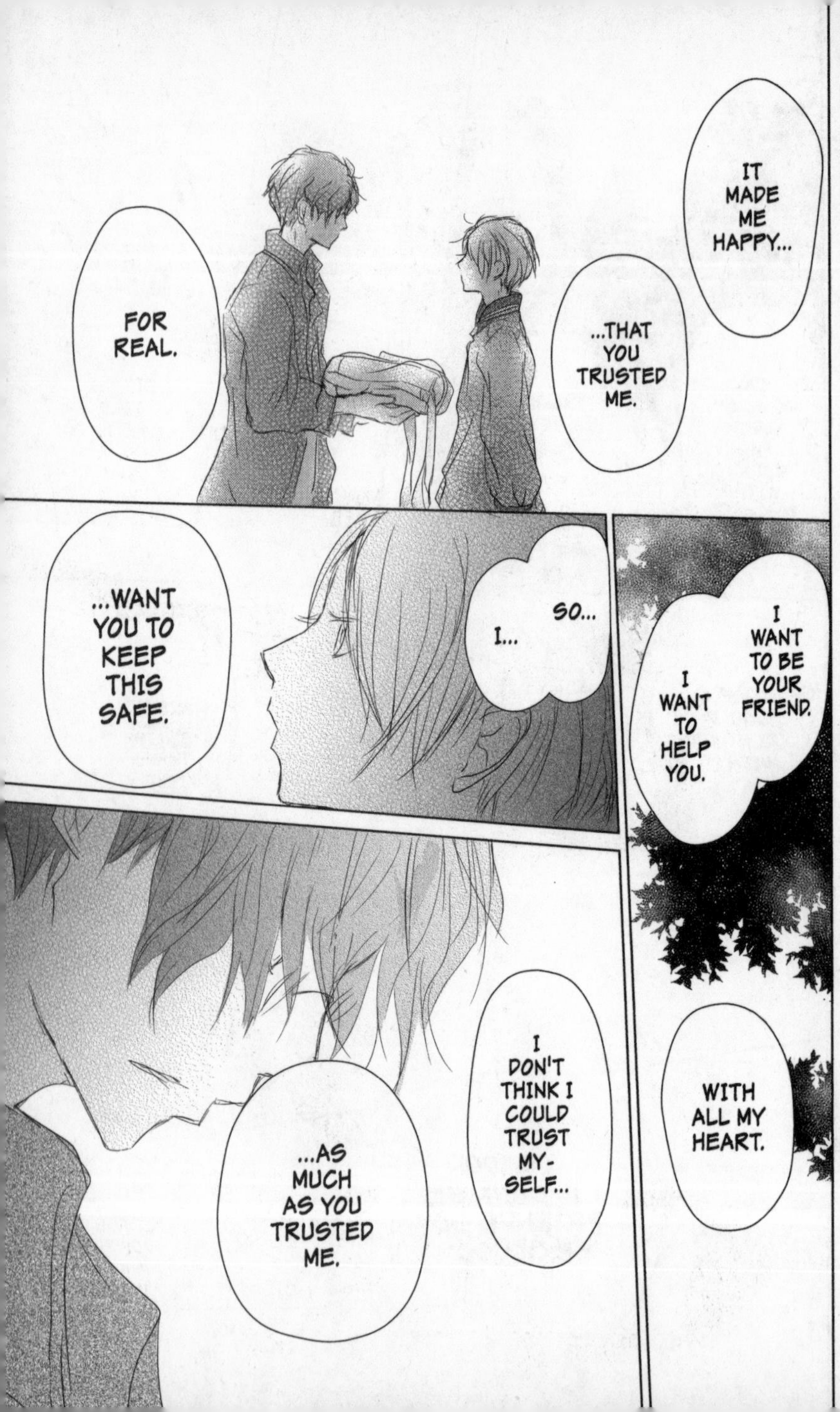
IT MADE ME HAPPY...
...THAT YOU TRUSTED ME.
FOR REAL.
I WANT TO BE YOUR FRIEND.
I WANT TO HELP YOU.
WITH ALL MY HEART.
SO...
I...
...WANT YOU TO KEEP THIS SAFE.
I DON'T THINK I COULD TRUST MY-SELF...
...AS MUCH AS YOU TRUSTED ME.

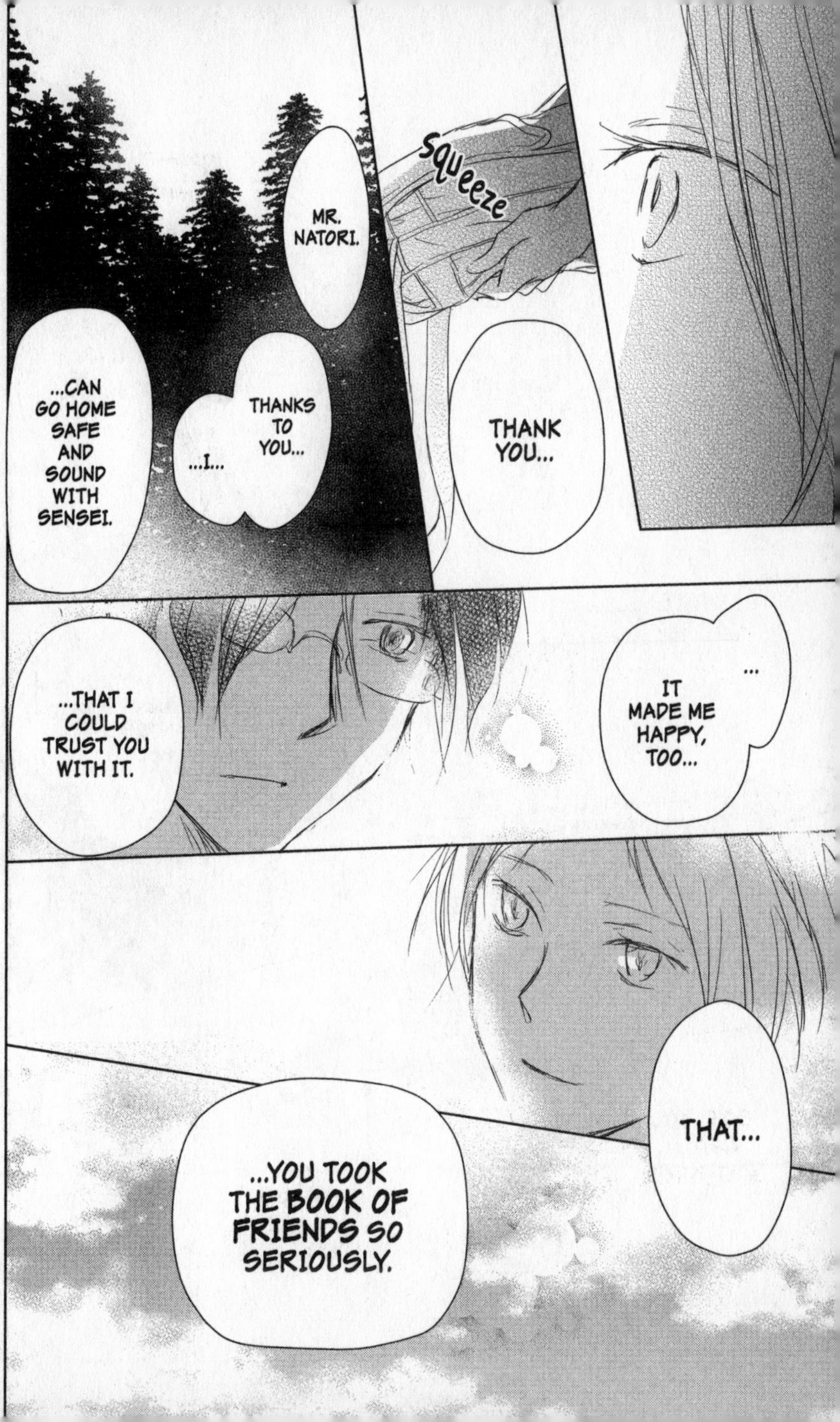
squeeze
THANK YOU...
MR. NATORI.
THANKS TO YOU...
...I...
...CAN GO HOME SAFE AND SOUND WITH SENSEI.
...
IT MADE ME HAPPY, TOO...
...THAT I COULD TRUST YOU WITH IT.
THAT...
...YOU TOOK THE BOOK OF FRIENDS SO SERIOUSLY.

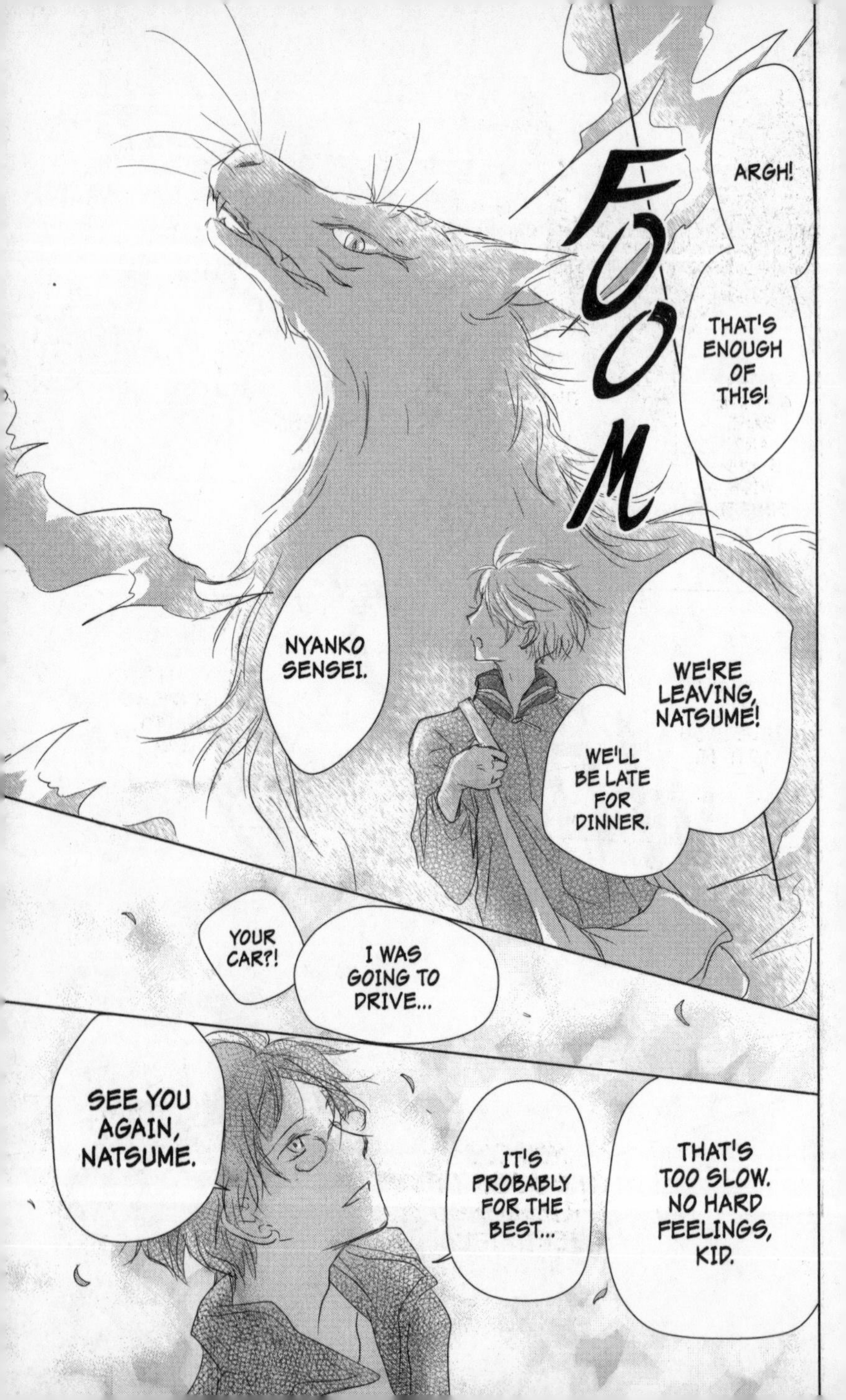
ARGH!
THAT'S ENOUGH OF THIS!
FOOM
WE'RE LEAVING, NATSUME!
WE'LL BE LATE FOR DINNER.
NYANKO SENSEI.
I WAS GOING TO DRIVE...
YOUR CAR?!
THAT'S TOO SLOW. NO HARD FEELINGS, KID.
IT'S PROBABLY FOR THE BEST...
SEE YOU AGAIN, NATSUME.

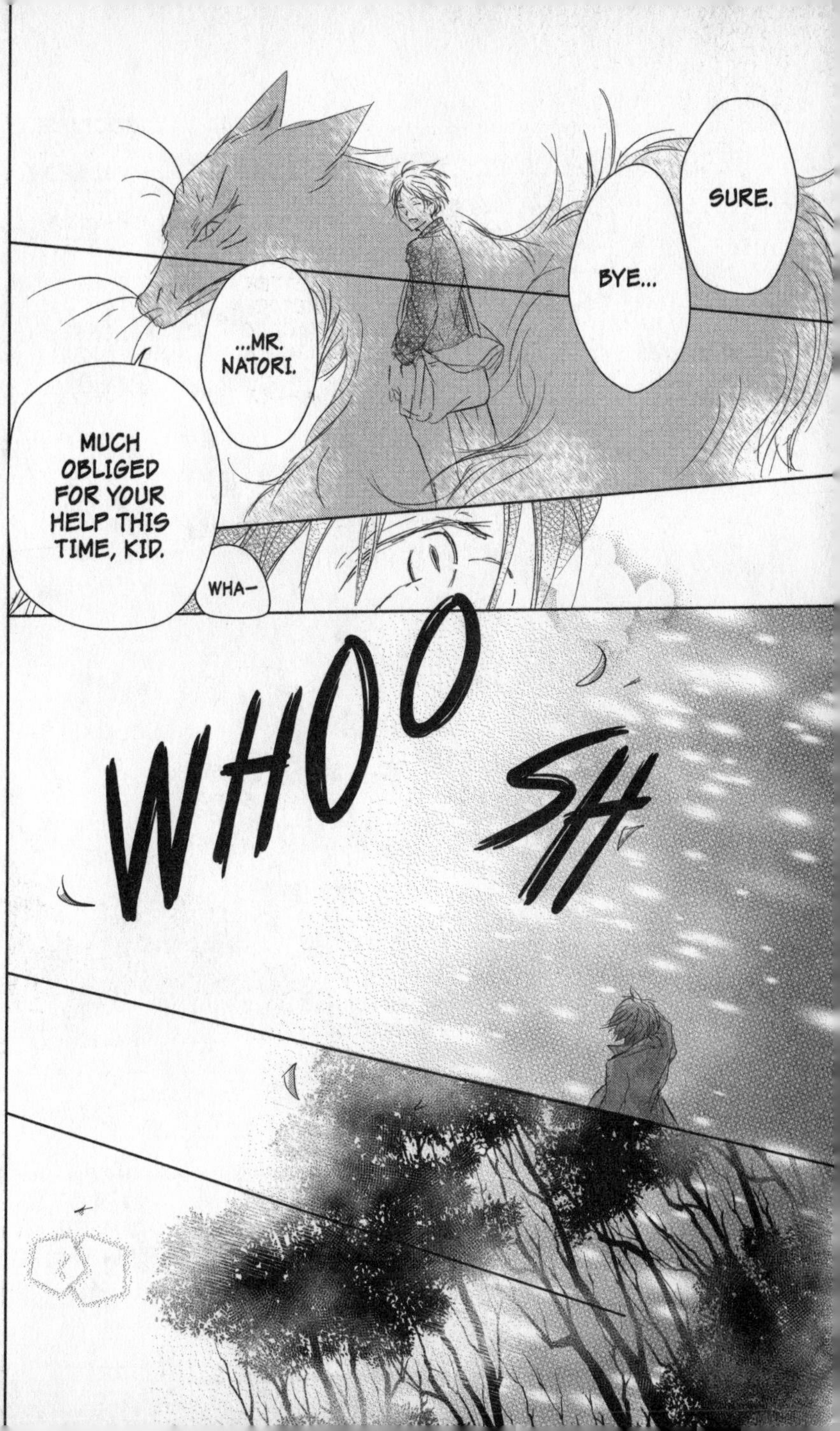
SURE.
BYE...
...MR. NATORI.
WHA-
MUCH OBLIGED FOR YOUR HELP THIS TIME, KID.
WHOOSH

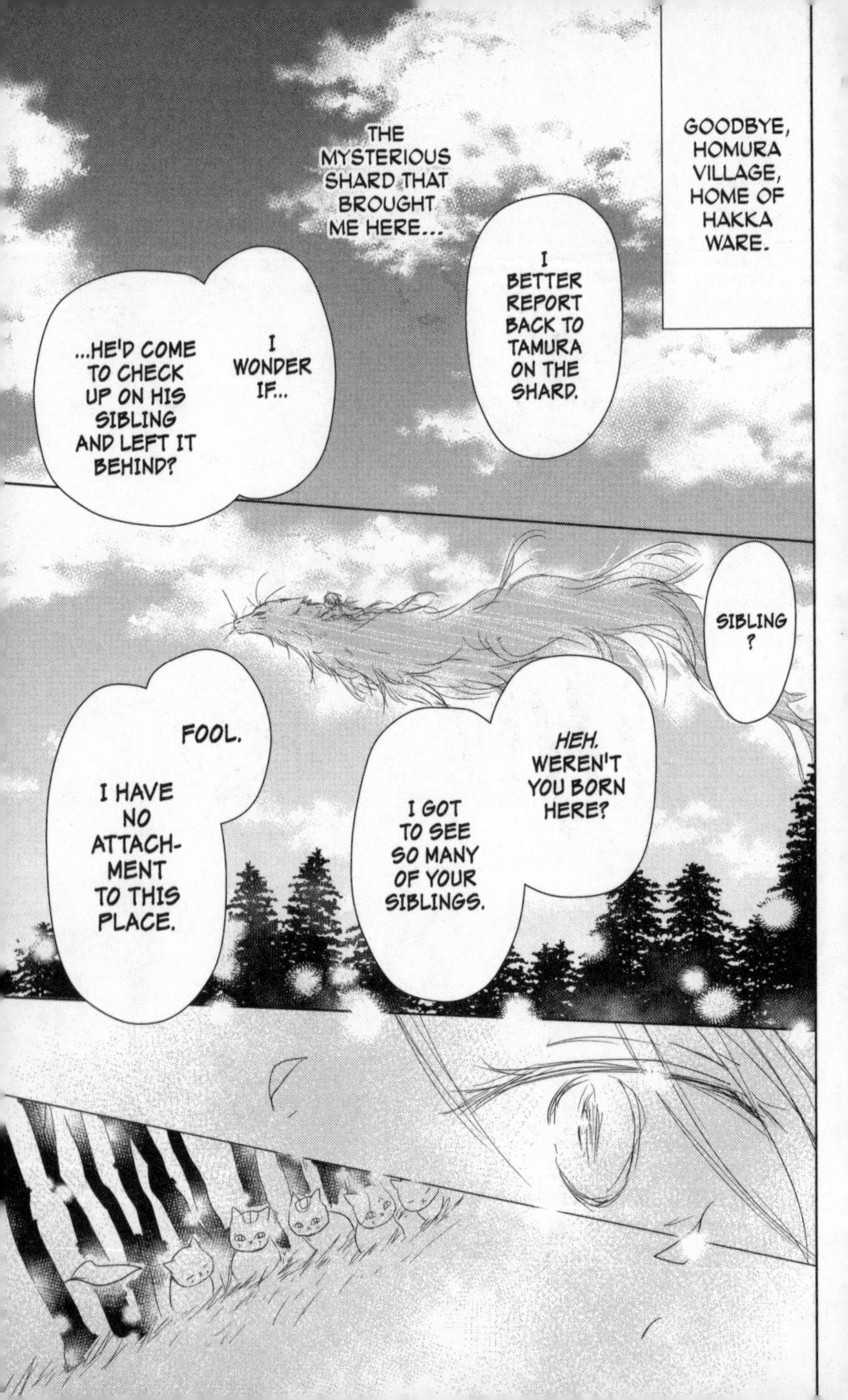
GOODBYE, HOMURA VILLAGE, HOME OF HAKKA WARE.
I BETTER REPORT BACK TO TAMURA ON THE SHARD.
THE MYSTERIOUS SHARD THAT BROUGHT ME HERE...
I WONDER IF...
...HE'D COME TO CHECK UP ON HIS SIBLING AND LEFT IT BEHIND?
SIBLING?
HEH. WEREN'T YOU BORN HERE?
I GOT TO SEE SO MANY OF YOUR SIBLINGS.
FOOL.
I HAVE NO ATTACHMENT TO THIS PLACE.

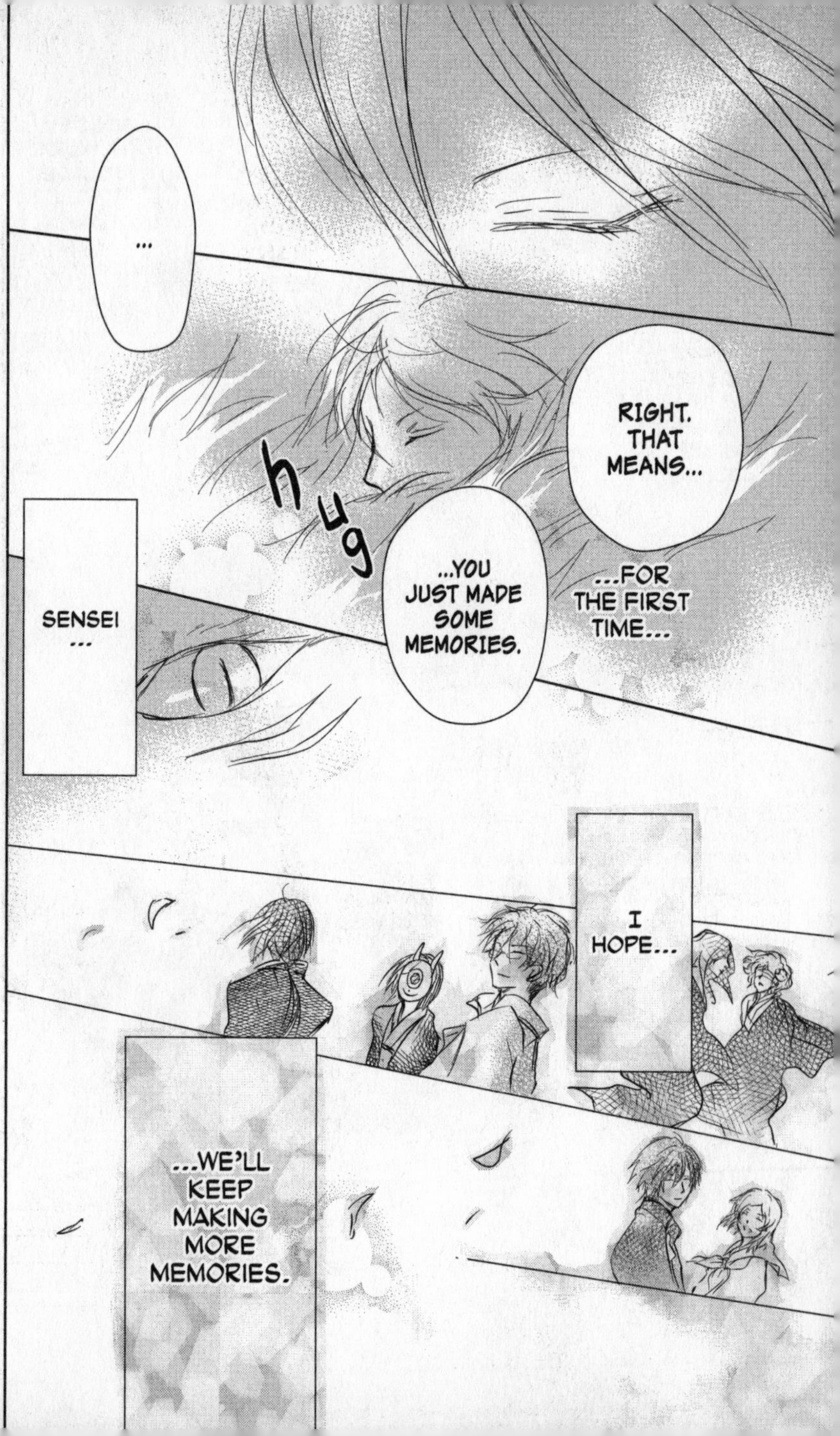
...
RIGHT. THAT MEANS...
...FOR THE FIRST TIME...
...YOU JUST MADE SOME MEMORIES.
hug
SENSEI ...
I HOPE...
...WE'LL KEEP MAKING MORE MEMORIES.

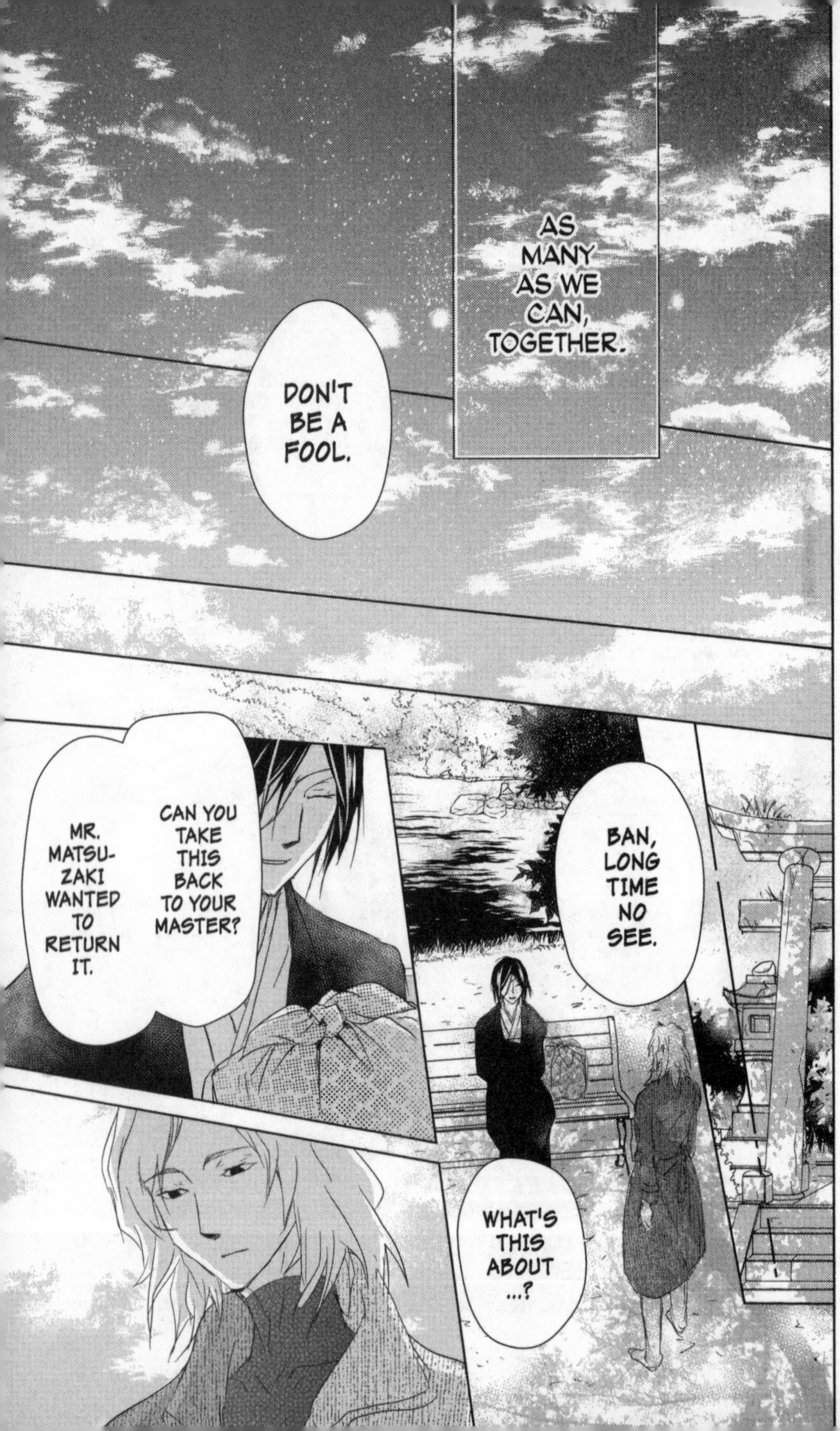
AS MANY AS WE CAN, TOGETHER.
DON'T BE A FOOL.
BAN, LONG TIME NO SEE.
WHAT'S THIS ABOUT ...?
CAN YOU TAKE THIS BACK TO YOUR MASTER?
MR. MATSU-ZAKI WANTED TO RETURN IT.

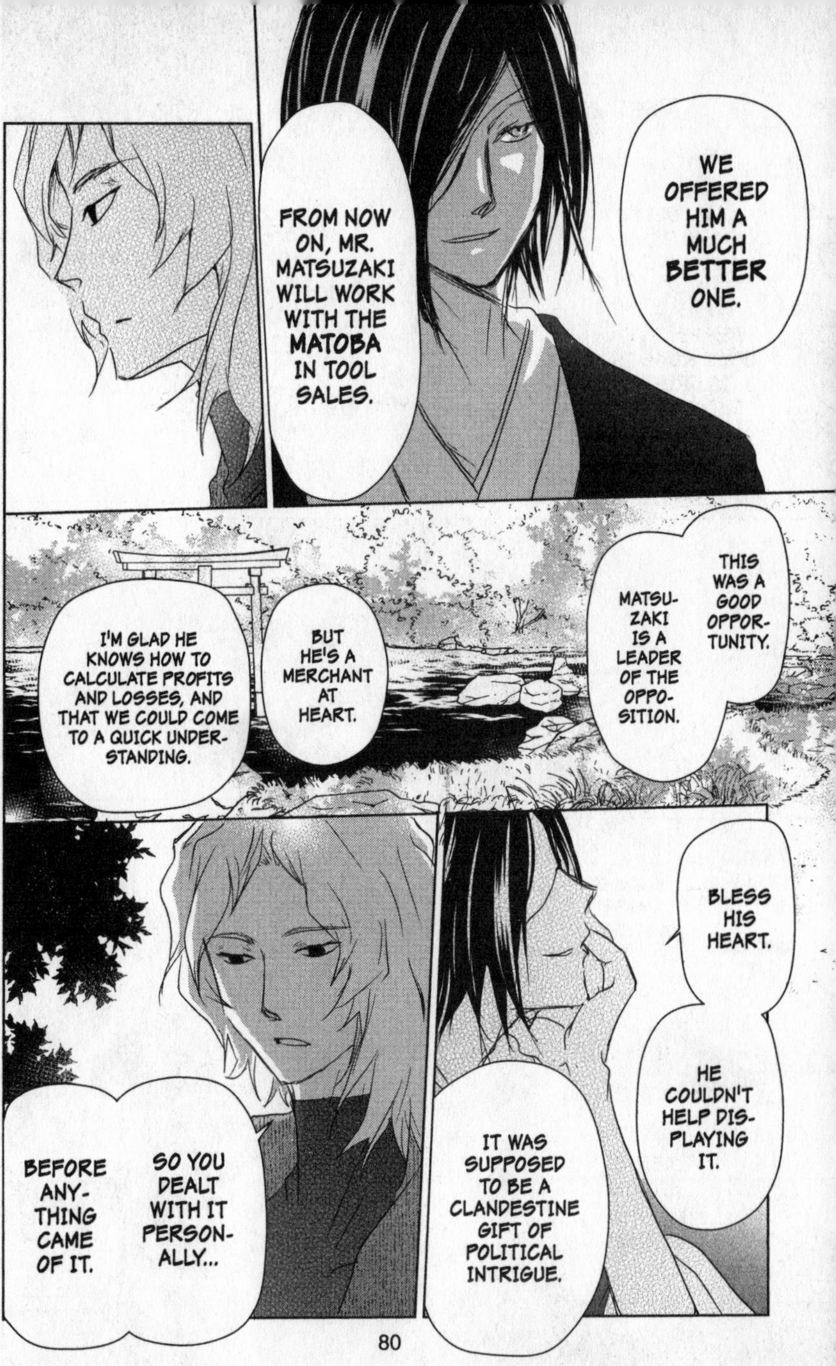

WE OFFERED HIM A MUCH BETTER ONE.
FROM NOW ON, MR. MATSUZAKI WILL WORK WITH THE MATOBA IN TOOL SALES.
THIS WAS A GOOD OPPOR-TUNITY.
MATSU-ZAKI IS A LEADER OF THE OPPO-SITION.
BUT HE'S A MERCHANT AT HEART.
I'M GLAD HE KNOWS HOW TO CALCULATE PROFITS AND LOSSES, AND THAT WE COULD COME TO A QUICK UNDER-STANDING.
BLESS HIS HEART.
HE COULDN'T HELP DIS-PLAYING IT.
IT WAS SUPPOSED TO BE A CLANDESTINE GIFT OF POLITICAL INTRIGUE.
SO YOU DEALT WITH IT PERSON-ALLY...
BEFORE ANY-THING CAME OF IT.

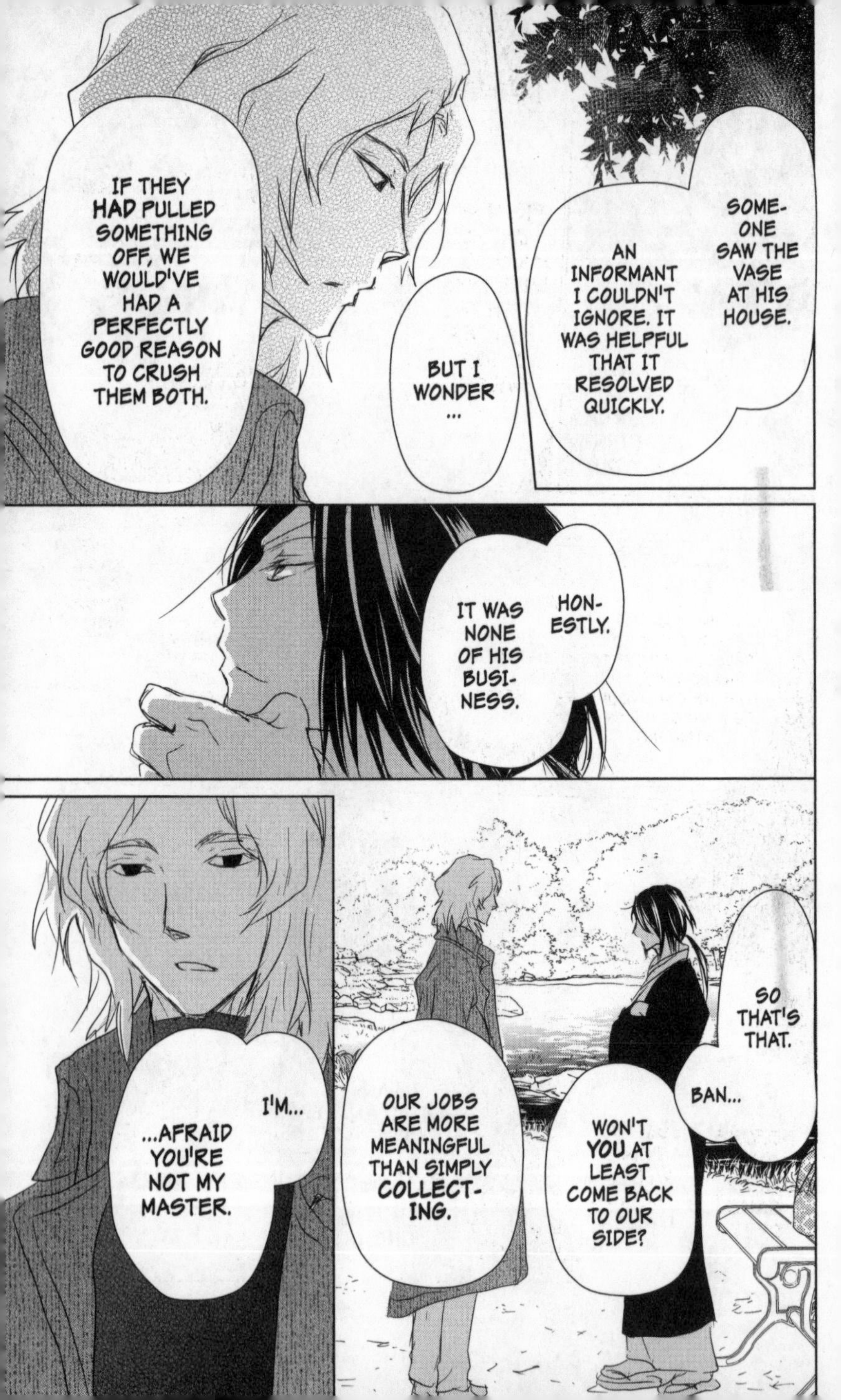
SOME-ONE SAW THE VASE AT HIS HOUSE.
AN INFORMANT I COULDN'T IGNORE. IT WAS HELPFUL THAT IT RESOLVED QUICKLY.
BUT I WONDER ...
IF THEY HAD PULLED SOMETHING OFF, WE WOULD'VE HAD A PERFECTLY GOOD REASON TO CRUSH THEM BOTH.
HON-ESTLY.
IT WAS NONE OF HIS BUSI-NESS.
SO THAT'S THAT.
BAN...
WON'T YOU AT LEAST COME BACK TO OUR SIDE?
OUR JOBS ARE MORE MEANINGFUL THAN SIMPLY COLLECT-ING.
I'M...
...AFRAID YOU'RE NOT MY MASTER.

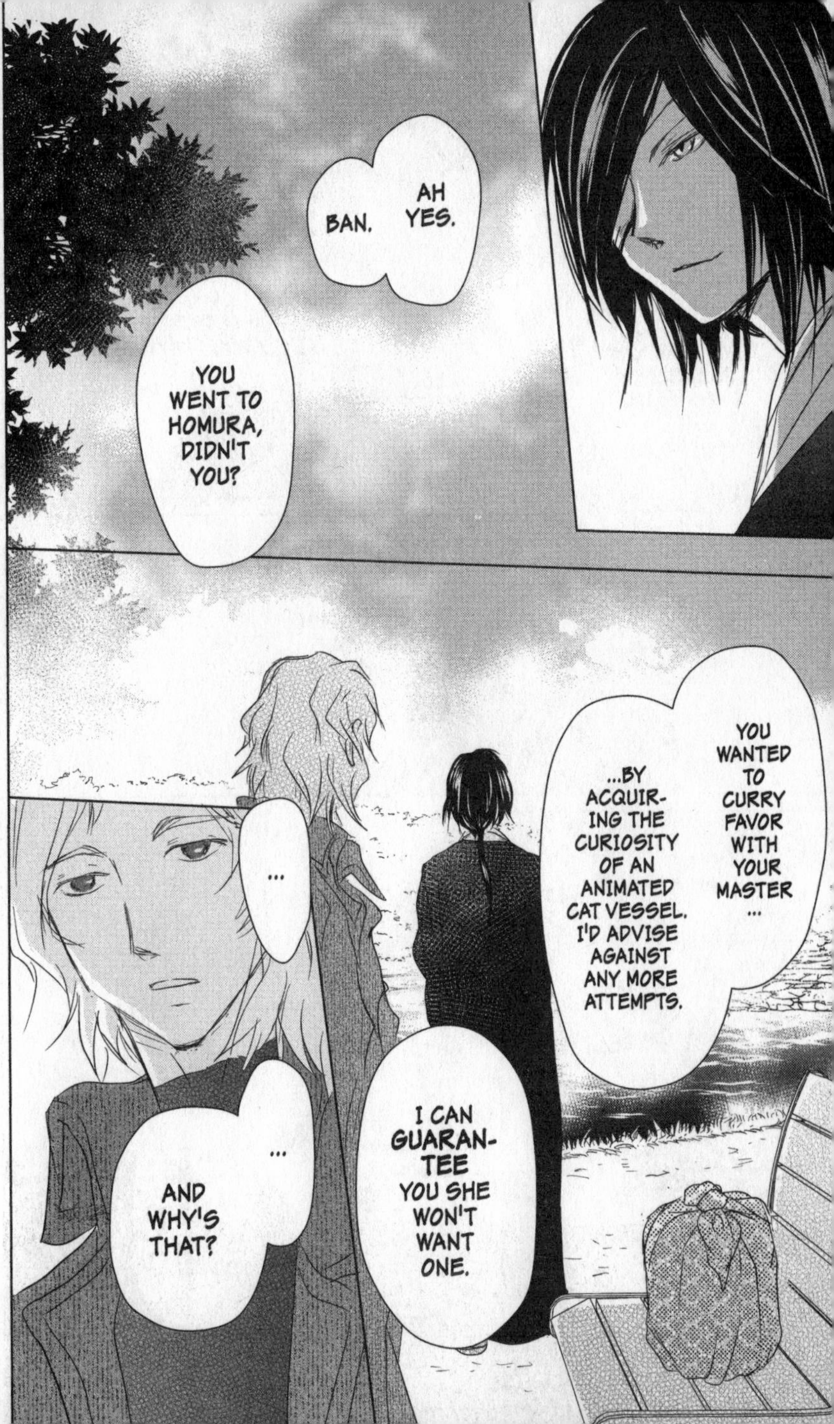
AH YES.
BAN.
YOU WENT TO HOMURA, DIDN'T YOU?
YOU WANTED TO CURRY FAVOR WITH YOUR MASTER ...
...BY ACQUIRING THE CURIOSITY OF AN ANIMATED CAT VESSEL. I'D ADVISE AGAINST ANY MORE ATTEMPTS.
...
I CAN GUARANTEE YOU SHE WON'T WANT ONE.
...
AND WHY'S THAT?

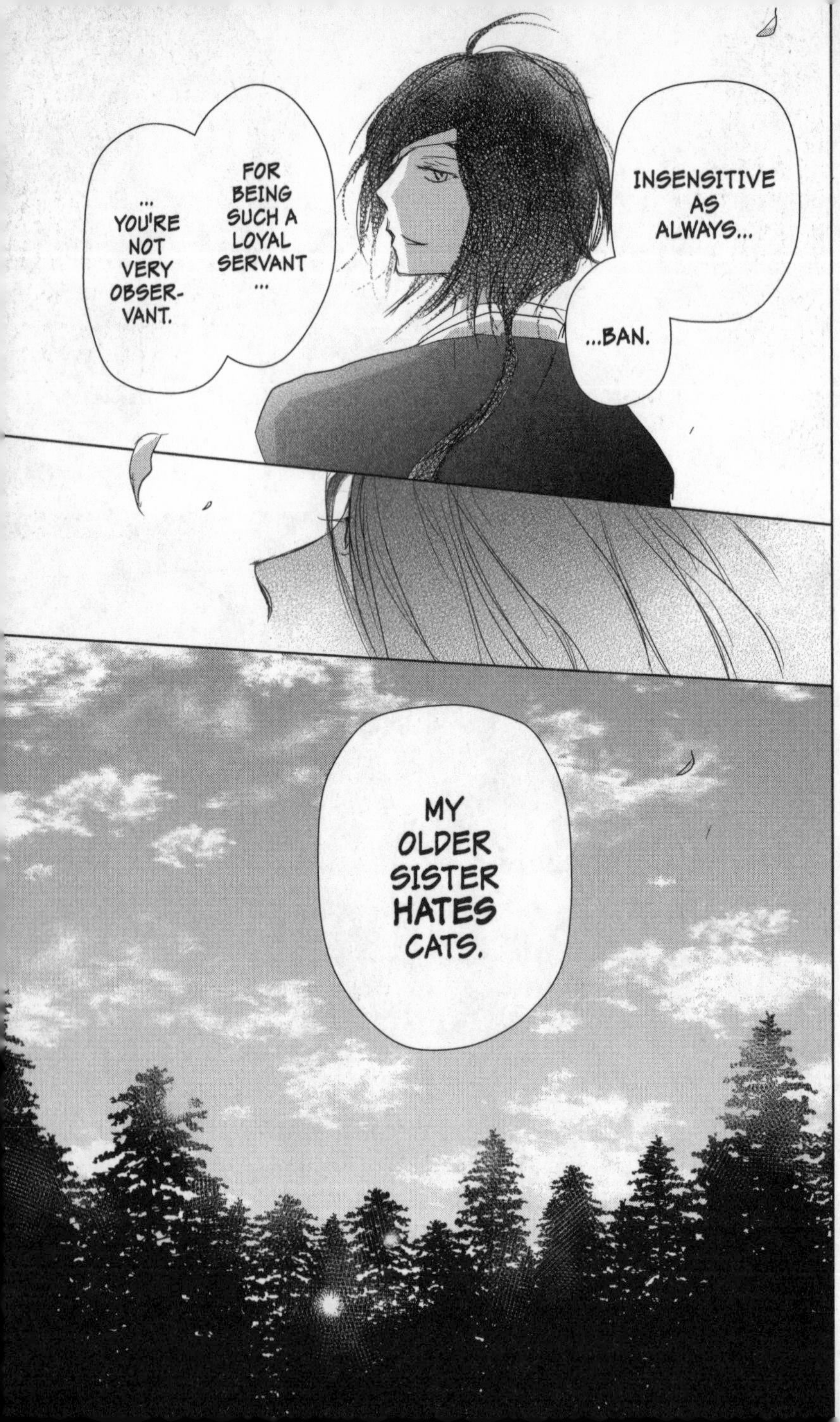
INSENSITIVE AS ALWAYS...
...BAN.
FOR BEING SUCH A LOYAL SERVANT...
...YOU'RE NOT VERY OBSER-VANT.
MY OLDER SISTER HATES CATS.

Hello, Midorikawa here. *Natsume's Book of Friends* has reached the 26th volume. Thank you so much for picking up this book. Because of space constraints, this afterword has to go in the middle of the book—to prevent spoilers, please read the entire volume before you read this.

CHAPTER 103-104 Where Vessels Lie in Slumber

I was so happy to work on a longer story for once. My head sta
filling up with what to do next while I'm still working on the curr
episode when I'm in one-shot mode. But being able to linger on
story arc reminded me of the excitement I felt back when I fir
wanted to be a manga artist. I still have a lot of storylines I'd pr
not to cut short, so I hope I get more opportunities like this.

I've wanted to do this particular story for a long time, but I fee
it could only be done now because of how Natsume's currently
feeling. I hope you can pick up on how Natori and Matoba's
relationship changes subtly depending on the situation, and that
get a feel for their solidarity as exorcist peers. It was so fun dr
everything I wanted to include: Natsume's faith in his friends; Na
tori's belief that he can still offer help even as an exorcist; Ma
who's sometimes prevented from action because he knows and
too much; Tanuma, who's surely able to help, but is unable to acco
pany Natsume; the cats protecting their secret; Nyanko Sense
of course there were even more things I wanted to expand o

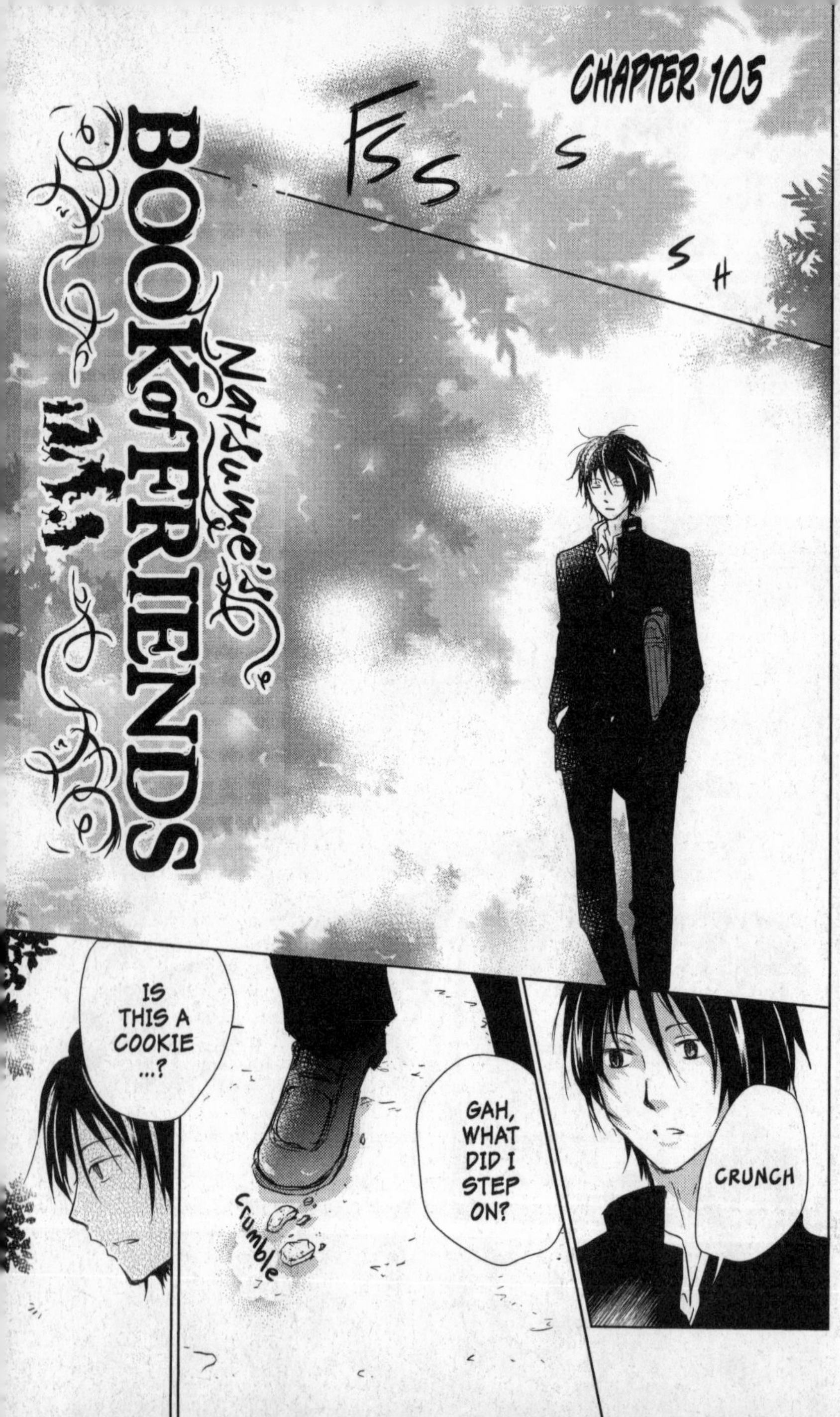
CHAPTER 105
FSSSSH
Natsume's BOOK of FRIENDS
CRUNCH
GAH, WHAT DID I STEP ON?
crumble
IS THIS A COOKIE ...?

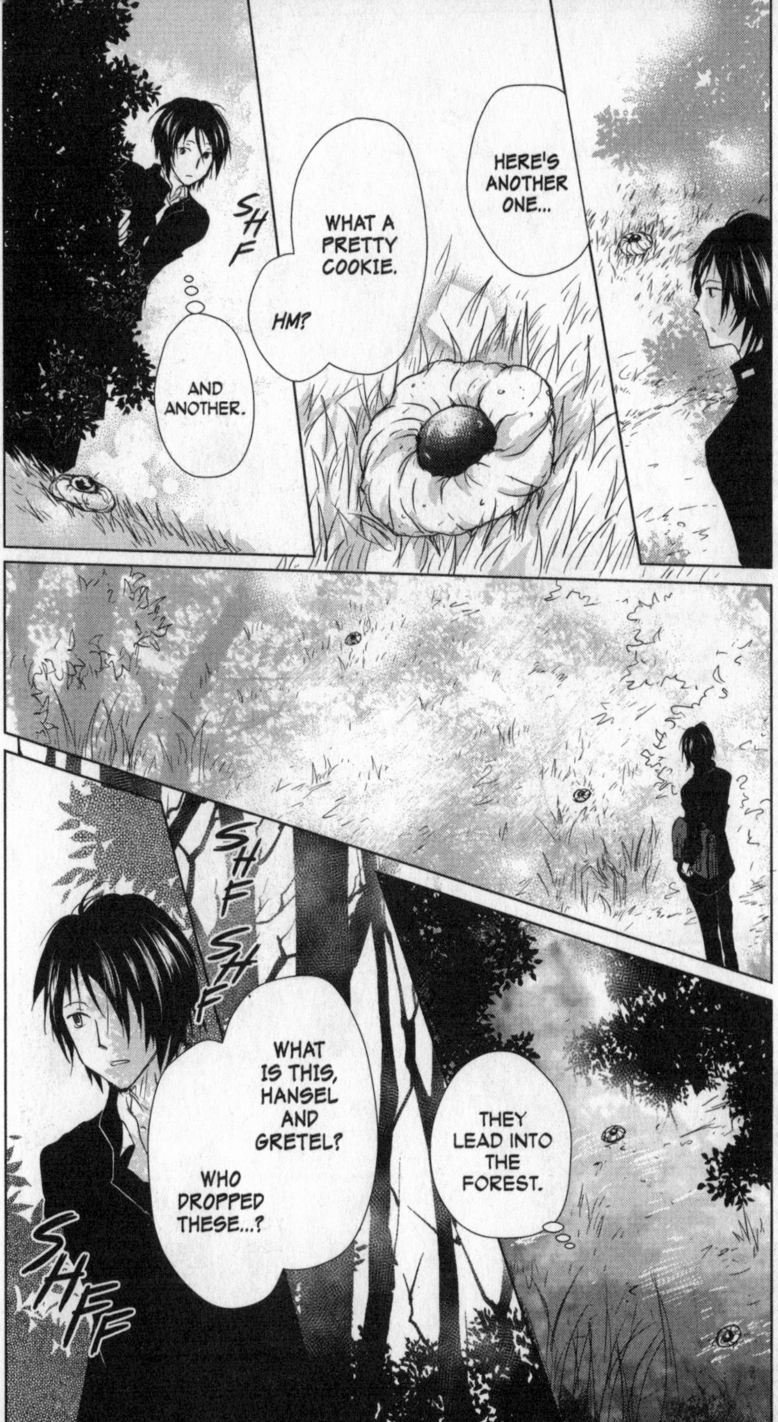

HERE'S ANOTHER ONE...
WHAT A PRETTY COOKIE.
HM?
SHF
AND ANOTHER.
THEY LEAD INTO THE FOREST.
SHF SHF
WHAT IS THIS, HANSEL AND GRETEL?
WHO DROPPED THESE...?
SHFF

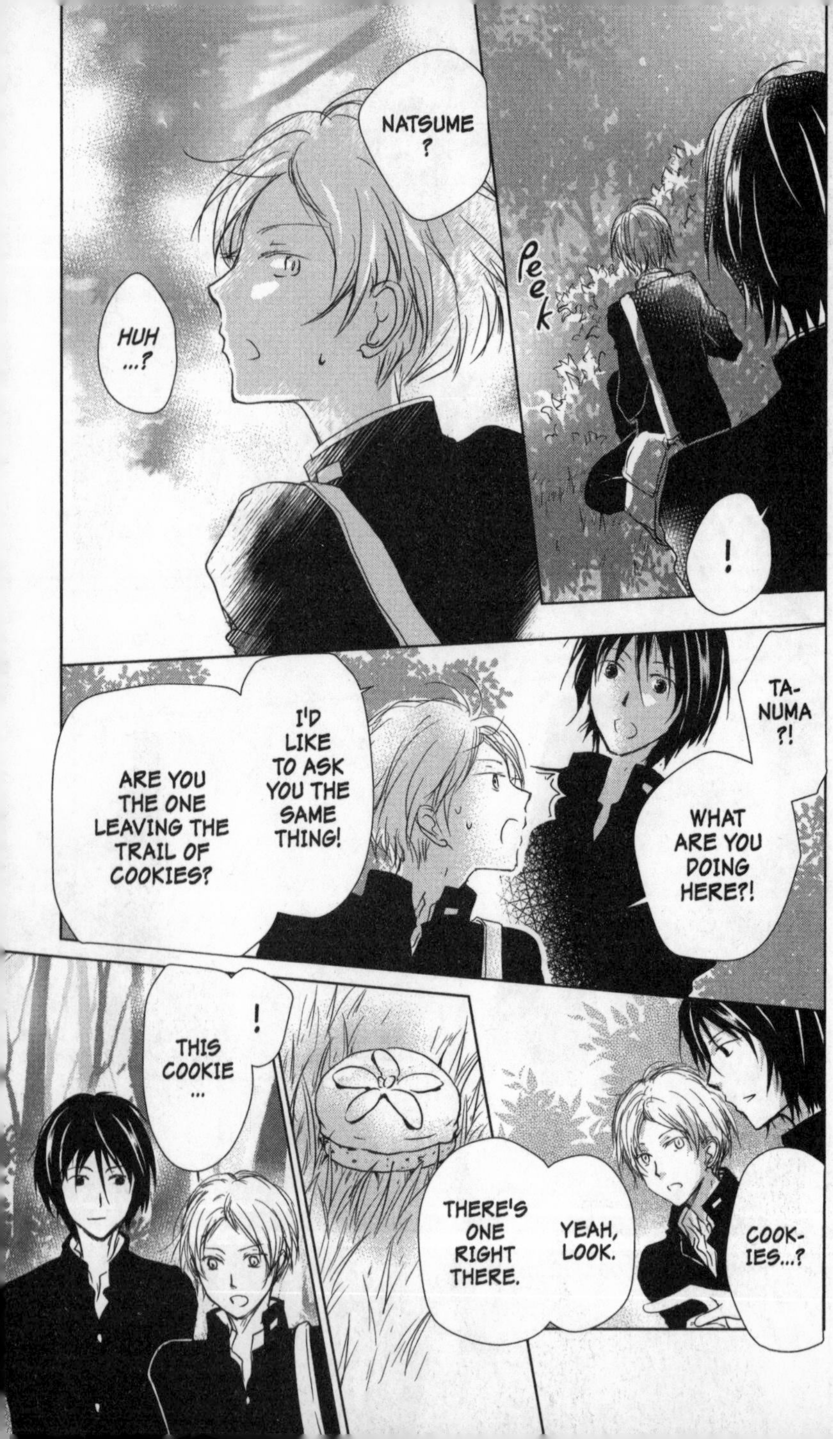
Peek
!
NATSUME ?
HUH ...?
TA-NUMA ?!
WHAT ARE YOU DOING HERE?!
I'D LIKE TO ASK YOU THE SAME THING!
ARE YOU THE ONE LEAVING THE TRAIL OF COOKIES?
COOK-IES...?
YEAH, LOOK.
THERE'S ONE RIGHT THERE.
!
THIS COOKIE ...

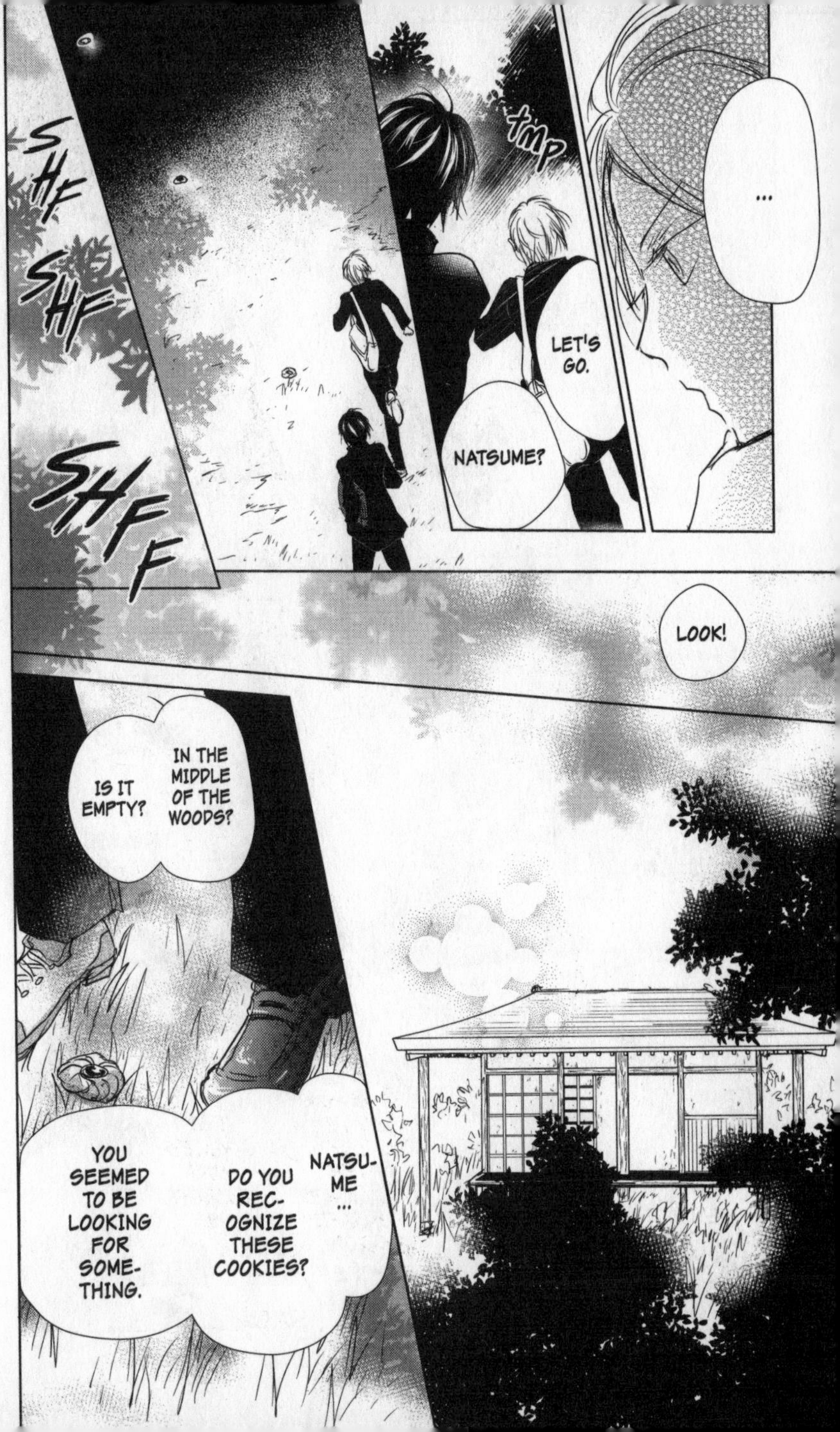
...
tmp
LET'S GO.
NATSUME?
SHF
SHF
SHFF
LOOK!
IN THE MIDDLE OF THE WOODS?
IS IT EMPTY?
NATSUME ...
DO YOU RECOGNIZE THESE COOKIES?
YOU SEEMED TO BE LOOKING FOR SOMETHING.

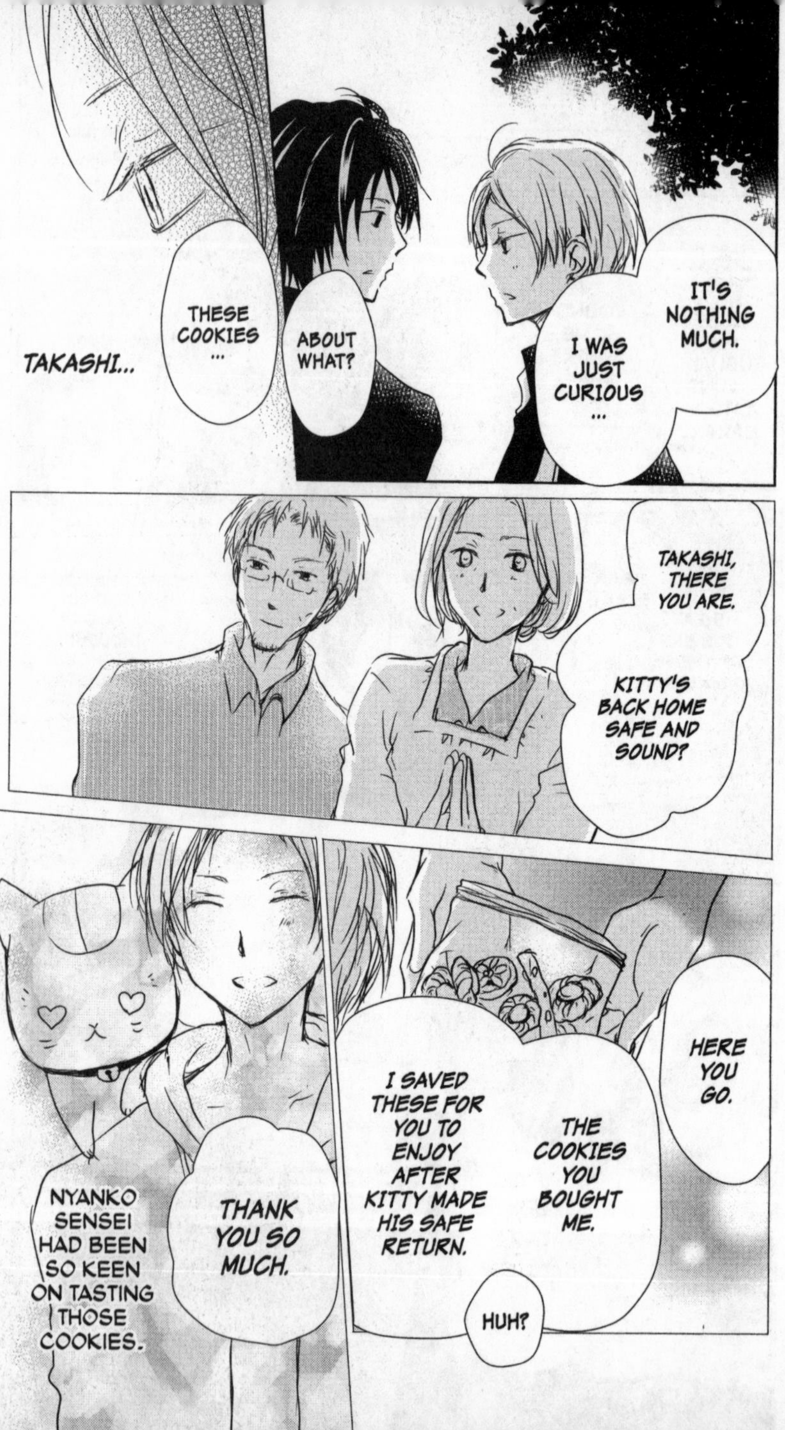
IT'S NOTHING MUCH.
I WAS JUST CURIOUS ...
ABOUT WHAT?
THESE COOKIES ...
TAKASHI...
TAKASHI, THERE YOU ARE.
KITTY'S BACK HOME SAFE AND SOUND?
HERE YOU GO.
THE COOKIES YOU BOUGHT ME.
I SAVED THESE FOR YOU TO ENJOY AFTER KITTY MADE HIS SAFE RETURN.
HUH?
THANK YOU SO MUCH.
NYANKO SENSEI HAD BEEN SO KEEN ON TASTING THOSE COOKIES.

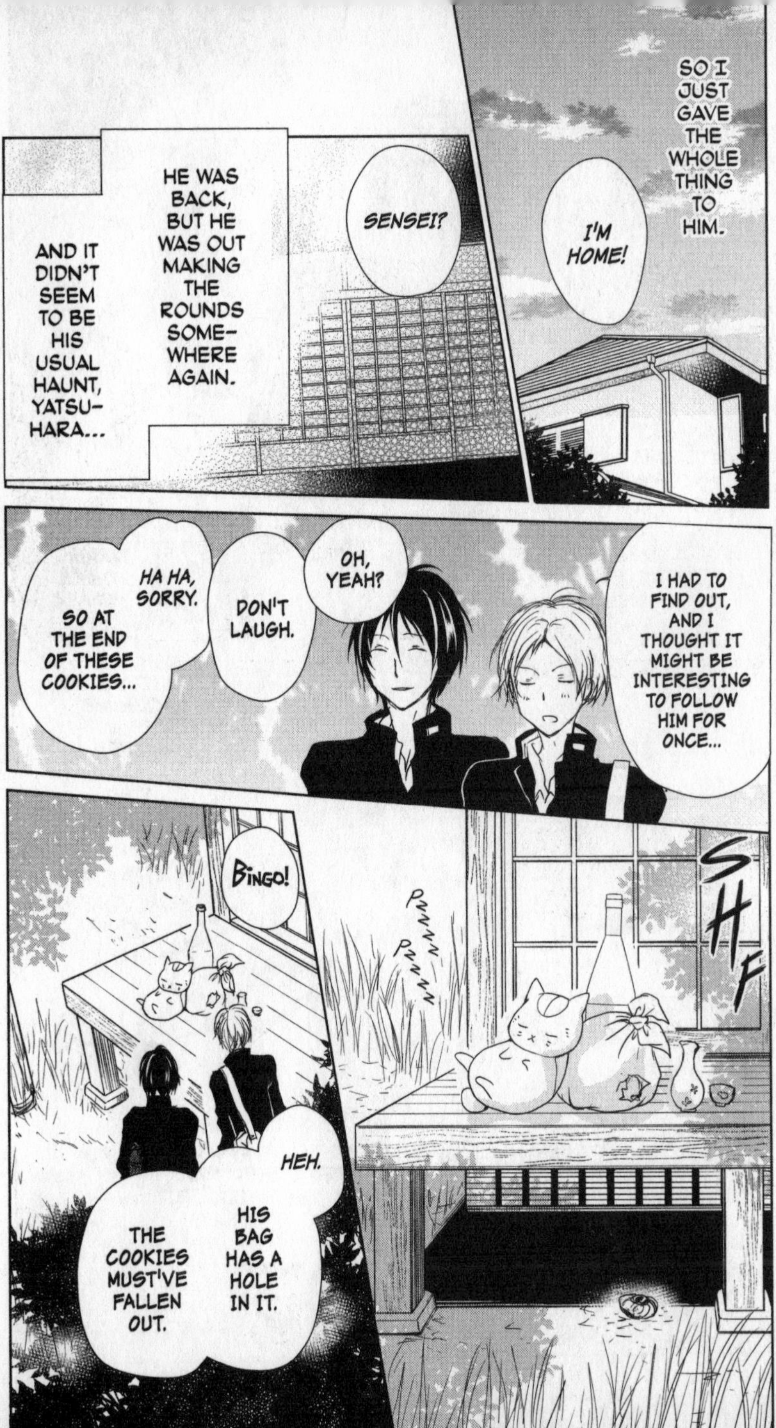
SO I JUST GAVE THE WHOLE THING TO HIM.
I'M HOME!
SENSEI?
HE WAS BACK, BUT HE WAS OUT MAKING THE ROUNDS SOME-WHERE AGAIN.
AND IT DIDN'T SEEM TO BE HIS USUAL HAUNT, YATSU-HARA...
I HAD TO FIND OUT, AND I THOUGHT IT MIGHT BE INTERESTING TO FOLLOW HIM FOR ONCE...
OH, YEAH?
DON'T LAUGH.
HA HA, SORRY.
SO AT THE END OF THESE COOKIES...
SHF
PZZZZ
PZZZZ
BINGO!
HEH.
HIS BAG HAS A HOLE IN IT.
THE COOKIES MUST'VE FALLEN OUT.

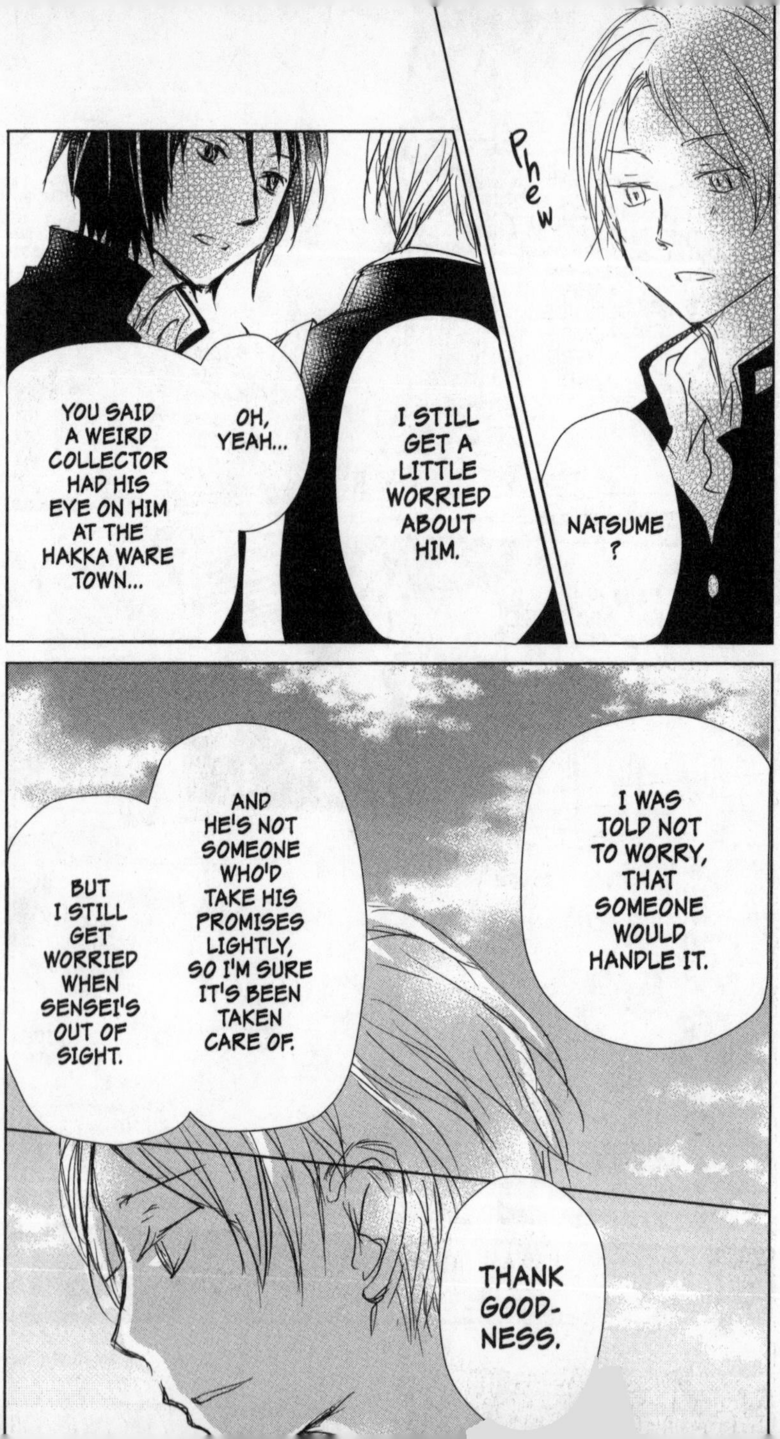
Phew
NATSUME?
I STILL GET A LITTLE WORRIED ABOUT HIM.
OH, YEAH...
YOU SAID A WEIRD COLLECTOR HAD HIS EYE ON HIM AT THE HAKKA WARE TOWN...
I WAS TOLD NOT TO WORRY, THAT SOMEONE WOULD HANDLE IT.
AND HE'S NOT SOMEONE WHO'D TAKE HIS PROMISES LIGHTLY, SO I'M SURE IT'S BEEN TAKEN CARE OF.
BUT I STILL GET WORRIED WHEN SENSEI'S OUT OF SIGHT.
THANK GOOD-NESS.

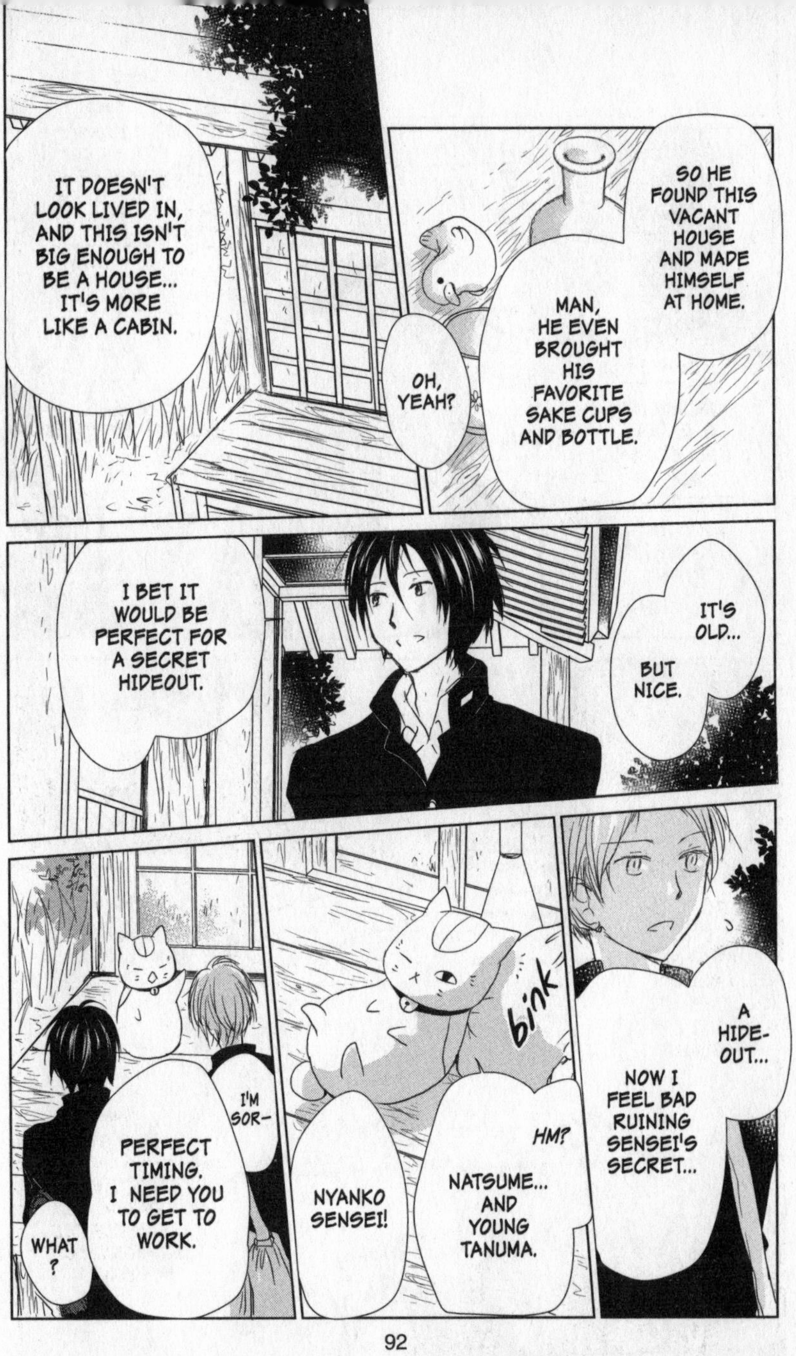
SO HE FOUND THIS VACANT HOUSE AND MADE HIMSELF AT HOME.
MAN, HE EVEN BROUGHT HIS FAVORITE SAKE CUPS AND BOTTLE.
OH, YEAH?
IT DOESN'T LOOK LIVED IN, AND THIS ISN'T BIG ENOUGH TO BE A HOUSE... IT'S MORE LIKE A CABIN.
IT'S OLD...
BUT NICE.
I BET IT WOULD BE PERFECT FOR A SECRET HIDEOUT.
A HIDE-OUT...
NOW I FEEL BAD RUINING SENSEI'S SECRET...
bink
HM?
NATSUME... AND YOUNG TANUMA.
NYANKO SENSEI!
I'M SOR-
PERFECT TIMING. I NEED YOU TO GET TO WORK.
WHAT?

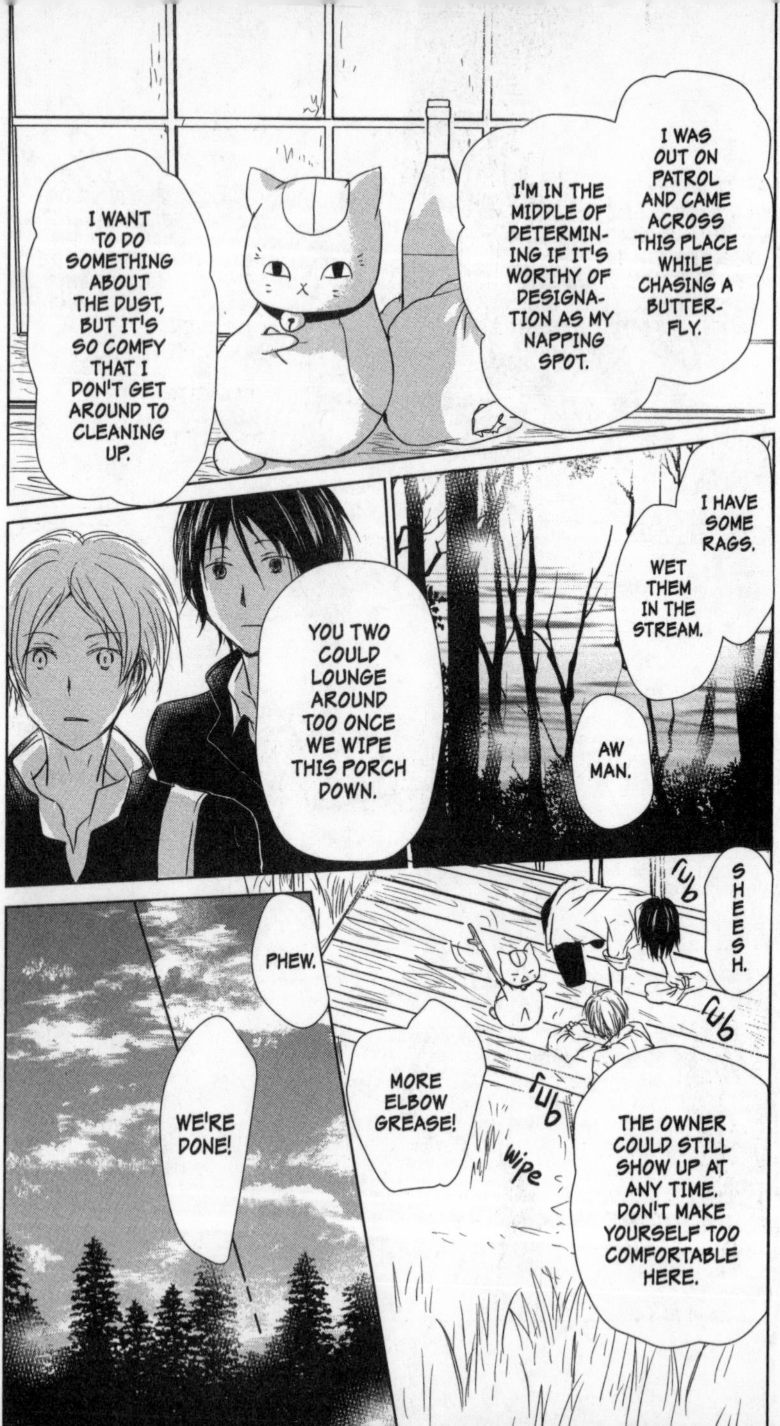
I WAS OUT ON PATROL AND CAME ACROSS THIS PLACE WHILE CHASING A BUTTERFLY.
I'M IN THE MIDDLE OF DETERMINING IF IT'S WORTHY OF DESIGNATION AS MY NAPPING SPOT.
I WANT TO DO SOMETHING ABOUT THE DUST, BUT IT'S SO COMFY THAT I DON'T GET AROUND TO CLEANING UP.
I HAVE SOME RAGS.
WET THEM IN THE STREAM.
AW MAN.
YOU TWO COULD LOUNGE AROUND TOO ONCE WE WIPE THIS PORCH DOWN.
SHEESH.
rub
rub
PHEW.
THE OWNER COULD STILL SHOW UP AT ANY TIME. DON'T MAKE YOURSELF TOO COMFORTABLE HERE.
MORE ELBOW GREASE!
rub
wipe
WE'RE DONE!

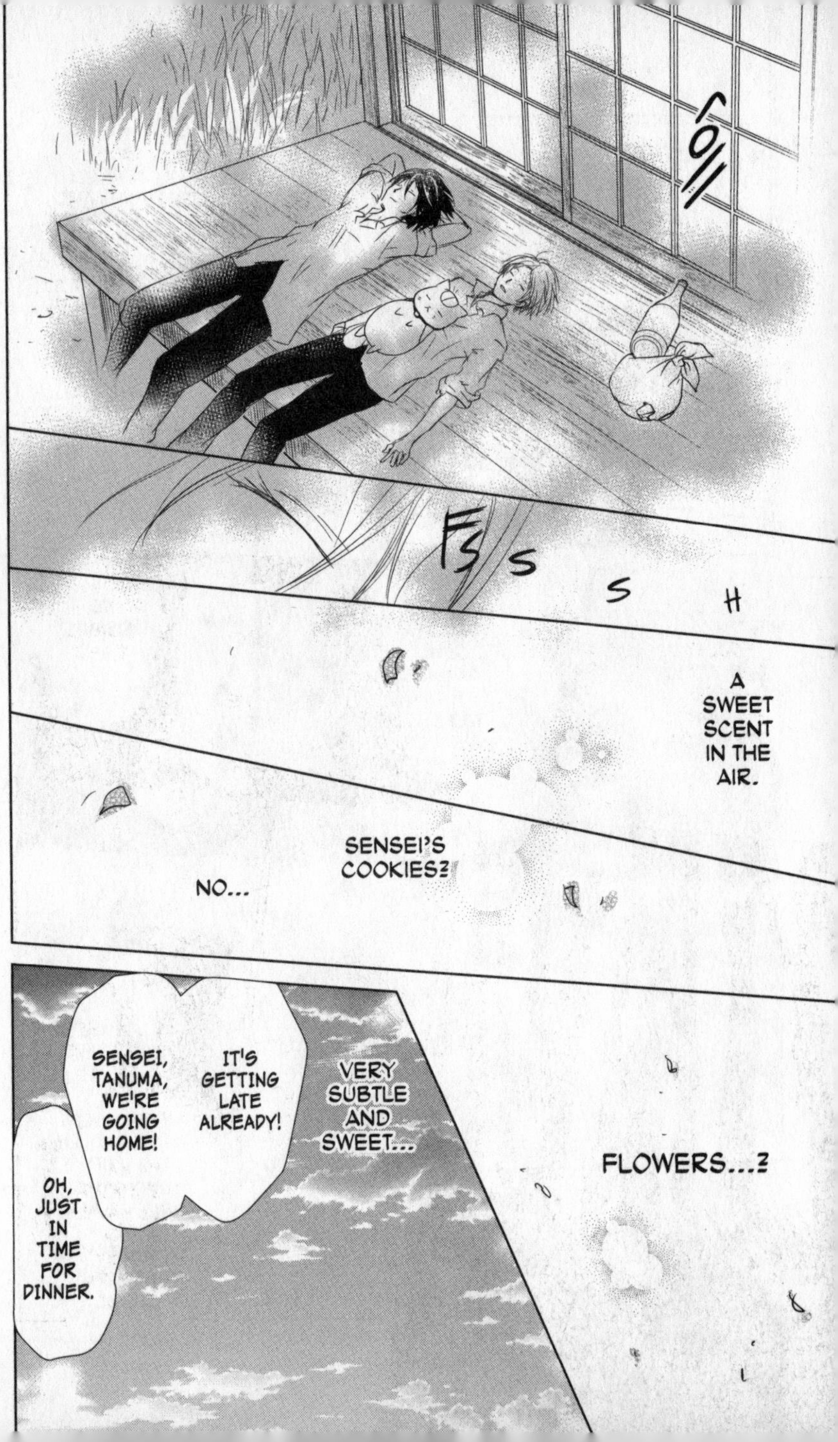
FSSSH
A SWEET SCENT IN THE AIR.
SENSEI'S COOKIES?
NO...
FLOWERS...?
VERY SUBTLE AND SWEET...
IT'S GETTING LATE ALREADY!
SENSEI, TANUMA, WE'RE GOING HOME!
OH, JUST IN TIME FOR DINNER.

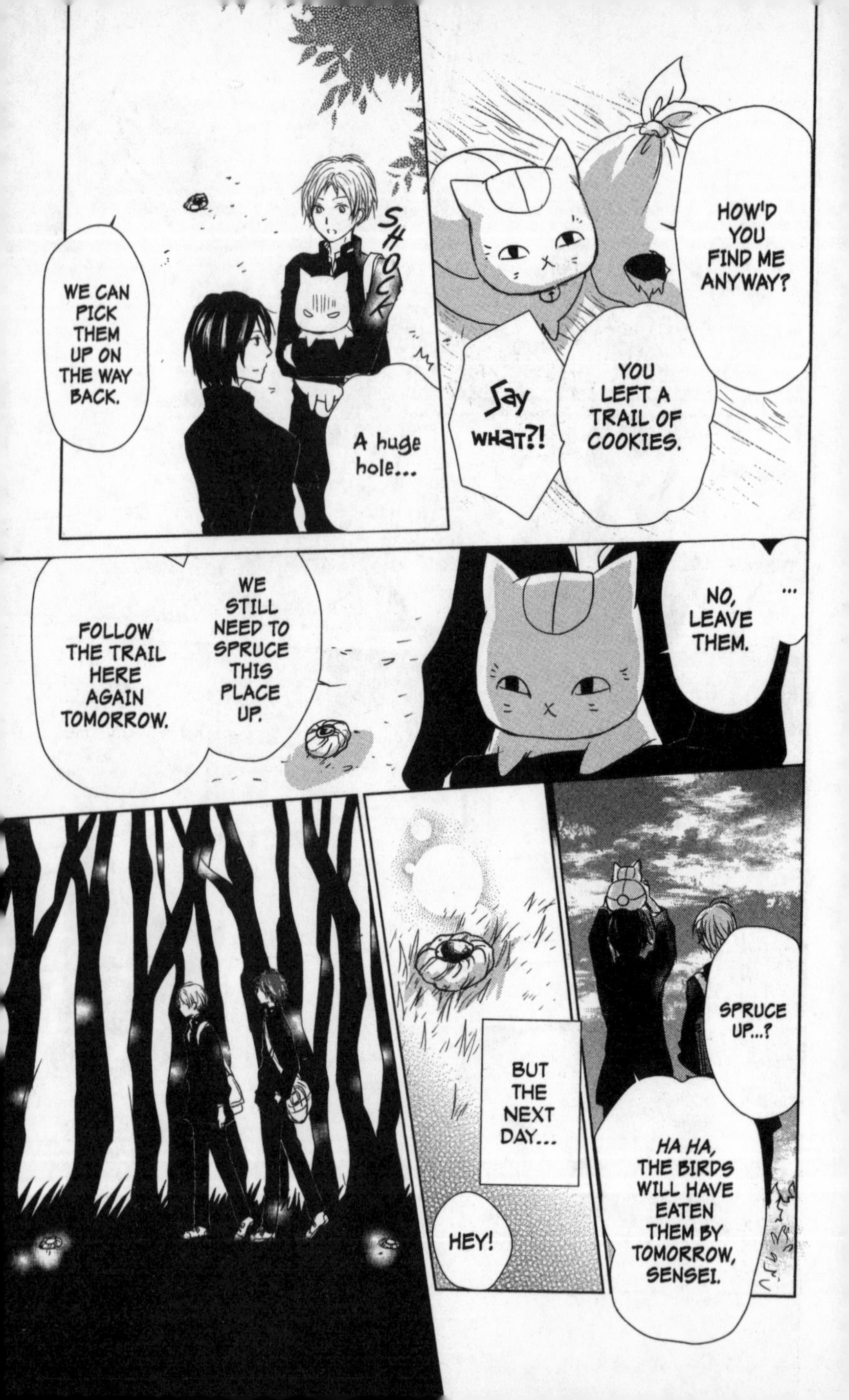
HOW'D YOU FIND ME ANYWAY?
YOU LEFT A TRAIL OF COOKIES.
Say WHAT?!
SHOCK
WE CAN PICK THEM UP ON THE WAY BACK.
A huge hole...
...
NO, LEAVE THEM.
WE STILL NEED TO SPRUCE THIS PLACE UP.
FOLLOW THE TRAIL HERE AGAIN TOMORROW.
SPRUCE UP...?
HA HA, THE BIRDS WILL HAVE EATEN THEM BY TOMORROW, SENSEI.
BUT THE NEXT DAY...
HEY!

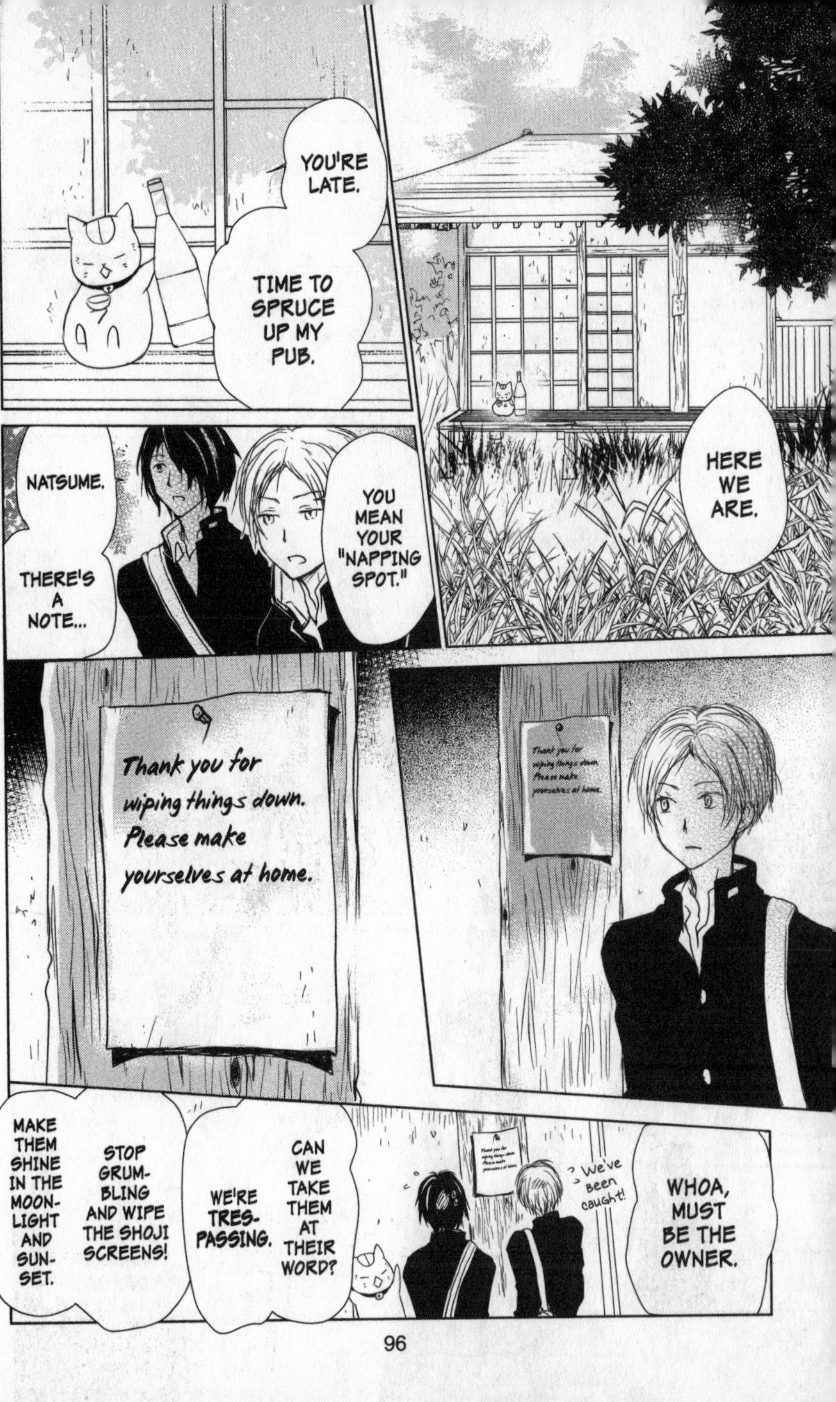
HERE WE ARE.
YOU'RE LATE.
TIME TO SPRUCE UP MY PUB.
YOU MEAN YOUR "NAPPING SPOT."
NATSUME.
THERE'S A NOTE...
Thank you for wiping things down. Please make yourselves at home.
WHOA, MUST BE THE OWNER.
We've been caught!
CAN WE TAKE THEM AT THEIR WORD?
WE'RE TRES-PASSING.
STOP GRUM-BLING AND WIPE THE SHOJI SCREENS!
MAKE THEM SHINE IN THE MOON-LIGHT AND SUN-SET.

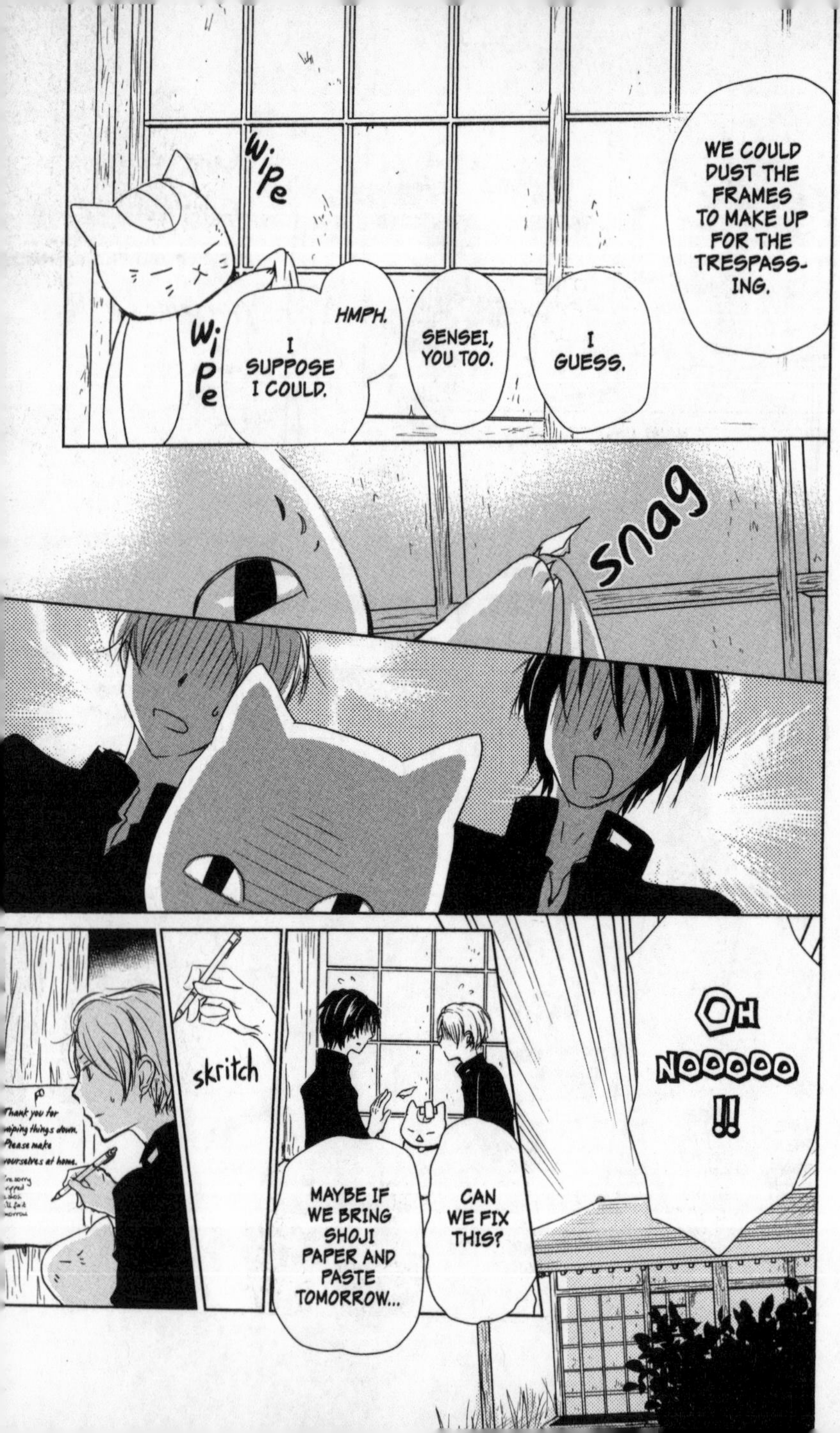
WE COULD DUST THE FRAMES TO MAKE UP FOR THE TRESPASS-ING.
I GUESS.
SENSEI, YOU TOO.
HMPH.
I SUPPOSE I COULD.
wipe
wipe
snag
OH NOOOOO!!
CAN WE FIX THIS?
MAYBE IF WE BRING SHOJI PAPER AND PASTE TOMORROW...
skritch
Thank you for wiping things down. Please make yourselves at home.

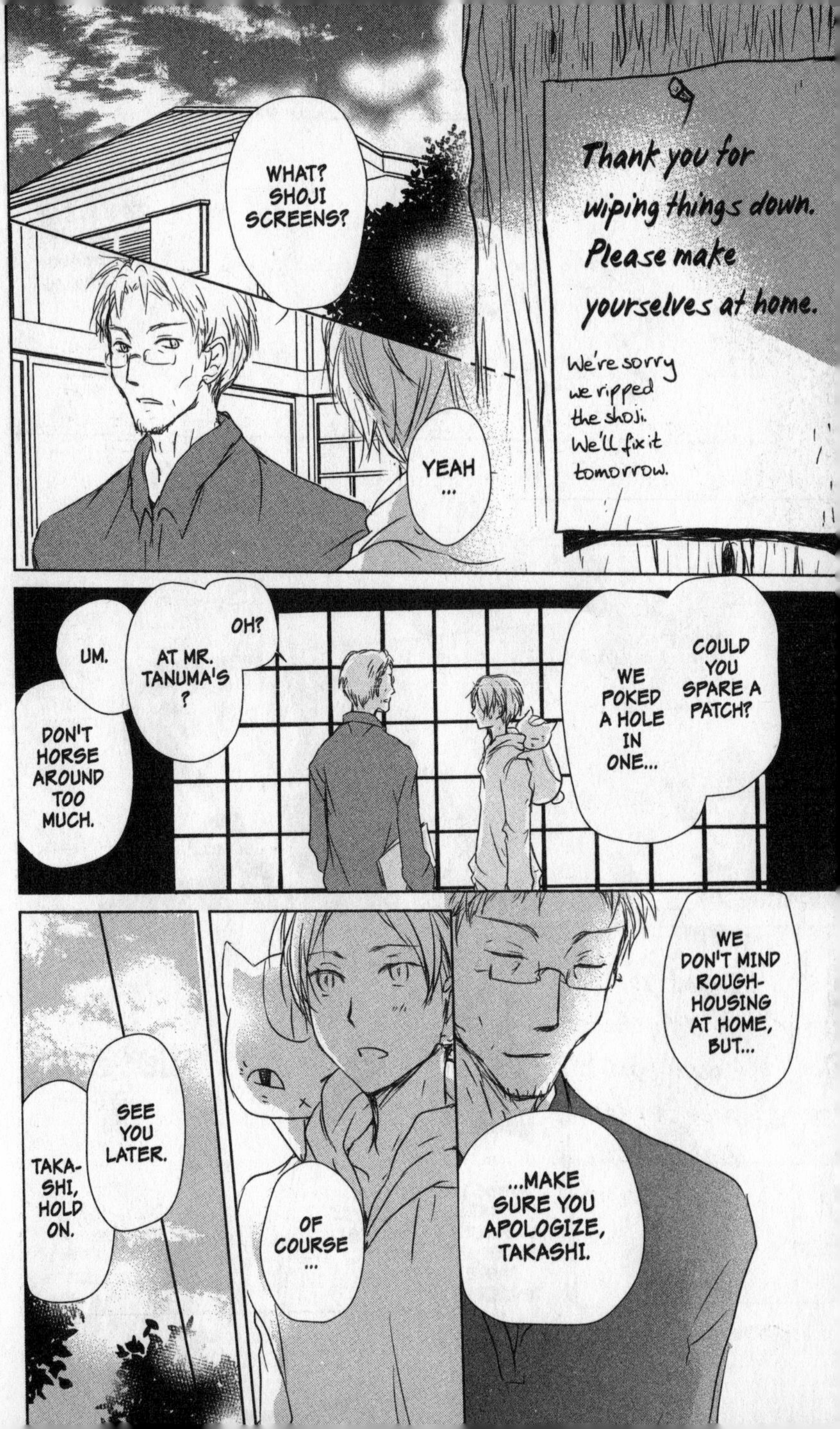

Thank you for wiping things down. Please make yourselves at home.
We're sorry we ripped the shoji. We'll fix it tomorrow.
WHAT? SHOJI SCREENS?
YEAH...
COULD YOU SPARE A PATCH?
WE POKED A HOLE IN ONE...
OH? AT MR. TANUMA'S?
UM.
DON'T HORSE AROUND TOO MUCH.
WE DON'T MIND ROUGH-HOUSING AT HOME, BUT...
...MAKE SURE YOU APOLOGIZE, TAKASHI.
OF COURSE...
SEE YOU LATER.
TAKA-SHI, HOLD ON.

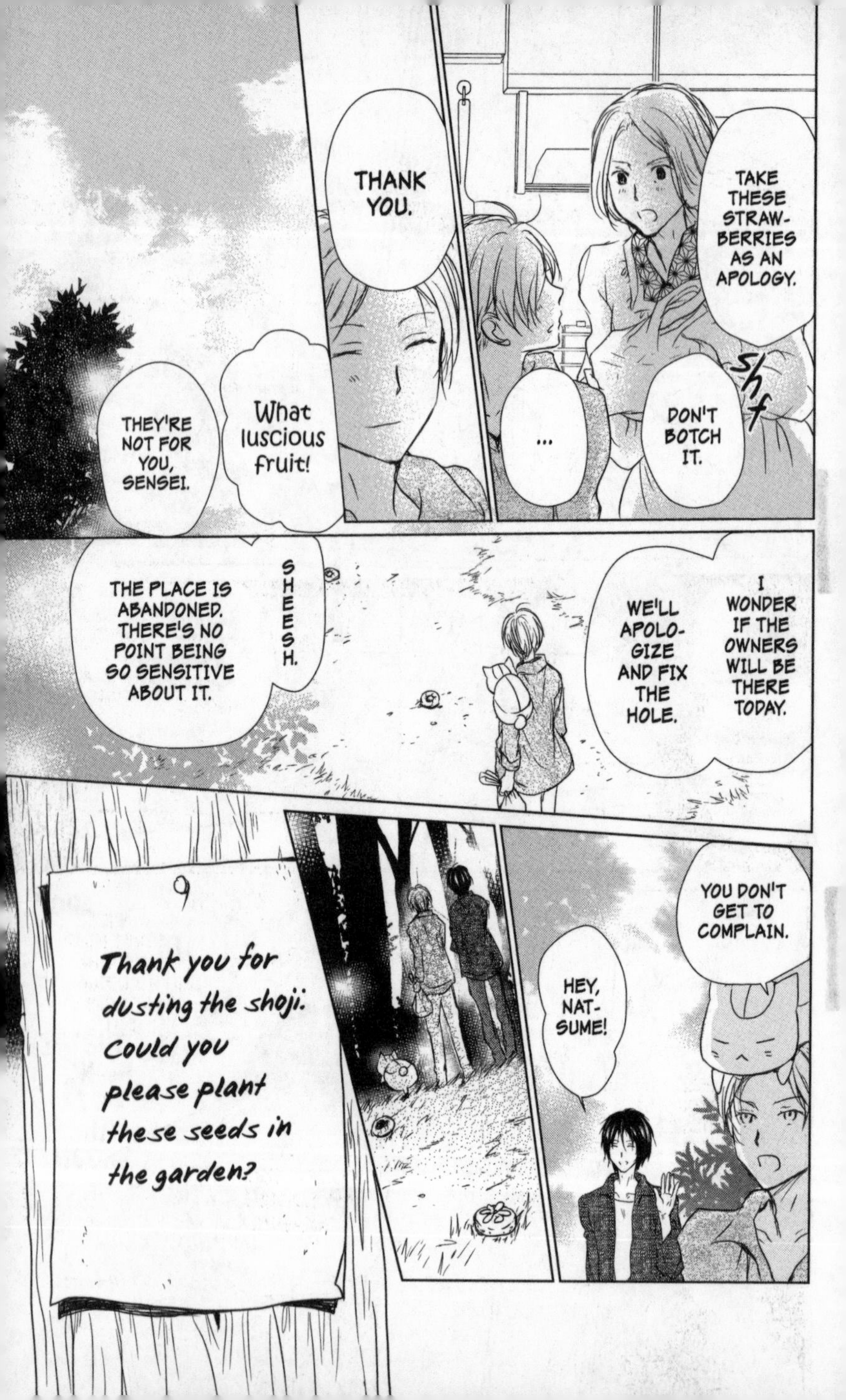
TAKE THESE STRAW-BERRIES AS AN APOLOGY.
Shf
DON'T BOTCH IT.
...
THANK YOU.
What luscious fruit!
THEY'RE NOT FOR YOU, SENSEI.
I WONDER IF THE OWNERS WILL BE THERE TODAY.
WE'LL APOLO-GIZE AND FIX THE HOLE.
SHEESH.
THE PLACE IS ABANDONED. THERE'S NO POINT BEING SO SENSITIVE ABOUT IT.
YOU DON'T GET TO COMPLAIN.
HEY, NAT-SUME!
Thank you for dusting the shoji. Could you please plant these seeds in the garden?

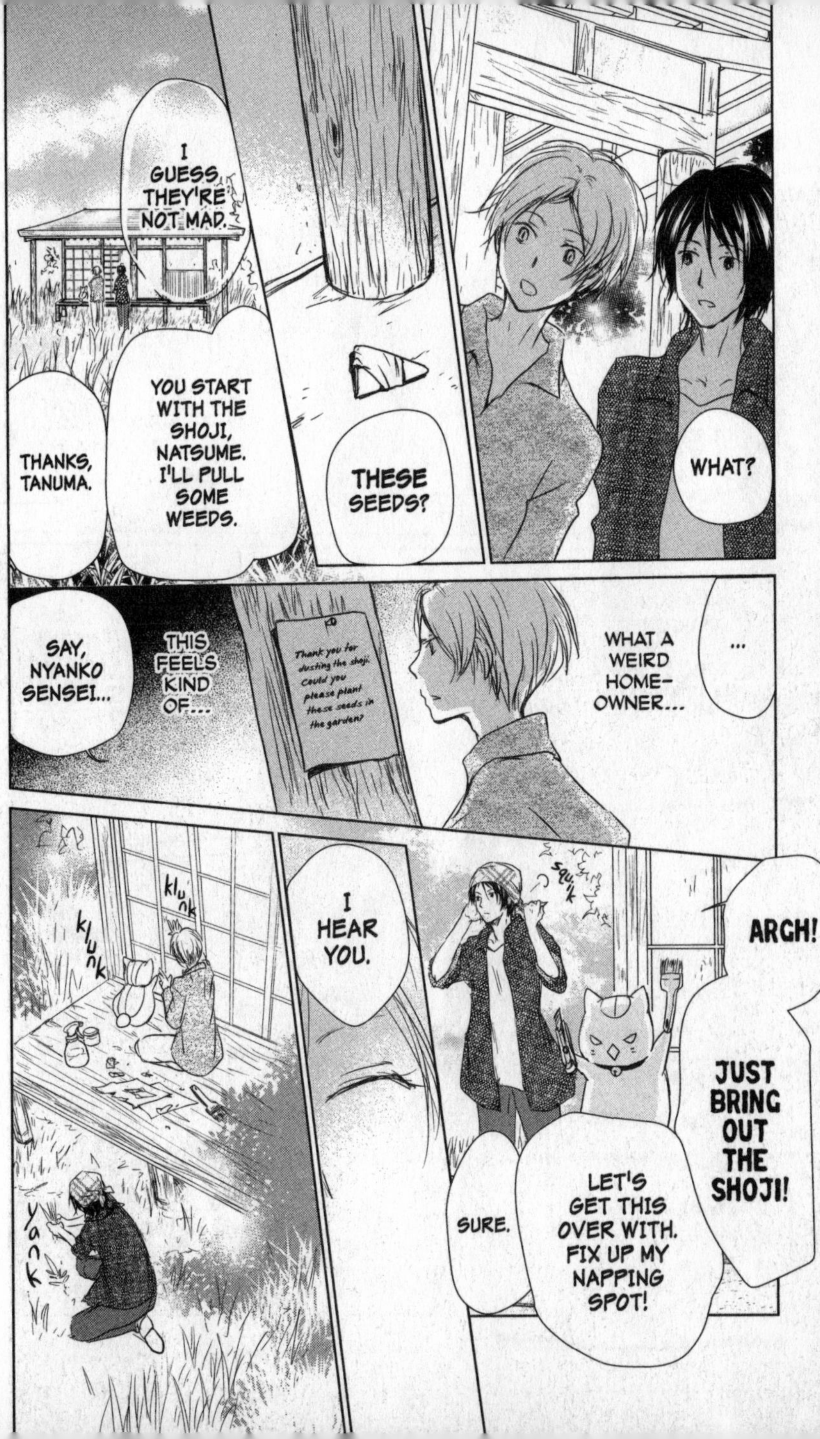
WHAT?
THESE SEEDS?
I GUESS THEY'RE NOT MAD.
YOU START WITH THE SHOJI, NATSUME. I'LL PULL SOME WEEDS.
THANKS, TANUMA.
...
WHAT A WEIRD HOME-OWNER...
Thank you for dusting the shoji. Could you please plant these seeds in the garden?
THIS FEELS KIND OF...
SAY, NYANKO SENSEI...
ARGH!
JUST BRING OUT THE SHOJI!
squik
LET'S GET THIS OVER WITH. FIX UP MY NAPPING SPOT!
SURE.
I HEAR YOU.
klunk
klunk
yank

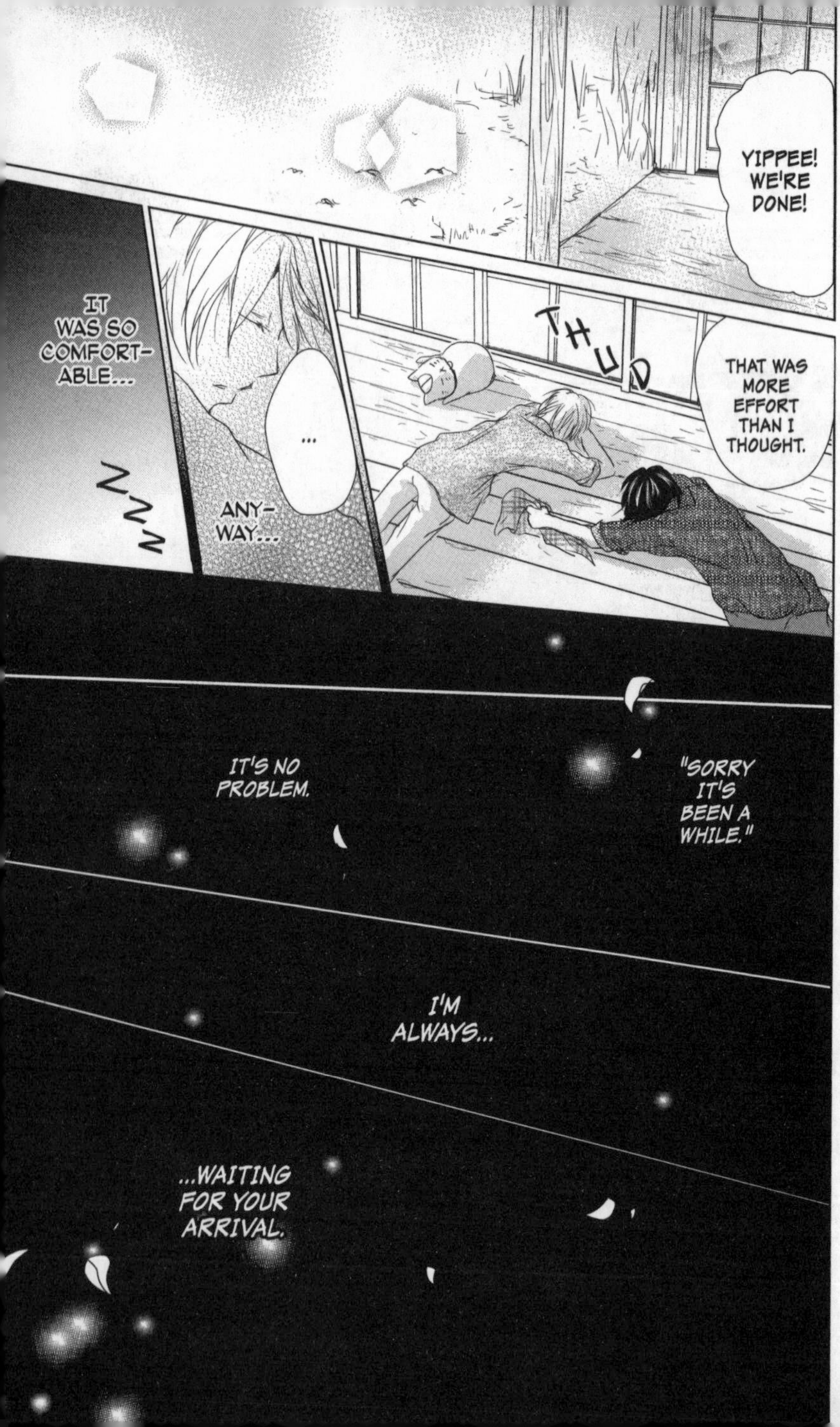
YIPPEE! WE'RE DONE!
THAT WAS MORE EFFORT THAN I THOUGHT.
THUD
...
ANY-WAY...
IT WAS SO COMFORT-ABLE...
ZZZ
"SORRY IT'S BEEN A WHILE."
IT'S NO PROBLEM.
I'M ALWAYS...
...WAITING FOR YOUR ARRIVAL.

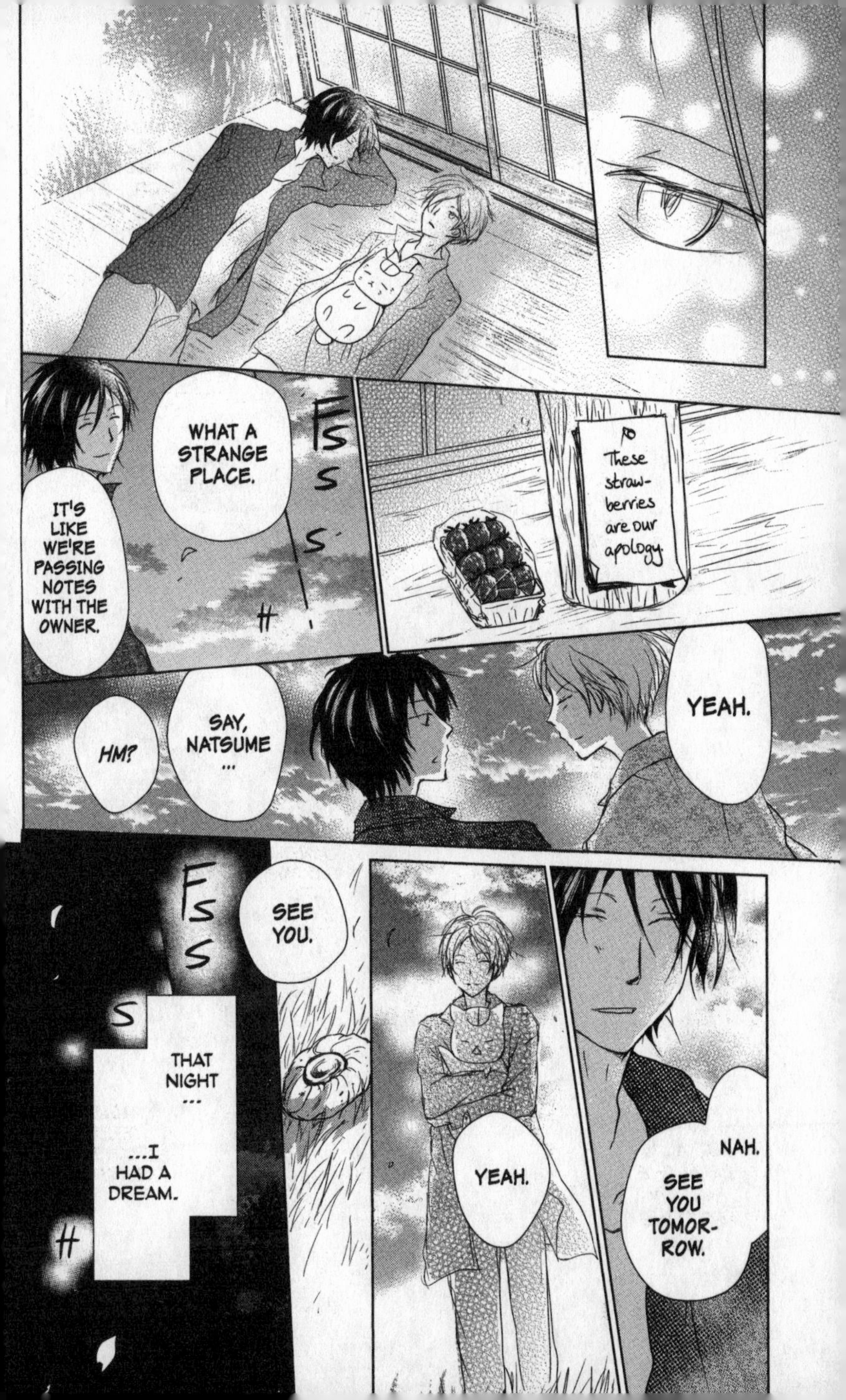
These strawberries are our apology.
WHAT A STRANGE PLACE.
IT'S LIKE WE'RE PASSING NOTES WITH THE OWNER.
FSSSH
YEAH.
SAY, NATSUME ...
HM?
NAH.
SEE YOU TOMORROW.
YEAH.
SEE YOU.
FSSSH
THAT NIGHT ...
...I HAD A DREAM.

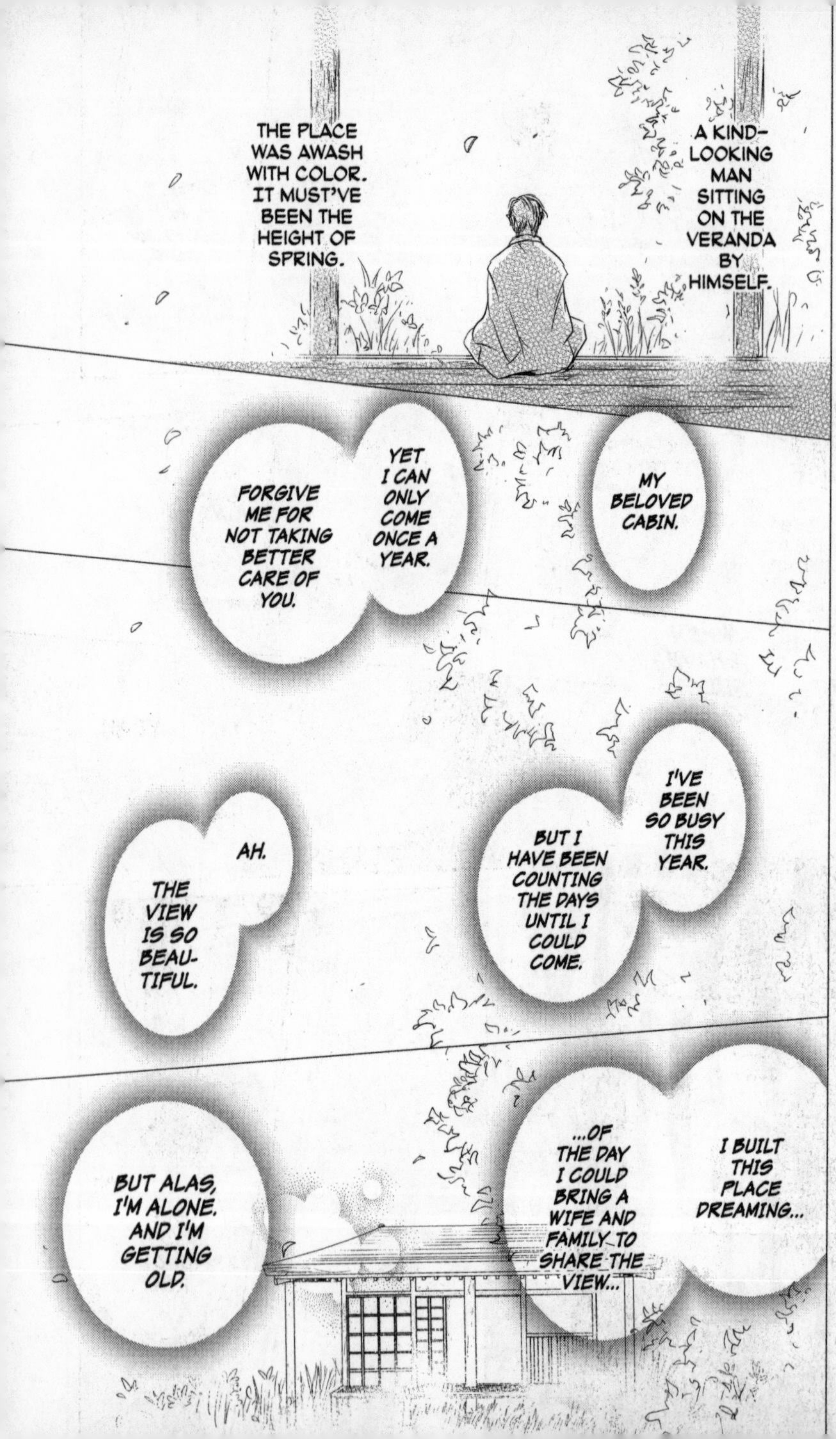
A KIND-LOOKING MAN SITTING ON THE VERANDA BY HIMSELF.
THE PLACE WAS AWASH WITH COLOR. IT MUST'VE BEEN THE HEIGHT OF SPRING.
MY BELOVED CABIN.
YET I CAN ONLY COME ONCE A YEAR.
FORGIVE ME FOR NOT TAKING BETTER CARE OF YOU.
I'VE BEEN SO BUSY THIS YEAR.
BUT I HAVE BEEN COUNTING THE DAYS UNTIL I COULD COME.
AH.
THE VIEW IS SO BEAUTIFUL.
I BUILT THIS PLACE DREAMING...
...OF THE DAY I COULD BRING A WIFE AND FAMILY TO SHARE THE VIEW...
BUT ALAS, I'M ALONE. AND I'M GETTING OLD.

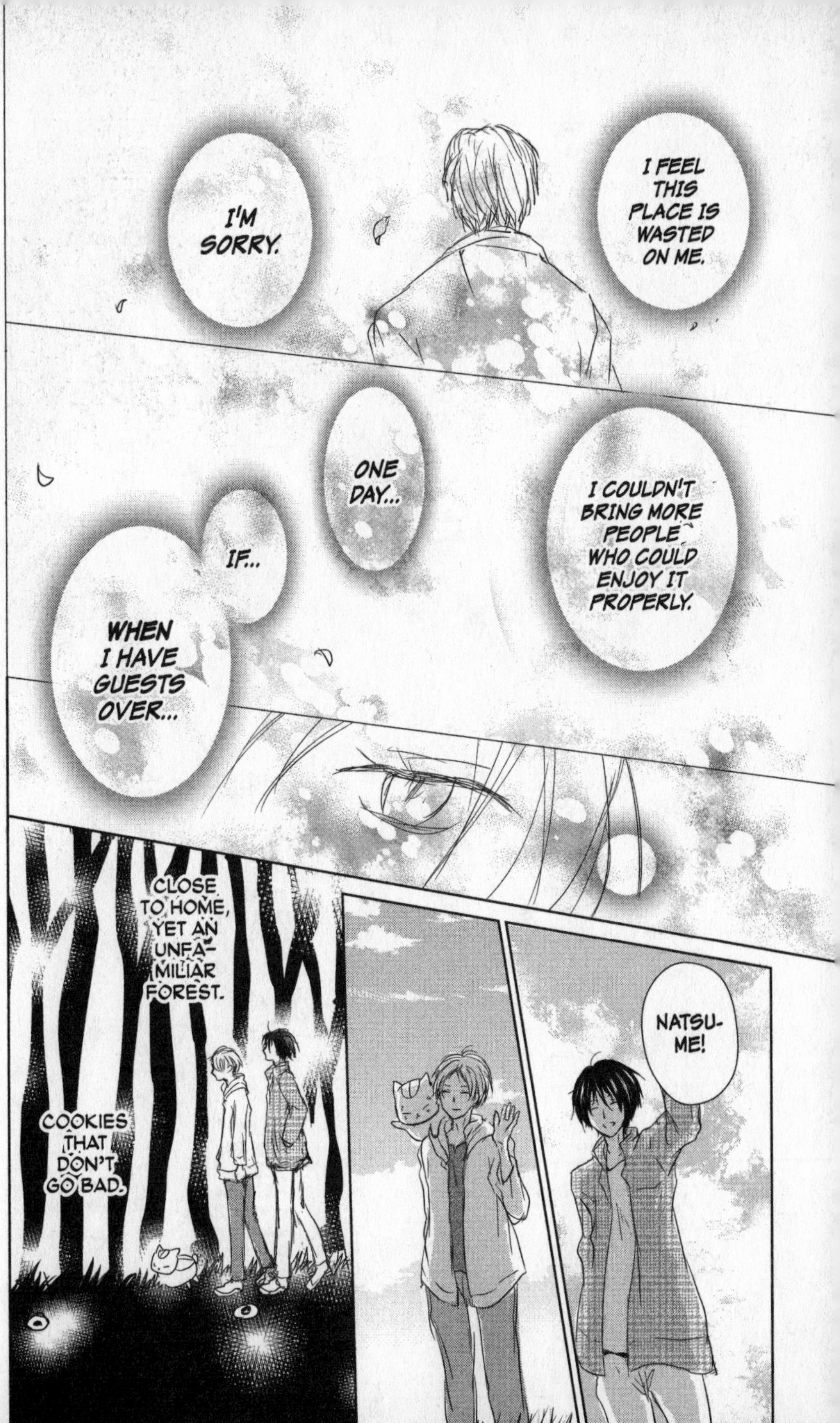
I FEEL THIS PLACE IS WASTED ON ME.
I'M SORRY.
I COULDN'T BRING MORE PEOPLE WHO COULD ENJOY IT PROPERLY.
ONE DAY...
IF...
WHEN I HAVE GUESTS OVER...
NATSU-ME!
CLOSE TO HOME, YET AN UNFA-MILIAR FOREST.
COOKIES THAT DON'T GO BAD.

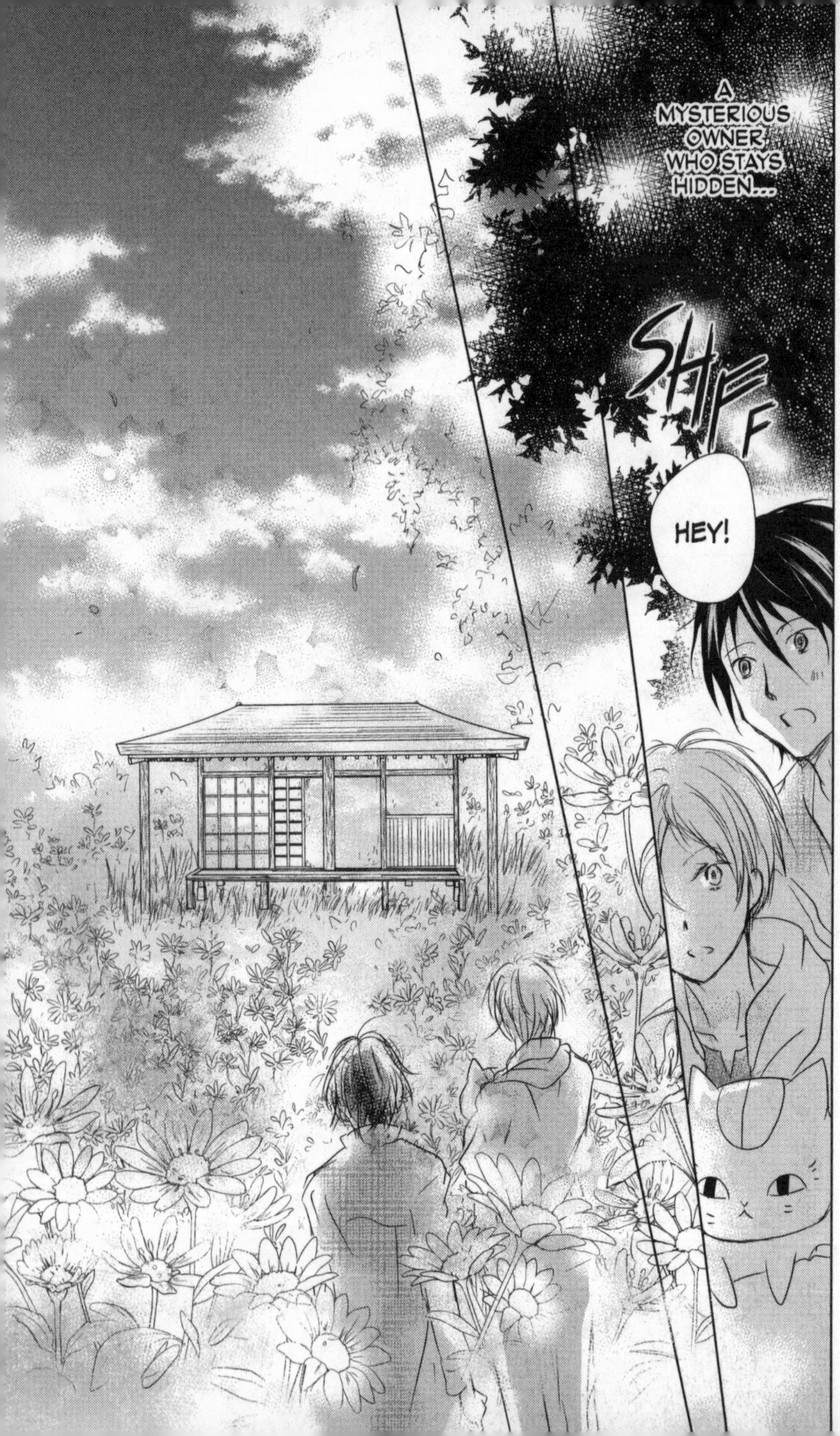
A MYSTERIOUS OWNER WHO STAYS HIDDEN...
SHFF
HEY!

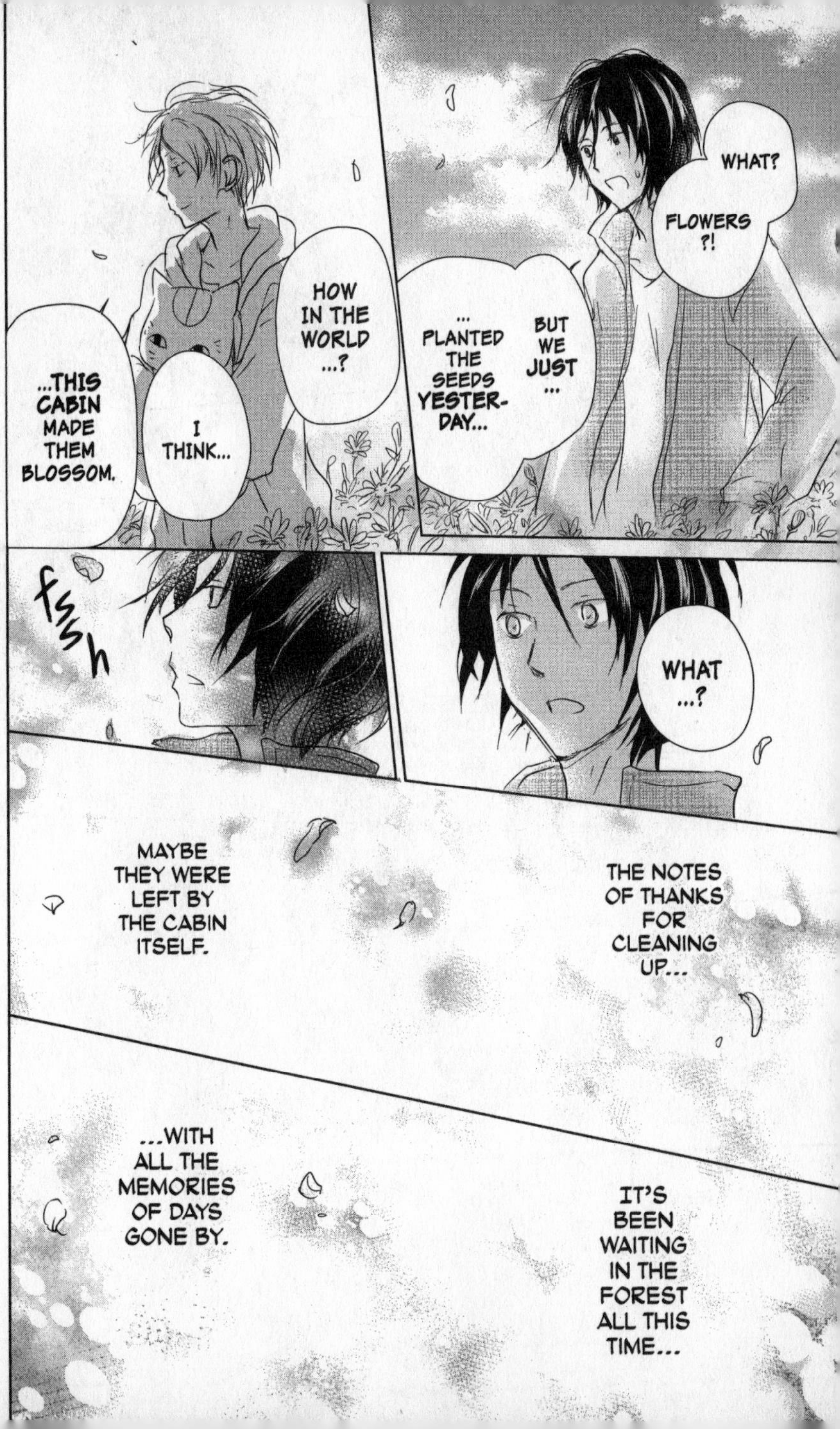
WHAT?
FLOWERS ?!
BUT WE JUST ...
... PLANTED THE SEEDS YESTER-DAY...
HOW IN THE WORLD ...?
I THINK...
...THIS CABIN MADE THEM BLOSSOM.
WHAT ...?
fssh
THE NOTES OF THANKS FOR CLEANING UP...
MAYBE THEY WERE LEFT BY THE CABIN ITSELF.
IT'S BEEN WAITING IN THE FOREST ALL THIS TIME...
...WITH ALL THE MEMORIES OF DAYS GONE BY.

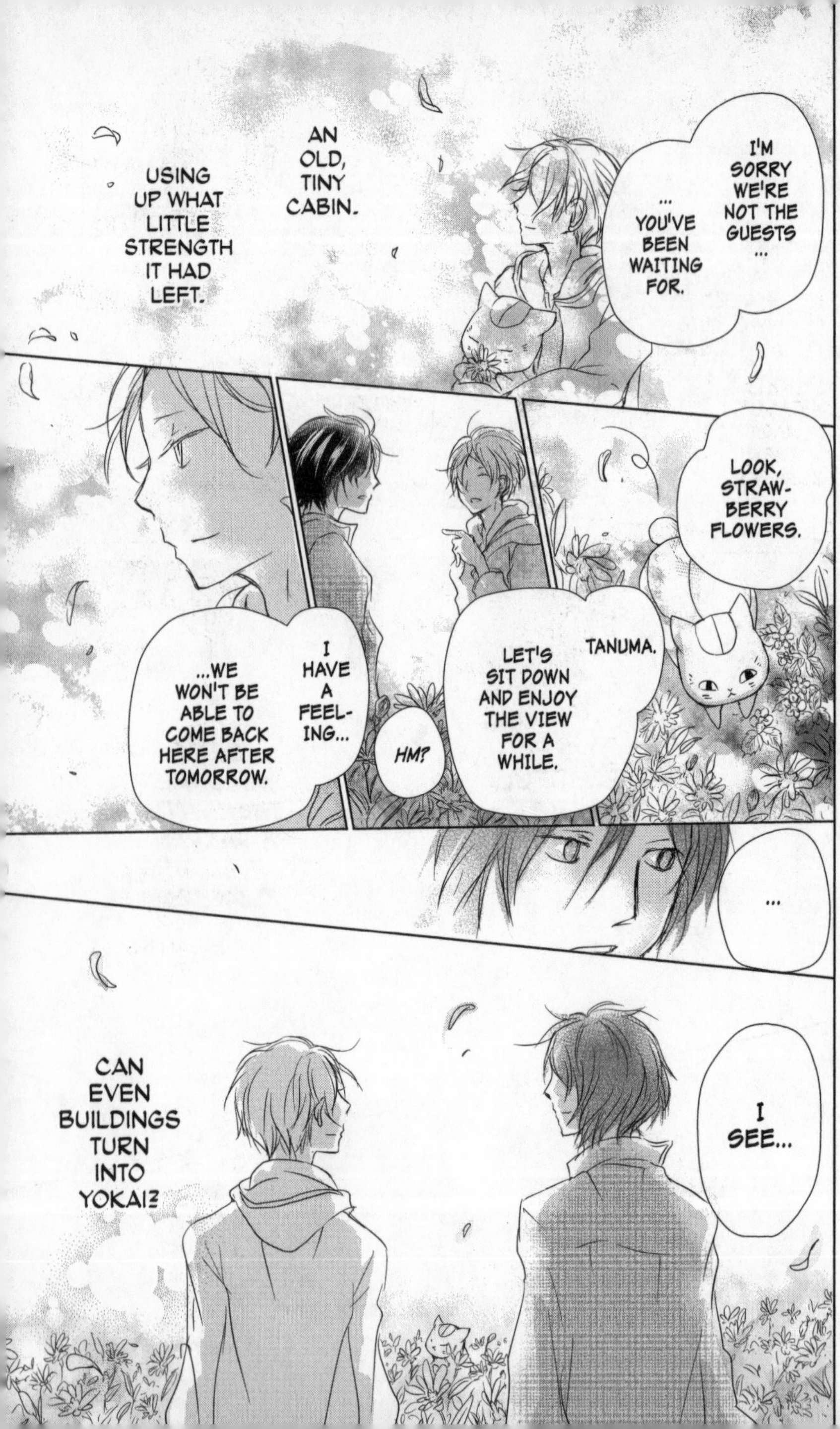

I'M SORRY WE'RE NOT THE GUESTS...
...YOU'VE BEEN WAITING FOR.
AN OLD, TINY CABIN.
USING UP WHAT LITTLE STRENGTH IT HAD LEFT.
LOOK, STRAW-BERRY FLOWERS.
TANUMA.
LET'S SIT DOWN AND ENJOY THE VIEW FOR A WHILE.
HM?
I HAVE A FEEL-ING...
...WE WON'T BE ABLE TO COME BACK HERE AFTER TOMORROW.
...
I SEE...
CAN EVEN BUILDINGS TURN INTO YOKAI?

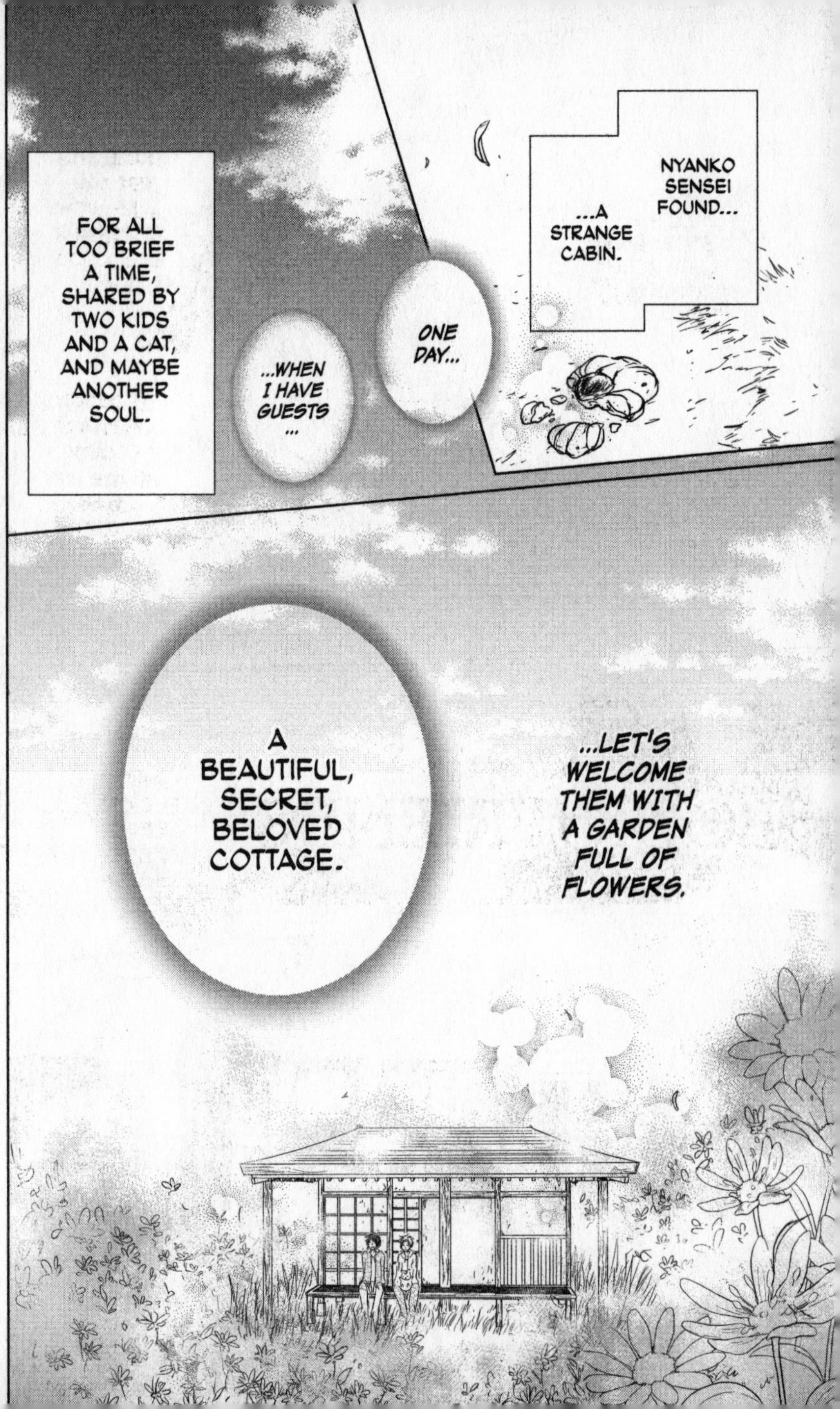
NYANKO SENSEI FOUND...
...A STRANGE CABIN.
ONE DAY...
...WHEN I HAVE GUESTS...
FOR ALL TOO BRIEF A TIME, SHARED BY TWO KIDS AND A CAT, AND MAYBE ANOTHER SOUL.
...LET'S WELCOME THEM WITH A GARDEN FULL OF FLOWERS.
A BEAUTIFUL, SECRET, BELOVED COTTAGE.

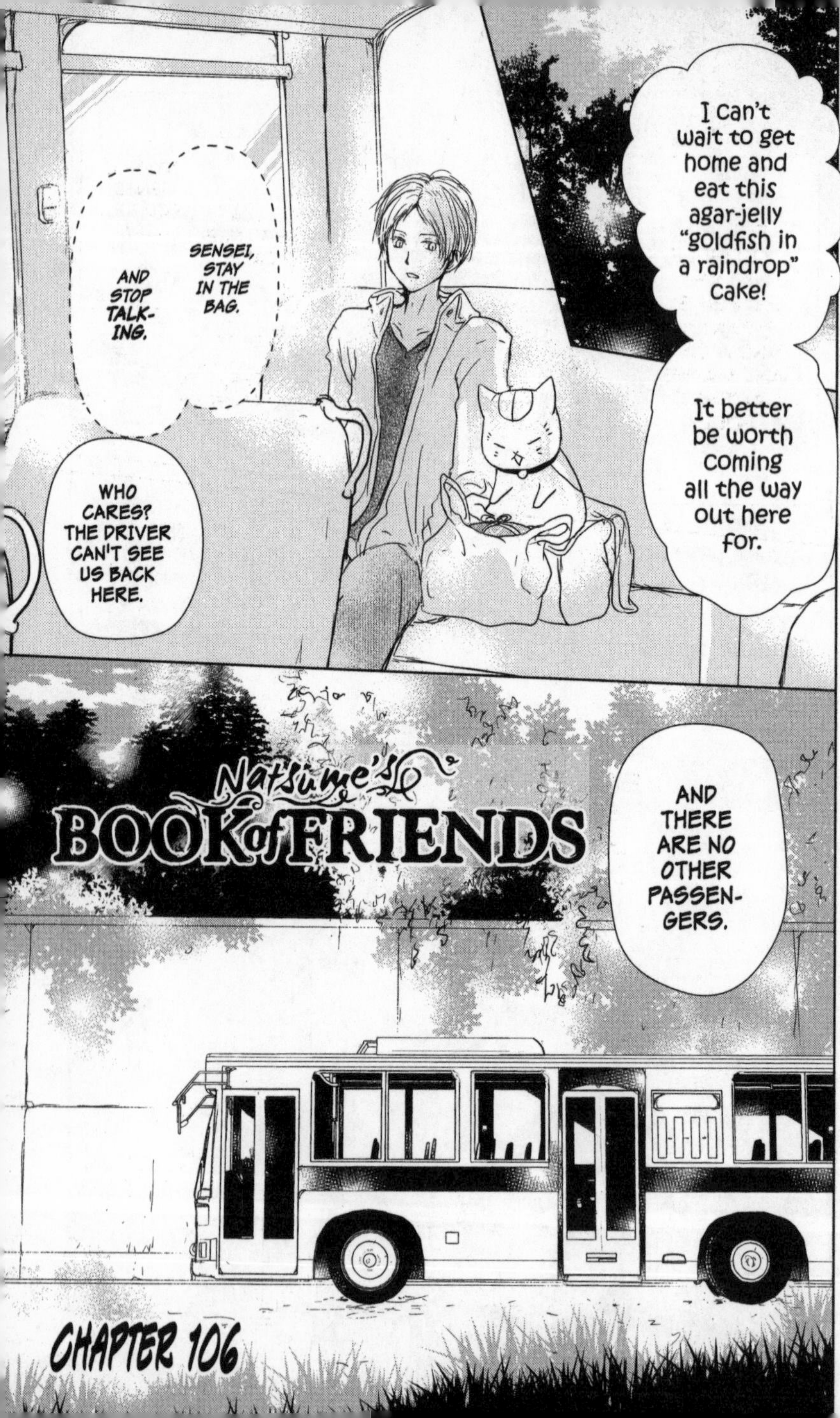
I can't wait to get home and eat this agar-jelly "goldfish in a raindrop" cake!
It better be worth coming all the way out here for.
SENSEI, STAY IN THE BAG.
AND STOP TALKING.
WHO CARES? THE DRIVER CAN'T SEE US BACK HERE.
AND THERE ARE NO OTHER PASSENGERS.
Natsume's BOOK of FRIENDS
CHAPTER 106

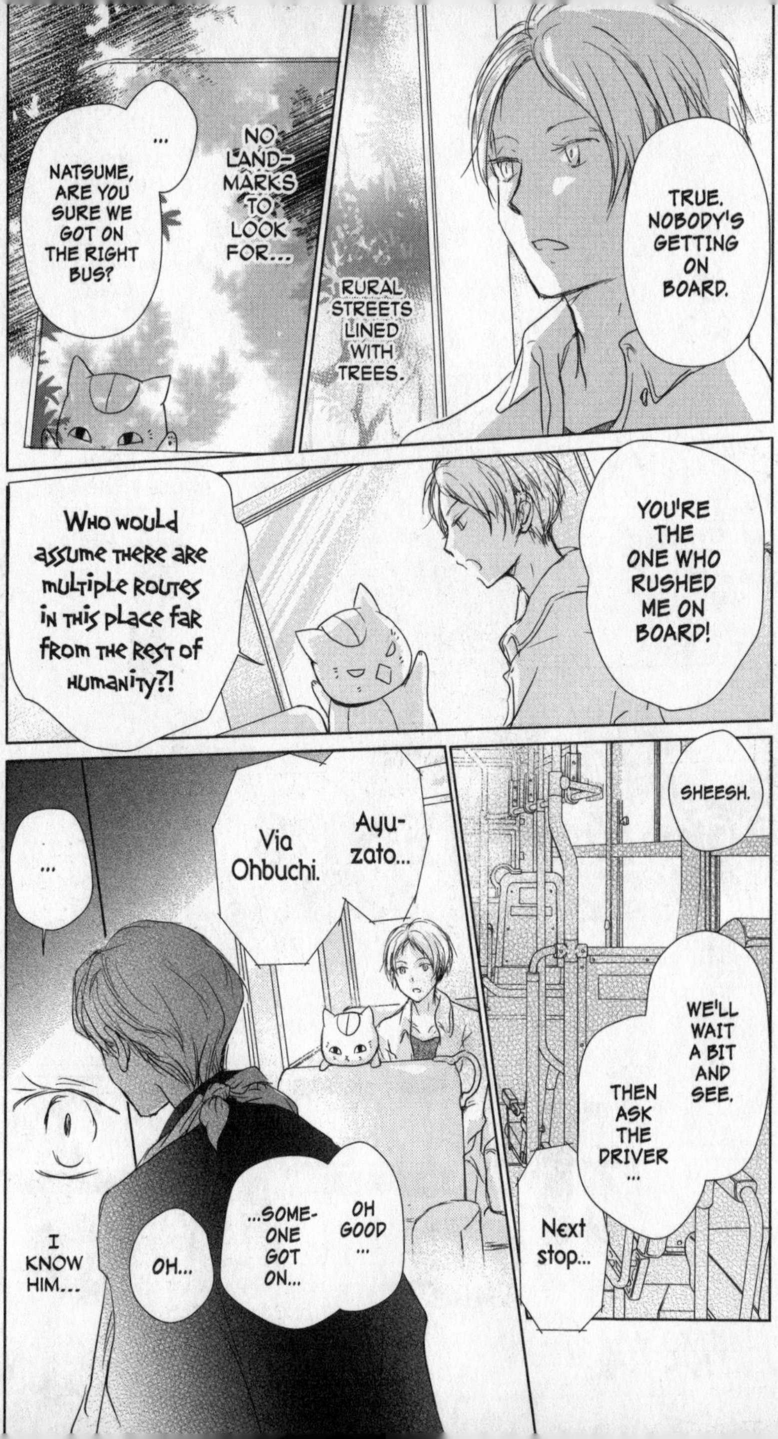
TRUE. NOBODY'S GETTING ON BOARD.
RURAL STREETS LINED WITH TREES.
NO LANDMARKS TO LOOK FOR...
...
NATSUME, ARE YOU SURE WE GOT ON THE RIGHT BUS?
YOU'RE THE ONE WHO RUSHED ME ON BOARD!
Who would assume there are multiple routes in this place far from the rest of humanity?!
SHEESH.
WE'LL WAIT A BIT AND SEE.
THEN ASK THE DRIVER...
Next stop...
Ayu-zato...
Via Ohbuchi.
...
OH GOOD...
...SOMEONE GOT ON...
OH...
I KNOW HIM...

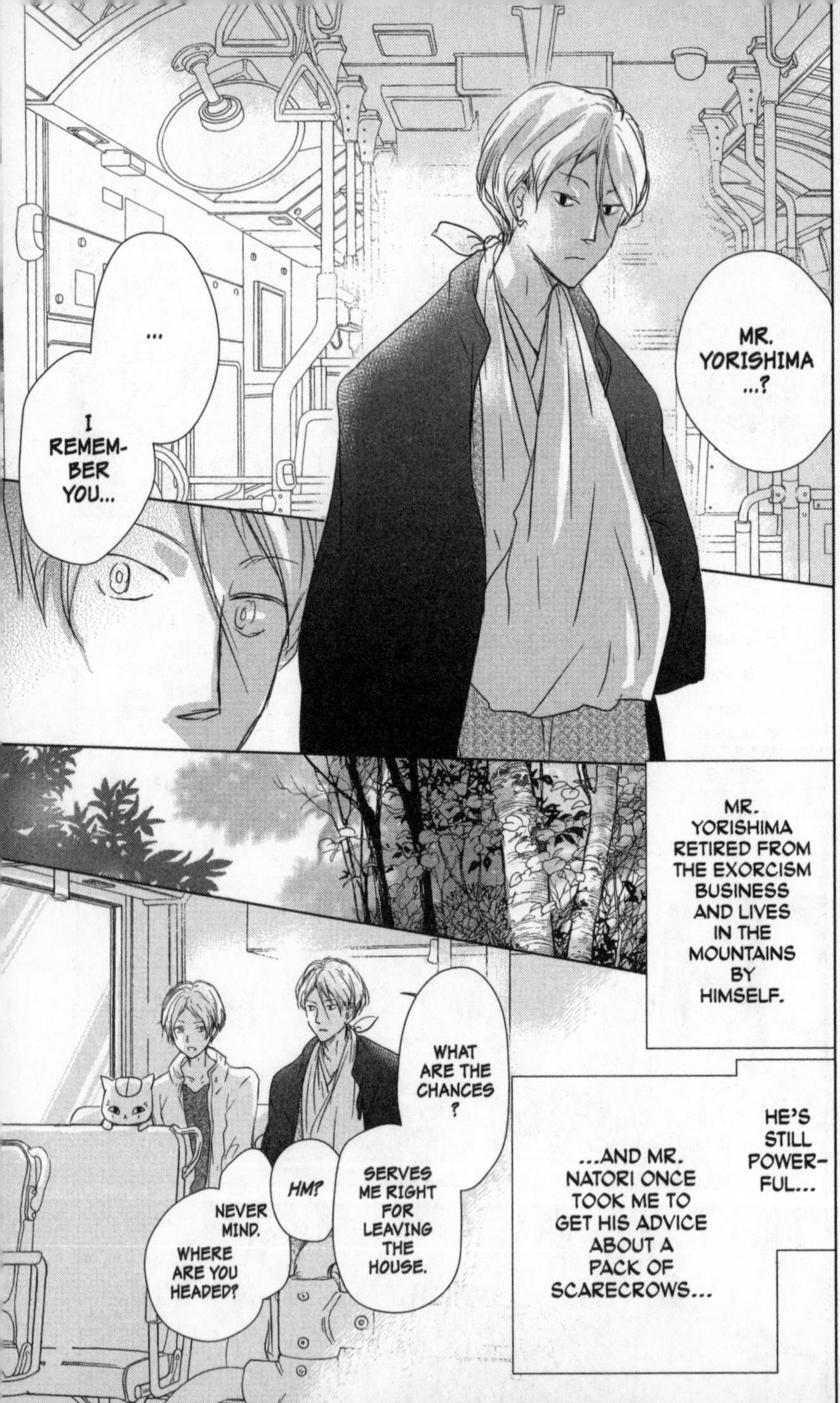
MR. YORISHIMA ...?
...
I REMEMBER YOU...
MR. YORISHIMA RETIRED FROM THE EXORCISM BUSINESS AND LIVES IN THE MOUNTAINS BY HIMSELF.
HE'S STILL POWERFUL...
...AND MR. NATORI ONCE TOOK ME TO GET HIS ADVICE ABOUT A PACK OF SCARECROWS...
WHAT ARE THE CHANCES?
SERVES ME RIGHT FOR LEAVING THE HOUSE.
HM?
NEVER MIND.
WHERE ARE YOU HEADED?

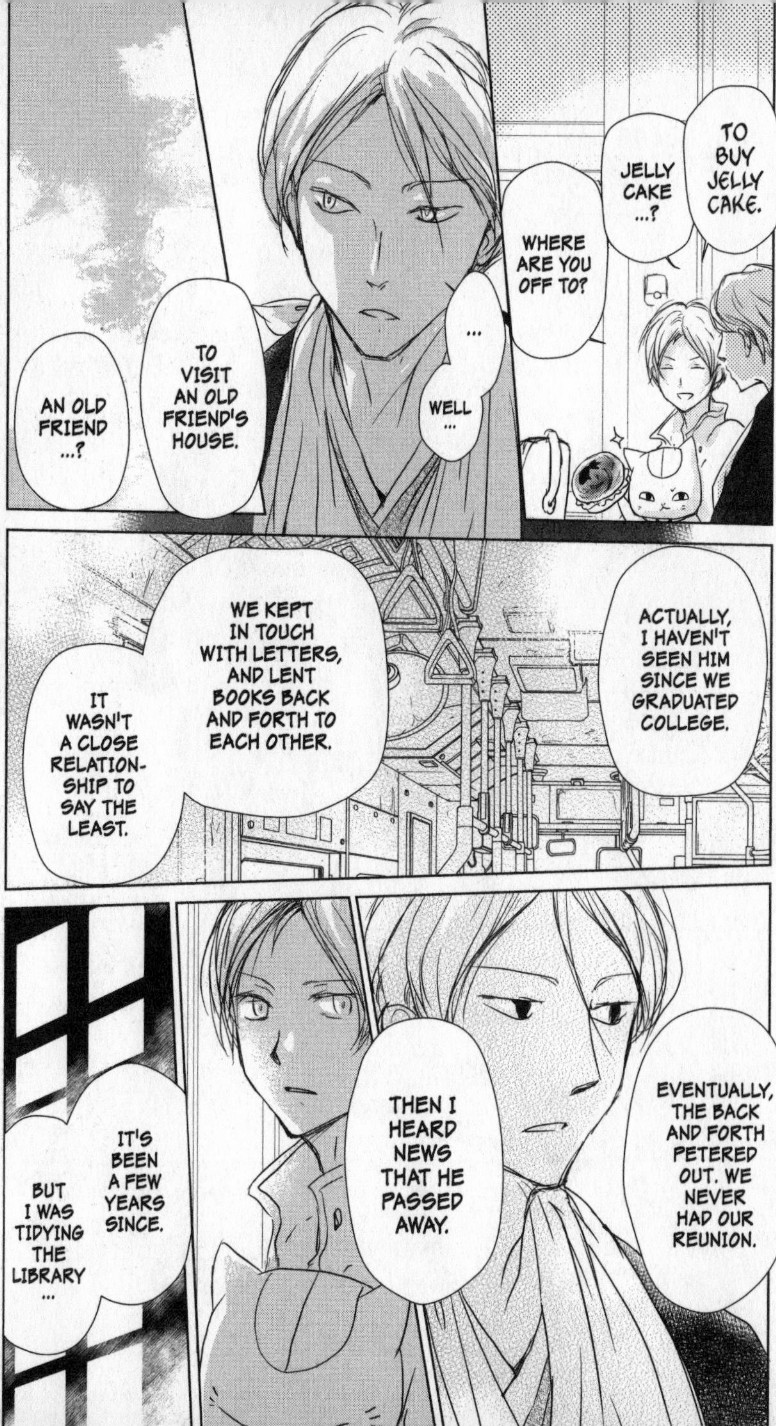
TO BUY JELLY CAKE.
JELLY CAKE ...?
WHERE ARE YOU OFF TO?
...
WELL ...
TO VISIT AN OLD FRIEND'S HOUSE.
AN OLD FRIEND ...?
ACTUALLY, I HAVEN'T SEEN HIM SINCE WE GRADUATED COLLEGE.
WE KEPT IN TOUCH WITH LETTERS, AND LENT BOOKS BACK AND FORTH TO EACH OTHER.
IT WASN'T A CLOSE RELATION-SHIP TO SAY THE LEAST.
EVENTUALLY, THE BACK AND FORTH PETERED OUT. WE NEVER HAD OUR REUNION.
THEN I HEARD NEWS THAT HE PASSED AWAY.
IT'S BEEN A FEW YEARS SINCE.
BUT I WAS TIDYING THE LIBRARY ...

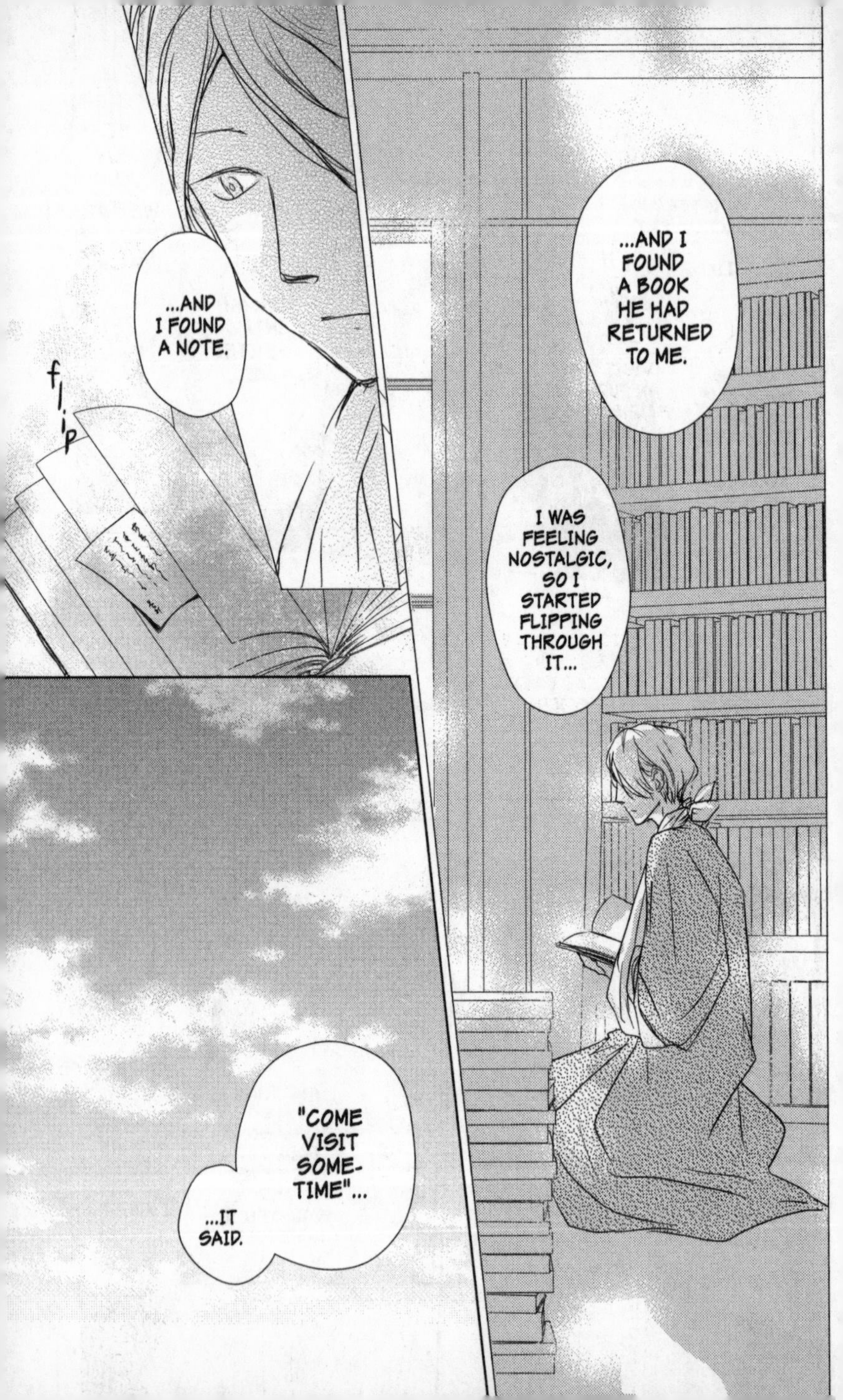
...AND I FOUND A BOOK HE HAD RETURNED TO ME.
I WAS FEELING NOSTALGIC, SO I STARTED FLIPPING THROUGH IT...
...AND I FOUND A NOTE.
flip
"COME VISIT SOME-TIME"...
...IT SAID.

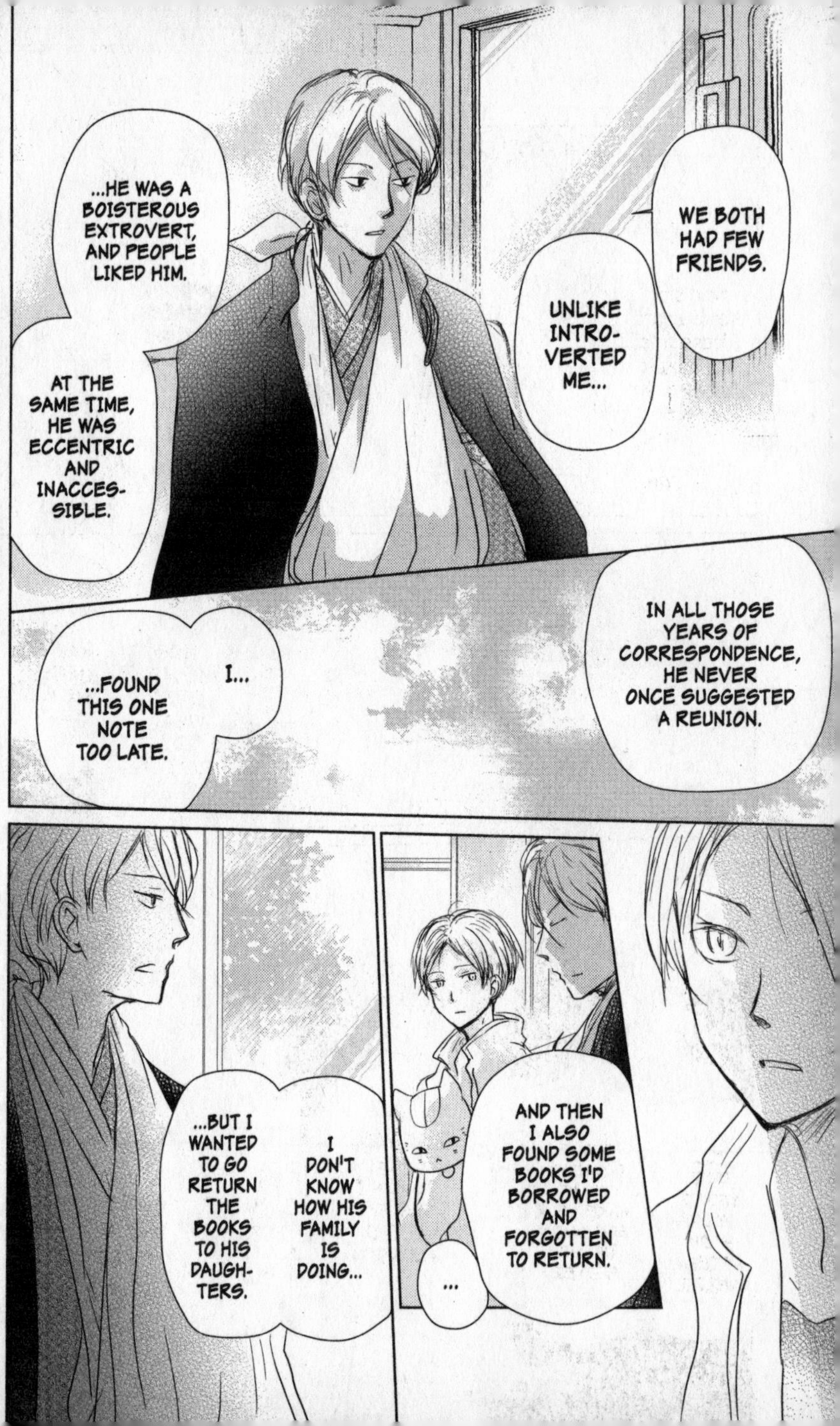
WE BOTH HAD FEW FRIENDS.
UNLIKE INTROVERTED ME...
...HE WAS A BOISTEROUS EXTROVERT, AND PEOPLE LIKED HIM.
AT THE SAME TIME, HE WAS ECCENTRIC AND INACCESSIBLE.
IN ALL THOSE YEARS OF CORRESPONDENCE, HE NEVER ONCE SUGGESTED A REUNION.
I...
...FOUND THIS ONE NOTE TOO LATE.
AND THEN I ALSO FOUND SOME BOOKS I'D BORROWED AND FORGOTTEN TO RETURN.
...
I DON'T KNOW HOW HIS FAMILY IS DOING...
...BUT I WANTED TO GO RETURN THE BOOKS TO HIS DAUGHTERS.

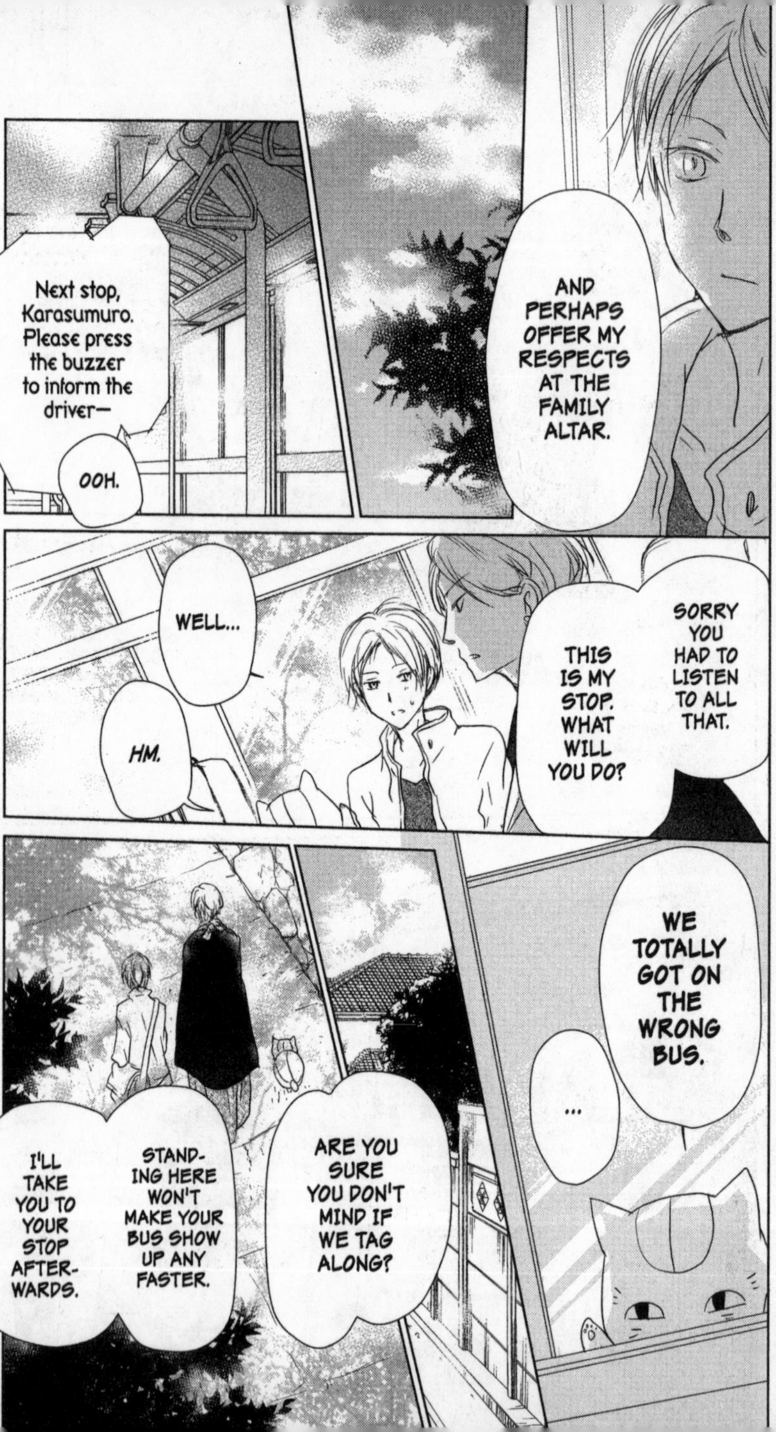
AND PERHAPS OFFER MY RESPECTS AT THE FAMILY ALTAR.
Next stop, Karasumuro. Please press the buzzer to inform the driver—
OOH.
SORRY YOU HAD TO LISTEN TO ALL THAT.
THIS IS MY STOP. WHAT WILL YOU DO?
WELL...
HM.
WE TOTALLY GOT ON THE WRONG BUS.
...
ARE YOU SURE YOU DON'T MIND IF WE TAG ALONG?
STANDING HERE WON'T MAKE YOUR BUS SHOW UP ANY FASTER.
I'LL TAKE YOU TO YOUR STOP AFTERWARDS.

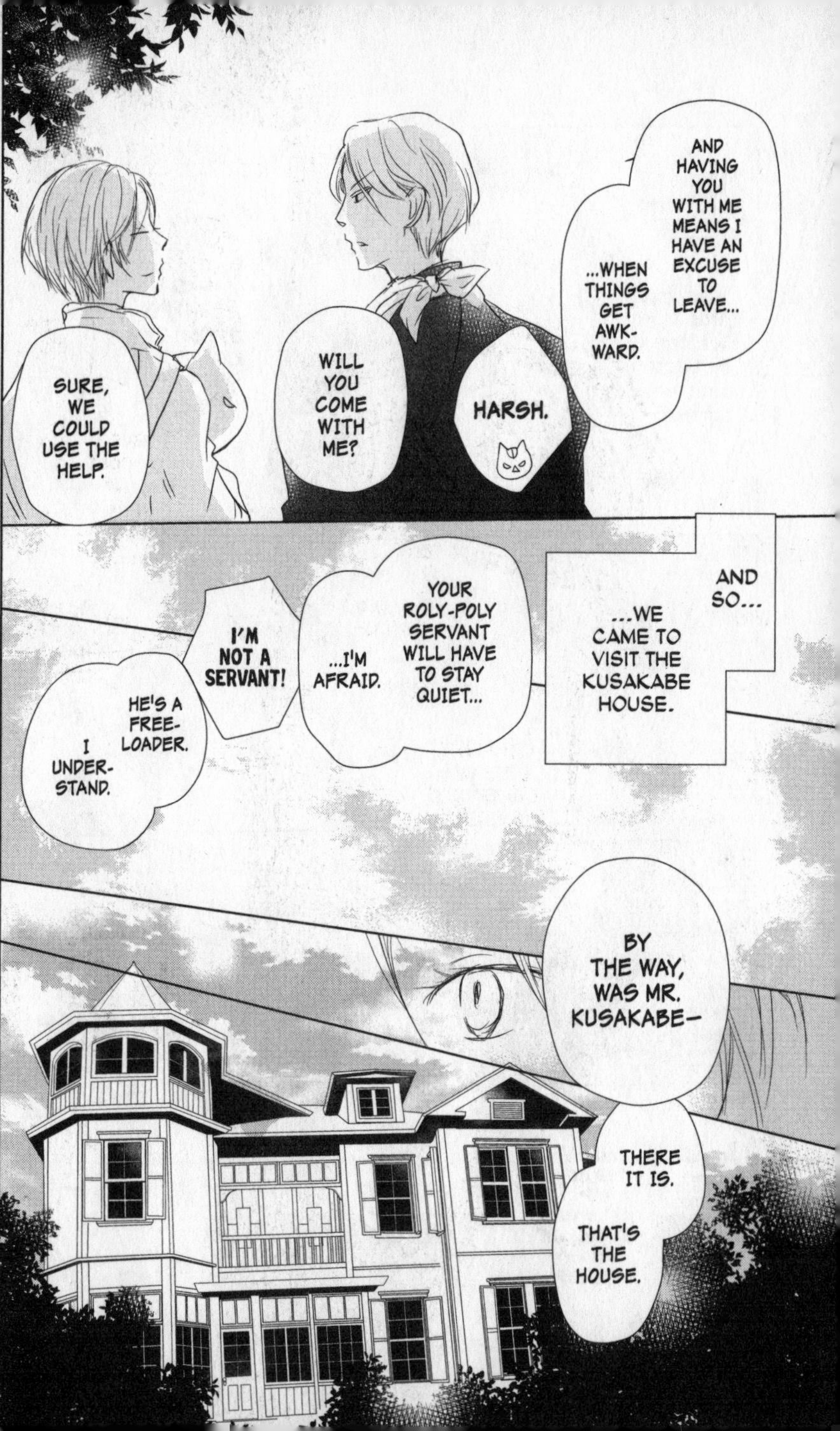
AND HAVING YOU WITH ME MEANS I HAVE AN EXCUSE TO LEAVE...
...WHEN THINGS GET AWK-WARD.
HARSH.
WILL YOU COME WITH ME?
SURE, WE COULD USE THE HELP.
AND SO...
...WE CAME TO VISIT THE KUSAKABE HOUSE.
YOUR ROLY-POLY SERVANT WILL HAVE TO STAY QUIET...
...I'M AFRAID.
I'M NOT A SERVANT!
HE'S A FREE-LOADER.
I UNDER-STAND.
BY THE WAY, WAS MR. KUSAKABE—
THERE IT IS.
THAT'S THE HOUSE.

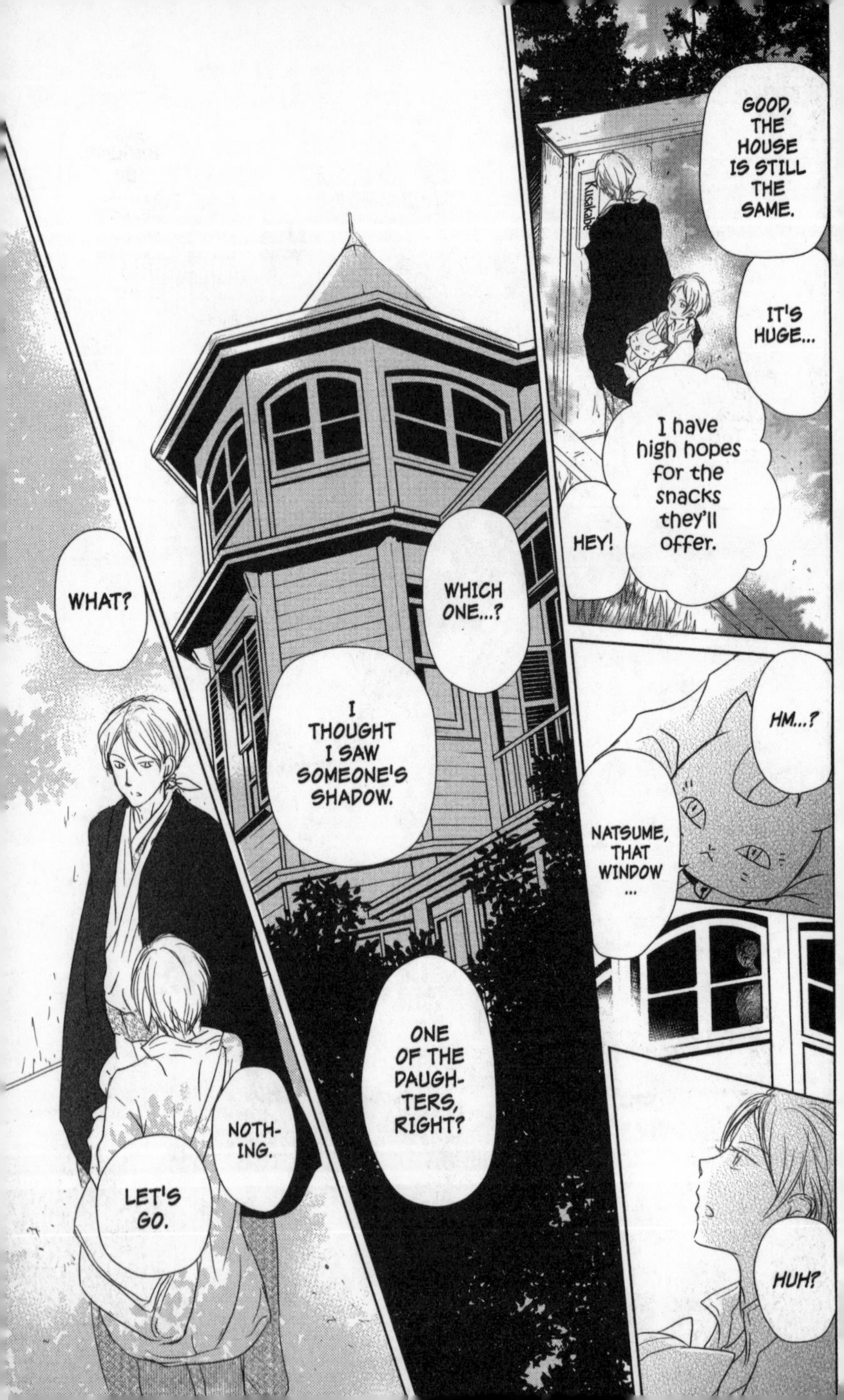
GOOD, THE HOUSE IS STILL THE SAME.
Kusakabe
IT'S HUGE...
I have high hopes for the snacks they'll offer.
HEY!
HM...?
NATSUME, THAT WINDOW ...
HUH?
WHICH ONE...?
I THOUGHT I SAW SOMEONE'S SHADOW.
ONE OF THE DAUGHTERS, RIGHT?
WHAT?
NOTHING.
LET'S GO.

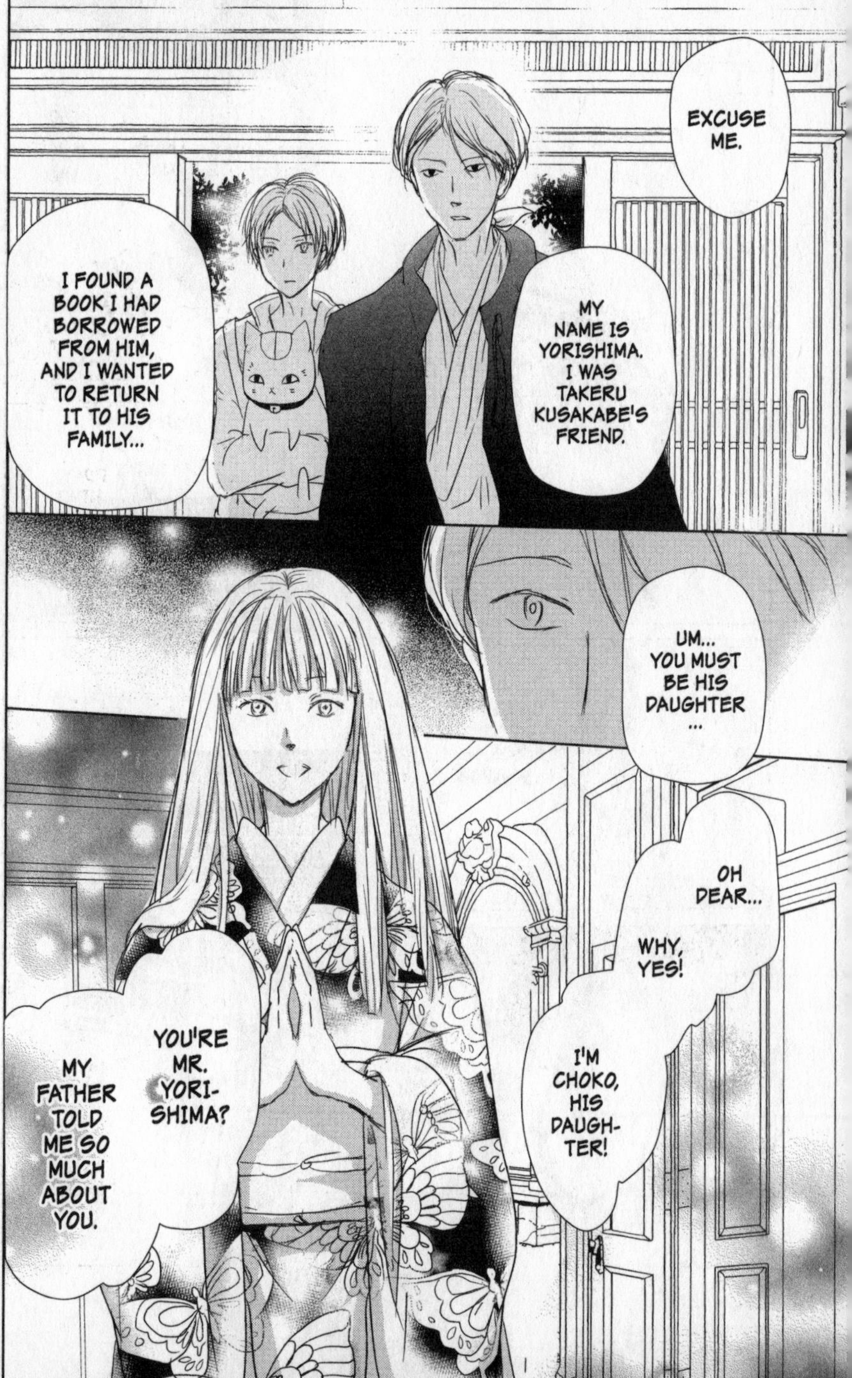
EXCUSE ME.
MY NAME IS YORISHIMA. I WAS TAKERU KUSAKABE'S FRIEND.
I FOUND A BOOK I HAD BORROWED FROM HIM, AND I WANTED TO RETURN IT TO HIS FAMILY...
UM... YOU MUST BE HIS DAUGHTER ...
OH DEAR...
WHY, YES!
I'M CHOKO, HIS DAUGH-TER!
YOU'RE MR. YORI-SHIMA?
MY FATHER TOLD ME SO MUCH ABOUT YOU.

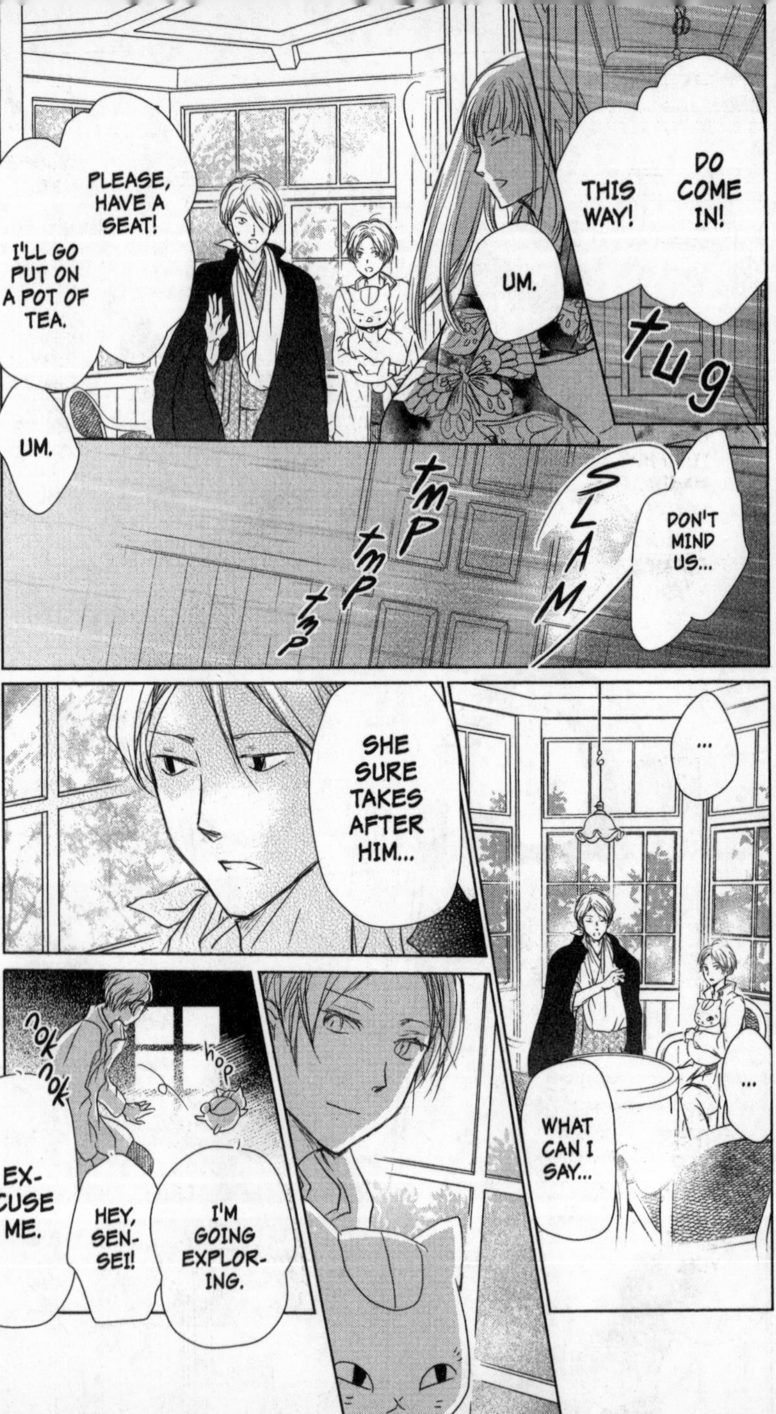
DO COME IN!
THIS WAY!
UM.
tug
PLEASE, HAVE A SEAT!
I'LL GO PUT ON A POT OF TEA.
UM.
DON'T MIND US...
SLAM
tmp tmp tmp
...
...
WHAT CAN I SAY...
SHE SURE TAKES AFTER HIM...
I'M GOING EXPLOR-ING.
HEY, SEN-SEI!
hop
EX-CUSE ME.
nok nok

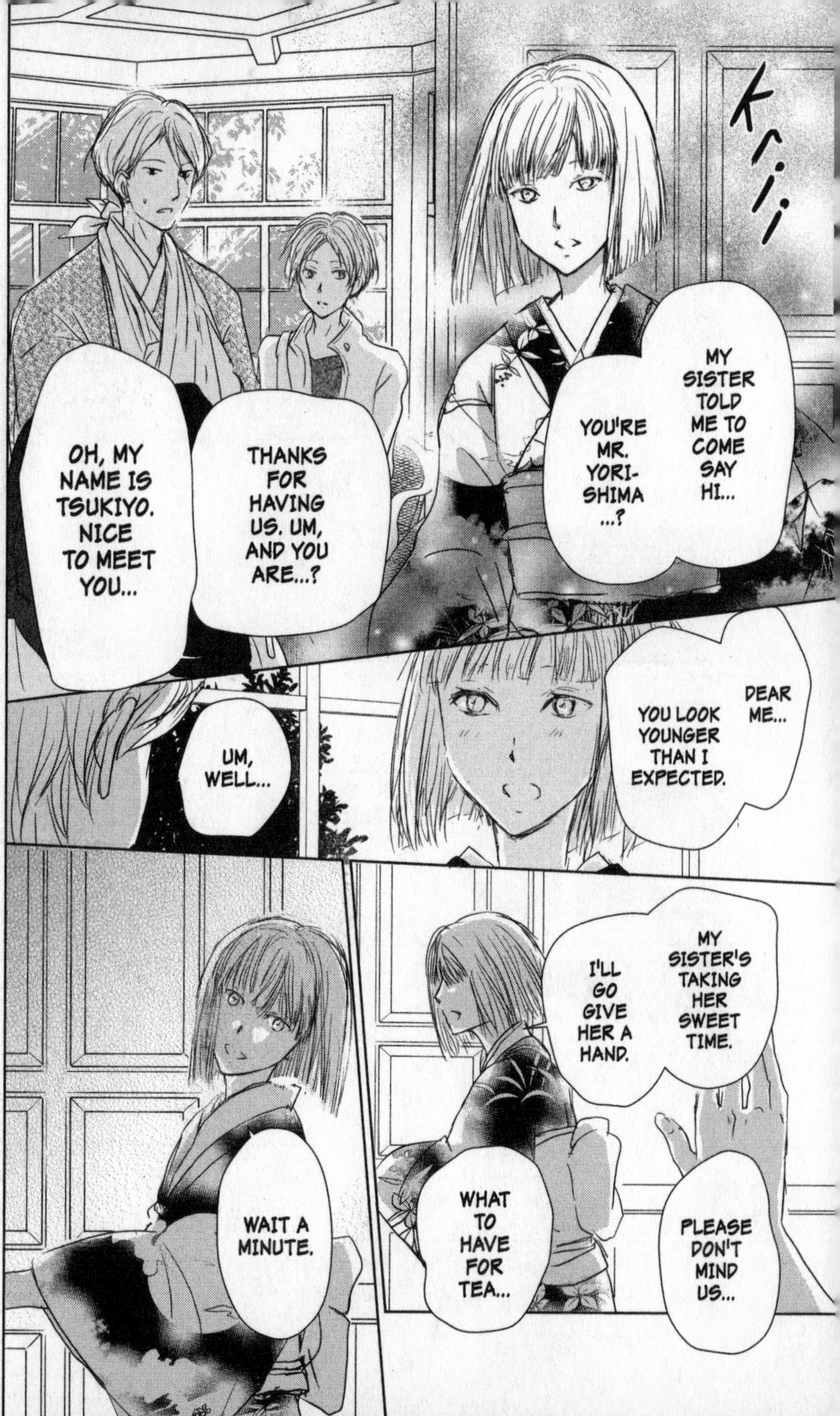
Krii
MY SISTER TOLD ME TO COME SAY HI...
YOU'RE MR. YORI-SHIMA ...?
THANKS FOR HAVING US. UM, AND YOU ARE...?
OH, MY NAME IS TSUKIYO. NICE TO MEET YOU...
DEAR ME...
YOU LOOK YOUNGER THAN I EXPECTED.
UM, WELL...
MY SISTER'S TAKING HER SWEET TIME.
I'LL GO GIVE HER A HAND.
PLEASE DON'T MIND US...
WHAT TO HAVE FOR TEA...
WAIT A MINUTE.

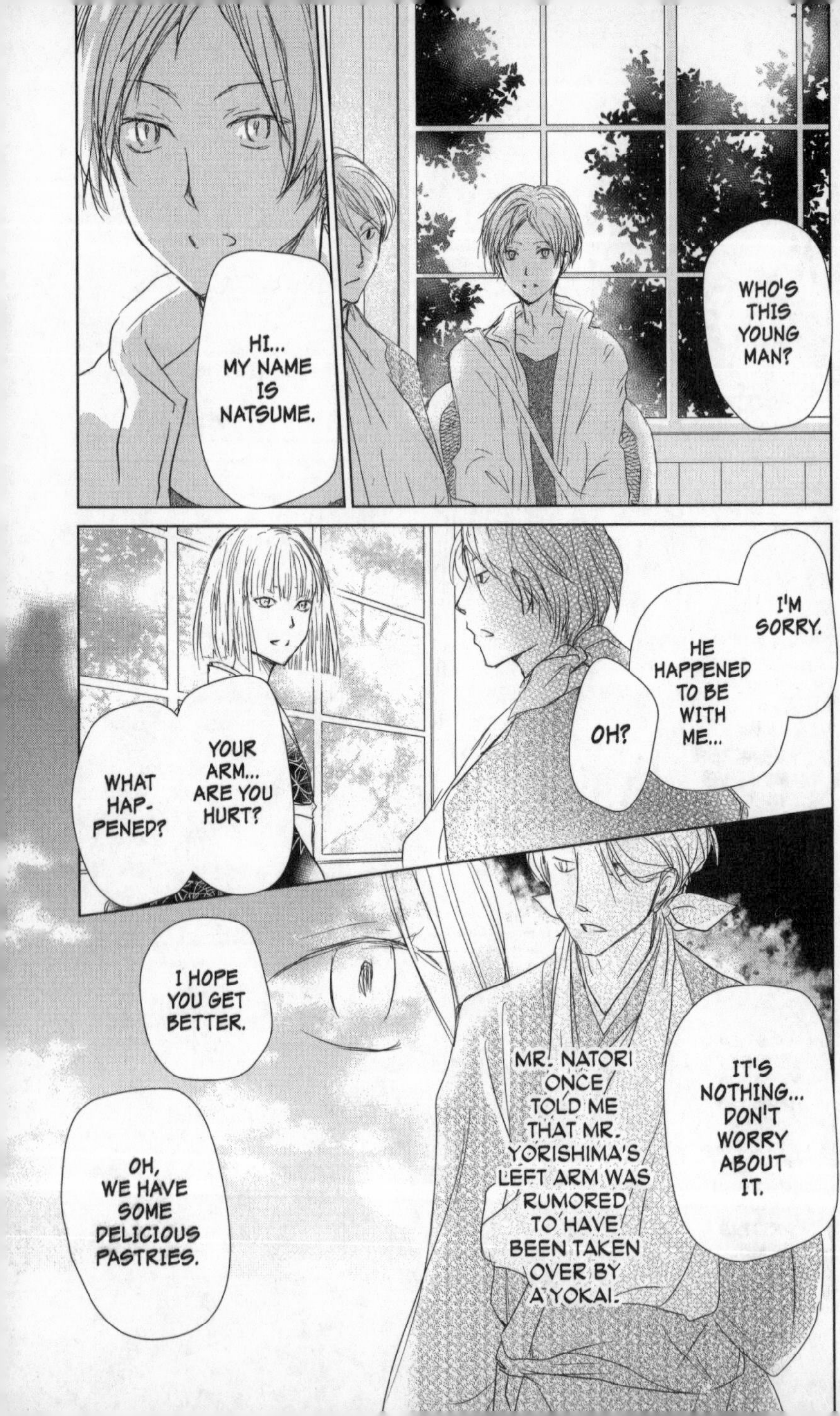
WHO'S THIS YOUNG MAN?
HI... MY NAME IS NATSUME.
I'M SORRY.
HE HAPPENED TO BE WITH ME...
OH?
YOUR ARM... ARE YOU HURT?
WHAT HAP-PENED?
IT'S NOTHING... DON'T WORRY ABOUT IT.
MR. NATORI ONCE TOLD ME THAT MR. YORISHIMA'S LEFT ARM WAS RUMORED TO HAVE BEEN TAKEN OVER BY A YOKAI.
I HOPE YOU GET BETTER.
OH, WE HAVE SOME DELICIOUS PASTRIES.

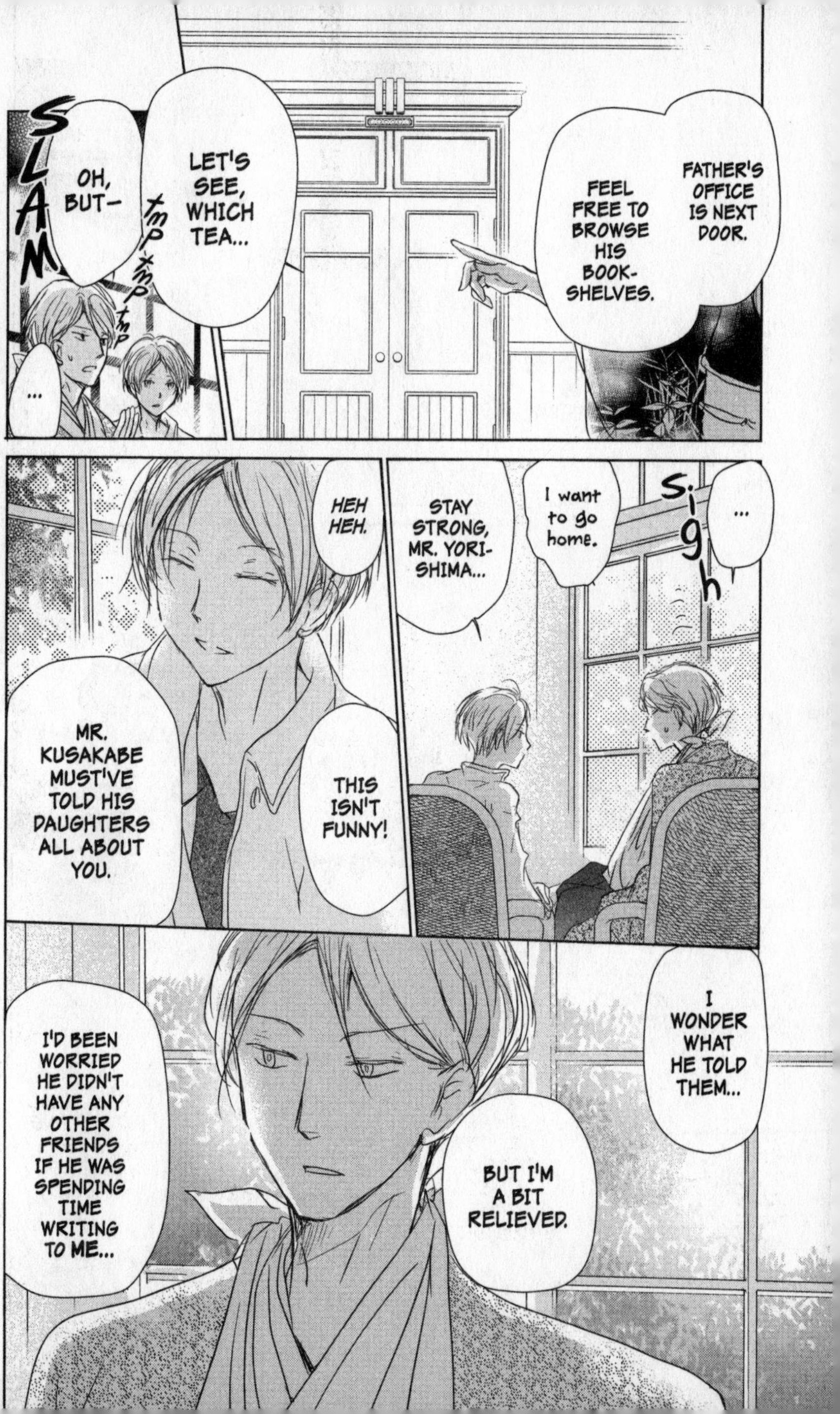
FATHER'S OFFICE IS NEXT DOOR.
FEEL FREE TO BROWSE HIS BOOK-SHELVES.
LET'S SEE, WHICH TEA...
tmp tmp tmp tmp
OH, BUT—
SLAM
...
...
Sigh
I want to go home.
STAY STRONG, MR. YORI-SHIMA...
HEH HEH.
...
THIS ISN'T FUNNY!
MR. KUSAKABE MUST'VE TOLD HIS DAUGHTERS ALL ABOUT YOU.
I WONDER WHAT HE TOLD THEM...
BUT I'M A BIT RELIEVED.
I'D BEEN WORRIED HE DIDN'T HAVE ANY OTHER FRIENDS IF HE WAS SPENDING TIME WRITING TO ME...

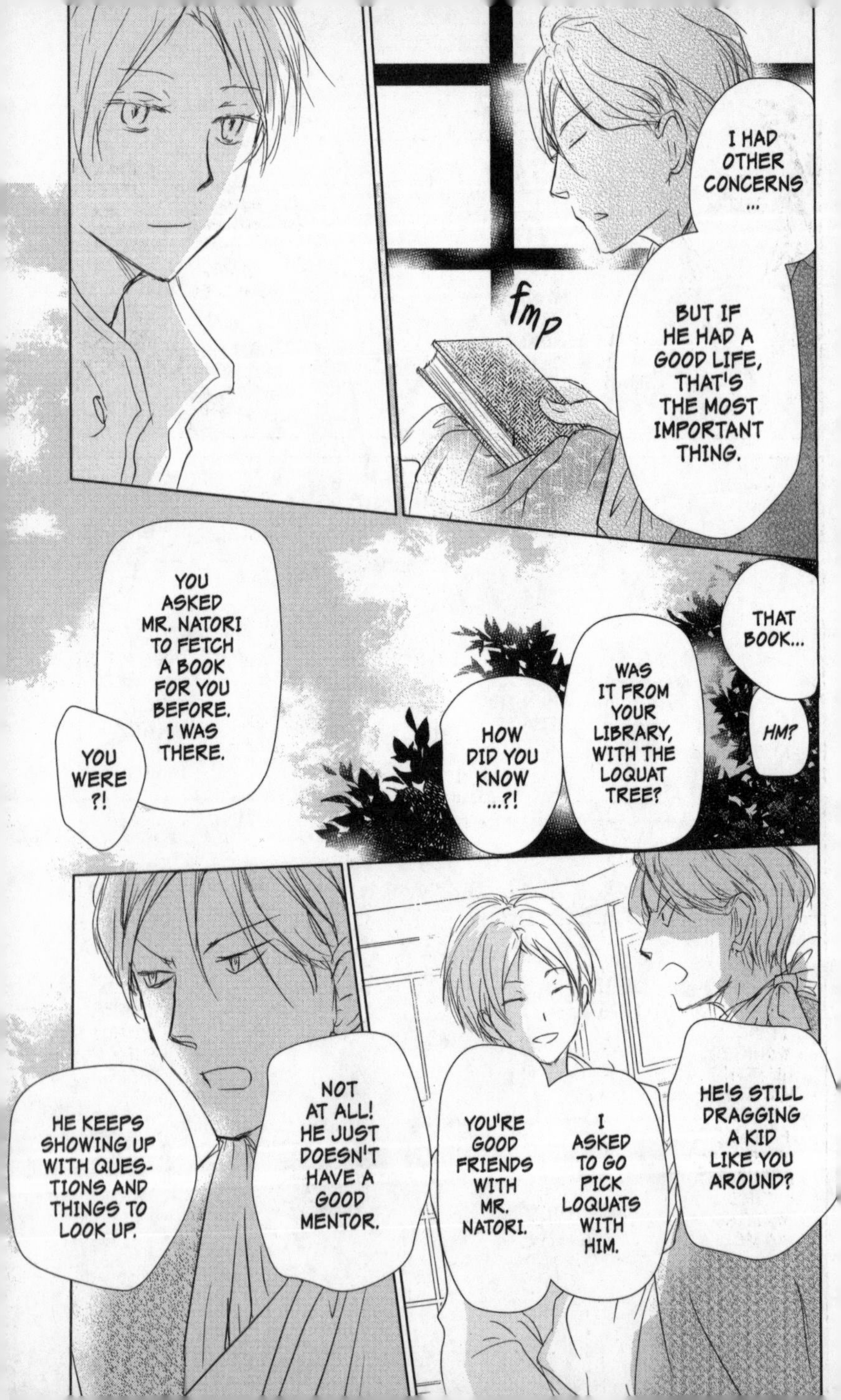
I HAD OTHER CONCERNS...
fmp
BUT IF HE HAD A GOOD LIFE, THAT'S THE MOST IMPORTANT THING.
THAT BOOK...
HM?
WAS IT FROM YOUR LIBRARY, WITH THE LOQUAT TREE?
HOW DID YOU KNOW...?!
YOU ASKED MR. NATORI TO FETCH A BOOK FOR YOU BEFORE. I WAS THERE.
YOU WERE?!
HE'S STILL DRAGGING A KID LIKE YOU AROUND?
I ASKED TO GO PICK LOQUATS WITH HIM.
YOU'RE GOOD FRIENDS WITH MR. NATORI.
NOT AT ALL! HE JUST DOESN'T HAVE A GOOD MENTOR.
HE KEEPS SHOWING UP WITH QUES-TIONS AND THINGS TO LOOK UP.

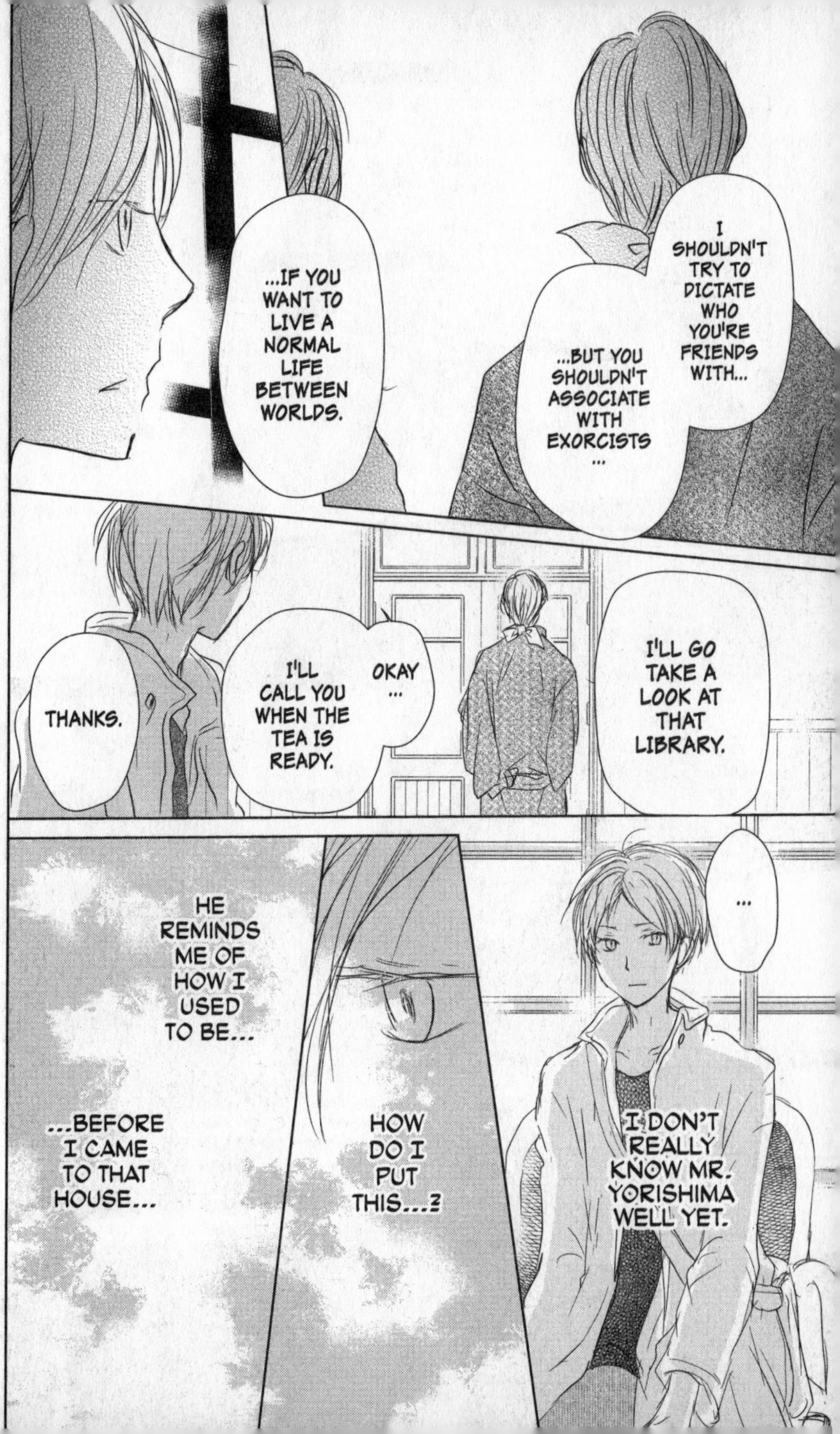
I SHOULDN'T TRY TO DICTATE WHO YOU'RE FRIENDS WITH...
...BUT YOU SHOULDN'T ASSOCIATE WITH EXORCISTS...
...IF YOU WANT TO LIVE A NORMAL LIFE BETWEEN WORLDS.
I'LL GO TAKE A LOOK AT THAT LIBRARY.
OKAY...
I'LL CALL YOU WHEN THE TEA IS READY.
THANKS.
...
I DON'T REALLY KNOW MR. YORISHIMA WELL YET.
HOW DO I PUT THIS...?
HE REMINDS ME OF HOW I USED TO BE...
...BEFORE I CAME TO THAT HOUSE...

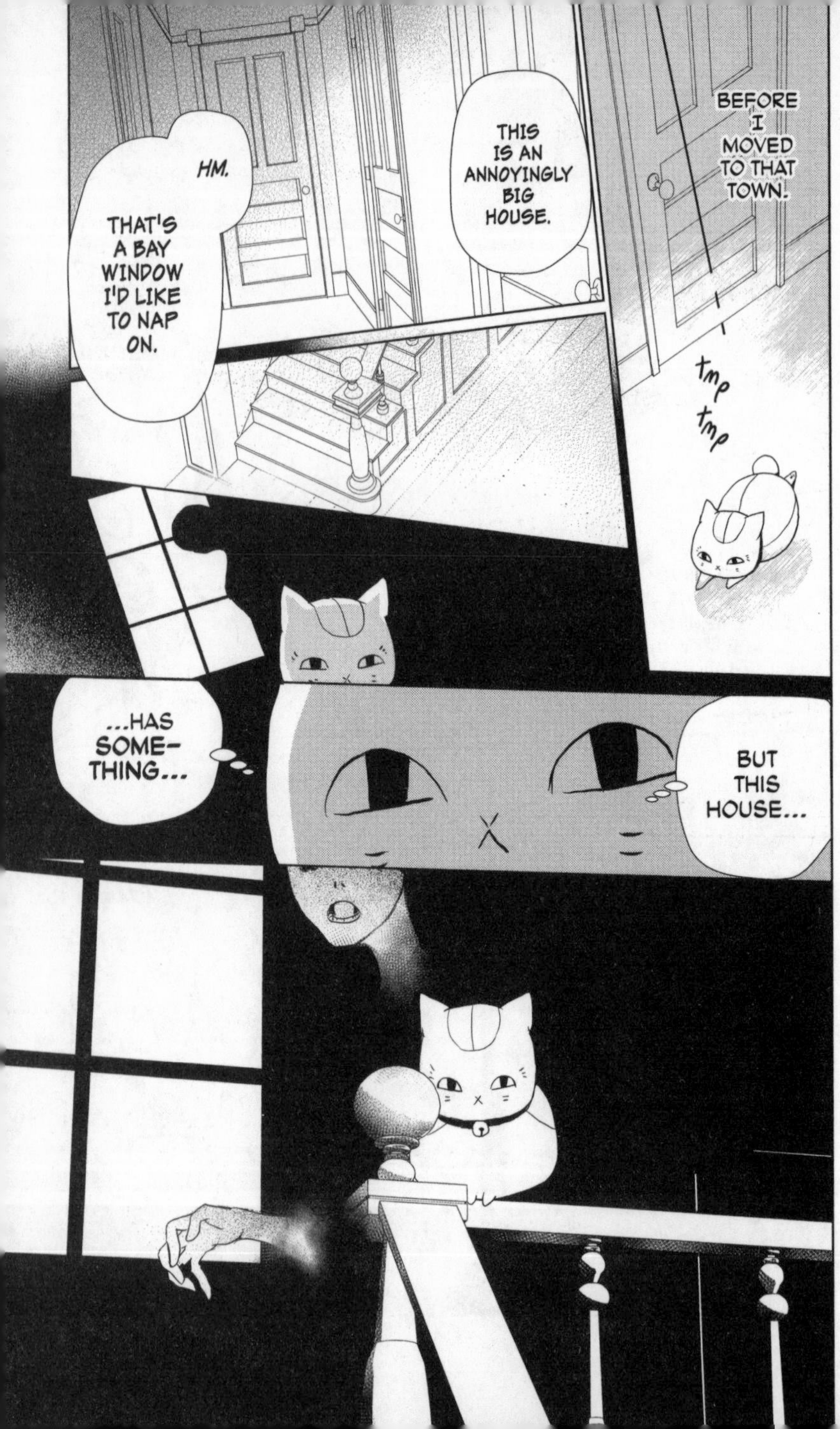
BEFORE I MOVED TO THAT TOWN.
TMP TMP
THIS IS AN ANNOYINGLY BIG HOUSE.
HM.
THAT'S A BAY WINDOW I'D LIKE TO NAP ON.
BUT THIS HOUSE...
...HAS SOME-THING...

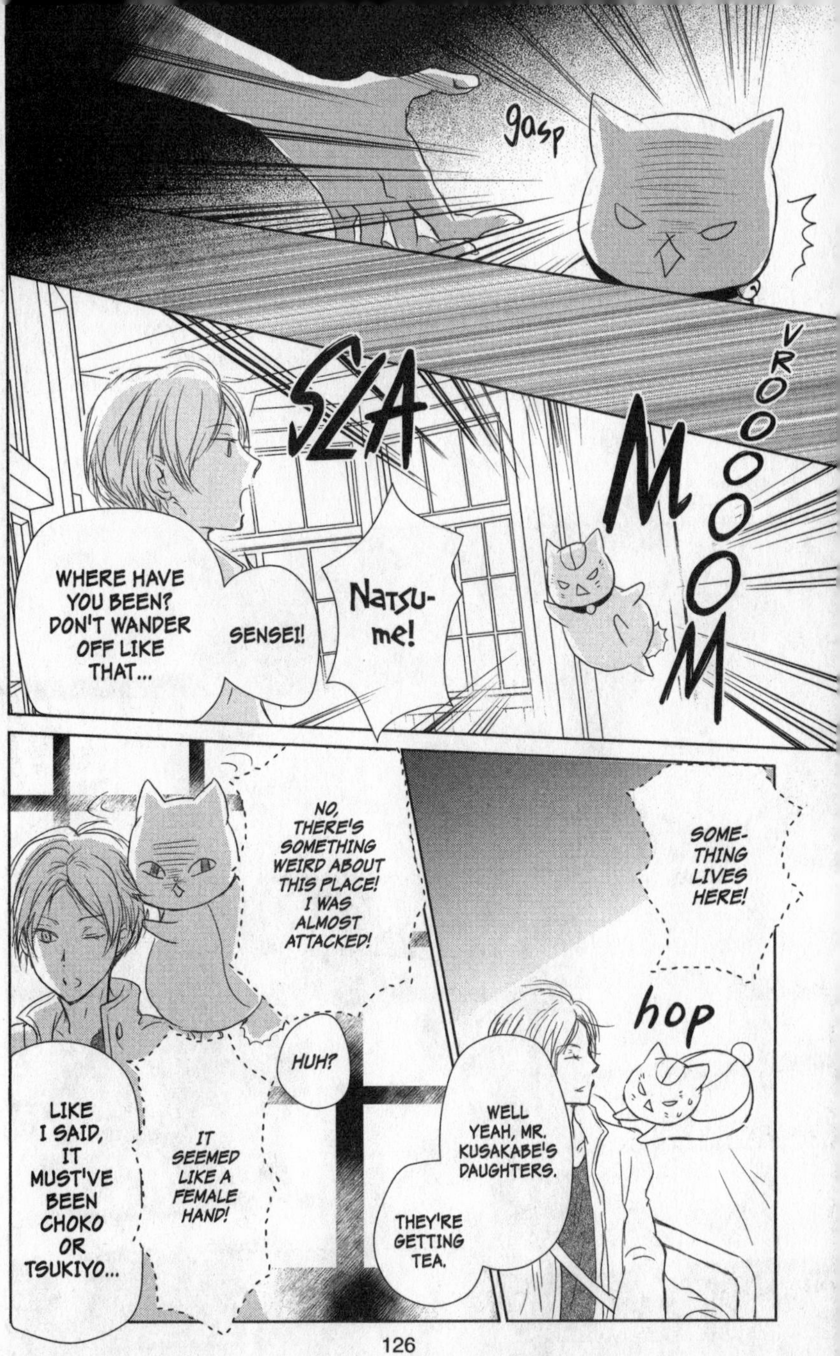
gasp
SLAM
VROOOOOOM
Natsu-me!
SENSEI!
WHERE HAVE YOU BEEN? DON'T WANDER OFF LIKE THAT...
SOMETHING LIVES HERE!
hop
WELL YEAH, MR. KUSAKABE'S DAUGHTERS.
THEY'RE GETTING TEA.
NO, THERE'S SOMETHING WEIRD ABOUT THIS PLACE! I WAS ALMOST ATTACKED!
HUH?
IT SEEMED LIKE A FEMALE HAND!
LIKE I SAID, IT MUST'VE BEEN CHOKO OR TSUKIYO...

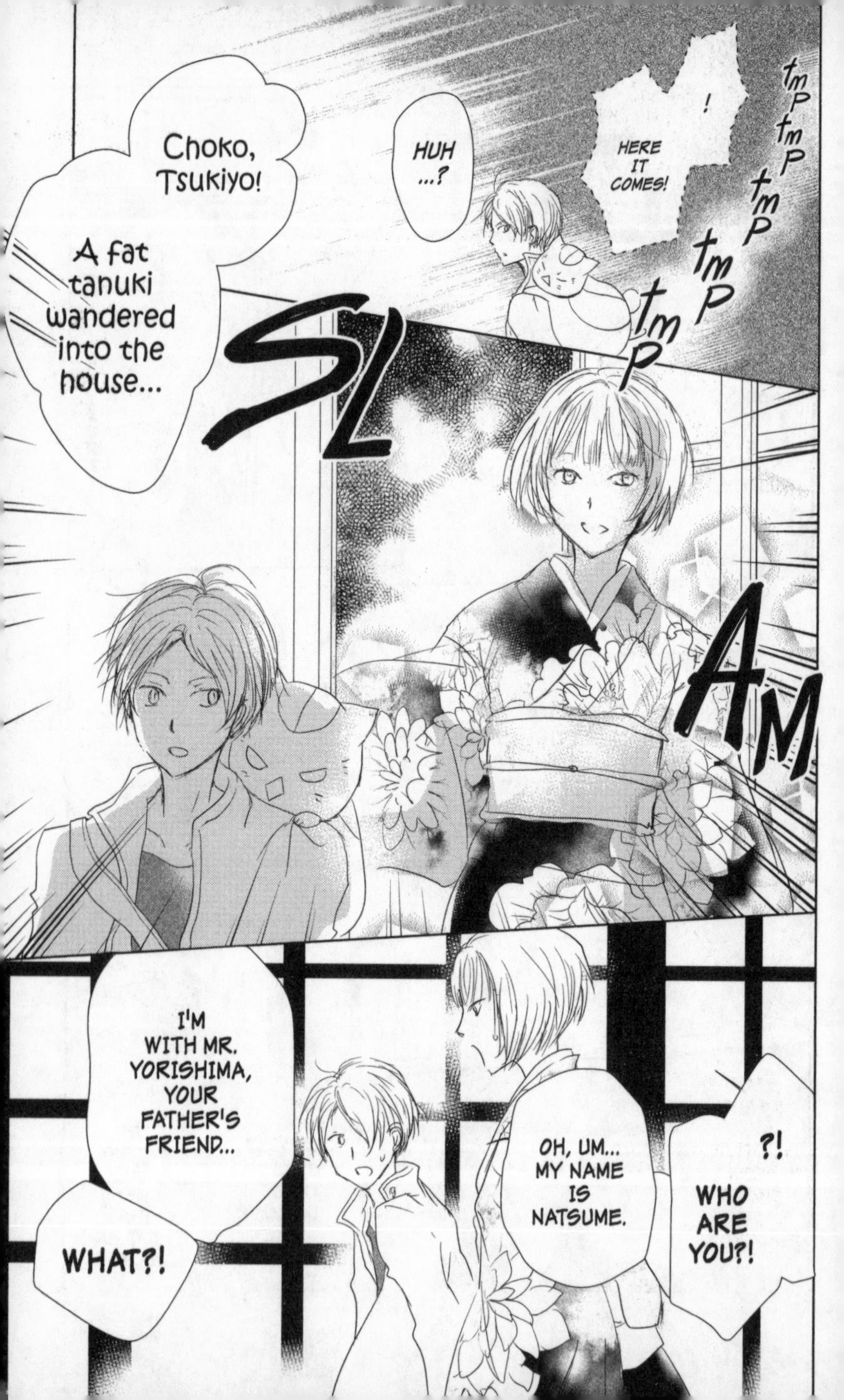
tmp tmp tmp tmp tmp
!
HERE IT COMES!
HUH ...?
Choko, Tsukiyo!
A fat tanuki wandered into the house...
SLAM
?!
WHO ARE YOU?!
OH, UM... MY NAME IS NATSUME.
I'M WITH MR. YORISHIMA, YOUR FATHER'S FRIEND...
WHAT?!

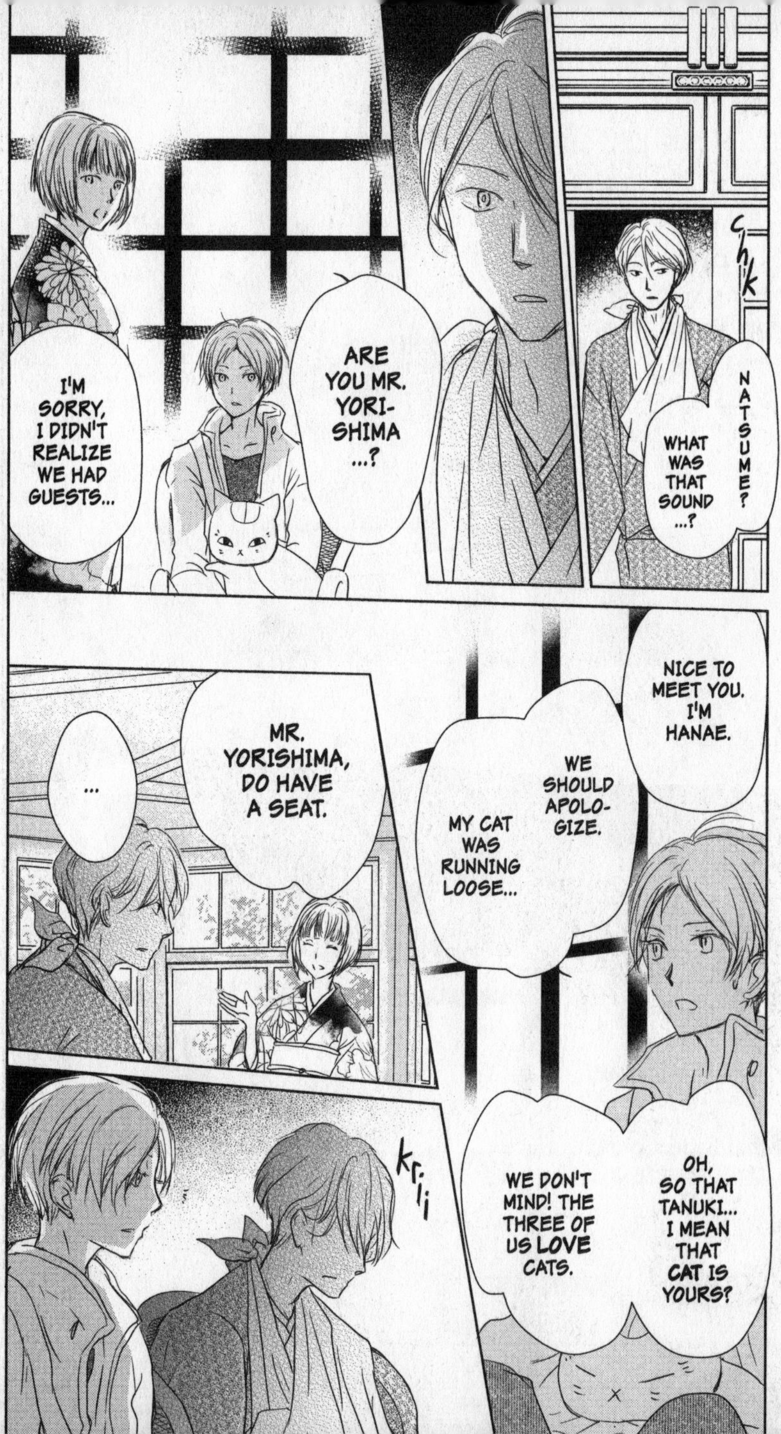
CHIK
NATSUME? WHAT WAS THAT SOUND...?
ARE YOU MR. YORISHIMA...?
I'M SORRY, I DIDN'T REALIZE WE HAD GUESTS...
NICE TO MEET YOU. I'M HANAE.
WE SHOULD APOLOGIZE.
MY CAT WAS RUNNING LOOSE...
MR. YORISHIMA, DO HAVE A SEAT.
...
OH, SO THAT TANUKI... I MEAN THAT CAT IS YOURS?
WE DON'T MIND! THE THREE OF US LOVE CATS.
KRII

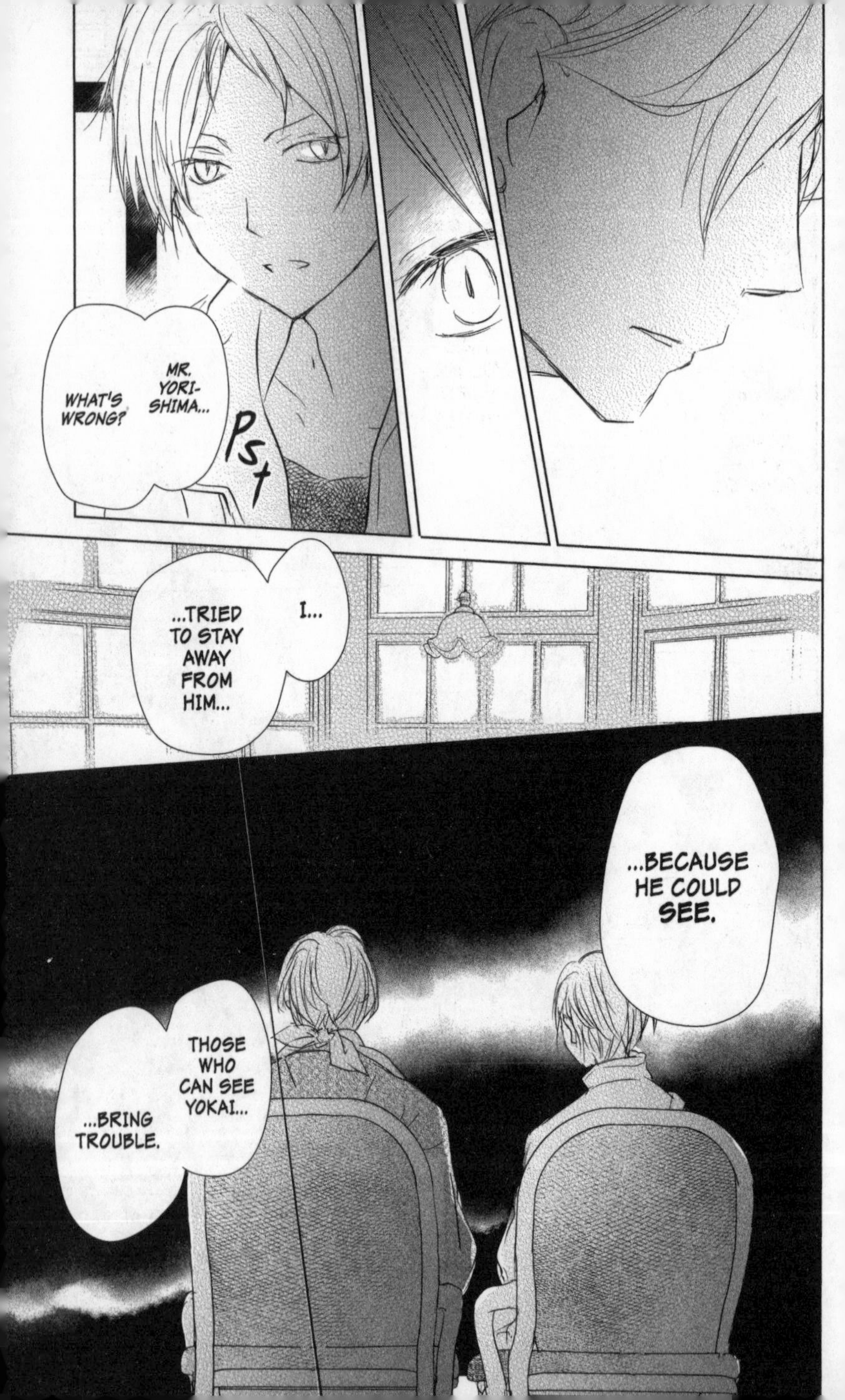
MR. YORI-SHIMA...
WHAT'S WRONG?
Pst
I...
...TRIED TO STAY AWAY FROM HIM...
...BECAUSE HE COULD SEE.
THOSE WHO CAN SEE YOKAI...
...BRING TROUBLE.

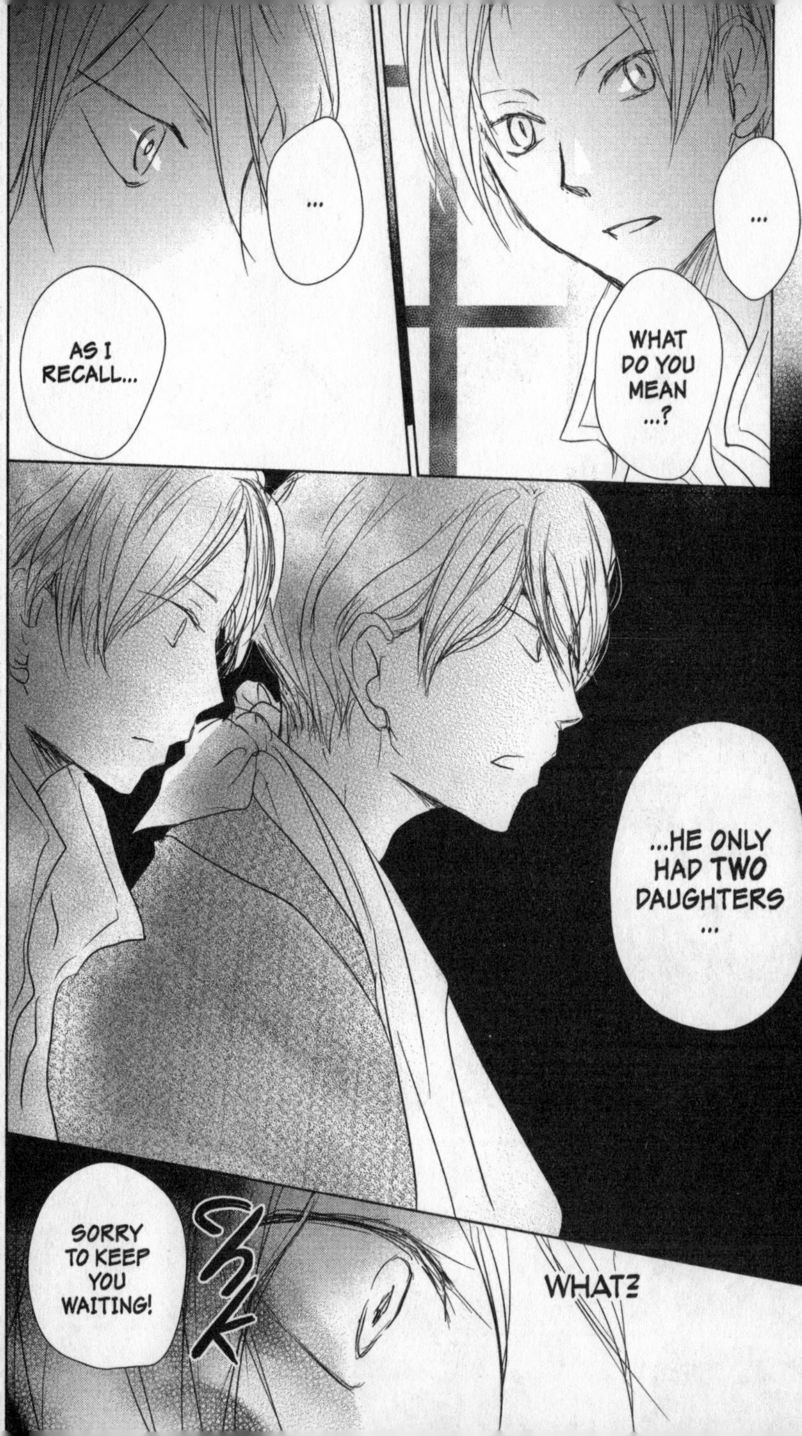
...
WHAT DO YOU MEAN ...?
...
AS I RECALL...
...HE ONLY HAD TWO DAUGHTERS ...
WHAT?
SORRY TO KEEP YOU WAITING!

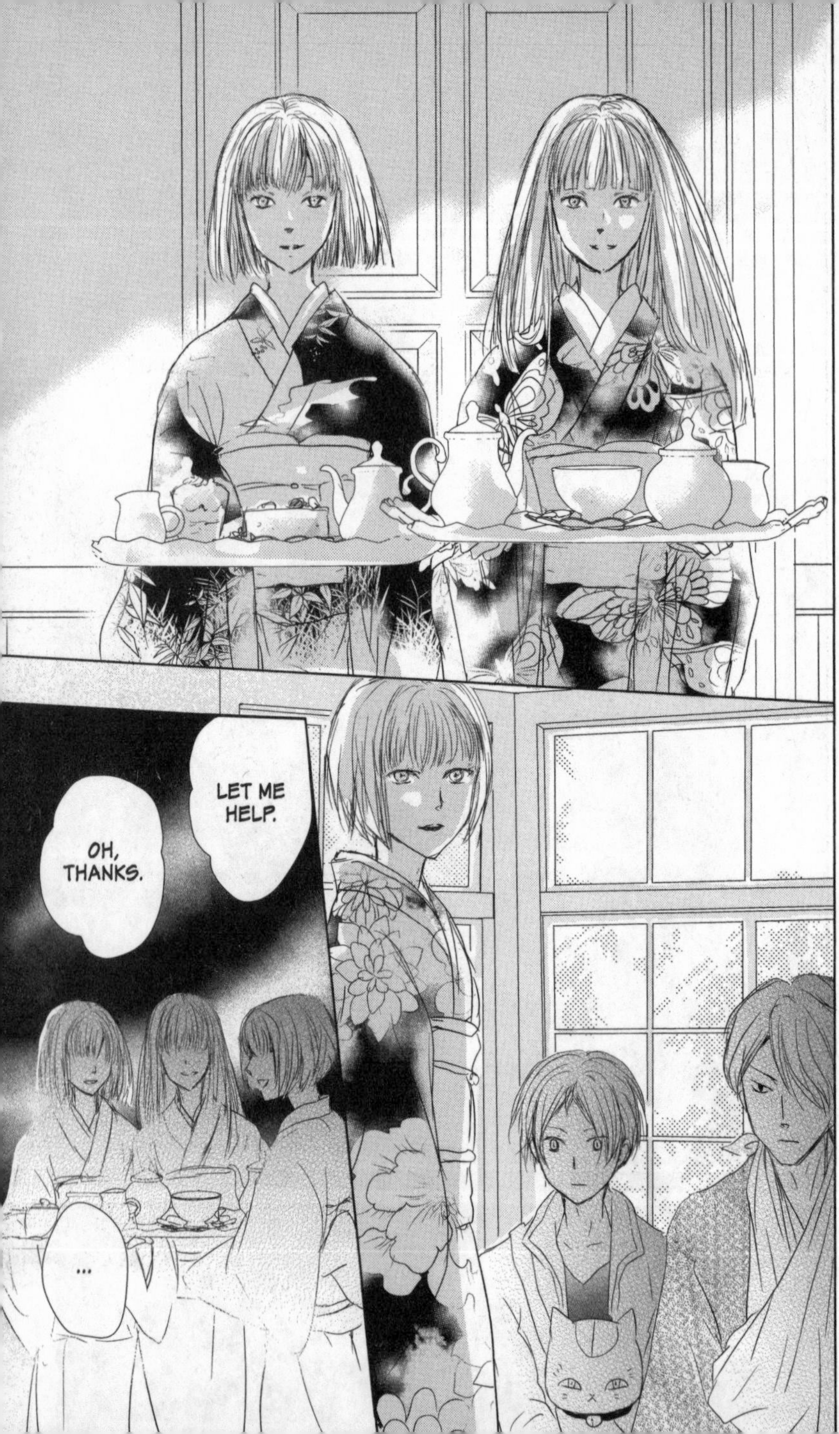
LET ME HELP.
OH, THANKS.
...

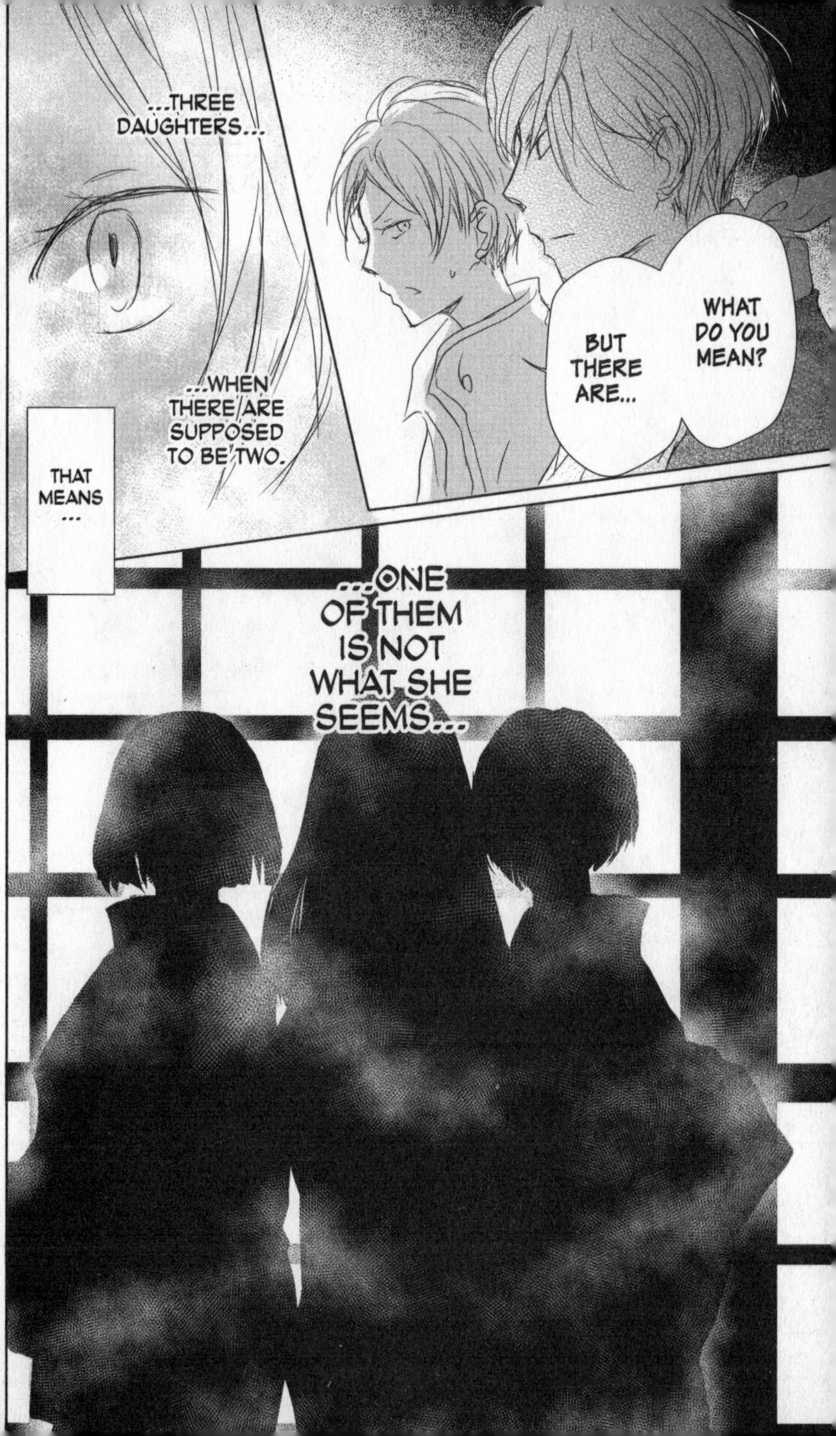
WHAT DO YOU MEAN?
BUT THERE ARE...
...THREE DAUGHTERS...
...WHEN THERE ARE SUPPOSED TO BE TWO.
THAT MEANS...
...ONE OF THEM IS NOT WHAT SHE SEEMS...

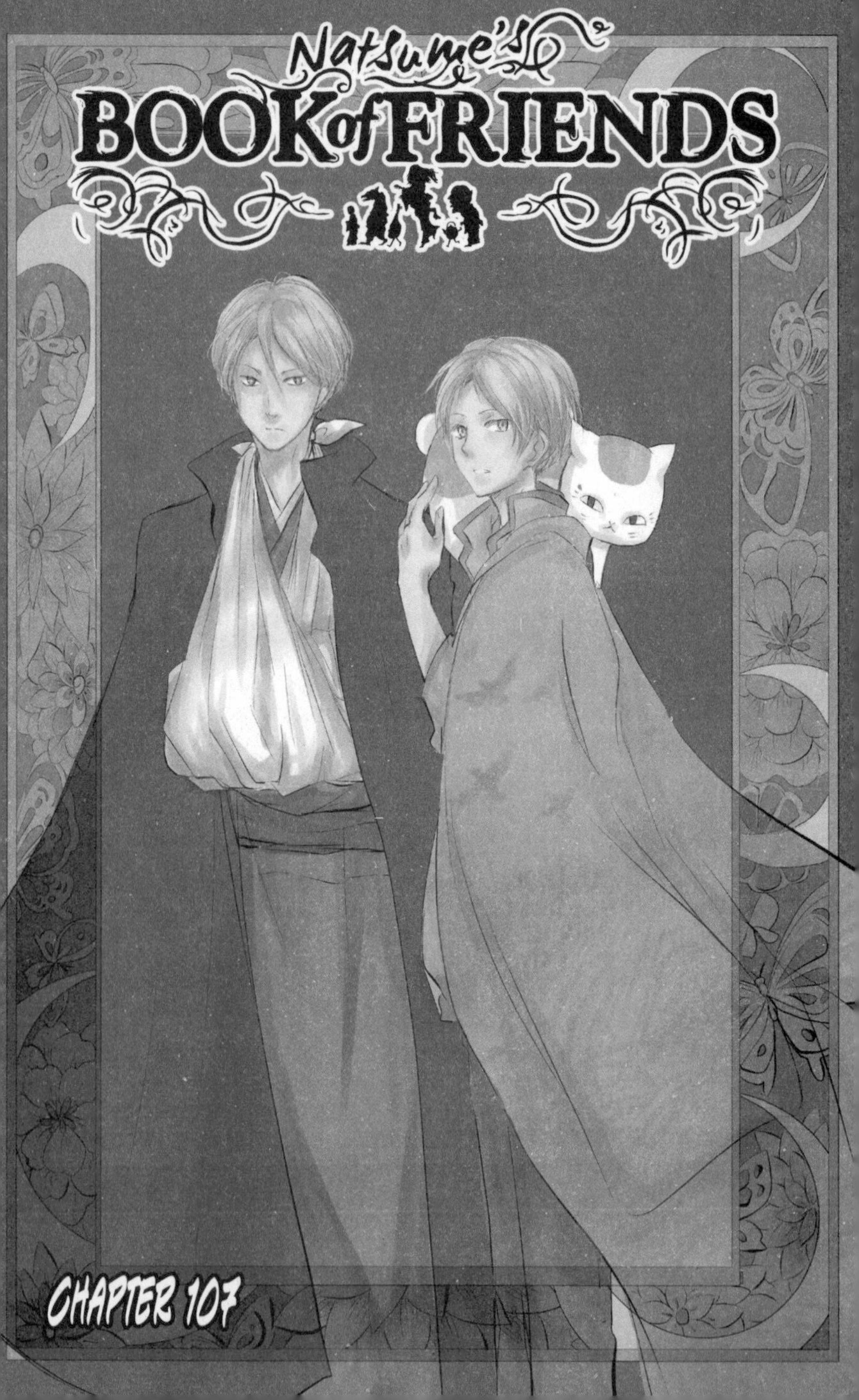
Natsume's
BOOK of FRIENDS
CHAPTER 107

CHAPTER 105 Cookies and the Entrance to the Forest

I wrote this story because I figured that after returning from the village, there were a lot of things Natsume had tell Tanuma about Nyanko Sensei and the people whose jobs revolve around yokai. But I felt that it would be better for them to be doing something together rather than just sitting and talking. And I remembered some merchandise that had a cute picture of Nyanko Sensei carrying a sack with a hole, spilling clementines.

CHAPTER 106-107 Visiting a Departed Friend

Mr. Yorishima is a former exorcist who appeared in vol. 20, in an chapter called "Ten Nights." I worried that two chapters of 24 and 32 pages might not be long enough to tell the story, but I was looking forward to working on it. I wanted to include it after having done the story on the village of vessels. Drawing Mr. Yorishima always feels timeless. And it was a new experience writing about someone who has as much power as Natsume. It must be complicated for the younger generation to see someone so powerful be retired and reclusive, no matter what the circumstances that brought it about. I wanted to draw lively daughters, a large mansion, and the moment you come to notice a whisper of loneliness in an otherwise radiantly beautiful space.

Thank you so much for reading. I'm very grateful that an animated movie of episodes "The Alarm" (vol. 21) and "A Suspicious Visitor" (vol. 24) was made in January 2021. Thank you so much to the director, staff, actors, fans, and everyone involved. I was so happy I found myself in tears when they told me the news. I hope you'll be able to enjoy Natsume and Sensei in the anime that everyone worked so hard on in these difficult times.

The manga *Natsume's Book of Friends* has continued for a long time. I'll work hard so you can have volume 27 in your hands! Thank you so much.

Thanks to

Lulu Eijo
Sachi Fujita
Mr. Kakiuchi
My sister
Mr. Nakamura
Mr. Nomura
Hoen Kikaku Ltd.

Thank you.

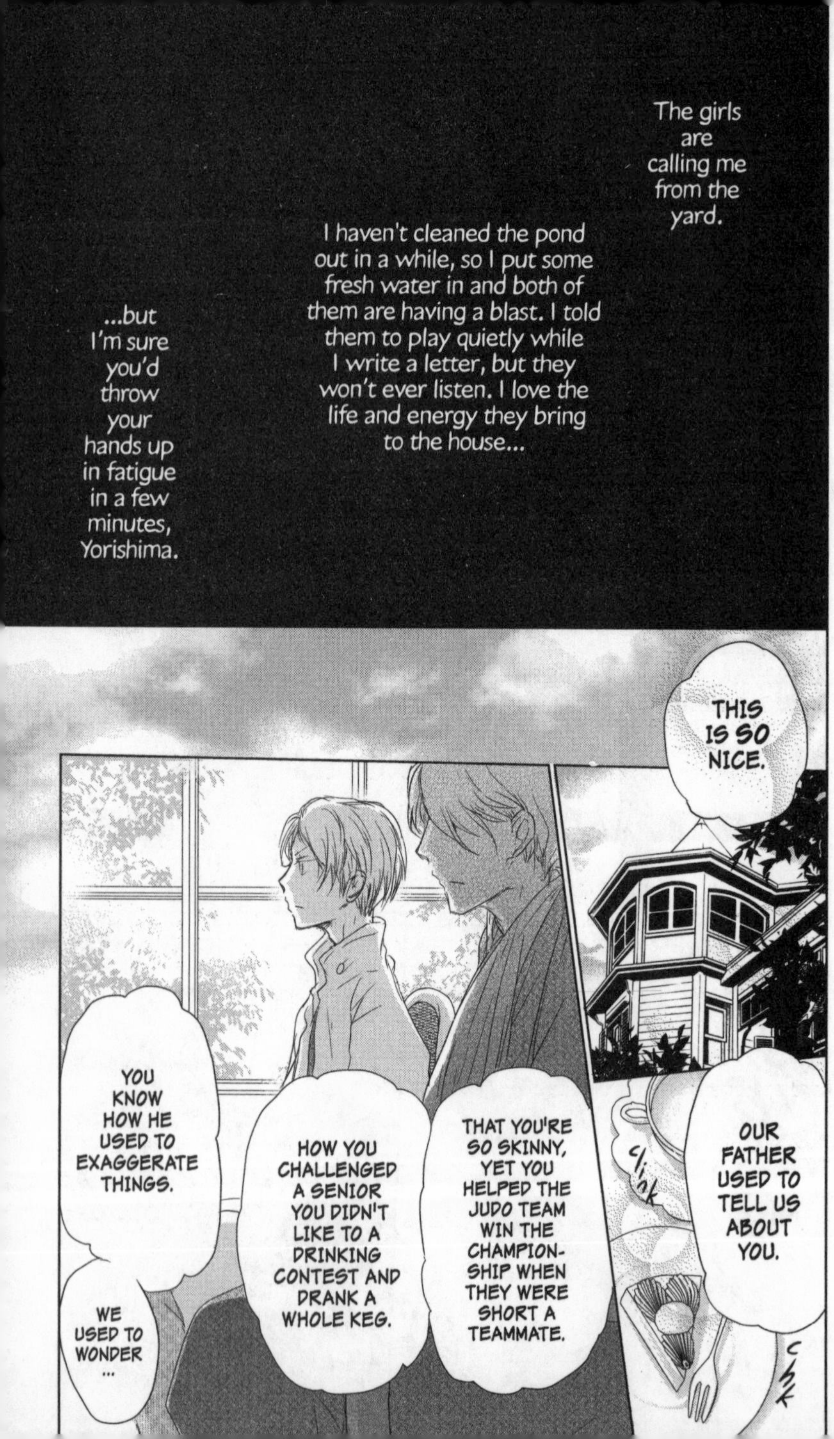
The girls are calling me from the yard.
I haven't cleaned the pond out in a while, so I put some fresh water in and both of them are having a blast. I told them to play quietly while I write a letter, but they won't ever listen. I love the life and energy they bring to the house...
...but I'm sure you'd throw your hands up in fatigue in a few minutes, Yorishima.
THIS IS SO NICE.
OUR FATHER USED TO TELL US ABOUT YOU.
clink
clink
THAT YOU'RE SO SKINNY, YET YOU HELPED THE JUDO TEAM WIN THE CHAMPION-SHIP WHEN THEY WERE SHORT A TEAMMATE.
HOW YOU CHALLENGED A SENIOR YOU DIDN'T LIKE TO A DRINKING CONTEST AND DRANK A WHOLE KEG.
YOU KNOW HOW HE USED TO EXAGGERATE THINGS.
WE USED TO WONDER...

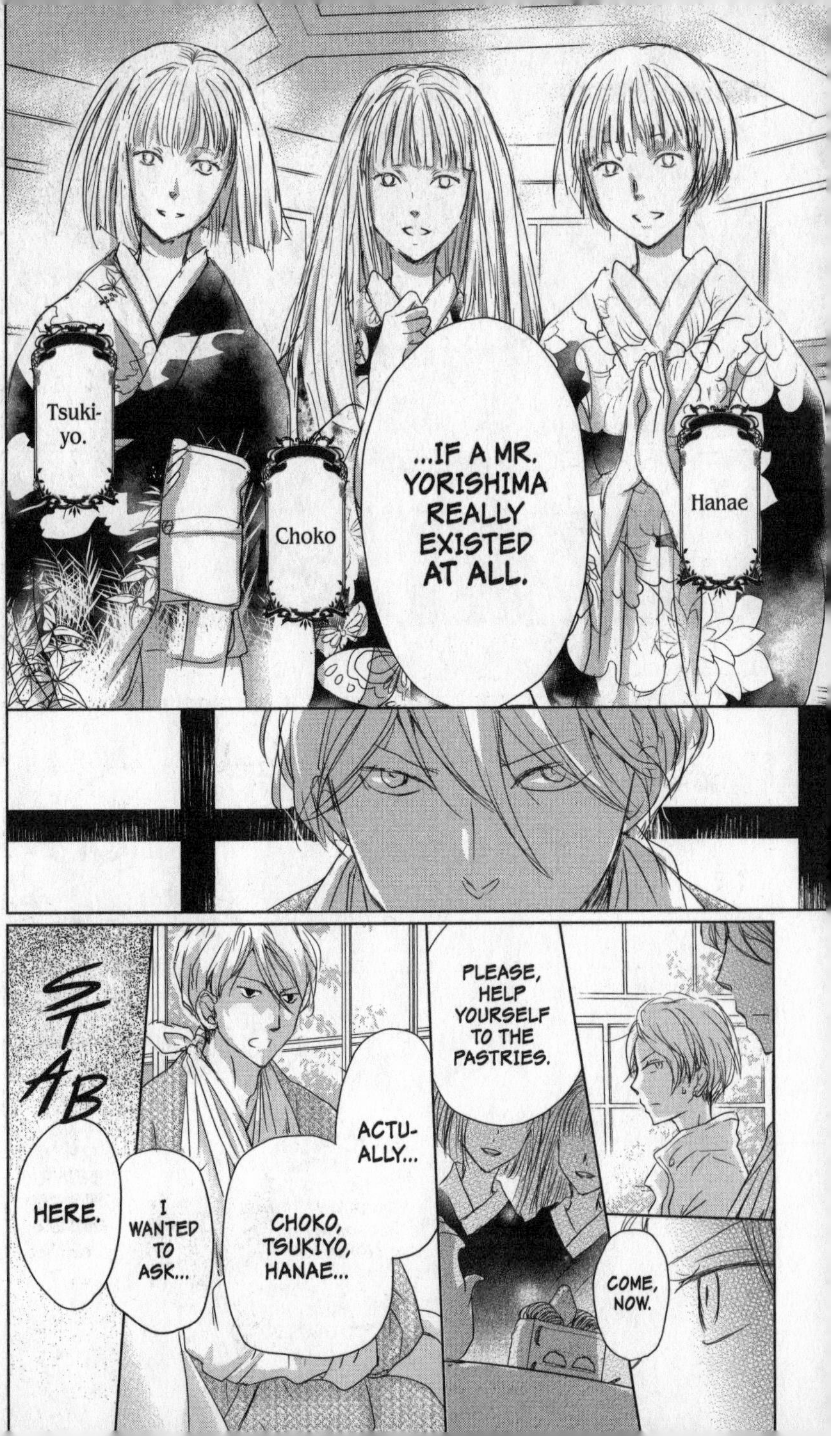
Hanae
...IF A MR. YORISHIMA REALLY EXISTED AT ALL.
Choko
Tsuki-yo.
PLEASE, HELP YOURSELF TO THE PASTRIES.
COME, NOW.
ACTU-ALLY...
CHOKO, TSUKIYO, HANAE...
I WANTED TO ASK...
HERE.
STAB

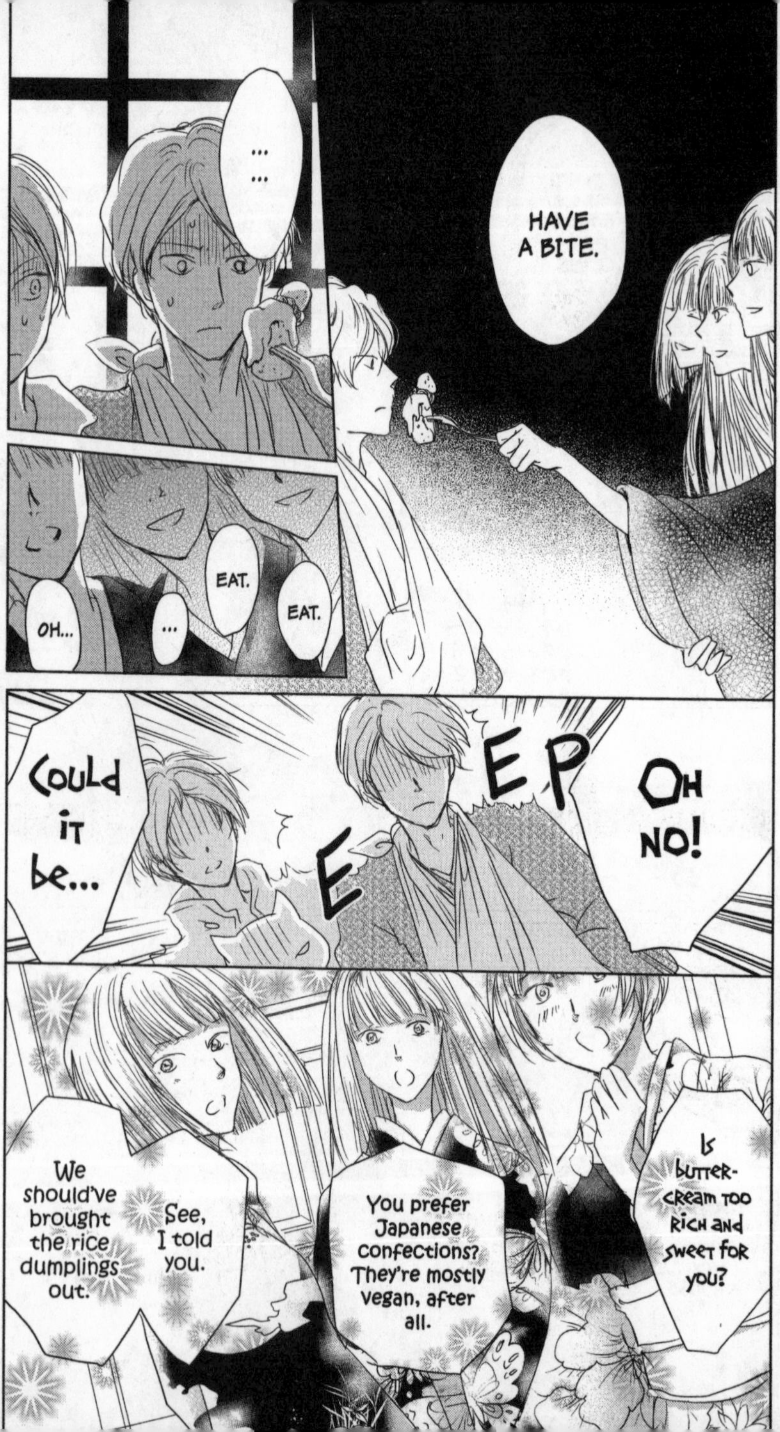
HAVE A BITE.
...
...
EAT.
EAT.
...
OH...
OH NO!
EEP
Could it be...
Is butter-cream too rich and sweet for you?
You prefer Japanese confections? They're mostly vegan, after all.
See, I told you.
We should've brought the rice dumplings out.

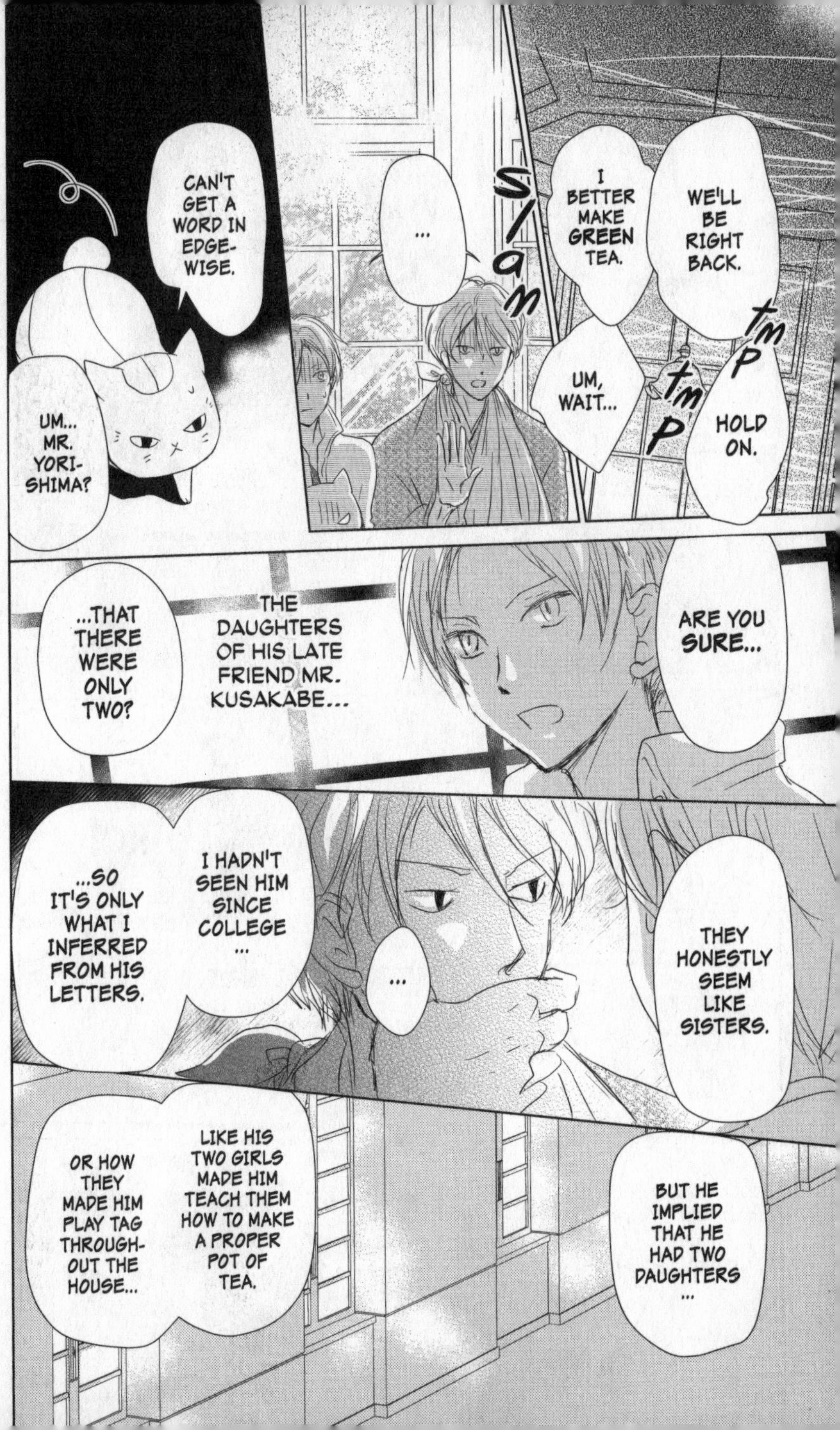
WE'LL BE RIGHT BACK.
I BETTER MAKE GREEN TEA.
tmp tmp
HOLD ON.
UM, WAIT...
Slam
...
CAN'T GET A WORD IN EDGE-WISE.
UM... MR. YORI-SHIMA?
ARE YOU SURE...
THE DAUGHTERS OF HIS LATE FRIEND MR. KUSAKABE...
...THAT THERE WERE ONLY TWO?
THEY HONESTLY SEEM LIKE SISTERS.
...
I HADN'T SEEN HIM SINCE COLLEGE...
...SO IT'S ONLY WHAT I INFERRED FROM HIS LETTERS.
BUT HE IMPLIED THAT HE HAD TWO DAUGHTERS...
LIKE HIS TWO GIRLS MADE HIM TEACH THEM HOW TO MAKE A PROPER POT OF TEA.
OR HOW THEY MADE HIM PLAY TAG THROUGH-OUT THE HOUSE...

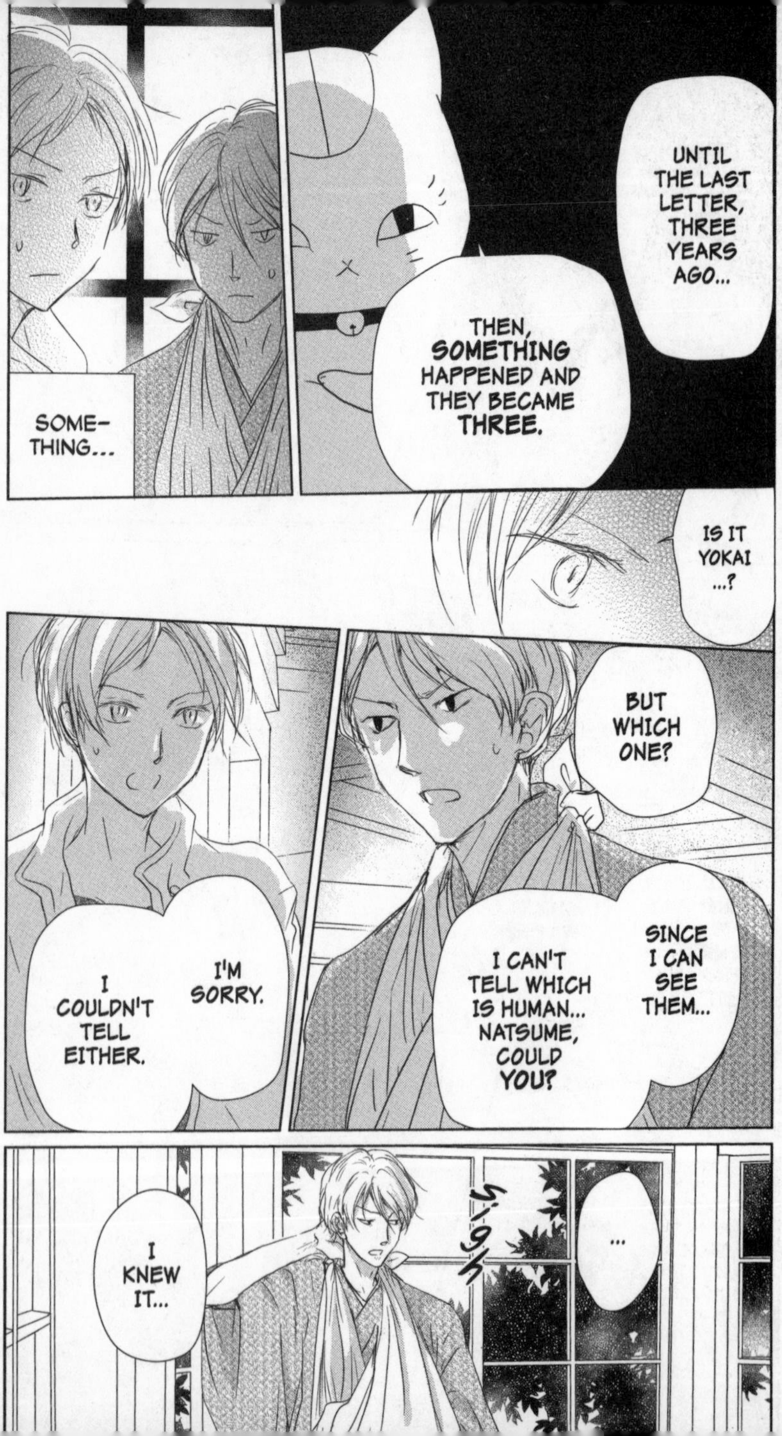
UNTIL THE LAST LETTER, THREE YEARS AGO...
THEN, SOMETHING HAPPENED AND THEY BECAME THREE.
SOME-THING...
IS IT YOKAI ...?
BUT WHICH ONE?
SINCE I CAN SEE THEM...
I CAN'T TELL WHICH IS HUMAN... NATSUME, COULD YOU?
I'M SORRY.
I COULDN'T TELL EITHER.
...
Sigh
I KNEW IT...

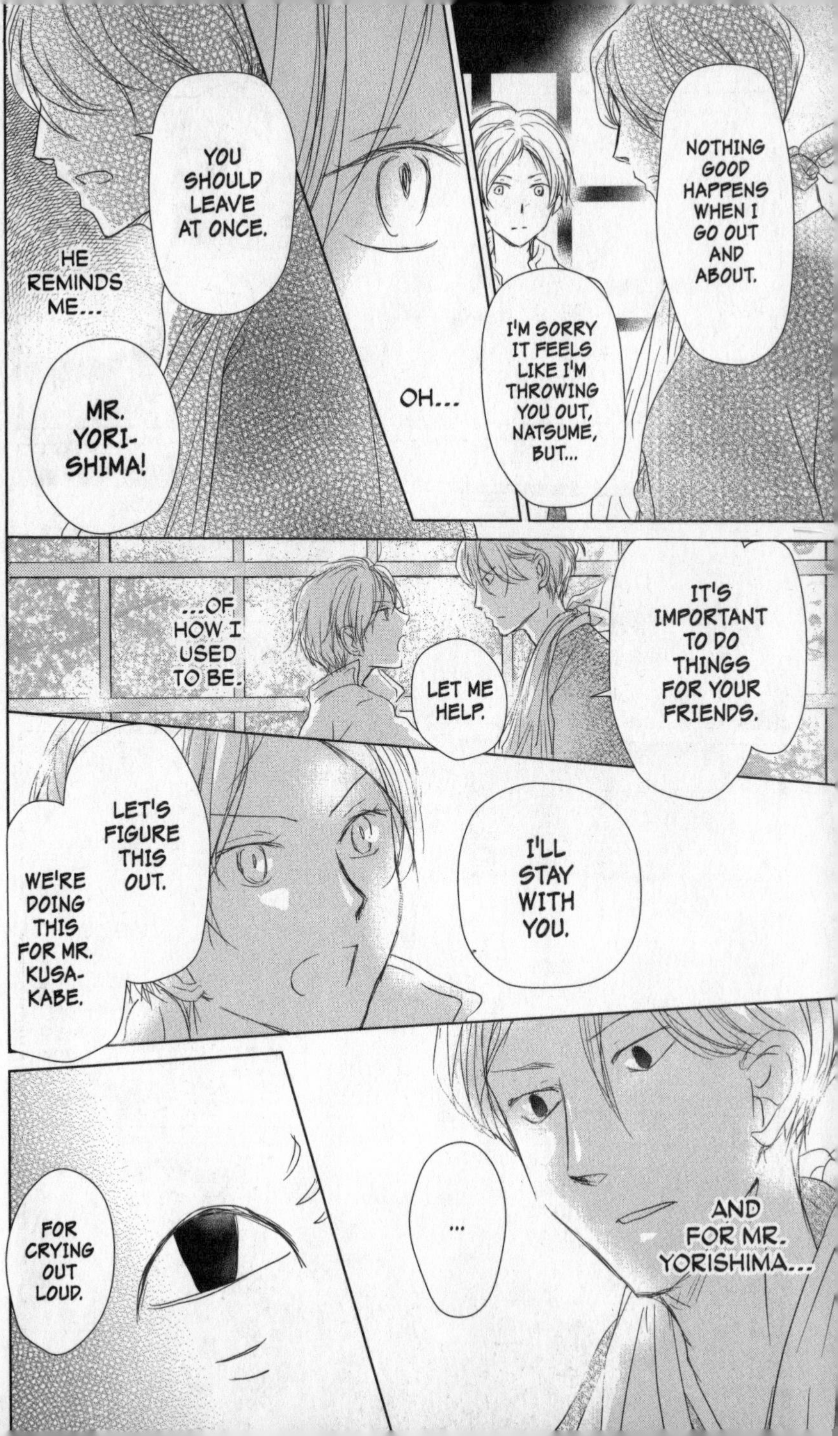
NOTHING GOOD HAPPENS WHEN I GO OUT AND ABOUT.
I'M SORRY IT FEELS LIKE I'M THROWING YOU OUT, NATSUME, BUT...
OH...
YOU SHOULD LEAVE AT ONCE.
HE REMINDS ME...
MR. YORI-SHIMA!
IT'S IMPORTANT TO DO THINGS FOR YOUR FRIENDS.
LET ME HELP.
...OF HOW I USED TO BE.
I'LL STAY WITH YOU.
LET'S FIGURE THIS OUT.
WE'RE DOING THIS FOR MR. KUSA-KABE.
AND FOR MR. YORISHIMA...
...
FOR CRYING OUT LOUD.

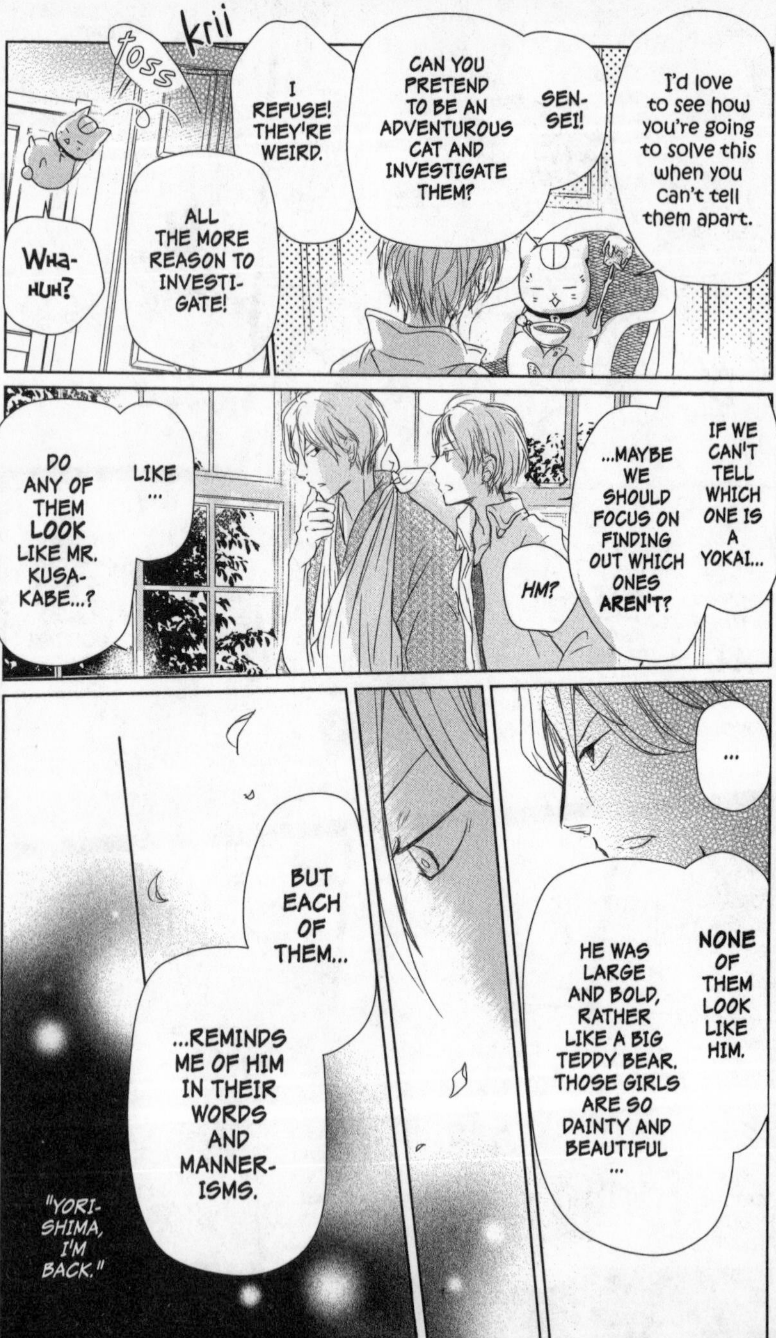
I'd love to see how you're going to solve this when you can't tell them apart.
SEN-SEI!
CAN YOU PRETEND TO BE AN ADVENTUROUS CAT AND INVESTIGATE THEM?
I REFUSE! THEY'RE WEIRD.
krii
toss
ALL THE MORE REASON TO INVESTI-GATE!
WHA-HUH?
IF WE CAN'T TELL WHICH ONE IS A YOKAI...
...MAYBE WE SHOULD FOCUS ON FINDING OUT WHICH ONES AREN'T?
HM?
LIKE ...
DO ANY OF THEM LOOK LIKE MR. KUSA-KABE...?
...
NONE OF THEM LOOK LIKE HIM.
HE WAS LARGE AND BOLD, RATHER LIKE A BIG TEDDY BEAR. THOSE GIRLS ARE SO DAINTY AND BEAUTIFUL ...
BUT EACH OF THEM...
...REMINDS ME OF HIM IN THEIR WORDS AND MANNER-ISMS.
"YORI-SHIMA, I'M BACK."

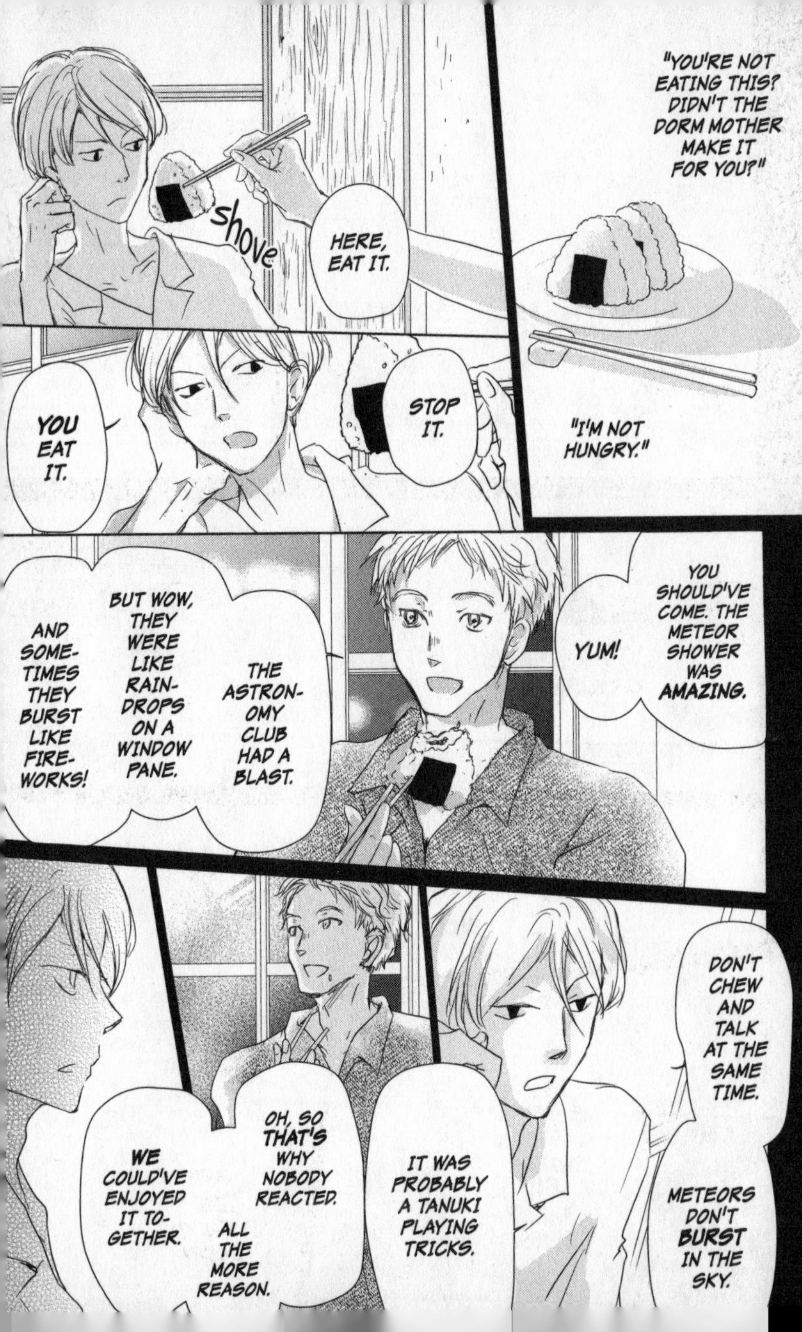
"YOU'RE NOT EATING THIS? DIDN'T THE DORM MOTHER MAKE IT FOR YOU?"
"I'M NOT HUNGRY."
shove
HERE, EAT IT.
STOP IT.
YOU EAT IT.
YOU SHOULD'VE COME. THE METEOR SHOWER WAS AMAZING.
YUM!
THE ASTRONOMY CLUB HAD A BLAST.
BUT WOW, THEY WERE LIKE RAINDROPS ON A WINDOW PANE.
AND SOMETIMES THEY BURST LIKE FIREWORKS!
DON'T CHEW AND TALK AT THE SAME TIME.
METEORS DON'T BURST IN THE SKY.
IT WAS PROBABLY A TANUKI PLAYING TRICKS.
OH, SO THAT'S WHY NOBODY REACTED.
ALL THE MORE REASON.
WE COULD'VE ENJOYED IT TOGETHER.

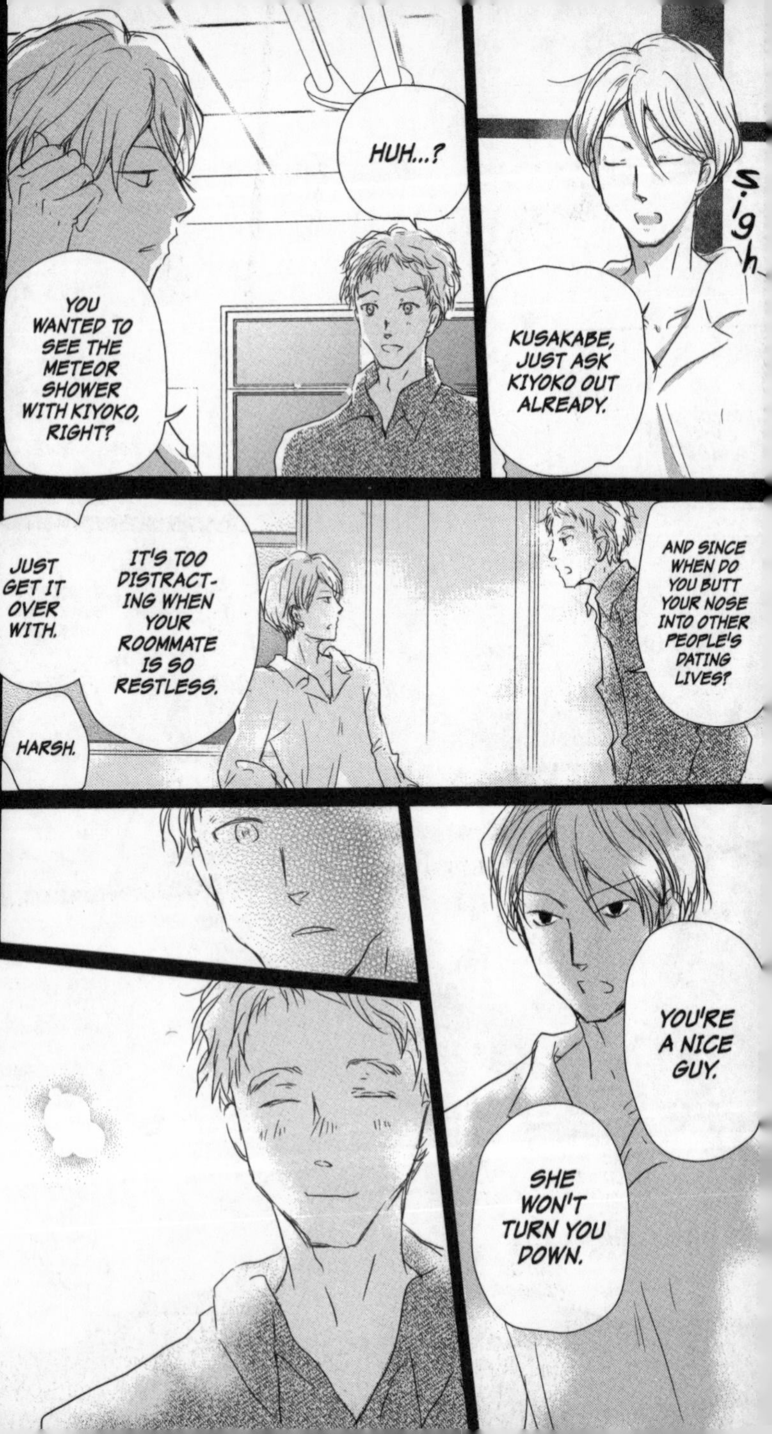
KUSAKABE, JUST ASK KIYOKO OUT ALREADY.
sigh
HUH...?
YOU WANTED TO SEE THE METEOR SHOWER WITH KIYOKO, RIGHT?
AND SINCE WHEN DO YOU BUTT YOUR NOSE INTO OTHER PEOPLE'S DATING LIVES?
IT'S TOO DISTRACTING WHEN YOUR ROOMMATE IS SO RESTLESS.
JUST GET IT OVER WITH.
HARSH.
YOU'RE A NICE GUY.
SHE WON'T TURN YOU DOWN.

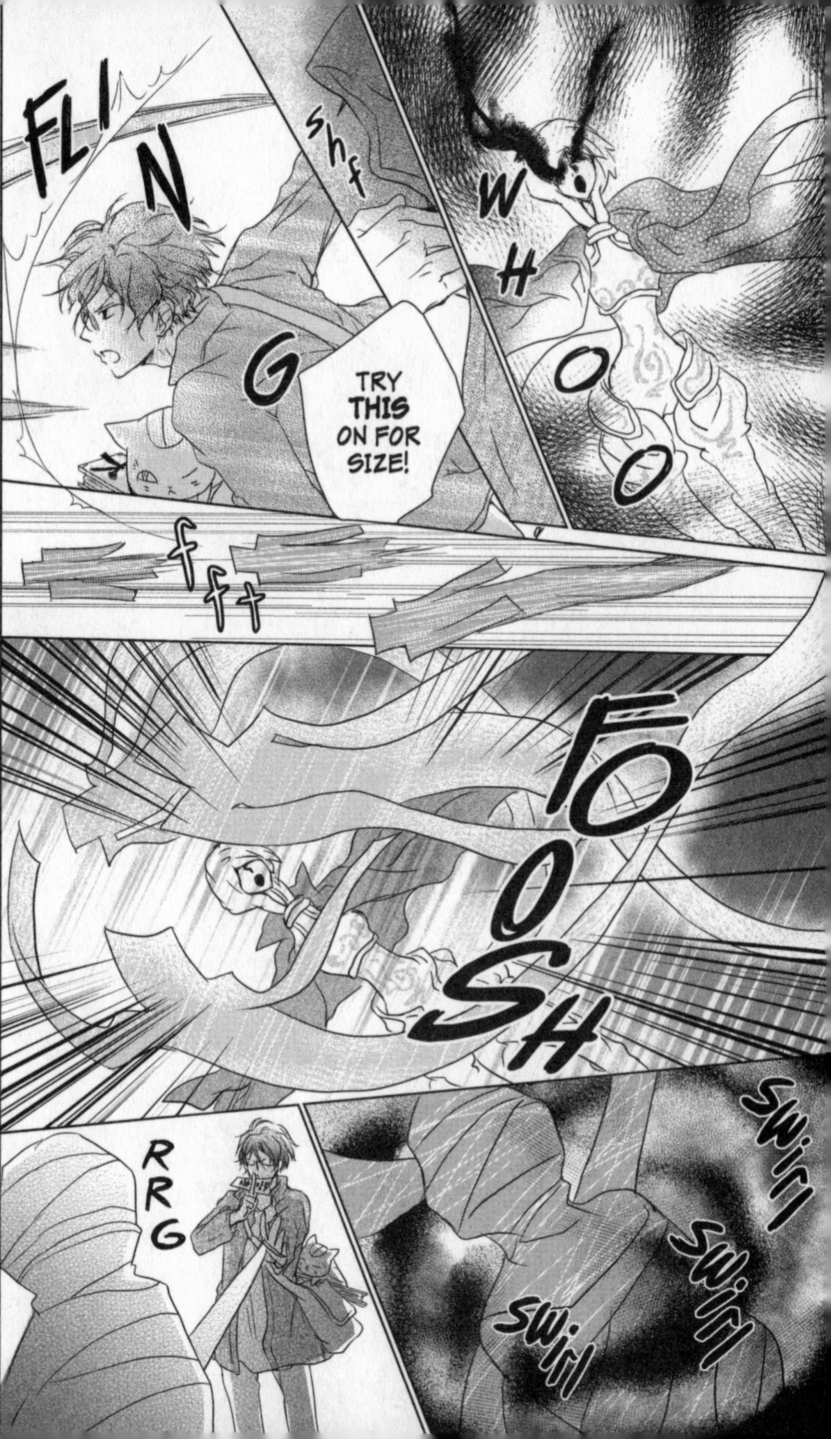
WHOOO
FLING
shf
TRY THIS ON FOR SIZE!
fff
FOOSH
swirl
swirl
swirl
RRG

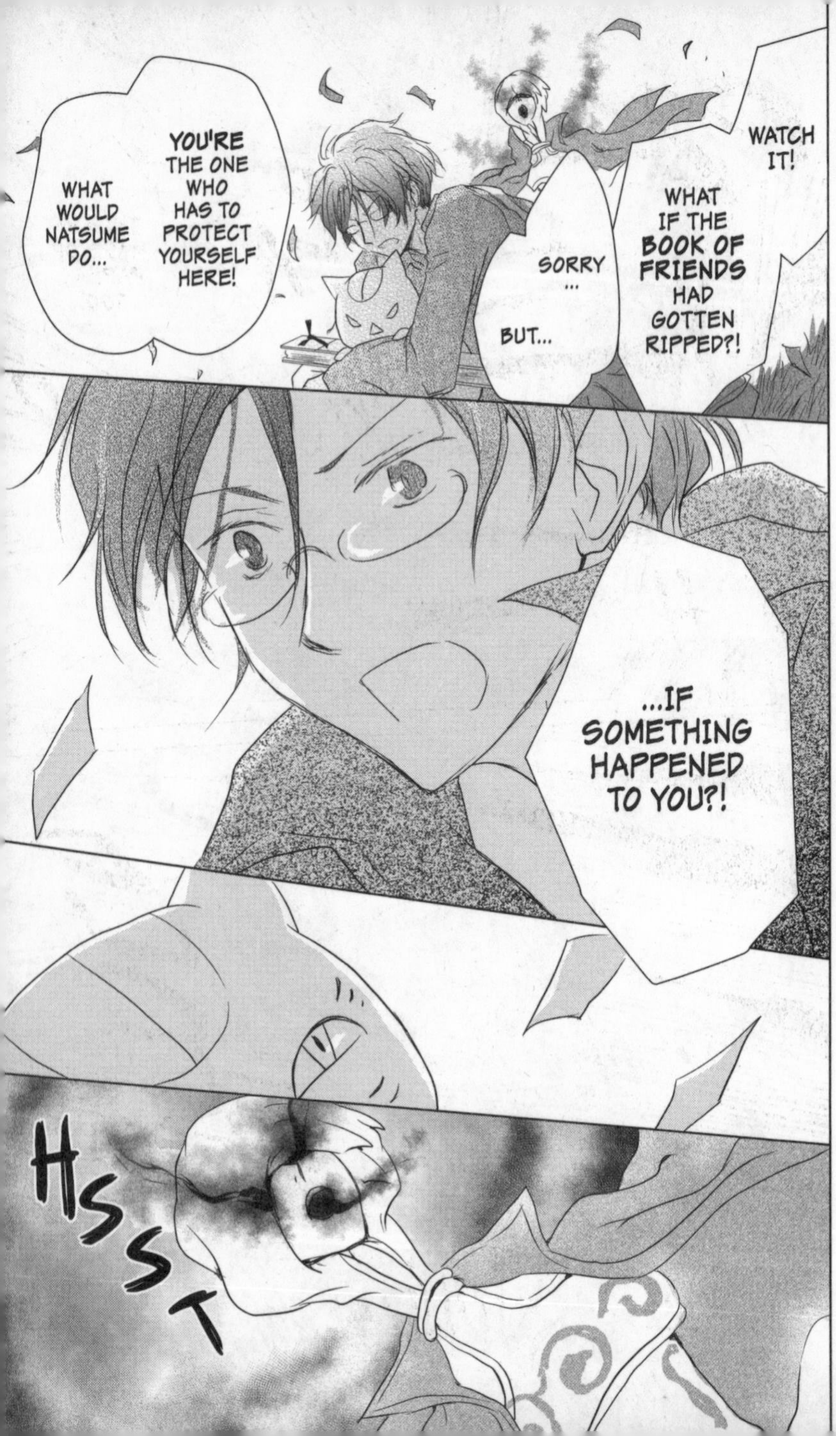
WATCH IT!
WHAT IF THE BOOK OF FRIENDS HAD GOTTEN RIPPED?!
SORRY...
BUT...
YOU'RE THE ONE WHO HAS TO PROTECT YOURSELF HERE!
WHAT WOULD NATSUME DO...
...IF SOMETHING HAPPENED TO YOU?!
HSSST

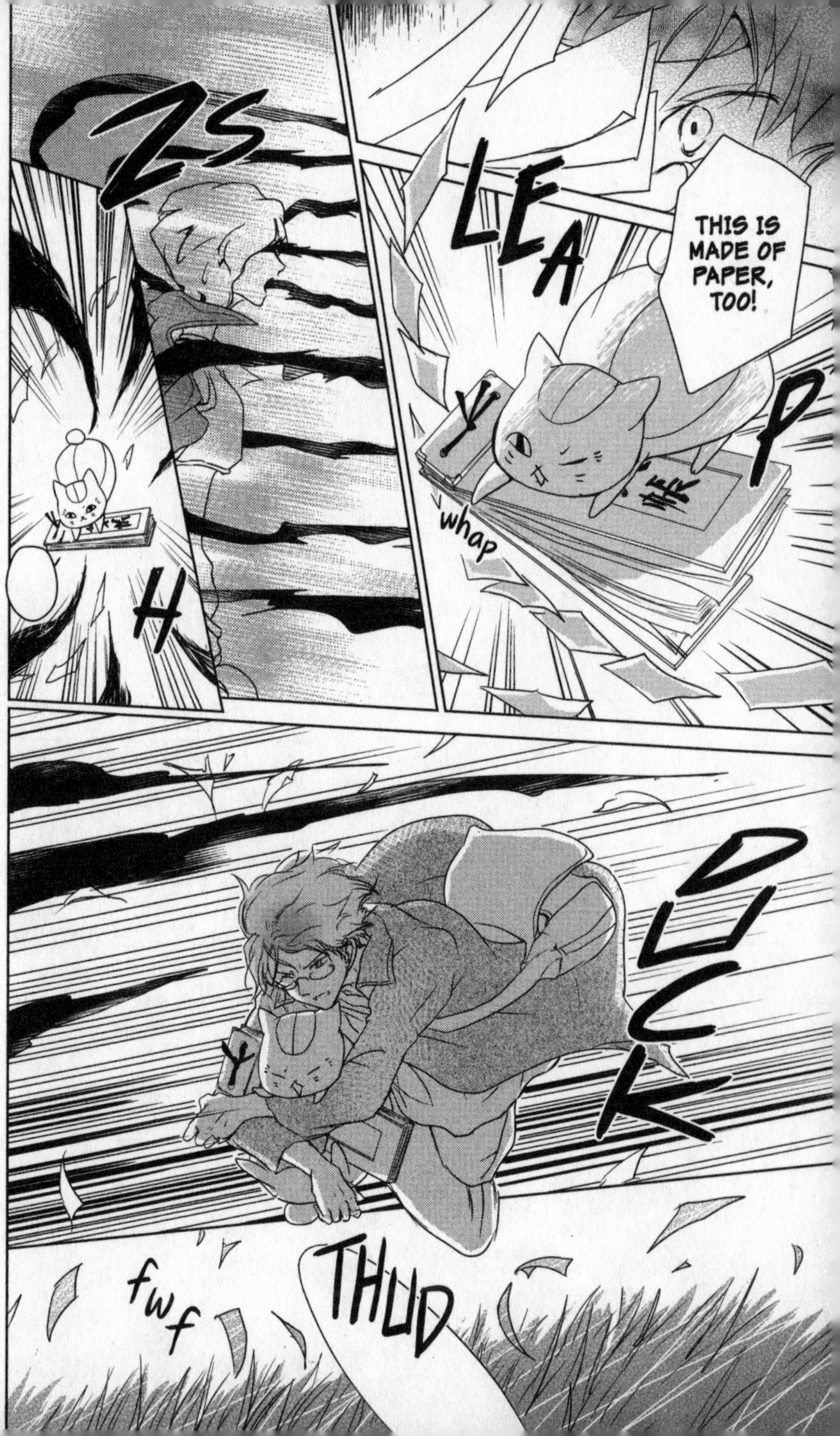
THIS IS MADE OF PAPER, TOO!
LEAP
whap
ZS
H
DUCK
THUD
fwf

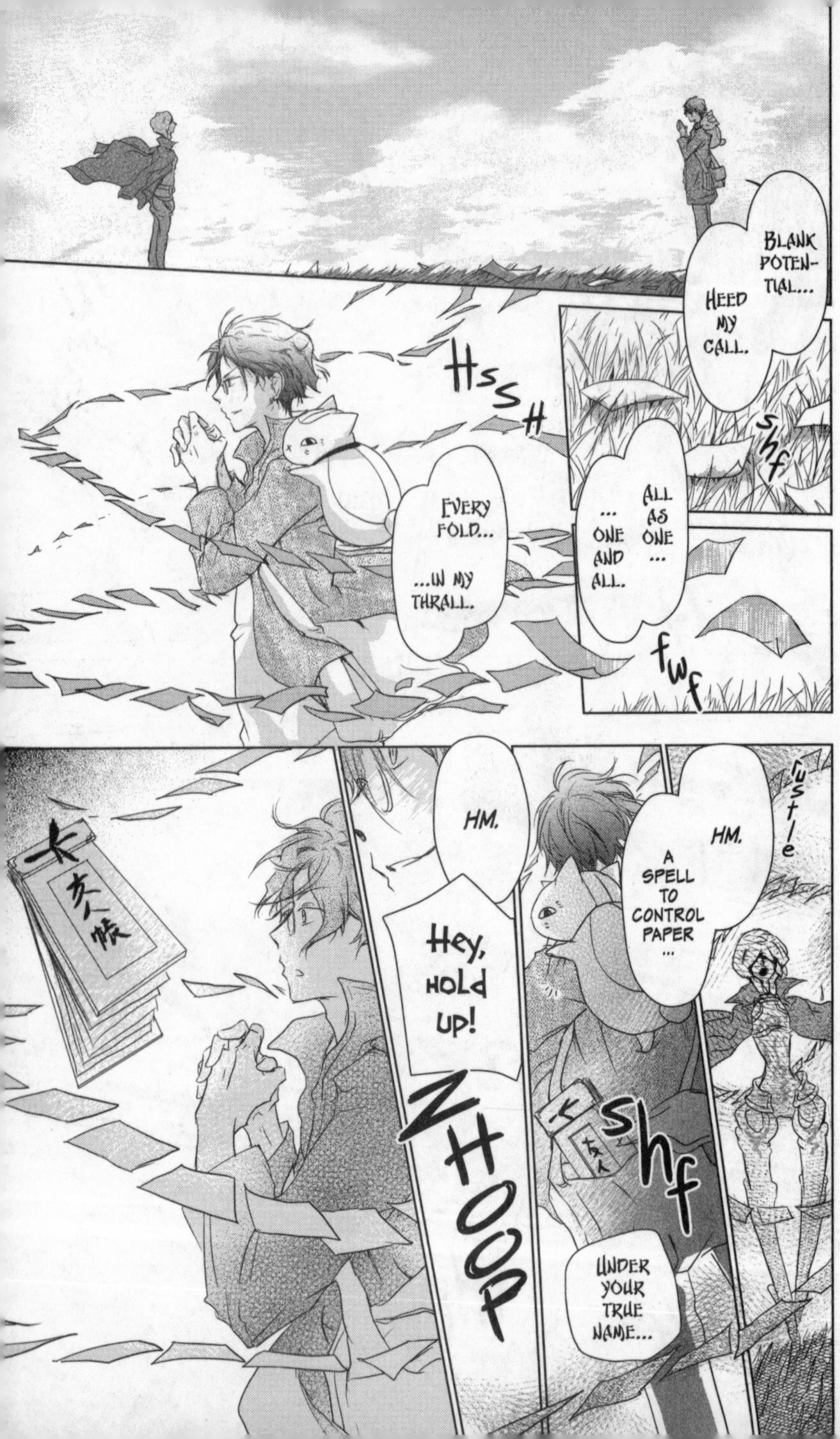

BLANK POTENTIAL... HEED MY CALL.
HSSH
shf
ALL AS ONE... ...ONE AND ALL.
EVERY FOLD... ...IN MY THRALL.
fwf
rustle
HM.
A SPELL TO CONTROL PAPER...
HM.
Hey, HOLD UP!
友人帳
ZHOOP
shf
UNDER YOUR TRUE NAME...

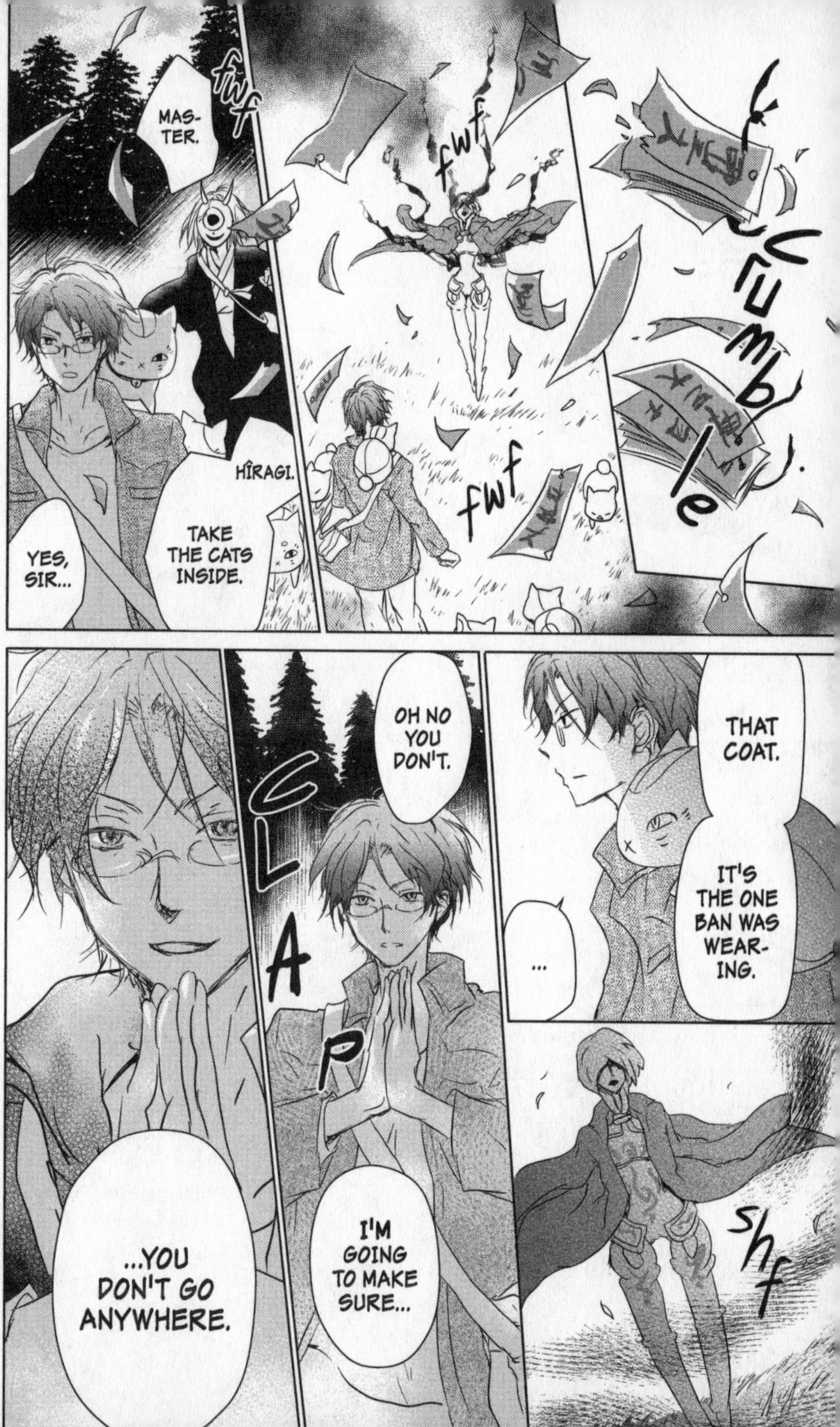
crumble
fwf
fwf
fwf
MAS-TER.
HÎRAGI.
TAKE THE CATS INSIDE.
YES, SIR...
THAT COAT.
IT'S THE ONE BAN WAS WEAR-ING.
...
shf
OH NO YOU DON'T.
CLAP
I'M GOING TO MAKE SURE...
...YOU DON'T GO ANYWHERE.

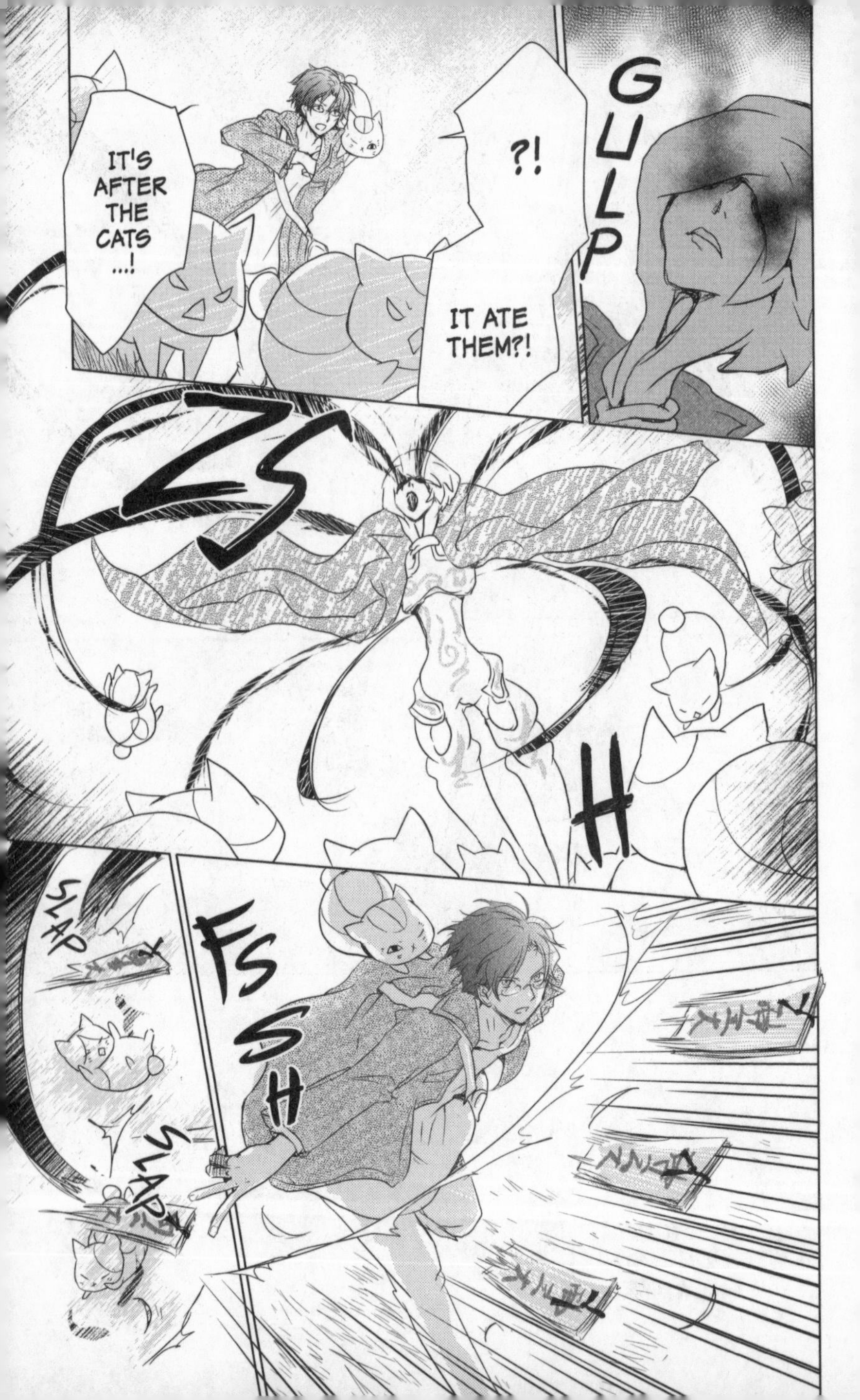
GULP
?!
IT ATE THEM?!
IT'S AFTER THE CATS ...!
ZSH
FSSH
SLAP
SLAP

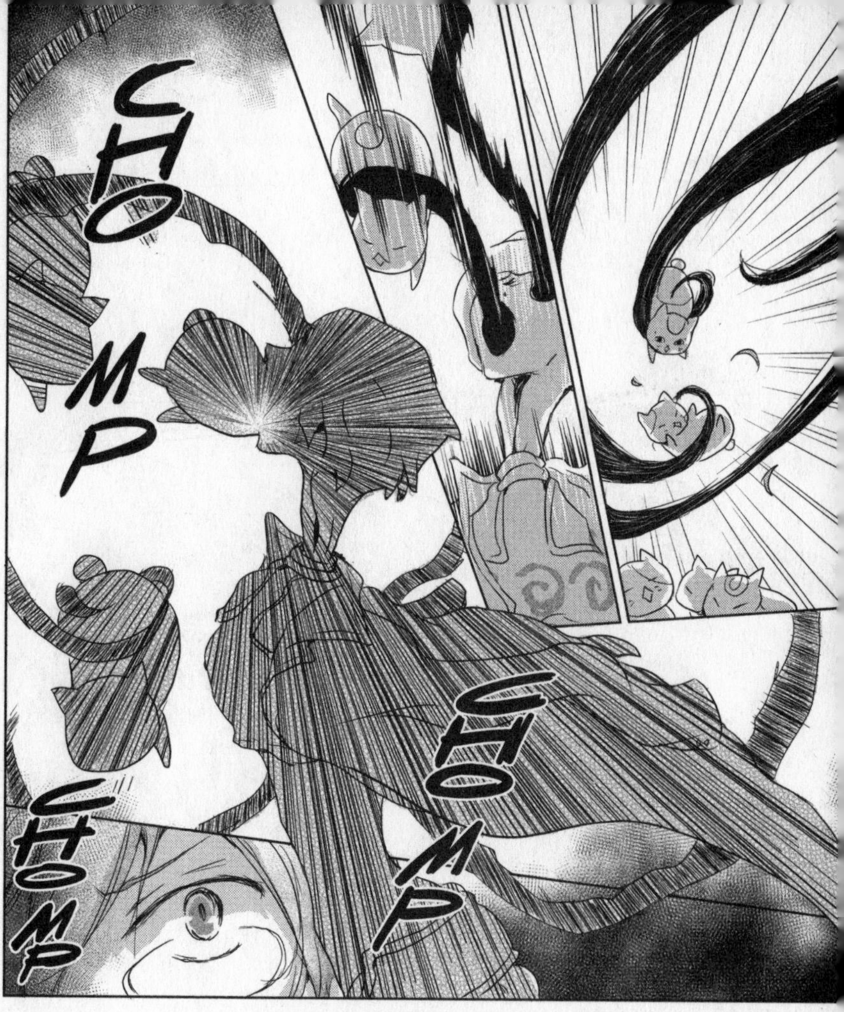
CHOMP
CHOMP
CHOMP

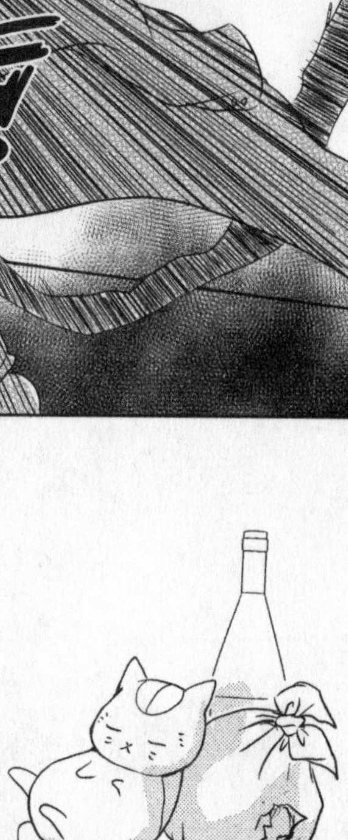

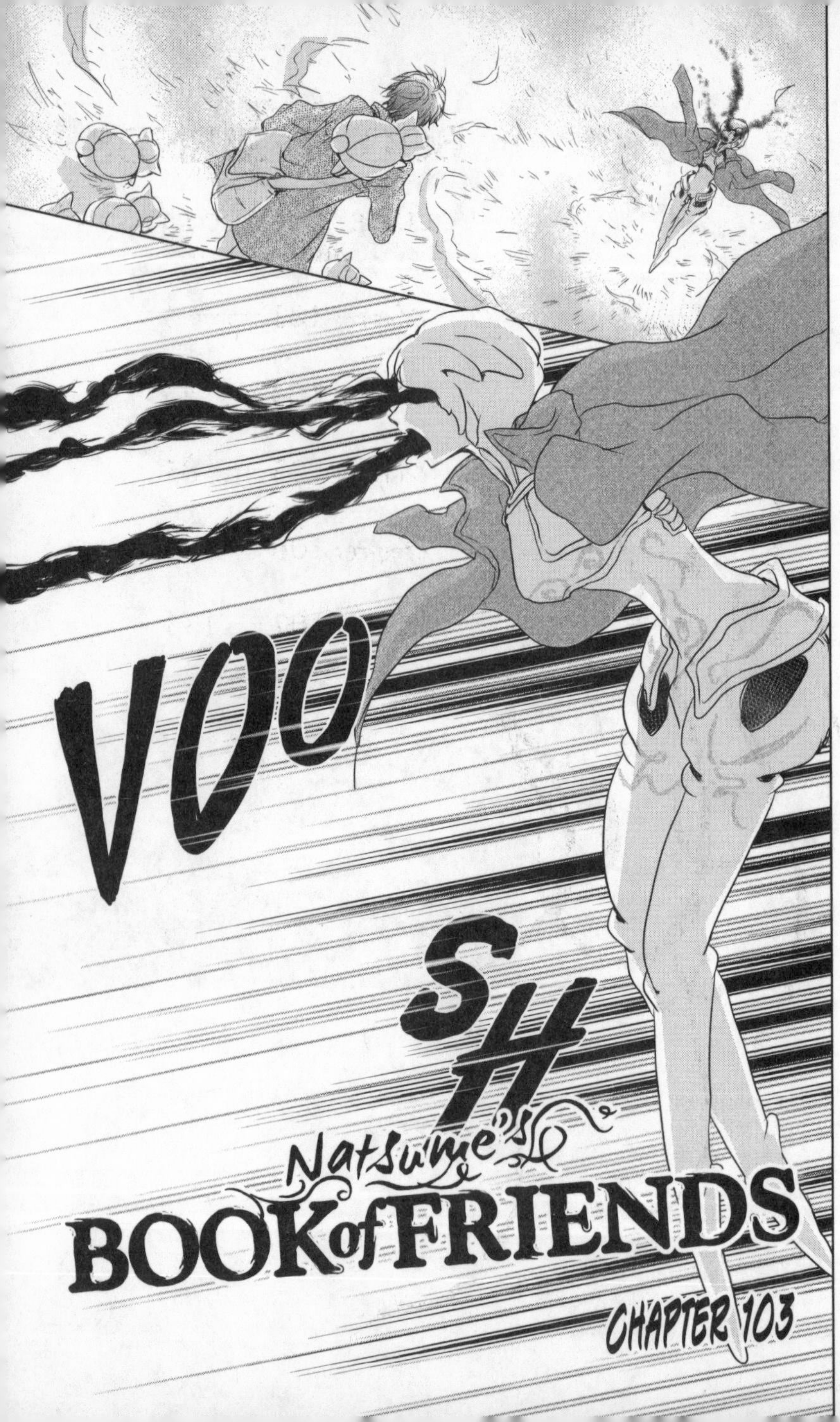
VOOSH
Natsume's BOOK of FRIENDS
CHAPTER 103

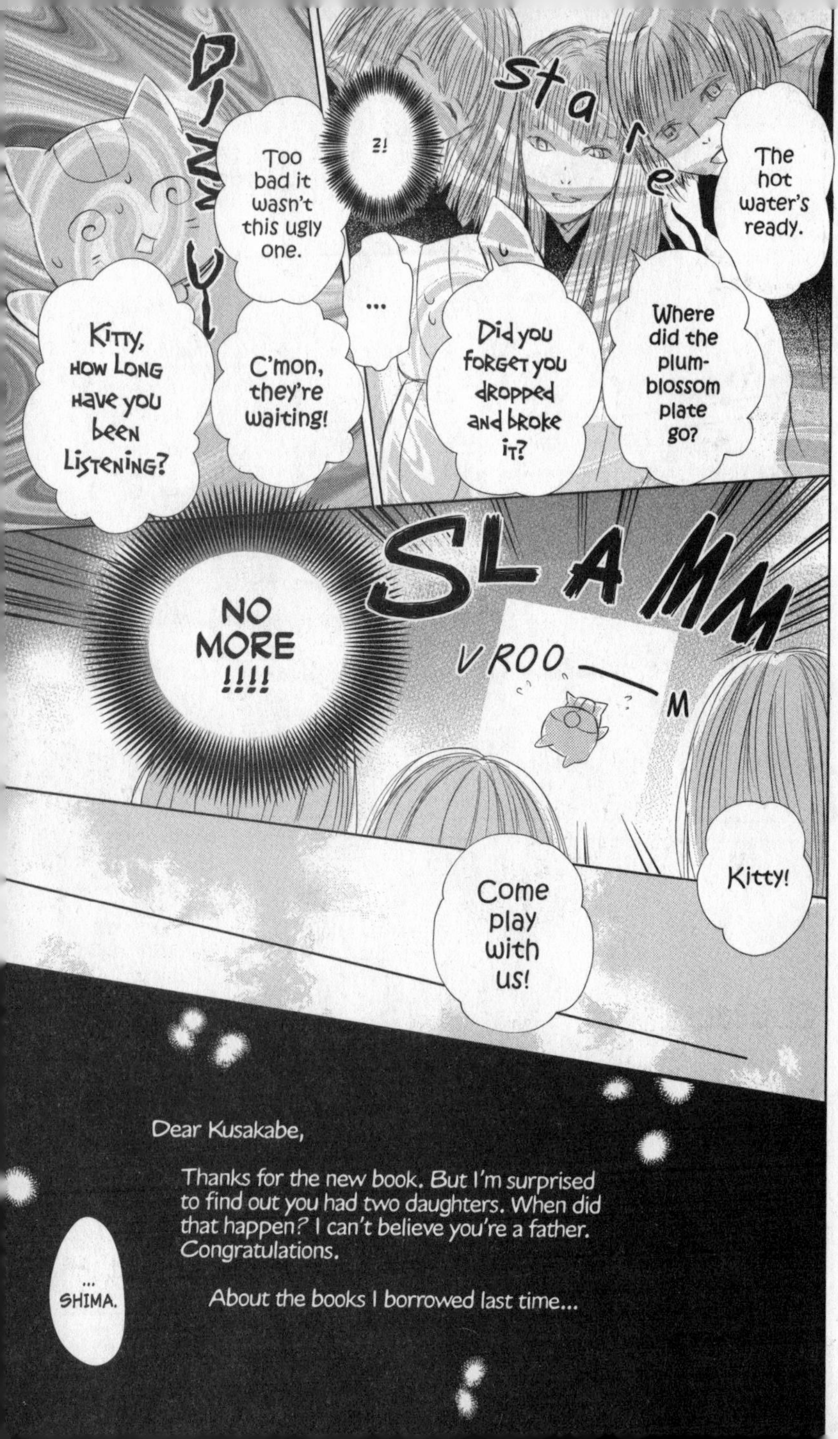

The hot water's ready.
stare
Where did the plum-blossom plate go?
Did you forget you dropped and broke it?
...
Too bad it wasn't this ugly one.
?!
C'mon, they're waiting!
Kitty, how long have you been listening?
NO MORE !!!!
SLAMM
VROO—M
Kitty!
Come play with us!
Dear Kusakabe,
Thanks for the new book. But I'm surprised to find out you had two daughters. When did that happen? I can't believe you're a father. Congratulations.
About the books I borrowed last time...
... SHIMA.

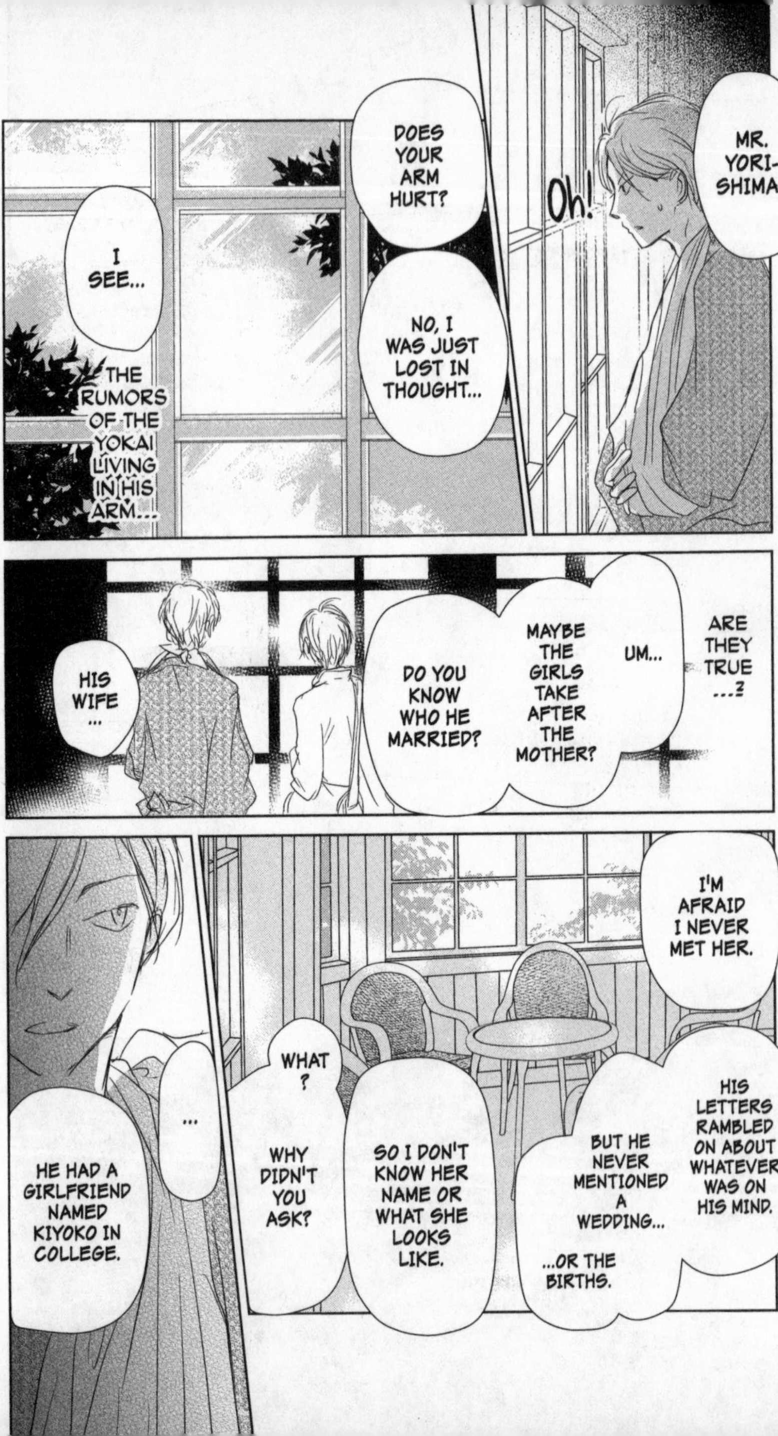
MR. YORI-SHIMA?
Oh!
DOES YOUR ARM HURT?
NO, I WAS JUST LOST IN THOUGHT...
I SEE...
THE RUMORS OF THE YOKAI LIVING IN HIS ARM...
ARE THEY TRUE ...?
UM...
MAYBE THE GIRLS TAKE AFTER THE MOTHER?
DO YOU KNOW WHO HE MARRIED?
HIS WIFE ...
I'M AFRAID I NEVER MET HER.
HIS LETTERS RAMBLED ON ABOUT WHATEVER WAS ON HIS MIND.
BUT HE NEVER MENTIONED A WEDDING...
...OR THE BIRTHS.
SO I DON'T KNOW HER NAME OR WHAT SHE LOOKS LIKE.
WHAT?
WHY DIDN'T YOU ASK?
...
HE HAD A GIRLFRIEND NAMED KIYOKO IN COLLEGE.

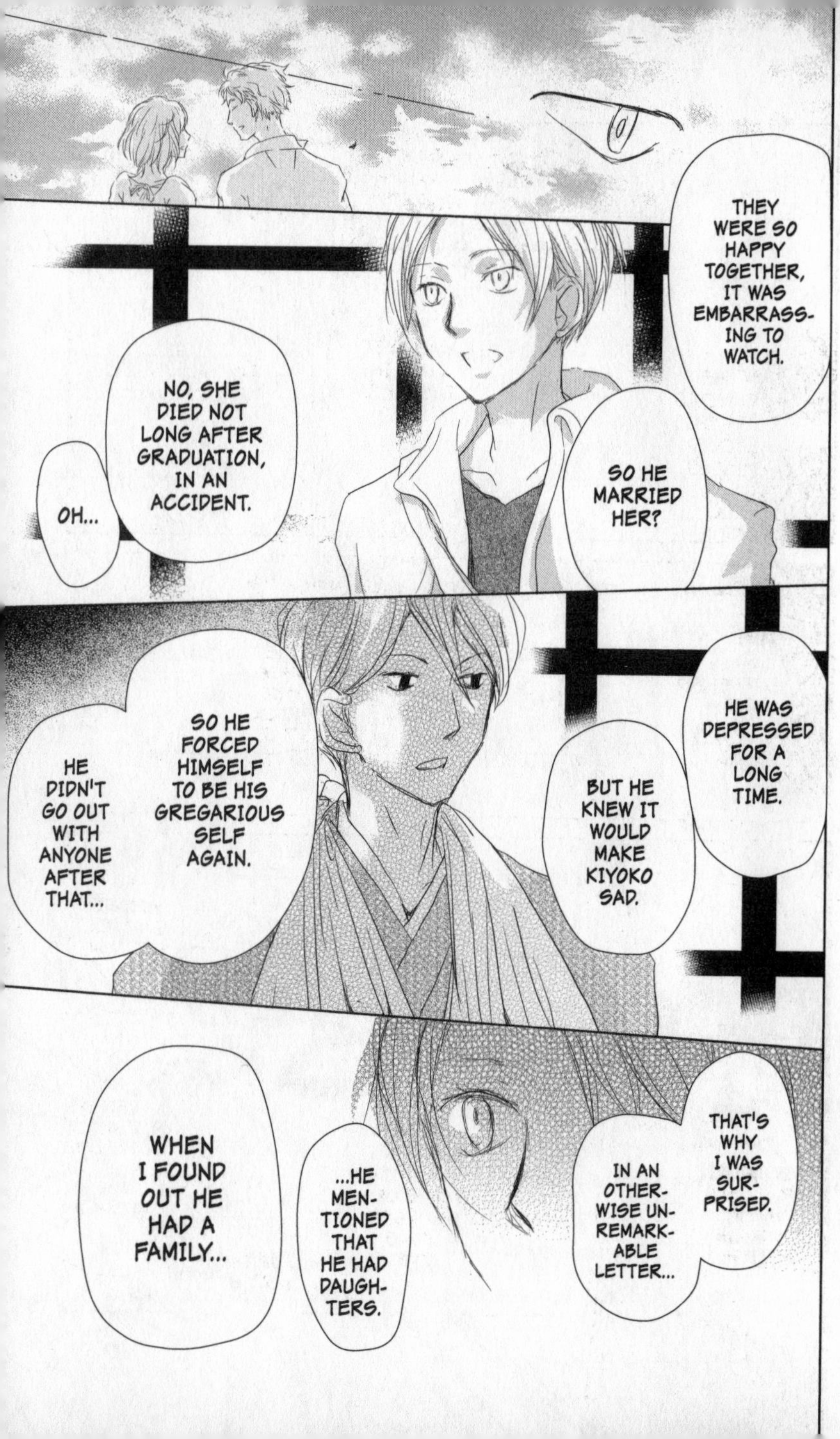
THEY WERE SO HAPPY TOGETHER, IT WAS EMBARRASSING TO WATCH.
SO HE MARRIED HER?
NO, SHE DIED NOT LONG AFTER GRADUATION, IN AN ACCIDENT.
OH...
HE WAS DEPRESSED FOR A LONG TIME.
BUT HE KNEW IT WOULD MAKE KIYOKO SAD.
SO HE FORCED HIMSELF TO BE HIS GREGARIOUS SELF AGAIN.
HE DIDN'T GO OUT WITH ANYONE AFTER THAT...
THAT'S WHY I WAS SURPRISED.
IN AN OTHERWISE UNREMARKABLE LETTER...
...HE MENTIONED THAT HE HAD DAUGHTERS.
WHEN I FOUND OUT HE HAD A FAMILY...

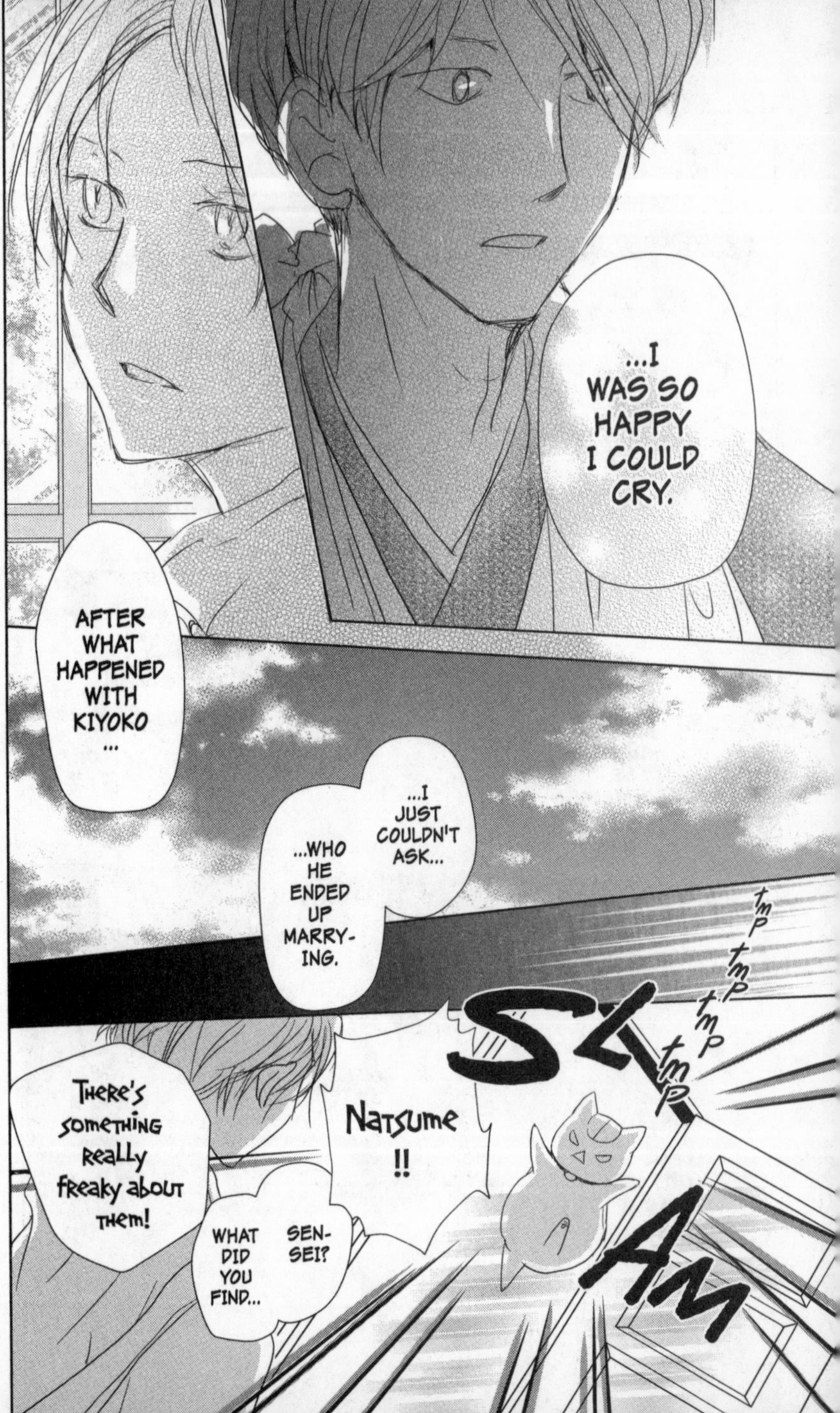
...I WAS SO HAPPY I COULD CRY.
AFTER WHAT HAPPENED WITH KIYOKO ...
...I JUST COULDN'T ASK...
...WHO HE ENDED UP MARRY-ING.
SLAM
tmp tmp tmp tmp
Natsume !!
SEN-SEI?
WHAT DID YOU FIND...
There's something really freaky about them!

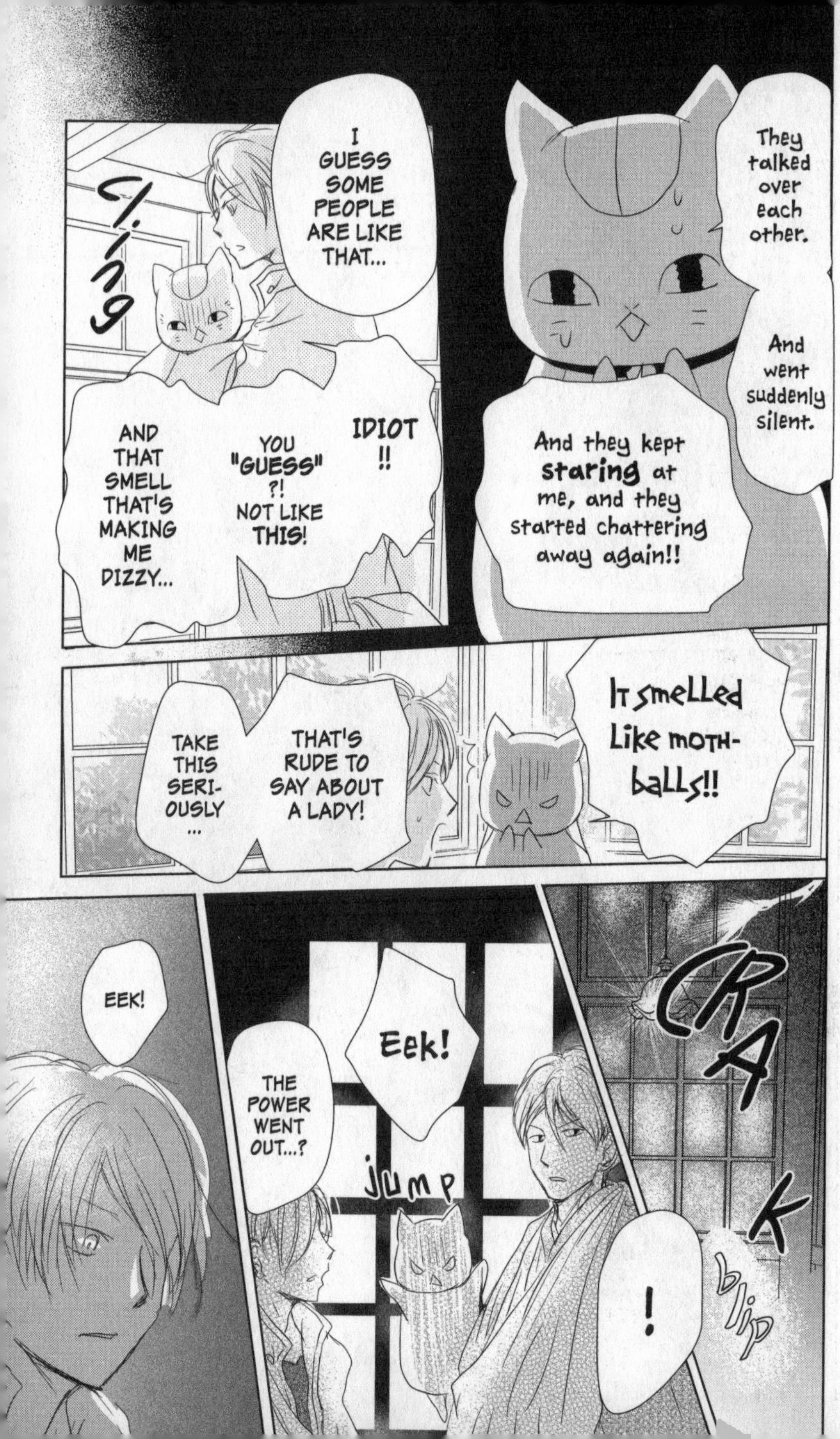
They talked over each other.
And went suddenly silent.
And they kept staring at me, and they started chattering away again!!
I GUESS SOME PEOPLE ARE LIKE THAT...
cling
IDIOT !!
YOU "GUESS" ?! NOT LIKE THIS!
AND THAT SMELL THAT'S MAKING ME DIZZY...
It smelled like moth-balls!!
THAT'S RUDE TO SAY ABOUT A LADY!
TAKE THIS SERI-OUSLY ...
CRAK
blip
!
Eek!
THE POWER WENT OUT...?
jump
EEK!

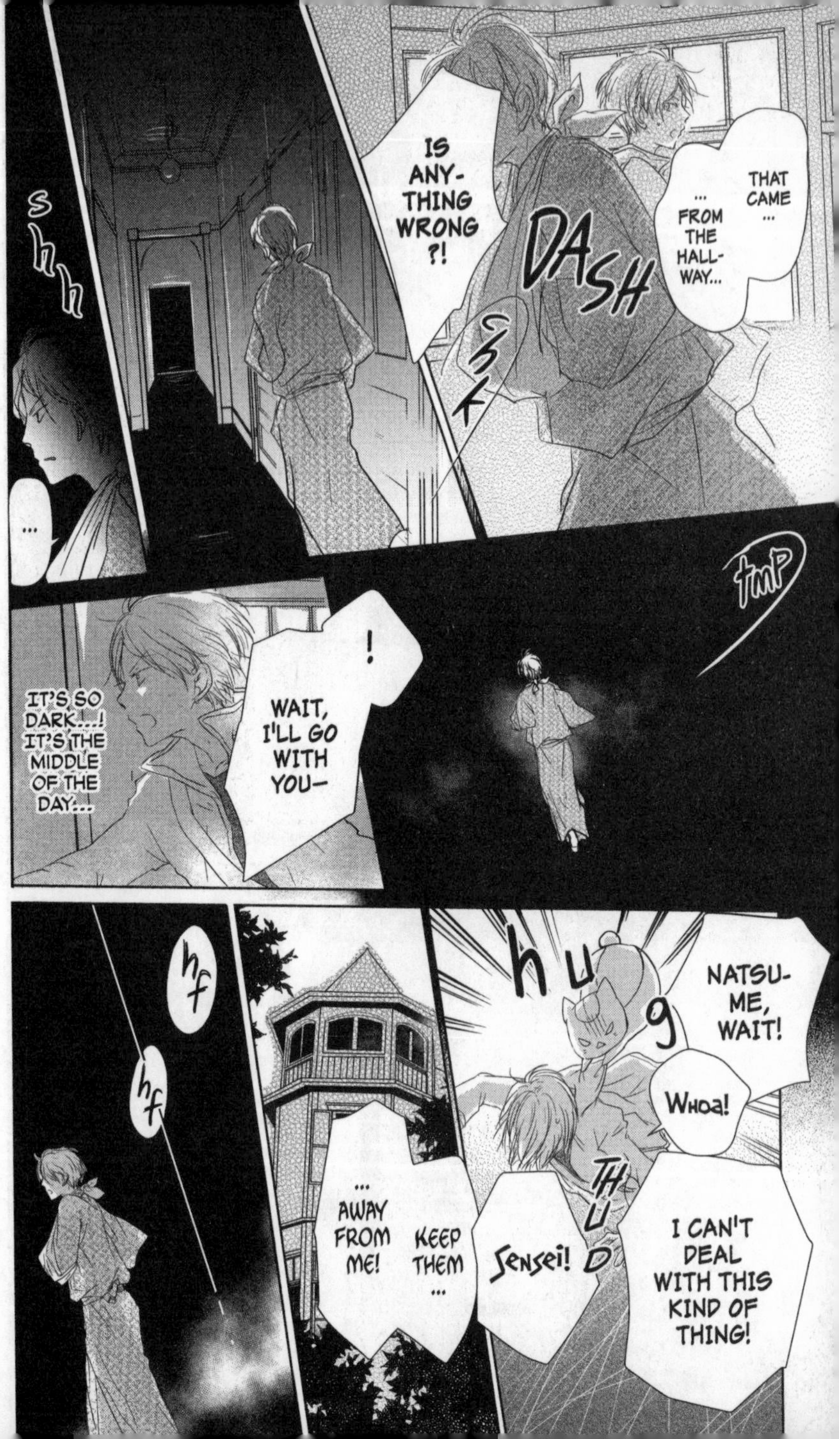
THAT CAME ...
... FROM THE HALL-WAY...
DASH
IS ANY-THING WRONG ?!
CHK
shh
...
tmp
!
WAIT, I'LL GO WITH YOU—
IT'S SO DARK...! IT'S THE MIDDLE OF THE DAY...
NATSU-ME, WAIT!
hug
Whoa!
I CAN'T DEAL WITH THIS KIND OF THING!
THUD
Sensei!
KEEP THEM ...
... AWAY FROM ME!
hf
hf

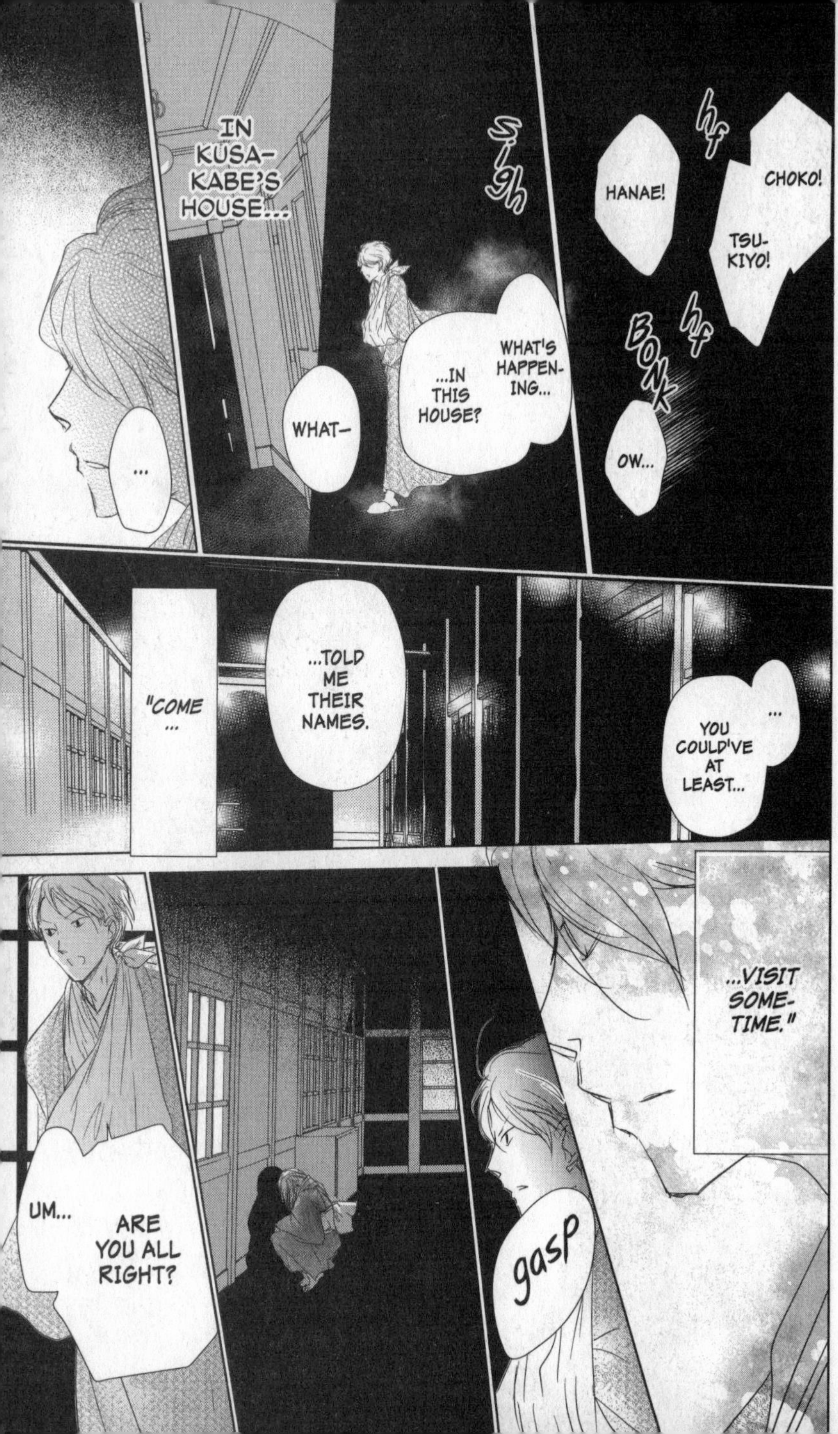
CHOKO!
TSU-KIYO!
HANAE!
hf
hf
BONK
OW...
WHAT'S HAPPEN-ING...
...IN THIS HOUSE?
WHAT—
Sigh
IN KUSA-KABE'S HOUSE...
...
...
YOU COULD'VE AT LEAST...
...TOLD ME THEIR NAMES.
"COME ...
...VISIT SOME-TIME."
gasp
UM...
ARE YOU ALL RIGHT?

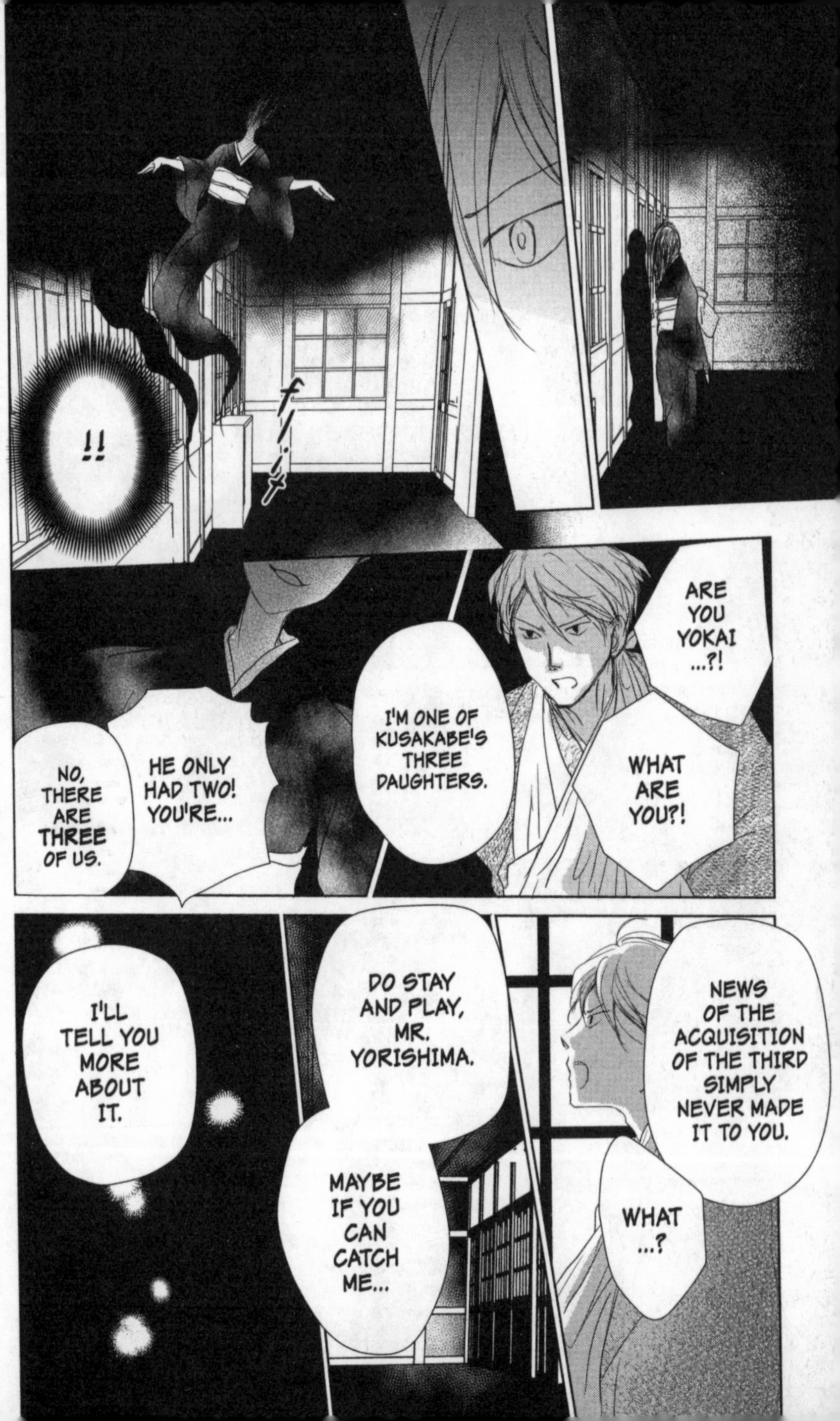
!!
ARE YOU YOKAI ...?!
WHAT ARE YOU?!
I'M ONE OF KUSAKABE'S THREE DAUGHTERS.
HE ONLY HAD TWO! YOU'RE...
NO, THERE ARE THREE OF US.
NEWS OF THE ACQUISITION OF THE THIRD SIMPLY NEVER MADE IT TO YOU.
WHAT ...?
DO STAY AND PLAY, MR. YORISHIMA.
MAYBE IF YOU CAN CATCH ME...
I'LL TELL YOU MORE ABOUT IT.

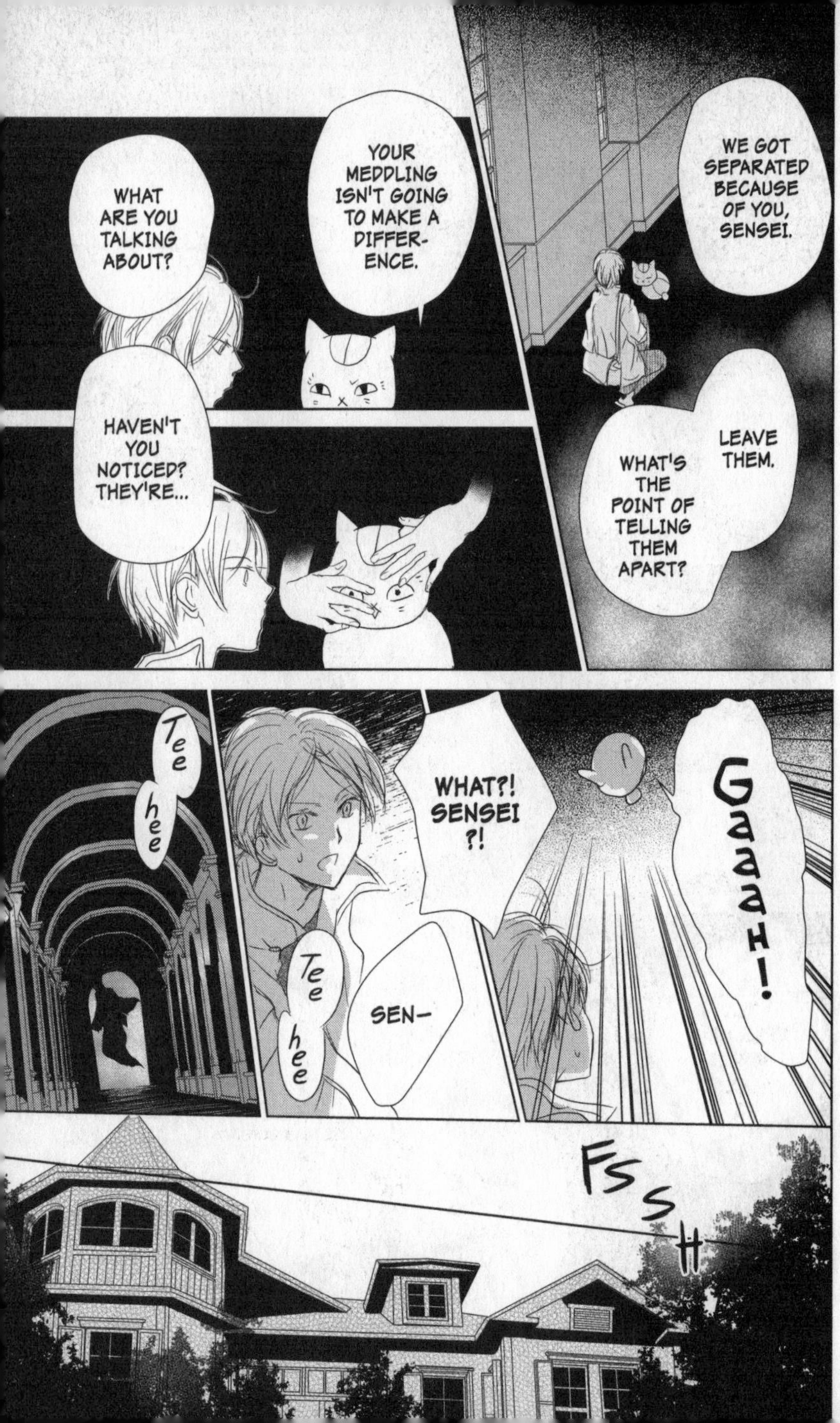
WE GOT SEPARATED BECAUSE OF YOU, SENSEI.
LEAVE THEM.
WHAT'S THE POINT OF TELLING THEM APART?
YOUR MEDDLING ISN'T GOING TO MAKE A DIFFER-ENCE.
WHAT ARE YOU TALKING ABOUT?
HAVEN'T YOU NOTICED? THEY'RE...
Gaaaah!
SEN-
WHAT?! SENSEI ?!
Tee hee
Tee hee
FSSH

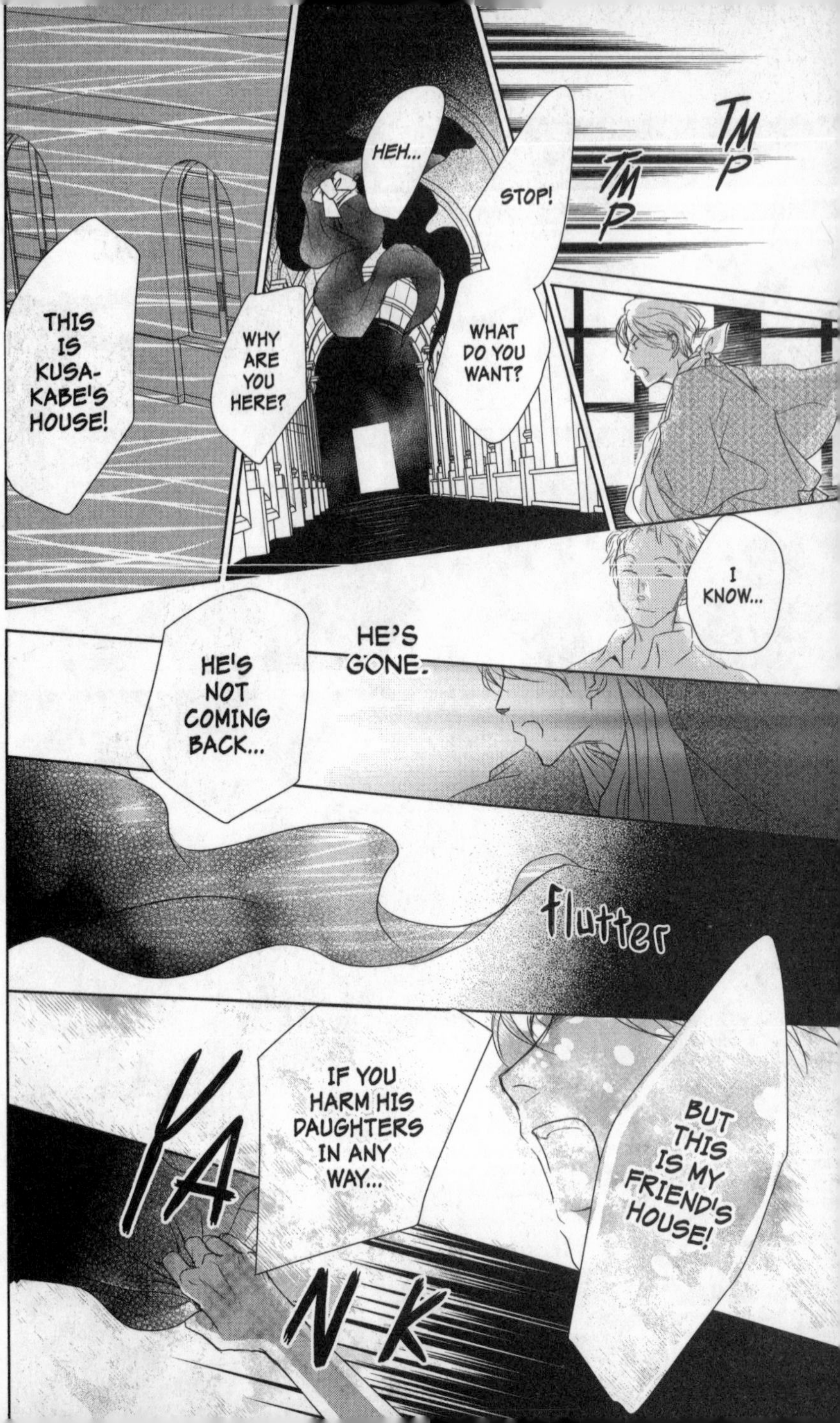
TMP
TMP
STOP!
HEH...
WHAT DO YOU WANT?
WHY ARE YOU HERE?
THIS IS KUSA-KABE'S HOUSE!
I KNOW...
HE'S GONE.
HE'S NOT COMING BACK...
flutter
BUT THIS IS MY FRIEND'S HOUSE!
IF YOU HARM HIS DAUGHTERS IN ANY WAY...
YANK

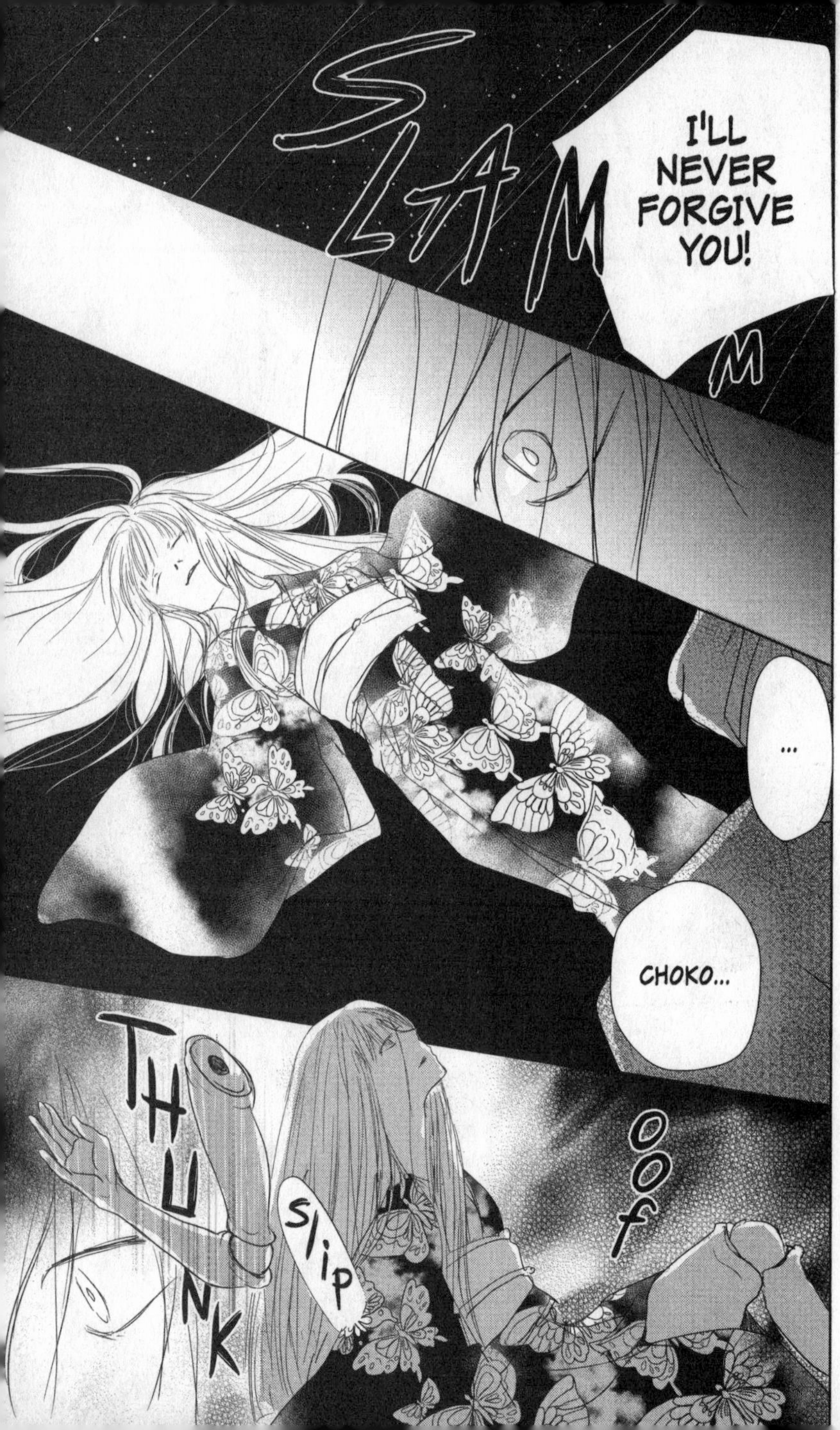
I'LL NEVER FORGIVE YOU!
SLAMM
...
CHOKO...
oof
slip
THUNK

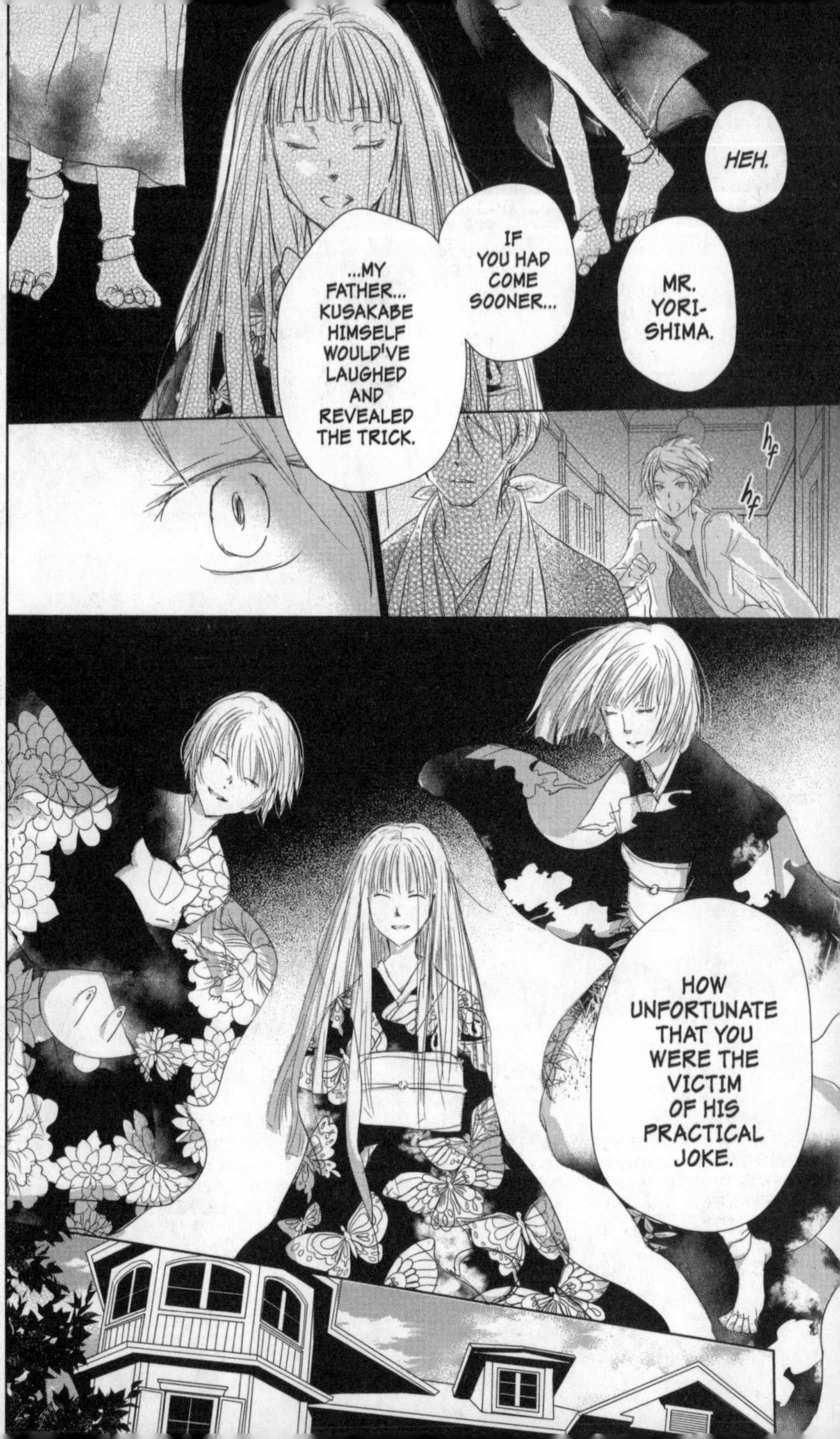
HEH.
MR. YORI-SHIMA.
IF YOU HAD COME SOONER...
...MY FATHER... KUSAKABE HIMSELF WOULD'VE LAUGHED AND REVEALED THE TRICK.
hf
hf
HOW UNFORTUNATE THAT YOU WERE THE VICTIM OF HIS PRACTICAL JOKE.

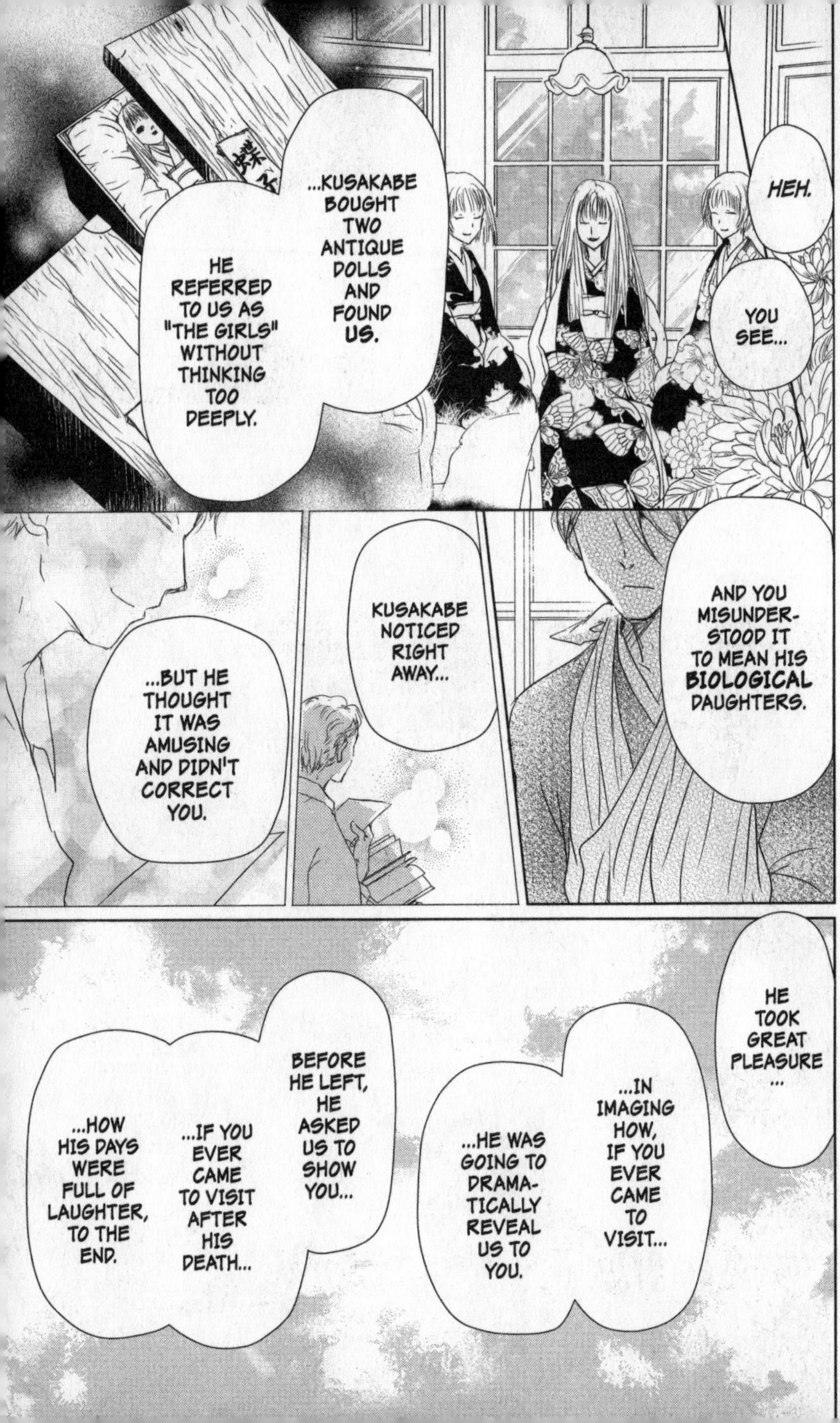
HEH.
YOU SEE...
...KUSAKABE BOUGHT TWO ANTIQUE DOLLS AND FOUND US.
HE REFERRED TO US AS "THE GIRLS" WITHOUT THINKING TOO DEEPLY.
AND YOU MISUNDER-STOOD IT TO MEAN HIS BIOLOGICAL DAUGHTERS.
KUSAKABE NOTICED RIGHT AWAY...
...BUT HE THOUGHT IT WAS AMUSING AND DIDN'T CORRECT YOU.
HE TOOK GREAT PLEASURE ...
...IN IMAGING HOW, IF YOU EVER CAME TO VISIT...
...HE WAS GOING TO DRAMA-TICALLY REVEAL US TO YOU.
BEFORE HE LEFT, HE ASKED US TO SHOW YOU...
...IF YOU EVER CAME TO VISIT AFTER HIS DEATH...
...HOW HIS DAYS WERE FULL OF LAUGHTER, TO THE END.

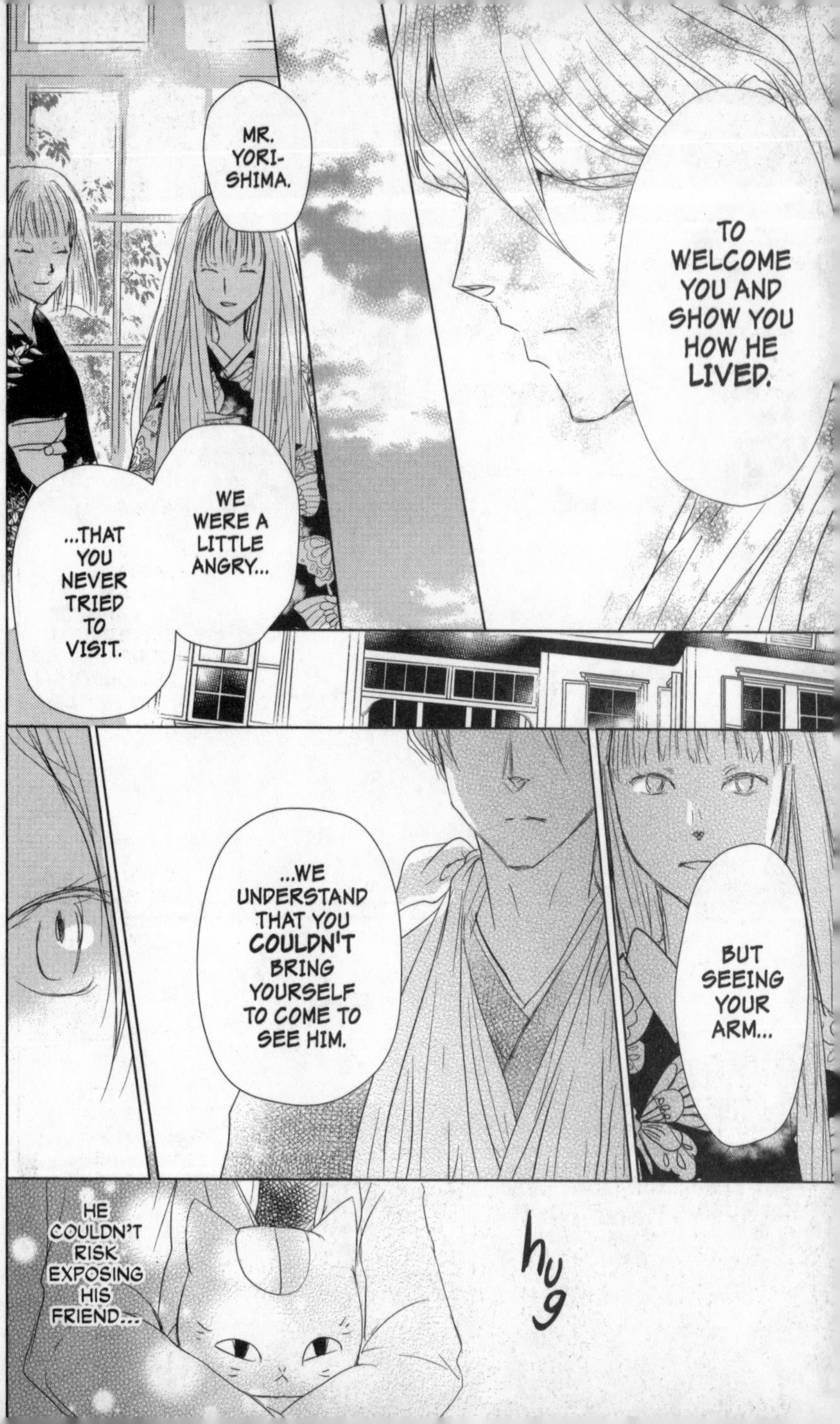
TO WELCOME YOU AND SHOW YOU HOW HE LIVED.
MR. YORI-SHIMA.
WE WERE A LITTLE ANGRY...
...THAT YOU NEVER TRIED TO VISIT.
BUT SEEING YOUR ARM...
...WE UNDERSTAND THAT YOU COULDN'T BRING YOURSELF TO COME TO SEE HIM.
hug
HE COULDN'T RISK EXPOSING HIS FRIEND...

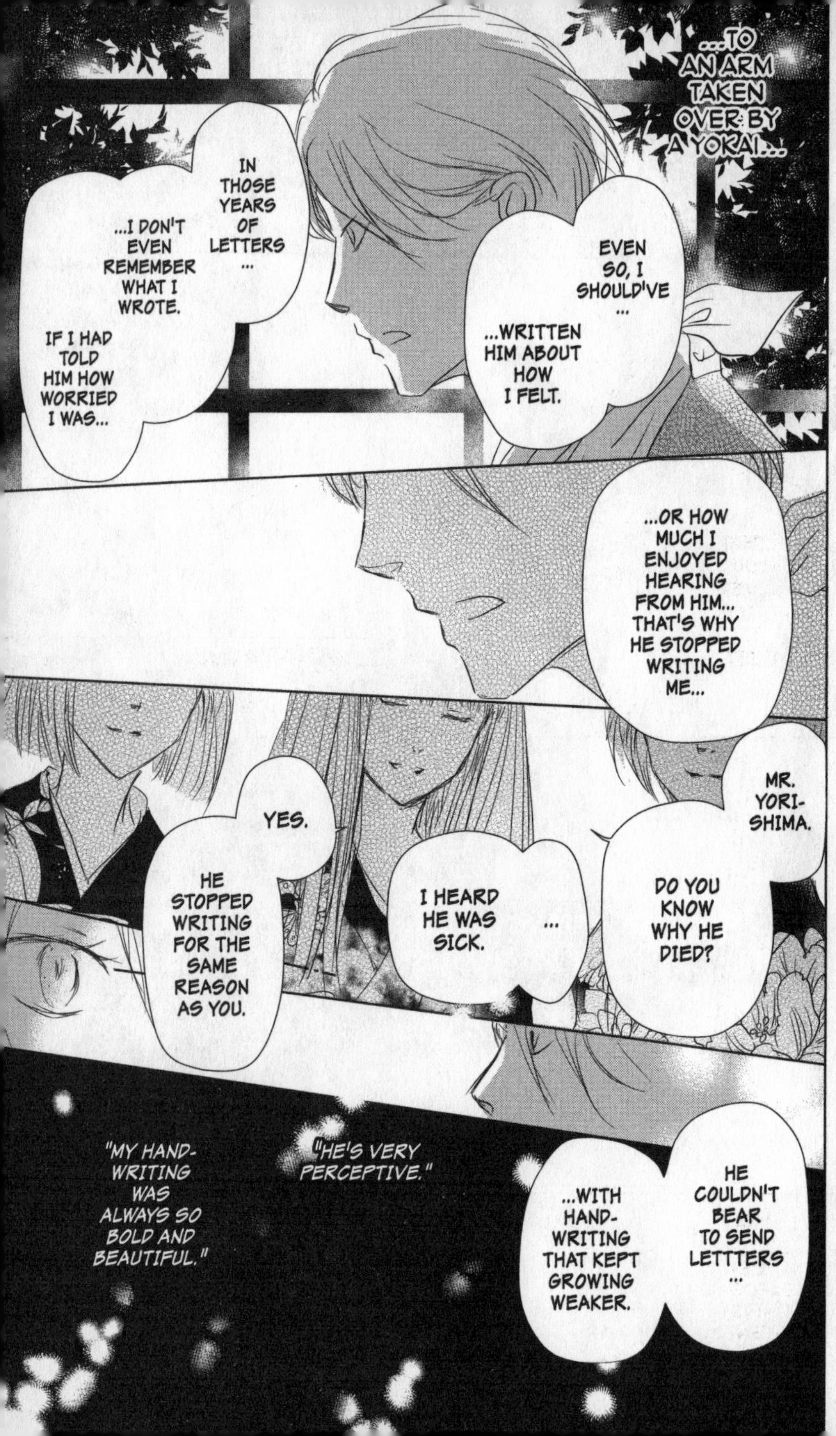
...TO AN ARM TAKEN OVER BY A YOKAI...
EVEN SO, I SHOULD'VE ...
...WRITTEN HIM ABOUT HOW I FELT.
IN THOSE YEARS OF LETTERS ...
...I DON'T EVEN REMEMBER WHAT I WROTE.
IF I HAD TOLD HIM HOW WORRIED I WAS...
...OR HOW MUCH I ENJOYED HEARING FROM HIM... THAT'S WHY HE STOPPED WRITING ME...
MR. YORI-SHIMA.
DO YOU KNOW WHY HE DIED?
I HEARD HE WAS SICK.
...
YES.
HE STOPPED WRITING FOR THE SAME REASON AS YOU.
HE COULDN'T BEAR TO SEND LETTTERS ...
...WITH HAND-WRITING THAT KEPT GROWING WEAKER.
"HE'S VERY PERCEPTIVE."
"MY HAND-WRITING WAS ALWAYS SO BOLD AND BEAUTIFUL."

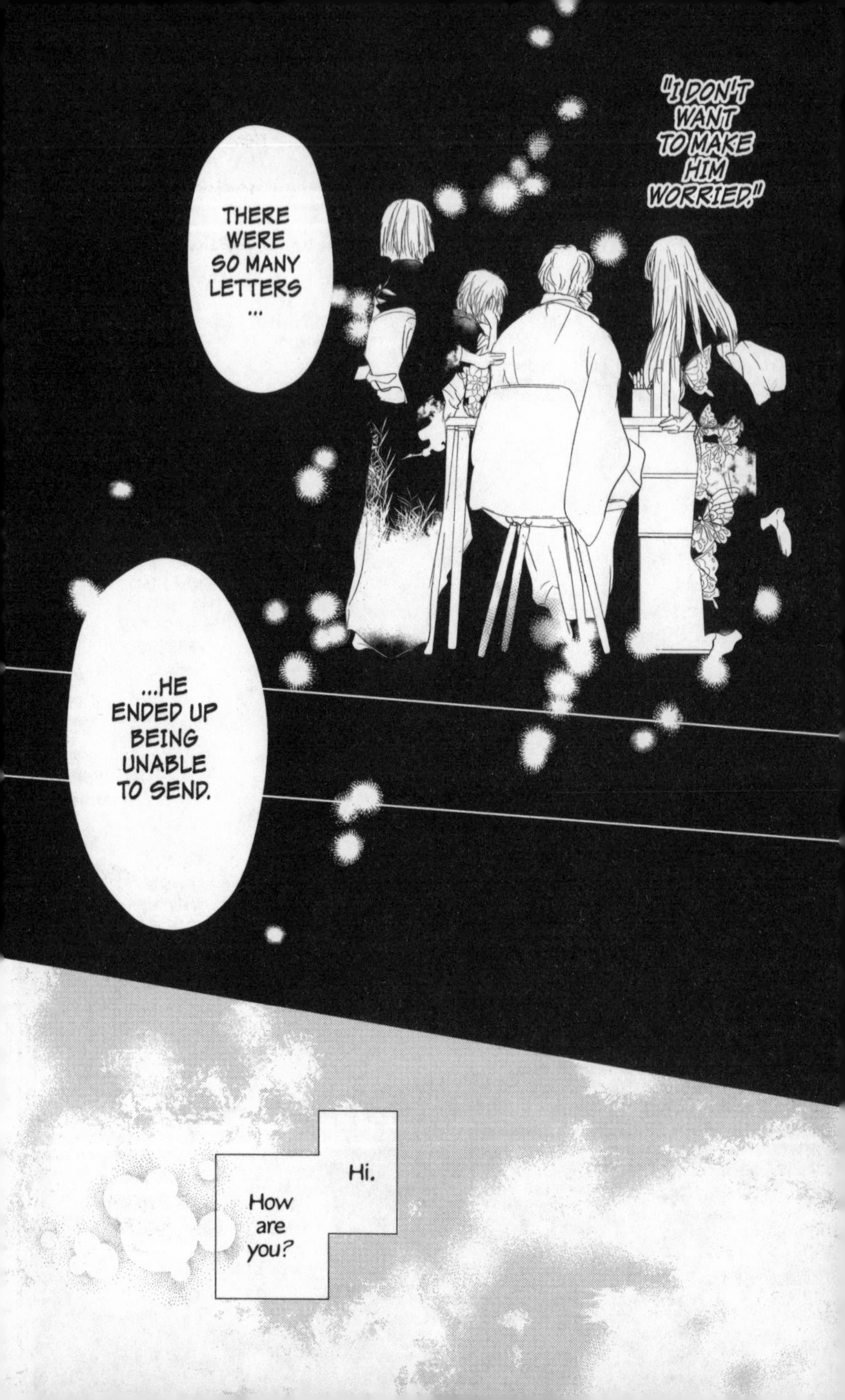
"I DON'T WANT TO MAKE HIM WORRIED."
THERE WERE SO MANY LETTERS ...
...HE ENDED UP BEING UNABLE TO SEND.
Hi.
How are you?

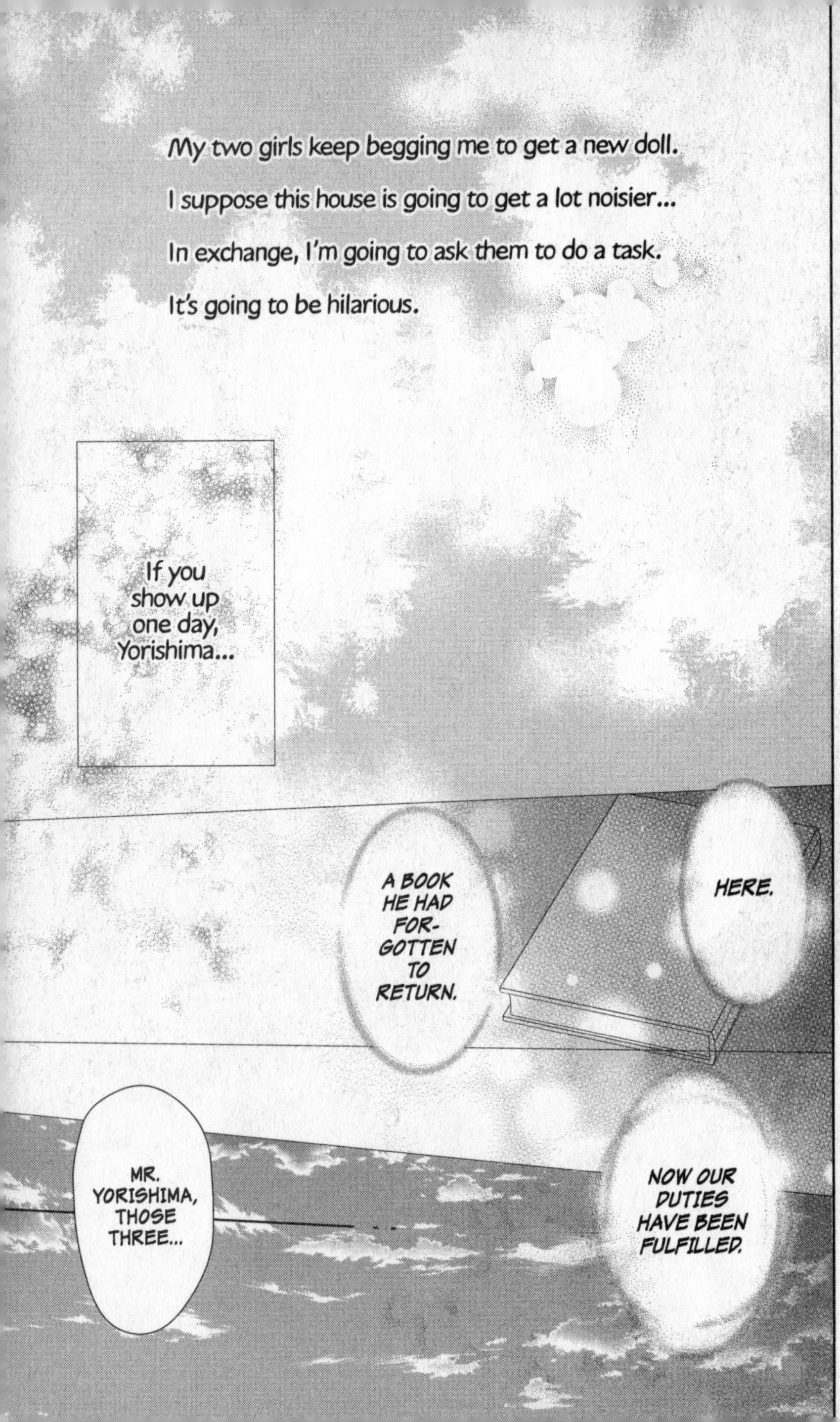
My two girls keep begging me to get a new doll.
I suppose this house is going to get a lot noisier...
In exchange, I'm going to ask them to do a task.
It's going to be hilarious.
If you show up one day, Yorishima...
HERE.
A BOOK HE HAD FOR-GOTTEN TO RETURN.
NOW OUR DUTIES HAVE BEEN FULFILLED.
MR. YORISHIMA, THOSE THREE...

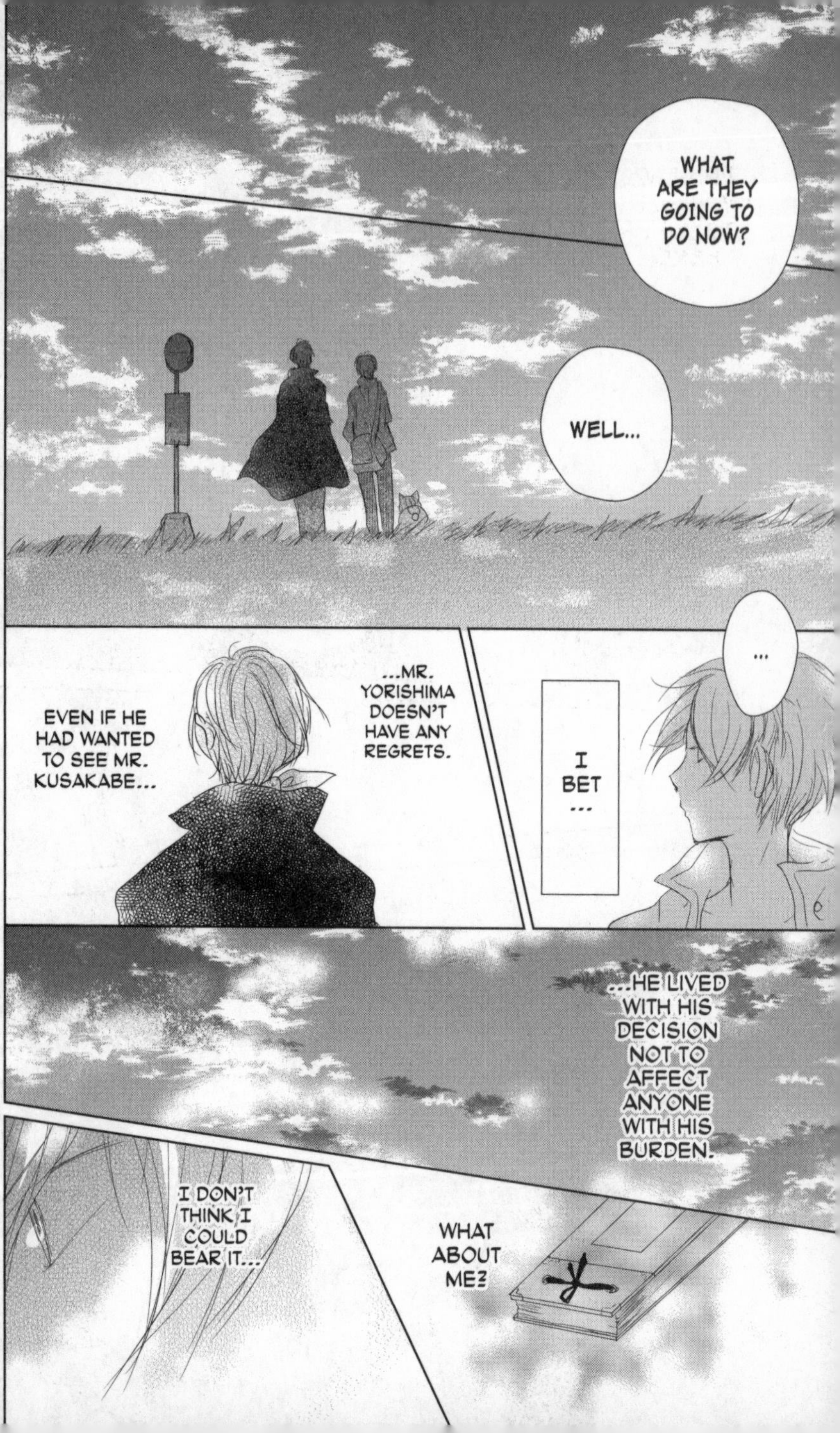
WHAT ARE THEY GOING TO DO NOW?
WELL...
...
I BET ...
...MR. YORISHIMA DOESN'T HAVE ANY REGRETS.
EVEN IF HE HAD WANTED TO SEE MR. KUSAKABE...
...HE LIVED WITH HIS DECISION NOT TO AFFECT ANYONE WITH HIS BURDEN.
WHAT ABOUT ME?
I DON'T THINK I COULD BEAR IT...

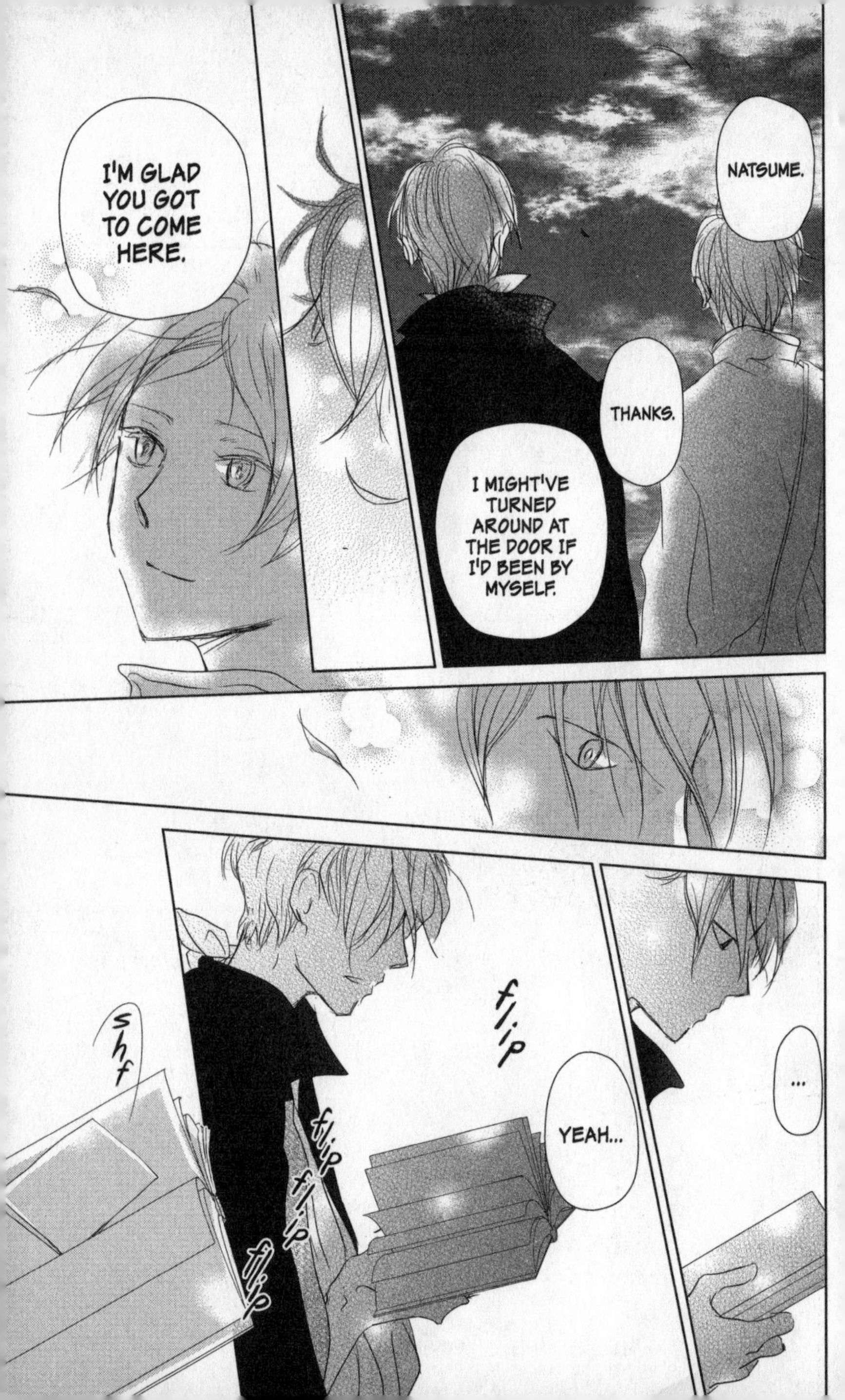
NATSUME.
THANKS.
I MIGHT'VE TURNED AROUND AT THE DOOR IF I'D BEEN BY MYSELF.
I'M GLAD YOU GOT TO COME HERE.
...
YEAH...
flip
flip flip flip
shf

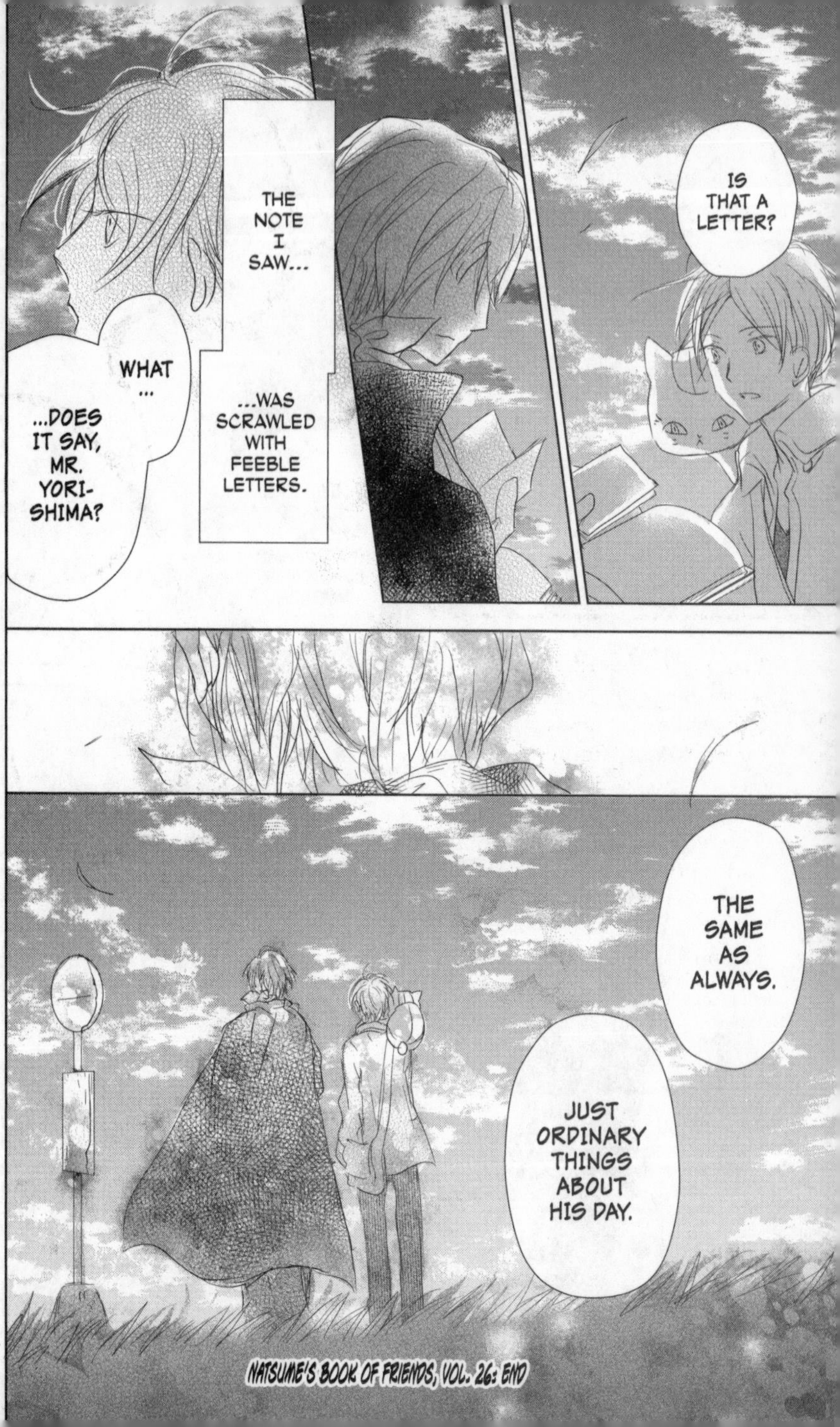
IS THAT A LETTER?
THE NOTE I SAW...
...WAS SCRAWLED WITH FEEBLE LETTERS.
WHAT ...
...DOES IT SAY, MR. YORI-SHIMA?
THE SAME AS ALWAYS.
JUST ORDINARY THINGS ABOUT HIS DAY.
NATSUME'S BOOK OF FRIENDS, VOL. 26: END